A SOCIAL
AND RELIGIOUS
HISTORY OF
THE JEWS

By SALO WITTMAYER BARON

Second Edition, Revised and Enlarged

INDEX
TO VOLUMES I-VIII

Columbia University Press
New York and London
The Jewish Publication Society of America
Philadelphia

LIBRARY OF CONGRESS CATALOG CARD NUMBER: 52-404

ⓒ COPYRIGHT 1960 BY COLUMBIA UNIVERSITY PRESS

First printing 1960
Second printing 1966

PRINTED IN THE UNITED STATES OF AMERICA

CHRONOLOGICAL TABLE OF
PRINCIPAL EVENTS AND PERSONALITIES

NOTE. Dates given for rulers indicate years during which they reigned. Dates followed by an asterisk (*) are approximate.

B.C.E.

2000*–1500*	Middle Bronze Age
1700*	Hammurabi
1675*–1560*	Hyksos period
1650*–1500*	Age of Patriarchs
1500*–1300*	Israel's sojourn in Egypt
1500*–1200*	Late Bronze Age
1490*–1436*	Thutmes III
1413*–1360*	El Amarna Age
1377*–1360*	Akhenaton (Amenhotep IV)
1300*	Exodus from Egypt
1225*–1020*	Period of Judges
1200*–1000*	Early Iron Age
1020*–1004*	Saul
1004*–965*	David; 1004*–998* in Judah only
965*–926*	Solomon
882*–871*	Omri of Israel
872*–852*	Jehoshaphat of Judah
871*–852*	Ahab of Israel; 853*–852*, participates in battle of Karkara. Elijah
800*–785*	Amaziah of Judah
793–753	Jeroboam II of Israel. Amos
746–737	Menahem of Israel. Hosea
785–747	Uzziah (Azariah) of Judah
742–725	Ahaz of Judah ⎱ Isaiah. Micah
725–697	Hezekiah of Judah ⎰
733–732	Assyrian invasions of Israel (Tiglath Pilesser)
721	Fall of Samaria
701	Assyrian invasion of Judah (Sennacherib)
696–642	Menasseh
663–609	Psammetichos I of Egypt
663* (586?)	Foundation of Elephantine Colony
639–609	Josiah
621	Deuteronomic Reformation
608–593	Jehoiakim
598	Nebukadrezzar's first invasion
598–597	Zedekiah
587	Nebukadrezzar's second invasion
586	Fall of Jerusalem
586–516* (538?)	Babylonian Exile
549–528	Cyrus the Great of Persia; 539, conquers Babylon
538	First return of exiles to Palestine
522–486	Darius I
520–516	Zerubbabel completes Second Temple. Haggai
500*	Malachi
486–465	Xerxes (Ahasuerus)

Jeremiah

Ezekiel

Deutero-Isaiah

465–425	Artaxerxes I	
458* (397?)	Ezra the Scribe. Second return of exiles to Palestine	⎫
445–433	Nehemiah governor of Judaea	⎪
419	Passover decree (Darius II)	Men of the
411–410	Destruction of Elephantine Temple	Great Synagogue
340*	Aristotle meets Jew of Coelesyria	
336–323	Alexander the Great; 332, in Palestine. Simon the Just. Samaritan schism deepens	⎭
323–283	Ptolemy I of Egypt	
312–311	Battle of Gaza and Egypt's rule over Palestine. Beginning of Seleucid Era	
312–280	Seleucus I of Syria	
260*–200*	Tobiads (Tobiah, his son Joseph, his grandson Hyrcanus)	
247	Rise of Parthia	
223–187	Antiochus III of Syria	
221–203	Ptolemy IV of Egypt; allegedly persecutes Jews (III Macc.)	
200*–100*	Letter of Aristeas; beginnings of Greek translation of Scripture (Septuagint)	
200–198	Antiochus III conquers Palestine and grants charter to Jews	
180*	Joshua ben Sirach	
175–163	Antiochus IV of Syria; Samaritans and Hellenizers collaborate with his regime.	
167	Outbreak of Maccabean Revolt	
165	Rededication of Temple (Ḥanukkah)	
160	Death of Judah Maccabeus	
160*	Onias IV founds temple in Leontopolis, Egypt	
160–142	Jonathan Maccabeus	
143–134	Simon Maccabeus; 141, named prince	
143	Palestine orders Egyptian communities to observe Ḥanukkah	
140–139	Rome's recognition of Judean independence; expulsion of Jews from city of Rome	
134–104	John Hyrcanus; his conflict with Pharisees	
128	Destruction of Samaritan temple on Mt. Gerizim	
103–76	Alexander Jannaeus	
76–67	Salome-Alexandra and her brother Simon b. Shetaḥ	
66–63	Aristobulus II	
63	Pompey's conquest of Palestine. Hyrcanus II, high priest	
59	Cicero's defense of Flaccus	
54	Crassus despoils Temple	
55*–43	Antipater, Idumaean unofficial ruler of Palestine	
49–48	Break between Julius Caesar and Pompey. Caesar's Jewish privileges	
44	Caesar's assassination	
40–38	Parthians conquer Jerusalem. Antigonus, high priest	
39–4	Herod the Great. Hillel and Shammai	
31–C.E.14	Augustus	

C.E.		
4	Judaea divided between Archelaus, Herod Antipas, and Philip	
6	Judaea under Roman procurators	
14–37	Tiberius. Ministries of John the Baptist and Jesus	
37–41	Gaius Caligula; 39, riots in Alexandria; Philo's mission to Rome	
40*–60*	Paul's missionary activities	
41–44	Agrippa I	

41-54	Claudius; edicts of toleration
48-53	Agrippa II (reigned in Jerusalem only to 53, but remained ruler of adjacent lands to his death in 100)
54-68	Nero
66-70	Roman-Jewish War; 66, Christians withdraw to Pella; 69, surrender of Joseph b. Matattiah (Josephus Flavius); 70, burning of the Second Temple

69-79   Vespasian; 70, allows Johanan b. Zakkai to establish academy at Yabneh (Jamnia); 73, closes Temple at Leontopolis

79-81   Titus. Princess Berenice

81-96   Domitian; 95, Gamaliel II and associates visit Rome

> Eliezer b. Hyrcanus and Joshua b. Ḥananiah

98-117	Trajan
115-17	Jewish revolts in Egypt, Cyrenaica, Cyprus
117-38	Hadrian. 'Aqiba begins compilation of Mishnah
132-35	Revolt of Bar-Kocheba. Death of 'Aqiba
134	Jerusalem renamed Aelia Capitolina
135	Fall of Bethar
138-61	Antoninus Pius. Reconstitution of Sanhedrin in Usha. Simon b. Gamaliel appointed patriarch. Simon b. Yoḥai. Meir continues work on Mishnah. Judah b. 'Ilai. Jose b. Ḥalafta. Jose the Galilean
161-80	Marcus Aurelius
170-217	Judah I, patriarch. Final redaction of Mishnah
180-92	Commodus
193-211	Septimus Severus
212	Caracalla's *Constitutio Antoniniana* universalizes Roman citizenship
217-25	Gamaliel III, patriarch
219-47	Abba Arikha establishes academy at Sura. Mar Samuel in Nehardea. Johanan and Simon b. Lakish in Tiberias
222-35	Alexander Severus
224-42	Ardashir I founds Sassanian empire of Persia
225-55	Judah II, patriarch
242-73	Shapur I
254-99	Judah b. Ezekiel founds academy of Pumbedita
255-75	Gamaliel IV, patriarch
263-72	Odenath and Zenobia of Palmyra
275-320	Judah III, patriarch
284-305	Diocletian
300*	Council of Elvira
309-30	Rabbah b. Naḥmani
310-79	Shapur II
311-37	Constantine the Great
313	Edict of Toleration and victory of Christianity
320-65	Hillel II, patriarch
321	Constantine's edict to Jewish community of Cologne
325	Council of Nicaea
337-61	Constantius II
338	Death of Abbaye
358*-359* (344?)	Hillel II proclaims perpetual calendar
361-63	Julian the Apostate
365-85	Gamaliel V, patriarch

375–427	Ashi of Sura begins redaction of Babylonian Talmud
379–95	Theodosius I
385–400	Judah IV, patriarch
395	Beginning of barbarian invasions
399–420	Yazdegerd I, of Persia, and his Jewish wife
400–429	Gamaliel VI, patriarch; 425*, suppression of patriarchate
408–50	Theodosius II; 438, Theodosian code
409–12	Vandal and Visigothic invasions of Spain
438–57	Yazdegerd II
459–84	Perez (Firuz) Shapur
471	Exilarch Huna Mari executed
474–99	Rabina II completes redaction of Babylonian Talmud
476	Odoacar ends Western Roman Empire
481–511	Clovis
485–507	Alaric II
488–531	Kavadh I. Rise and fall of Mazdak
491*–518*	Mar Zuṭra II's execution; end of his Jewish principality. Mar Zuṭra III emigrates to Tiberias
493–526	Theodoric the Great; 500, confirms Jewish privileges
500–650	Age of Saboraim
516*–25	Dhu Nuwas, Jewish king of South Arabia
527–65	Justinian I; 553, *Novella* 146
529	Samaritans declared a Christian sect
531–79	Khosroe I
555	Italy conquered by Belisarius
566	Lombard occupation of Italy
569–632	Mohammed; 622, hejira to Medina; 627–28, destroys Jewish tribes
575	Persian penetration of southern Arabia
586–601	Reccared I of Spain; 587, converted to Catholicism
590–604	Gregory I, pope
590–628	Khosroe II
604–30	Perso-Byzantine wars; Persian conquest and loss of Palestine; Jewish uprisings
610–41	Heraclius, Byzantine emperor; 632, forces conversion of Jews
612–20	Sisebut of Spain; 613, forces conversion of Jews
628–38	Dagobert I of France; 629–33, forces conversion of Jews
633	Fourth Council of Toledo
634–44	'Umar I, caliph; conquers Syria, Egypt, and Persia
638	Sixth Council of Toledo attempts to suppress Judaism in Spain
641*	Bustanai, exilarch
649–72	Recceswinth of Spain enacts *Leges Visigothorum*
650–1038	Age of Geonim
661	Perctarit's forced conversion of North Italian Jews
673	Kairuwan founded. Temporary suppression of Judaism in Narbonne
685–705	'Abd al-Malik, caliph
687–702	Egica
692	Trullan Council (Quinisext)
693–94	Sixteenth and Seventeenth Councils of Toledo
701	Dahya al-Kahina defeated in North Africa
711–15	Muslim conquest of Spain
717–20	'Umar II, caliph
717–41	Leo III, the Isaurian; 723, forces conversion of Byzantine Jews
730*–740*	Bulan of Khazaria; 740, converted to Judaism

732	Battle at Tours and Poitiers
752	Death of Aḥai of Shabḥa
754–75	Al-Manṣur, caliph
755	Abu 'Isa dies in battle
755–88	'Abd ar-Raḥman I of Spain
760–64	Yehudai Gaon of Sura
763–66	Baghdad becomes capital of Caliphate
767	'Anan's schism
768–814	Charlemagne; 787, sends Isaac to Harun ar-Rashid; 800, crowned emperor
772	Exilarch Naṭronai b. Ḥabibai in Spain
786–809	Harun ar-Rashid, caliph
813–33	Al-Ma'mun, caliph
814–40	Louis the Pious
820–29	Michael II
820*–40*	Agobard of Lyons, archbishop
825*	Simon of Qayyara's code
827–1061	Sicily under Muslim rule
830*	Benjamin an-Nahawendi
839	Bodo's conversion to Judaism
842–58	Palṭoi Gaon of Pumbedita
843	Treaty of Verdun
846–61	Al-Mutawakkil, caliph; 849–50, issues anti-dhimmi decree
853–56	Naṭronai b. Hilai Gaon of Sura
853–953	Isaac b. Solomon Israeli
856–74	Amram Gaon of Sura
867–86	Basil I; 873–74, forces conversion of Byzantine Jews
875–76	Expulsion of Jews from Sens, France
878	Palestine is part of Tulunid Egypt
880*	Ḥivi al-Balkhi's Bible criticism
882–942	Saadiah b. Joseph; 928–42, gaon of Surah
885*	Eldad ha-Dani's appearance in North Africa
886–912	Leo VI
892*–930*	Neṭira and his children
895	Magyar occupation of Hungary
900*	Daniel al-Qumisi
908–32	Al-Muqtadir, caliph
910–70	Menaḥem b. Saruq
912–59	Constantine VII
912–61	'Abd ar-Raḥman III of Spain
913–82	Shabbetai b. Abraham Donnolo
916–40	David b. Zakkai, exilarch
919–44	Romanos I
920*–90*	Dunash (Adonim) b. Labraṭ
921–22	Saadiah–Ben Meir controversy
932	Doge Petrus II promotes forced conversion of Jews in Germany
937–38	Pope Leo VII permits expulsion of Jews from Mayence
940*–66	Ḥisdai ibn Shapruṭ; 958, negotiates treaty with Ordoño III
941–43	Jews of Tibet mentioned
960*	Moses b. Ḥanokh arrives in Cordova
960–1028	Gershom b. Yehudah, "Light of the Exile"
963–92	Mieszko I of Poland
965	Sviatoslav's occupation of Kertch (Panticapaeum)
968–98	Sherira Gaon of Pumbedita; 987, writes Epistle

969	Faṭimid conquest of Egypt and Palestine; Jauhar-Palṭiel (?)
980–1015	Vladimir of Kiev; 989, adopts Christianity
980*–1053	Ḥananel b. Ḥushiel
985–1040	Jonah ibn Janaḥ (Abu'l Walid ibn Merwan)
987	Capetian dynasty established in France
993–1056	Samuel b. Joseph ibn Nagrela ha-Nagid
996–1021	Al-Ḥakim, caliph of Egypt; 1012–20, persecutes Jews and Christians
998–1038	Hai Gaon of Pumbedita
1000*–1050*	Nissim b. Jacob ibn Shahin
1012	Expulsion of Jews from Mayence
1013–1103	Isaac b. Jacob Alfasi
1021*–58	Hezekiah, exilarch; 1038–58, also Gaon of Pumbedita
1021–69	Solomon b. Joseph ibn Gabirol
1035–1106	Nathan b. Yeḥiel of Rome, 1101, writes dictionary 'Arukh
1038–73	Badis of Granada
1040–1105	Solomon b. Isaac (Yiṣḥaqi or Rashi)
1056–1106	Henry IV, emperor; 1090–97, enacts privileges for Jews of Spires, Worms, and Ratisbon
1061–73	Alexander II, pope; 1063, praises Spanish Church for defending Jews against Crusaders
1065–1109	Alphonso VI of Castile; 1085, conquers Toledo
1065–1136	Abraham b. Ḥiyya Savasorda
1066	Massacre of Granada Jewry
1066–87	William the Conqueror in England
1070*–1130	Yehudah b. Barzillai of Barcelona
1070*–1139	Moses ibn Ezra
1077–1141	Joseph b. Meir ibn Megas
1084	Invitation of Jews to Spires; first formal Jewish quarter
1086–1141	Yehudah b. Samuel Halevi
1089	Death of Yehudah b. Isaac ibn Ghayyat
1092–1167	Abraham ibn Ezra
1096–99	First Crusade; 1099, establishment of Latin Kingdom of Jerusalem
1100–1135	Henry I of England
1101–54	Roger II of Sicily; 1147, transplants Jews from Balkans
1103	Imperial "peace" for Jews and others
1106–42	'Ali, Almoravid ruler of Spain
1109	Anti-Jewish riots in Castile and Leon
1110*–80	Abraham ibn Daud
1119–24	Calixtus II, pope; enacts first Constitutio pro Judaeis
1120–90	Yehudah b. Saul ibn Tibbon
1125–86	Abraham b. David of Posquières
1126–57	Alphonso VII of Castile
1130–38	Anacletus II, pope
1135–1204	Moses b. Maimon; 1180*, completes Mishneh Torah; 1195*, completes Guide
1137–80	Louis VII of France
1144	First Blood Accusation, in Norwich
1145–53	Eugenius III, pope
1146–47	Second Crusade; massacres of Jews; intervention by St. Bernard of Clairvaux; Peter of Cluny attacks Jews
1146–48	Almohades conquer Muslim Spain; force conversion of Jews and Christians
1148	Decretum Gratiani

1152–90	Frederick I, "Barbarossa"
1154–89	Henry II of England
1158–1214	Alphonso VIII of Castile; 1205, Pope Innocent III censures his pro-Jewish policies
1159–81	Alexander III, pope
1160–73	Benjamin b. Jonah of Tudela's journey
1170	Death of Joseph Qimhi
1171	Blood Accusation at Blois. Death of Jacob b. Meir Tam
1179	Third Lateran Council
1180*	Petahiah b. Jacob of Ratisbon's journey
1180–1223	Philip II of France; 1182, expels Jews from royal France; 1198, recalls them
1187	Saladin recaptures Jerusalem
1189–92	Third Crusade
1189–99	Richard Lion-Heart; 1189–90, anti-Jewish massacres in England; 1195, English chirograph offices established

INDEX

INDEX

A

Aaron, I, 318; "Death of Aaron," midrashic apocryphon, VIII, 278; priestly descent from, V, 173
Aaron, Egyptian priest, *Pandects*, VIII, 242
Aaron, scholar of Baghdad, V, 56 f.
Aaron, *see* Abu Aaron
Aaron b. Amram, III, 152
Aaron b. Asher, *see* Ben Asher
Aaron b. Elijah, V, 261, VIII, 195
Aaron b. Jacob ha-Kohen of Lunel, VI, 74
Aaron b. Joseph the Elder, V, 234
Aaron b. Meir, *see* Ben Meir
Aaron of Lincoln, IV, 79, 82, 84, 214; home, IV, 85; *scaccarium Aronis*, IV, 203 f.
Aaron of Toledo, VII, 139
Ab, *see* Ninth of Ab
Abacus, VIII, 353
'Abar Nahara, I, 377
'Abassids, III, 198; feud with 'Umayyads, III, 107; period of transition to rule of, III, 121 ff.; policy toward minority groups, III, 120 f., 140
Abba, R. (Amora), II, 249
Abba, R. (Tanna), II, 227, 230
Abba, R., identified with R. Abbahu, VIII, 21; *see also* Raba
Abba, surgeon, VIII, 233
Abba, Mar, patriarch, VI, 4
Abba Arikha, *see* Rab
Abba b. Memel, R., II, 311
Abba b. Zabda, R., II, 309
Abba Benjamin, II, 281
Abba Eliyahu, Palestinian sage, VI, 402
Abbahu, R., VI, 155, 181; Caesarean academy, II, 175, VI, 248; friendly to Greek studies, II, 142; on Graeco-Roman vaudeville, I, 264; political attitudes, II, 178, 197; on prayers by proselytes, I, 376; relations to Gentiles, II, 430; sayings, II, 123, 138, 309, 310,

311, 313, 409; uncertain identification, VIII, 21
Abba Mari Astruc of Lunel, VIII, 145
Abba Saul, II, 314
Abbaye, II, 251, 278
'Abd al-Ḥaqq, Jewish convert to Islam, V, 85 ff.; attack on Jews, V, 97
'Abd Allah, emir, III, 103
'Abd Allah, Spanish king, III, 170
'Abd Allah ibn 'Ali, III, 121 f.
'Abdallah ibn Saba, V, 168; 'Ali's Jewish adviser, VI, 12
'Abd al-Latif, Saladin's court physician, VIII, 346; on the *Guide*, VIII, 314
'Abd al-Malik, caliph, III, 88, V, 182, VI, 153, VIII, 224; construction of mosques, III, 134; employment of Jew as fiscal adviser, III, 150; monetary reform, IV, 210; re Muslim-*dhimmi* relations, III, 146; *see also* Mosque of the Rock
'Abd al-Masi'h, VIII, 246
'Abd al-Mu'min, Almohade ruler: and "original" Almohades, III, 127; religious persecution in Fez, III, 124 f.
'Abd ar-Raḥman III, Spanish caliph, III, 107, 155, 183; gift from Romanos II, VIII, 246
'Abd as-Salam, astronomer, III, 133
Abdera, Spain, *see* Adra
Abdiḥipa of Jerusalem, I, 34
'Abd Isho ('Ebedjesu) b. Berikha, Syriac poet, VIII, 260
Abel, I, 22, 230, II, 136, 382
Abelard, Peter: apologia of Christianity, VIII, 67; biblical studies, VI, 272 f.
Abenalazar, *see* Ibn Eleazar
Abgar IX of Edessa, II, 165
Abiathar, priest, I, 149, 330, 340
Abiathar b. Elijah ha-Kohen, V, 33, 38, 306; vs. David b. Daniel, VI, 215 f.; Scroll, V, 31, 37, VI, 215; on moon's first nativity, VIII, 203
Abiathar family, II, 343
Abimelech, I, 75
Abin, R., II, 284
Abin the Levite, R., II, 424

Abisha Scroll, V, 372

Abjuration, converts' oath of, III, 41 f., 184, 194, 322

Ablution: ritualistic, V, 29 f., VI, 14, 182; conversion through, IV, 187 f., 334; general hygiene, VIII, 262

'Abodah, service, VII, 91

Abraham, patriarch, I, 34-38 passim, 136, 203, 301, 376, II, 82, 364, V, 137, VIII, 134; alleged falsification of story of, V, 88; Apocalypse of, VIII, 20; Arab traditions re customs introduced by, III, 273; astrology and, VIII, 176; bilingualism, I, 20; contribution to astral sciences, II, 16; dependence on lunar month, I, 44; descent from, II, 31, III, 201, V, 99; Egyptian sojourn, I, 304; formulation of monotheism, VI, 229; God's blessing of, V, 99 f., VI, 300; God's visit to, VI, 302 f.; importance to Mohammed, III, 81, 85 f., 266; journey "toward the South," V, 329; Judeo-Christian rival claims, II, 137 f., 383; and Lot, VI, 39; at Mamre, V, 106 f., 121; and Melchizedek, I, 312; missionary activities, I, 51, 315; names of family, I, 44, VI, 170; "religion of," III, 201, VIII, 124; religious league organized by, I, 51; revelation to, V, 93; role of, in mysticism, VIII, 20

Abraham (Ibrahim) Abu Sa'ad, Jewish banker, III, 158

Abraham b. David of Posquières, II, 408, VI, 101, 179 f., VIII, 24; commentaries, VI, 62; correspondence with Zerahiah, VI, 87 f., 118; criticism of Maimonides, VI, 105 f., 380 f., VIII, 40 f., 100 f.; on influence of the stars, VIII, 181; monographs, VI, 73 f., 354, 385; and mysticism, VIII, 39 f.; on the Tosafists, VI, 56, 350

Abraham b. Hillel: re Saladin, IV, 116; vs. Zutta, VI, 215

Abraham b. Hiyya, see Bar Hiyya

Abraham b. Isaac, "Father of the Court," VI, 73; and Yehudah b. Barzillai, VIII, 38

Abraham b. Isaac b. Meborakh, Hebrew poet, VII, 118, 139, 192

Abraham b. Maimon, R., VII, 311; see also Abraham Maimonides

Abraham b. Nathan ha-Yarhi of Lunel, VI, 129 f., 391 f.

Abraham b. Nathan ibn Ata, V, 40

Abraham b. Samuel ibn Hisdai, see Ibn Hisdai

Abraham b. Shabbetai, VI, 57, 256

Abraham b. Sherira, V, 15

Abraham b. Solomon of Torrutiel, VI, 209

Abraham ha-Kohen, Baghdad scholar, VI, 119, 127

Abrahamites, ancestors of, I, 44

"Abraham Judaeus," name denoting Ibn Ezra and Bar Hiyya, VIII, 170

Abraham Maimonides, Nagid, V, 47 f., 72, 366, VI, 104, 313, 401, VIII, 63; and Aggadah, VI, 412 f.; on bans, V, 48; biblical authorship, I, 308; biblical law, VI, 143; categories of midrashic lore, VI, 180 f.; on eschatological folklore, V, 165; and his father, VI, 120, 297, VII, 120 f., VIII, 70; re Karaites, V, 281; on local customs, VI, 127 f., 131; marriage contract issued by, VI, 138; on masoretic text, VI, 293; on piyyutim, VII, 102 f.; on segregation and autonomy, V, 4

Abraham of Saragossa, IV, 48 f.

Abraham the Babylonian, grammarian, VII, 46

Abraham Zutra of Thebes, VI, 278

Ab-Ram, see Abraham

Abram, meaning, I, 311

Abravanel, Isaac: condemnation of Martini, VI, 172; on rational law, VI, 144

Abrogation, of biblical law, V, 91, 124, VI, 145 f.

Absentee landlordism, I, 72, 277, II, 246

Abtalyon and Shemaya, II, 346

Abu Aaron (or Ahron), Babylonian mystic, VIII, 44, 293

Abu 'Ali ibn Fadhlan, see Ibn Fadhlan

Abu Bakr, caliph, III, 122, VI, 151; death of, V, 294; suppression of Jews, III, 76

Abu Bakr al-'Attar, scholar, VI, 243

Abu-Bekr, see Ibn Bajja

Abudarham, David, VII, 105 f.

Abu Dulaf, III, 115

Abu Hanifa, Muslim jurist, V, 210, 211, 213, VI, 107, 325; re expression of condolence to a dhimmi, III, 147; re property of a convert, III, 144

Abu Huraira, VI, 13

Abu Ibrahim b. Joseph ibn Benveniste, see Ibn Baron

Abu-'Imram al-Tiflisi, *see* Za'frani, Musa
al-

Abu 'Isa al-Isfahani (Obadiah), V, 182,
185, 191 f.; seven daily services instituted by, VII, 64

Abu-Ishaq of Elvira, III, 158, V, 93

Abu Kathir of Tiberias, VI, 265

Abulafia, Meir ha-Levi, R., jurist-poet,
VII, 164

Abulafia, Todros b. Yehudah, VII, 147,
196

Abu'l 'Ataluj, Baghdad court poet, VII,
169

Abu'l Barakat Hibbat Allah ibn Malka
al-Baghdadi, Jewish philosopher, III,
158, VI, 477, VIII, 63, 141, 249; doctrine of impetus, VIII, 223

Abu'l Fadail ibn an-Nagid, Jewish eye-
doctor, VIII, 237, 254 f.

Abu'l Fadhi, *see* Ibn Hisdai, Abu'l
Fadhi

Abu'l Fadl, Muslim scholar, VII, 87

Abu'l Faraj Harun, Karaite grammarian
and exegete, V, 233, VII, 3, 26, 38 f.,
VIII, 60; commentaries, VI, 206;
grammatical works, VI, 290

Abu'l-Fath, chronicle of, II, 29, 340, V,
175 f., 367, 371, VI, 212

Abu'l Kamal Tamim, Moroccan rebel,
III, 108, 122

Abu'l Ma'ali ibn Hibbat Allah, Jewish court physician, VIII, 249

Abu'l-Ma'ali Juwayni (Imam al-Hara-
mein), VIII, 333

Abu'l Mina ha-Kohen al-'Attar, VIII,
257

Abu'l Walid ibn Merwan, *see* Ibn Janah

Abu Mansur adh-Dhamari, VII, 181

Abu Mansur al-Baghdadi, V, 327

Abun (or Bun), R., II, 13, VIII, 34

Abu Salih, Christian chronicler, III, 136,
297

Abu Shuja, vizier, III, 141

Abu Tahir, Qarmatian chief, V, 104

Abu Tahir ibn Shibr, Jewish leader, V,
295

Abu 'Ubaid, III, 168

Abu Yusuf, fiscal authority, III, 162,
295, 299, 302, 309, 310, IV, 181, VI,
112

Abu Zakariya Yahya ibn Daud Hayyuj,
see Hayyuj, Yehudah b. David

Abyss, meaning of, VI, 285

Abyssinia, *see* Ethiopia

Academies, ancient, II, 120 f., 205, 206,
207, 399, 425; Babylonian leaders of,
in Palestine, II, 208; Caesarea, II, 175;
calendar proclamations issued by, II,
198; decline of, and growth of synagogue, VII, 62; funds, II, 194; Hira,
III, 61; *kallah* gatherings, II, 245,
247, 276, 277; leadership, II, 196, 197,
403; Pumbedita, II, 207; Sura, II, 207;
Tiberias, II, 196; Usha, II, 126, 378;
Yabneh, II, 115, 120, 126, 377

—— medieval Babylonian, IV, 215; V,
10, 16, 282; at assemblies, V, 19 f.;
authority of, V, 13-20, 51, VI, 22, 26 ff.,
VII, 147 f.; and Caliphate, V, 14;
courts, V, 20, VI, 9 f.; decline of, VI,
119, VIII, 4; differences between Sura
and Pumbedita, VI, 389; and evolution
of law, V, 22, VI, 16 ff., 25; and the exilarchate, V, 6; explanations of talmudic terms, VI, 27 ff.; guardians of
oral tradition, VI, 427; hereditary
principle of leadership, V, 50, 300;
investiture of gaon, V, 24; *kallah*
gatherings, VI, 111, 154; Karaites and,
V, 230 ff., 237, 274; legal decisions, V,
22 ff., 211, VI, 55, 301, 384; on local
customs, VI, 124 ff.; loss of archives,
VI, 112; mystics among leaders, VIII,
7 ff.; neglect of Hebrew philology,
VII, 19; and proclamation of leap year,
VIII, 194 ff.; re prophets and sages, VI,
202, VIII, 130; revenue of, III, 154,
V, 19, 23 f., 33, 40, 51 f., 237, 306, VI,
111; on ritualistic innovations, VII,
64 f., 78; titles awarded by, V, 52; use
of Arabic, VII, 6; work on biblical
texts, VI, 238 ff., 248 f., 253, 261

—— medieval Palestinian, IV, 215, V,
32 ff.; aggadic studies, VI, 153; calendar
proclamations, VI, 216, VIII, 193 f.;
homiletical and biblical studies, VI,
152 ff., 245; controversies over regional
leadership, VI, 214; halakhic monographs, VI, 63 ff.; talmudic commentaries, VI, 56 f.; vernacular versions of
Bible, VI, 239

—— medieval, Western, IV, 26, 45, 215,
VI, 56; founded by captive scholars, V,
46; ordinance re communal establishment of, VI, 140 f.; responsa, VI, 117 ff.

—— Muslim, VII, 138

Accadian dialect, I, 20

Accents: masoretic, VII, 126, 283; musi-

Accents (*Continued*)
cal, VII, 126 f.; in punctuation, VI, 237, 249, 259 f.
Acco, Palestine, I, 255, IV, 116, VIII, 249; *see also* Ptolemais
Accursius, VI, 55
Achaemenids, dynasty, I, 107, 341; and Babylonia, I, 355, II, 206; and chronology, II, 26; effects of, I, 131, II, 317; and Egypt, I, 354; *see also* Persia, Achaemenid
Achillas Rufus, II, 98
Acmonia, synagogue in, II, 24
Acoustics, and music, VII, 209
Acre, *see* Acco; Ptolemais
Acropolis of Athens: burned, I, 348; statue to Herod, I, 262
Acrostics: alphabetic, VII, 88, 91; double, VII, 92; list of words for, VII, 14; on names, VII, 99, 141, 144, 289; related to Haduta or Ḥaduta, VII, 259
Active Intelligence, VIII, 115, 128, 338
"Acts of Pilate," II, 379
Acts of the Apostles, Ebionite, II, 75
"Acts of the Heathen Martyrs," I, 190, 381, II, 108
Adalbert (Wojtech), bishop of Prague, III, 219
Adalbert, bishop of Worms, IV, 99
Adam, VIII, 203; allegorical meaning of, VIII, 86, 338; "Book of Adam," VI, 17, 197; dualist critique of story of, V, 106; and Eve, V, 235, VI, 283; and future ideas, I, 10, 52; midrash on the speech of, VI, 269; sin and punishment, VI, 303; sons and daughters, VI, 170; years of life, VIII, 149
Adam of Bremen, VIII, 224; re Kiev, III, 217
Adam zakhar, phrase, VIII, 149 f.
Adda, R., talmudic sage, VIII, 189, 193, 198 f., 358
Adelard of Bath, VIII, 174
Aden, Arabia, III, 115; dynasty of communal officials, V, 51
Adfuwi, al-, commentator on the Qur'an, VI, 282
Adharbaijan, Khazar invasion, III, 199
Adhémar de Chabannes, IV, 57
Adhémar de Monteil, bishop of Le Puy, IV, 98
Adiabene, kingdom, I, 168, II, 213
Adiabene, royal house of, I, 173, 183, 210,

III, 63, VI, 257; opposition to Trajan, II, 371; tombs, II, 333
Adjectives, multiplication of, VIII, 14
Adler papyri, I, 261
Administration, communal, *see* Communal control; Communities, Jewish
Adon, king of Ascalon, I, 334
Adonai, divine name, I, 244, II, 18, 361, VI, 449; *see also* Names, divine; Yahweh
Adonim, *see* Dunash b. Labraṭ; Ibn Tamim
Adoniram, servant of Solomon, III, 244; alleged tombstone of, III, 34
Adonizedek, I, 45
Adora, I, 224
Adoram, I, 74
Adra (Abdera), Spain, III, 34
Adrianeion of Tiberias, II, 108, 400
Adult education, II, 275 f., 421 f.; *see also* Education
Adultery, V, 240 f., VI, 324; Muslim law on, III, 142 f.; punishment for, I, 361, II, 222, 228; *see also* Sex
Adventure stories, VII, 183 ff., VIII, 211 f.
Aelia Capitolina, Jerusalem renamed, II, 107, III, 269
Aelius Gallus, III, 64
Aeon, cosmic, II, 60, 351, 436
Afdhal, Abu'l Hasan 'Ali al-, sultan, VIII, 260 f.
Afdhal, Abu'l Qasim al-, vizier, V, 203
Afendopolo, Caleb b. Elijah, V, 234, 410
Afghanistan, VI, 299; inscription, III, 282; Jews in, III, 110
Africa: Christians in, II, 165, 188, 393; commercial relations with Rome, I, 410; gold and silver mines, IV, 211; Jewish communities, I, 262, III, 106 f., 116, IV, 174; Semitic civilization, I, 64, 176, 374; size of, VIII, 215
Africa, North: abandonment of Aramaic Targum, VI, 264; Arab expansion in, III, 90 ff.; Canaanite-Phoenician antecedents, III, 214, 271; Graeco-Roman linguistic heritage, VII, 12; Jewish communities, V, 25; Karaite settlement, VII, 226; resistance to Belisarius, III, 7; *see also* individual countries
Africanus, (Sextus) Julius, *see* Julius Africanus
Agag, the Amalekite, III, 63

Agapios of Alexandria, VIII, 241

Agapius (Mahbub) of Menbidj, III, 98, 236; re forced conversion to Christianity, III, 176 ff.; re sack of Damascus, III, 121 f.

Agathias Scholasticus, III, 54; quoted, II, 183, 399

Agde, Council of, III, 36, 245, IV, 241

Agents: business, IV, 180; merchant travelers as, IV, 174 ff.; slaves as, IV, 196

Age of maturity, II, 219, 421 f.

Agga, name, I, 120

Aggadah, I, 205, II, 293, 298, 429; on Abraham, VI, 39; III, 71, 273; anthropomorphism in, VI, 178, 268, VIII, 99; debates recorded in, II, 310; doctrine of the Exile, V, 101; on Elijah, V, 195; form of transmission, II, 65; re fasting, VI, 14; German students of, VI, 422, VIII, 44 f.; on God's love, VIII, 114; handmaid of the Halakhah, II, 298, 429, VI, 178; on the Hereafter, VIII, 105; historical outlook, VI, 231; on humility, VIII, 121; liturgical poets and, V, 151, VII, 83; messianic concepts, V, 139, 164, 185; mixed reactions to, VI, 43, 152 ff., 160 f., 175-81; Mohammed's familiarity with, III, 83, 265; Palestinian and Babylonian positions on, II, 316 f.; reappraisal of older teachings, II, 362; secular stories and romances, VI, 181 ff.; "seventy nations," VIII, 216; source of philosophic speculation, VIII, 4 ff.; transition from mystical to rationalist, II, 426; Yosephon III, 240; see also Ethics; Midrash; Rabbis and rabbinate; Talmud

Aggadic Midrash, see Midrash

Aghlabids, Moroccan dynasty, III, 108

Agnosticism, VIII, 79; in the Renaissance of Islam, V, 103 ff.; views on matter and space, VIII, 88

Agobard, archbishop of Lyons, IV, 14, 18, 26, 51 f., 220, VI, 153, VIII, 26; anti-Jewish writings, IV, 263, V, 123, 126 f.; dilemma re canon law, IV, 263 f.; on magister Judaeorum, V, 63

Agriculture: ancient, I, 42, 250-55, 406-7; in Babylonia, II, 244, 246, 257, 414; changing attitudes and laws, II, 263 f., IV, 151; effect of antisemitism, II, 244; Essenes' occupation, II, 48; evolution from nomadic life to, I, 55 ff.; exiles engaged in, I, 109; laborers, I, 70, 281; in Palestine, I, 277, II, 245, 246; rate of production, I, 65, 251, 253, 265

—— medieval: Jewish contributions to, III, 70 f., 197, 260, IV, 161; Jewish settlements, IV, 29; Jewish share in, IV, 151 ff.; Karaites and, V, 272 f.; laws, V, 257

—— see also Farmers; Land; Peasants

Agrippa I, king, I, 66, 219, 236, 246, 261, 264, 372, II, 131; economic blockade of Tyre and Sidon, I, 277; family's statues, I, 401; letter to Caligula, I, 218; no right to be king of Judaea, I, 223

Agrippa II (Marcus Julius Agrippa), II, 82, 91, 105, 123; imaginary arguments by, II, 99, 101

Agrippa, Marcus Vipsanius, I, 215, 218, II, 17, 402; protection of temple funds, I, 215, 393

Agrippenses, congregation of, II, 402

'Agunah, II, 238, IV, 184

Agur b. Jakel, VI, 160

Aha, R. (Amora), II, 392

Aha, R. (Sabora), VI, 20 f.

Aha, R., "the fort commander," II, 259

Ahab, king, I, 68, 77, 78, 93, 318, 327; chariots, I, 332; and Jezebel, I, 322; in battle of Karkara, I, 67

Aha b. Adda, R., VI, 238

Aha b. Jacob, R., prayer of thanksgiving, VII, 109

Aha b. Hanina, R., II, 287

Ahai of Shabha, R., V, 15, 32, 212, VI, 22 f., 81, 156; juridico-homiletical work, VI, 37 ff., 169, 174, 202, 336 ff.; on liturgical problems, VII, 68, 110; weekly homilies, VI, 91

Ahasuerus-Xerxes, I, 354

Ahaz, king, I, 326, VIII, 361

Ahimaaz, ancestor of Ahimaaz of Oria, V, 376 f., VI, 216 f.

Ahimaaz of Oria, III, 180, IV, 23, VIII, 44; chronicle of, III, 154, IV, 157, 216 f.; re Paltiel, V, 40 f.

Ahiqar story, I, 187; VII, 183

Ahmad, numerical equivalent of, V, 86

Ahmad as-Sinhaji al-Qarafi, see Qarafi

Ahuramazda, I, 130, 348, II, 316

Ahwaz, city, IV, 201, 340

Ai, city, I, 299

'Ain Fashkha cave, see Dead Sea Scrolls
Air, cosmic principle, VIII, 22
Aix-en-Provence, IV, 58
Ajal, doctrine, VIII, 259
Akhenaton unodeistic reform, I, 45 f., 53
Akko, see Acco
Alabarch, office of, I, 261, 409, 410
Alaçar, IV, 39
Alans, III, 98, 203; Jewish influence on, III, 200, 208
Alaric II, Breviarium, III, 35, 49
Al-Balia, see Isaac b. Baruch
Alban, Saint, shrine of, IV, 84
Albert of Aix, IV, 111
Albertus Magnus, VIII, 167
Albigensian Crusade, IV, 61, 132, VIII, 32
Albigensianism, IV, 9
Al-Biruni Ḥamza al-Isfahani, Arab historiographer and astronomer, V, 13, 327, VI, 199, 307, 437, VIII, 148; chronological computations, VIII, 189 f., 194, 209; Chronology of Creation, VIII, 377; collector of scientific material, VIII, 370; Table, VIII, 368
Albo, Joseph, VII, 207, VIII, 99
Alcaeus, poet, I, 184
Alcala de Henares, Spain, IV, 32 f.
Alchemy, VIII, 223 ff.
Alcuin, IV, 26, 44 f.
Alduin, bishop of Limoges, IV, 57; conversion of Jews, IV, 284
'Alenu, prayer, IV, 138, VII, 75 f., 89
Aleppo (Ḥaleb; Ṣobah), Syria, III, 104 f.; biblical manuscript, VI, 447; exilarch, V, 311; Rabbanite community, V, 50, VI, 247
Alexander, alabarch, I, 261, 265
Alexander II, pope, IV, 94, 122, 131; crusade against Spanish Islam, IV, 284; intervention for Spanish Jewry, V, 361; against forced conversion, IV, 236
Alexander III, pope, IV, 14, 434; re Christian nurses, IV, 15; re Jewish officials, IV, 15; re Judeo-Christian litigation, IV, 16, 240; and St. Augustine monastery, IV, 84; re tithes, IV, 153 f.; welcomed by Jewish elders, V, 59
Alexander Jannaeus, king, I, 167, 215, 218, 221 ff., 235 f., 276, II, 13, V, 255, VI, 207

Alexander b. Moses, IV, 119
Alexander of Aphrodisias, VIII, 76
Alexander Severus, emperor: donor to synagogues, II, 87, 191, 402; religious syncretism, II, 390
Alexander the Great, II, 4, 311-12; Alexander Romance, VIII, 306; alleged conversion of, VIII, 306; conquest of western Asia, I, 184, 228, 338; Du'l Qarnayim, V, 329; encounter with Simon the Pious, VI, 207; era of, VIII, 205; established communities, II, 34, 341; Hebraic paraphrase of Romance, VI, 192; and Jewish quarter, I, 188; Samaria, rebuilt by, II, 27; and Temple of Bel, I, 168
Alexandria, ancient: antisemitism, I, 188, 191, 216, 219, 246, 372, 381, II, 159, 189, 365, 402, see also "Acts of the Heathen Martyrs"; center of trade with India and China, II, 249; Claudius' edict, I, 240, 403; early capitalistic system, I, 201, 411; intellectual center extinguished, II, 163; intermarriages in, II, 233; largest Jewish community, I, 185, 188, 393; necropolis, II, 286; omitted from Paul's journeying, II, 84, 365; Phoenician ghetto, I, 176; population, I, 171, 371; religious customs, I, 200, II, 306; shipowners' guild, II, 261; a "sister" of Jerusalem, I, 219; status of Jews, I, 190, 221, 240, 248, 403, II, 419; uprising suppressed, II, 95
—— medieval, III, 271, VIII, 57, 241; Arab conquest, II, 402, III, 90; Coptic church, III, 9; Jewish community, II, 402, III, 106; medical treatise concerning, VIII, 226; prohibition of new synagogue, III, 9; schools of, VIII, 61, 76
—— see also Egypt
Alexis Comnenus, Byzantine emperor, III, 186; and the papacy, IV, 95
Aleyan Epic, I, 312
Al-Fasi, see David b. Abraham al-Fasi
Alfasi, Isaac b. Jacob, Spanish jurist, II, 295, 425, IV, 213, VI, 27, 48; on Babylonian Talmud, VI, 25; birthplace, VI, 367; re celebration of the New Year, V, 29, 49; compilation of laws, VI, 84-90; influence in southern France, VIII, 292; legalization of drafts, IV, 213; Maimonides and, VI,

59; manuscripts, VI, 368; prohibition of Arabic tunes, VII, 205; on ransom of captives, IV, 178; responsa, VI, 117; on Saadiah's Book of Pledges, VI, 69

Al-Fellaḥi, vizier, III, 158

Alfonso, Spanish kings, see Alphonso

Al-Gasum, see Ibn al-Jasus

Algebra, VIII, 153 ff.

Algeria: dialect of Berber tribes, VII, 12; preservation of Saadiah's texts, VI, 296

Al-Ghazzali, see Ghazzali, al-

Al-Haitham, see Ibn 'Adi

Al-Hajjaj, governor, III, 120

Al-Ḥakim, caliph of Cordova, VI, 61

Al-Ḥakim bi-Amrillah, Egyptian caliph, III, 122 ff., 289, VIII, 248

Al-Ḥanbali, Abu 'Ali, V, 296

Al-Ḥaqir an-Nafi', court physician, VIII, 248

Al-Ḥaqq, see 'Abd al-Ḥaqq

Al-Ḥarith, Khaibar leader, III, 87

Al-Ḥarizi, Yehudah b. Solomon, poet and traveler, VII, 155, VIII, 64, 306 f., 340; on cantor-preachers, VII, 58 ff., 81; linguistic feats, VII, 191; on medical quack, VIII, 238; original Hebrew work, VII, 185 f.; paraphrase of Hariri's Maqamas, VII, 184 ff.; poem reading backward and forward, VII, 151, 197; on R. 'Uzziel of Ḥamat, III, 159; translations into Hebrew, VI, 60, VII, 7

Al-Ḥijr, city, III, 64

Al-Ḥimyari, re Granada, III, 109

'Ali, Mohammed's son-in-law, V, 168, VI, 12; greeting from Jews of Mosul, III, 276; marriage of his son Ḥusain, III, 89; violent death, III, 122

'Ali aṭ-Ṭabari, see Ṭabari, 'Ali aṭ-

'Ali b. Israel Alluf, V, 298 f.

'Ali b. Suleiman, VI, 287 f.; dependence on Rabbanite exegetes, VI, 291

'Ali b. Yehudah 'Alan of Tiberias, VII, 34

'Ali b. Yusuf, Almoravid ruler, III, 145

'Alides, Muslim faction, V, 375, VI, 12

"Alien law," theory of, and "serfdom," IV, 262

Aliens: resident, I, 179, 325, 375; status in Carolingian Empire, IV, 50

'Ali ibn 'Isa, vizier, III, 146, 153, 158; and his Jewish bankers, IV, 201, 208

Al-Idrisi, see Idrisi, al-

Al-Isfahani, see Abu 'Isa al-Isfahani

Aliturus, actor, II, 9

Al-Jaḥiẓ, VIII, 67 f.; on bilingualism, VII, 10; on his lack of success, VIII, 237; on interfaith animosities, V, 108; on intermarriage, III, 143; study of zoology, VIII, 386

Al-Jauhari, Arab lexicographer, VII, 26

Al-Jubai, Jewish rationalist, VIII, 67

Al-Khwarizmi, Mohammed ibn Musa, Muslim mathematician, VIII, 147; Algebra, VIII, 149, 153

Allegory: in biblical interpretation, I, 205-7, II, 144, 158, VI, 297, VII, 167 f., VIII, 100; harmonization of revelation and logic, VIII, 85 f.

Allodia, hereditary, IV, 47

Al-Malik az-Azhir Khoshkadem, Mameluk sultan, V, 268

Al-Ma'mun, caliph: decree re sects, V, 9 f., 222; expulsion of many Jews from Baghdad, III, 100; founder of libraries, VII, 138; Judeo-Christian debates, V, 83, 85, 110; promoter of scientific studies, VIII, 162, 167, 198

Almanac, Latin treatise on, VIII, 362

Al-Manṣur, caliph: building of Baghdad, III, 99, IV, 170, VIII, 148; employment of non-Muslims, III, 126, 152; stamp of tax receipts, III, 168; transplanting of Armenians to Syria, III, 98

Al-Manṣur, Muslim regent of Cordova: decree re clothing of Jews, III, 141; and Ibn Jau, V, 44

Al-Mas'udi, VI, 192, 199; on differences between Hebrew and Arabic, VI, 453; on Saadiah's Bible translation, VI, 458

Al-Mawardi, VI, 150

Almeria, city, IV, 332

Almohades, Berber sect, III, 173; conquest of Spain, IV, 21; influence on Jewish theology, VIII, 96; Jewish refugees, III, 291, IV, 3 ff.; mass conversions, III, 127, 176; religious persecution by, III, 108, 111, 124, 132, 281; Saladin's appeal to, IV, 298

Almoravids, Moroccan dynasty, III, 108, 124 f., 289; conquest of Spain, VII, 153, 186; persecution of dhimmis, IV, 3, V, 200

Alms, see Charity

Al-Mu'izz, Faṭimid caliph, III, 154, VI, 325, VIII, 167

Al-Muqammiṣ, David ibn Merwan, III, 295; classification of the sciences, VIII, 141 f.; commentary on Genesis, VI, 284; on eschatological retribution, VIII, 104; quoted on oneness of God, VIII, 97 f.; "Twenty Tractates," VIII, 58

Al-Muqtadir, caliph, III, 88, 158; characterized by Suyuti, III, 153; decree re public office, VIII, 236; eunuchs of, IV, 191 f.

Al-Musta'in, ruler of Saragossa, VIII, 248

Al-Mustanṣir, Faṭimid caliph, III, 190

Al-Mu'tadhid, caliph, III, 152 f.; re taxation of Jews, III, 167

Al-Mu'tadhim, caliph, III, 166

Al-Mu'tamin, III, 158

Al-Muzaffar 'Umar ibn Nur ad-Din, VIII, 251

Alphabet: Cyrillic, III, 208 f.; Glagolitic, III, 209, 330; Hebrew-Phoenician, I, 307; Ugaritic, I, 307; Western Slavonic, III, 218; see also individual alphabets, e.g., Arabic alphabet

"Alphabet of Ben Sira," VI, 159, 169

Alphonsine tables, VIII, 161

Alphonso I, king of Aragon and Navarre, IV, 30; godfather of Petrus Alphonsi, V, 116; marriage to Doña Urraca, IV, 252 f.; privilege for merchants, IV, 179; see also Alphonso VII

Alphonso II, king of Aragon, IV, 159

Alphonso III (Alphonso the Great), king of Asturias, IV, 35

Alphonso VI, king of Castile and Leon, IV, 9, 36, 254; re moneylending, IV, 207; re Mozarabs, III, 127

Alphonso VII, king of Castile and Leon: amnesties, IV, 39 f.; and Christian merchants, IV, 179 f.; coronation, IV, 28; egalitarian policy, IV, 254; see also Alphonso I

Alphonso VIII, king of Castile: egalitarian policy, IV, 254; Jewish mistress, IV, 37; papal threats, IV, 42, 188 f.

Alphonso X, king of Castile and Leon, IV, 37, VIII, 161

Alqabeṣ, Solomon, VII, 251

Al-Qali, Armenian philologist in Cordova, VII, 19, 20

Al-Qasim ibn Ibrahim, a Zaidite, V, 7, 12 f.

Al-Quds, Muslim name of Jerusalem, IV, 109

Al-Qumisi, Daniel, see Qumisi, Daniel al-

Alroy, David (Menahem b. Solomon Al-Roḥi), III, 204; messianic movement, V, 202 ff.

Altars: of the patriarchs, I, 48; prohibited outside of Jerusalem, I, 128; see also Bamot

Al-Tell, city, I, 299

Altercatio Jasonis et Papisci, II, 133

Altercation (Theophilus), II, 138

Al tiqri, formula of, VI, 166

Al-Zarqali, Muslim scientist, VIII, 358; Ibn Ezra and, VIII, 173; "Toledan Tables," VIII, 171

Amadia, city, V, 203

Amah, see Slaves and slavery

Amalekites, I, 57, 317, III, 63

Amalfi, Italy, IV, 24

Amalfitans, in Cairo, IV, 331 f.

Aman, see Passport

Amarna Age, see El-Amarna age

Amaziah, king of Judah, VII, 313

Amaziah, priest of Bethel, I, 86

Ambrose, Saint, II, 172, V, 133; and Gregory I, III, 243; victory over Theodosius, II, 189, 192, 401, III, 30

Amel-Marduk (Evil Merodach), I, 115, 116; pacific policy, I, 132

Amen: congregational chant, VII, 125; repetition of, VI, 130

Amen-em-ope, I, 363, VII, 165

'Am ha-areṣ, I, 278, 280, III, 263; discrimination against, discontinued, II, 272; enmity of scholars, II, 242, 282, 286, IV, 167, V, 178, 284, VI, 342, VII, 109; and Karaites, V, 219, 394

Amida, Mesopotamia, Church of, III, 10; contributions of Jews to, III, 231

'Amidah, prayer, I, 186, 351, 376, II, 61, 112, 115, 282, 351, V, 26, 248, 303, VI, 14 f.; accuracy of oral transmission, VII, 112; benedictions, VII, 66 ff., 244, 247; date of, II, 40, 61, 345; definitive form, II, 119, VII, 101; Musaf, VII, 107 f., 127, 172; prayer against heretics, II, 135, 381; prayer for peace, II, 115; substitution of new prayers for, VII, 69, 95 f.; targum of, VII, 67; texts, II, 376, VII, 105 f.; see also Prayers

Amittai b. Shefaṭiah, poet, V, 152, VII, 176 ff., VIII, 30, 60

Amixia, II, 223; *see also under* Marriage
Ammi, R., VI, 441
Ammianus Marcellinus, II, 257
'Ammiel, name of Messiah's father, V, 153
Ammon and Ammonites, I, 55, 56, 156, 162, 190, III, 61; endogamous exclusion of, II, 232, VI, 303
Amnesty, general, in Castile, IV, 39 f.
Amon, king, I, 78, 155
Amorai, R., VIII, 35 f.
Amoraim, I, 386, II, 295, 296, VI, 17 ff., 30, 65, 240, VIII, 21; and ancient Babylonian traditions, II, 207; authority of, VI, 201; debates, V, 180 f., VI, 63; end of age, VI, 17; and geonim, VI, 334, VII, 108; mystics among, VIII, 6; ritualistic autonomy, VII, 65; status of first generation, VI, 29; support of synagogue, VII, 62; tombs of, VI, 436; and written midrashim, VI, 158; *see also* Talmud
Amos, prophet, I, 79, 94, 128; expelled from Bethel, I, 86; sycamore grower, I, 87, 89; teachings of, I, 25, 72, 340, 360
Amphictyonies: Greek, I, 319; Israelitic, I, 61
Amram b. Sheshna, gaon of Sura, IV, 187; anti-Karaite bias, VII, 70; on congregational leaders, VII, 80; letter to Barcelona community, V, 19 f.; prayer book, V, 28, 248, VI, 15, 69, 112, 264, VII, 69, 81, 111 ff.; re prayers, V, 26, VII, 65, 250; on thanksgiving for education, VII, 109
Amraphel, king of Shinear, I, 301
Amulets, protective, II, 20, 336, 337, 390, 435, VIII, 29
Amulo, French churchman, IV, 14, 18; antisemitism, IV, 53, 54; appeal for obedience to canon law, IV, 54
Amun hymns, Egyptian, I, 52
Anacharsis, the Scythian, I, 228
Anacletus II, pope, IV, 121; family background, IV, 10 f.; and Roger II, IV, 21
Anagrams, in poems, VII, 49 f.
Analogy: approach to philology, VII, 34, 52, 58; in biblical interpretation, V, 213
'Anan b. David, founder of Karaism, II, 221, III, 161, 202, V, 181, 210-22; approach to Jewish law and life, V, 216-22; Book of Commandments, V, 212, 219 f., 227, 231; claim re his copy of Deuteronomy, VI, 243 f.; conflict with brother Ḥananiah, V, 9; genealogy, VI, 200 f., 446; and his successors, V, 256 f.; Ibn Daud's discussion of, VI, 481; liturgical reforms, VII, 64, 72 f., 110 f.; on medical practice, VIII, 247; observation of new moon, VIII, 194; in Persia, V, 183; predecessors of, VI, 363; reading vs. spelling of biblical words, VI, 243; on the soul, VIII, 107; on the Talmud, V, 276; writings hidden in caves, V, 255; Yannai as legal source, VII, 94
Ananel, I, 216
Ananias, general, I, 215
Ananias, high priest, I, 272
Ananias, merchant-missionary, I, 173, 183
'Ananites: attitude toward Jesus, V, 262; doctrine of catenation, VI, 69; *see also* Karaites
Ananus, high priest, II, 131
Anapa, *see* Gorgippia
'Anaqim, biblical giants, III, 63
Anarchy, in Roman society, II, 234
Anastasios the Sinaite, III, 175, VI, 304; anti-Jewish dialogues, V, 350
Anastasius, Byzantine emperor: and Antioch, III, 6; capture of Yotabe, III, 69 f.
'Anat, 'Anati, 'Anat-Yahu, goddess, I, 128
Anathema, *see* Curse; Excommunication
Anatoli b. Joseph, Sicilian judge and poet, VII, 176
Anavim, I, 152, 364, II, 269
Anbari, 'Ubaid Allah al-, Muslim philosopher, VI, 472
Ancestor worship, I, 148
Anchorets, VIII, 119 f.
Andalusians: in Fez, III, 145; quotation re children and Jews of, III, 148
Andreas, archbishop of Bari: alleged conversion to Judaism, III, 189 f., IV, 294
Andrew II, king of Hungary, III, 213
Angelos stones of Thera, II, 25
Angels, I, 139, 140, II, 17 ff., 32, 44, 335, VII, 180, 275; antagonism to man, VII, 251; Babylonian-Persian, in Arabia, III, 82; in Book of Jubilees, II, 43; heavenly family, II, 317, VIII, 23; as intermediaries, V, 228, 259, VI, 469, VII, 76, VIII, 3 ff., 93 ff.; intervention

Angels (*Continued*)
of, II, 67; knowledge of Aramaic, VII, 193; in messianism, V, 142; ministering, VII, 66, 193; in magic formulas, VIII, 8 f., 21; in poetry, VII, 181 f.; on Sinai, VIII, 6; singing, VII, 77; winged, II, 332; *see also* Heavenly hosts

Angers, France, IV, 182

'*Ani*, I, 152, 364, II, 269

Anilaeus, principality, I, 168, III, 63

Animal figures in art, II, 9, 10, 13, 15, 154, 402

Animals, VI, 103; castration of, V, 174; compensation for suffering of, VIII, 103 f., 230; consumption of, V, 92 f., VIII, 227; first-born, V, 53; life-endangering illness of, VIII, 228, 387; names of, VIII, 226; ritualistic slaughtering, II, 306; in stories, VI, 182 f.; VII, 189; tithe of, V, 399; *see also* Meat; Monsters; Slaughtering

Animal sacrifice, V, 123, 273, 249, VI, 125, VII, 78 f., VIII, 228; in Armenia, III, 110; in Khazaria, III, 202; *see also* Paschal lamb; Sacrifices

Animal worship, Egyptian, I, 199, 402

Annona, I, 410

Anointed priest, term, I, 152, 364

Anomaly, approach to philology, VII, 34, 58

Ansegisus, archbishop of Sens, IV, 56

Anselm, Saint: treatise on incarnation, V, 115; motto, VIII, 113 f.

Ansuvannam, India, III, 114 f.

Anthropomorphism, V, 249; in aggadic works, VI, 178, 268, 342; biblical, I, 196, V, 90, 106, 197, 226, VI, 267 f., 300 ff., VIII, 99 ff.; defense of, I, 13; and divine attributes, VIII, 97; Karaite and Muslim charges, V, 121, 258 f.; in mystic literature, V, 258, VI, 175, VIII, 25 ff., 29 ff.; Rashi and, VI, 51; rejection of, I, 49, 335, VI, 45 f., VIII, 57 ff.; in Septuagint, I, 383, VI, 258 f.

Anthropopathism, VIII, 98

Antichretic transactions, II, 302, 431

Antichrist, *see* Armilus; *Dajjal*

Antifeminism, VIII, 53

Antigonus of Socho, II, 41

Anti-intellectualism, VIII, 17

Anti-Jewish riots, *see* Antisemitism

Antimonarchical trends, I, 91-93, 336-38

Antinomianism, V, 80, 122, 194, 235, VI, 3, 143, VIII, 49; Jewish attitude toward, II, 310, VIII, 17 ff., 295; in magic arts, VIII, 11; Qur'an and, VI, 7

Antinoupolis, I, 410

Antioch: antisemitism, I, 188, II, 189; archaeological excavations, III, 230; cemeteries, II, 286; Christians, II, 188, 189, 366, 401, III, 38, 161; Crusaders in, IV, 243, 285; decline, III, 105; earthquake, III, 234 f.; Hannah and sons buried in, VI, 417; Herod's work in, I, 236; Jerusalem named after, I, 229, 398; Jews in, I, 216, 248, III, 3, 58, 73; loot from Temple in Jerusalem, I, 217; Persian conquests of, II, 178, III, 19, 56; political and religious riots, III, 6, 21, 38, 161; *see also* New Antioch; Syria

Antiochians: in Jerusalem, I, 399; vilification of Jews and Judaism, I, 192

Antiochus, renegade, II, 3

Antiochus III (Antiochus the Great), king of Syria, I, 239, 369, 373, 397; charter extended to Palestine Jews, I, 216

Antiochus IV (Antiochus Epiphanes), king of Syria, I, 166, 185, 220, 244, 369, II, 30, 81, 98, 100; conflict with Jews, I, 193, 216, 217, 230, VI, 189; desecration of Temple, I, 192; homily on, VIII, 278; identification with Zeus, I, 229, 398; oppressive measures, I, 229, 398; story of ritual murder, I, 193; *see also* Maccabees, revolt by

Antiochus V, king of Syria, I, 216

Antiochus, Scroll of, *see* Hasmoneans, Scroll of

Anti-oriental sentiment, I, 212

Antipater, king VI, 192

Antirationalism, and progress of medical science, VIII, 248

Antisemitism, ancient: in Alexandria, I, 188, 191, 209, 216, 219, 381, II, 189; in Asia Minor, I, 283; Christian teachings and, II, 353; and economic motivations, I, 194, 383, II, 241; in Egypt, I, 381, 383, II, 89, 159; fountainhead of literature, II, 427; Hellenistic, I, 188-95, 283, 379-83, II, 55, 170, 401; and historic beliefs, II, 55; Marcionite, II, 167 f., 394, VIII, 288; in Persia, I, 116; pogroms, I, 191, 266, II, 189, 402; in Syria, I, 283, II, 89

—— medieval, III, 3 f., 91-94; accusation of demonic powers, V, 132; characterizations of Jews, V, 131 ff.; of clergy, IV, 14 ff., 53 ff., 121 ff.; economic basis, III, 194, IV, 85, 206, V, 96 ff.; imperial oppression, VII, 94 f., 266; of Jewish converts, V, 115 f.; and Jewish legalism, VIII, 52; liturgical, V, 352, VI, 42, VII, 85; millenary movements and, IV, 91 f.; of Nicetas, IV, 166; in periods of crisis, V, 111 f.; of Peter the Venerable, IV, 122; of Petrus II Candiano, IV, 25; popular, IV, 67, 69 f.; and protected minorities, III, 170 ff.; Qarafi on Christian, V, 108 f., 346; reaction of poets to, VII, 177 ff.; and royal protection, IV, 79 f.; social, III, 139-49, V, 96 ff., 125-34; tanners as targets of, IV, 166 f.

—— see also Massacres; Persecution; Pogroms

Antitalmudic movements, II, 264

Antonia, fortress, I, 239, II, 284

Antonines, dynasty, II, 109

"Antoninus," friend of R. Judah, II, 187, 374, 400

Antoninus Martyr, II, 355, 412

Antoninus Pius, emperor, II, 107, 108, 110, 126, 132, 187, 193, 374, 400; encouragement of scholars, II, 243

Antonius, Marcus, I, 237

Apamaea, surname, II, 338

Apamaea, city (Asia Minor), I, 393; coins, II, 24

Apamaea, city (Syria), II, 199

Aphraates, bishop, II, 149, 191, V, 109 f., 114, 358; anti-Jewish polemics, VI, 322; censure of Judeo-Christian relations, VI, 241

Aphrodite, I, 374

Apion of Alexandria, I, 192, 233, 242; antisemitism, I, 195, II, 170

Apiphior, equation with pope, IV, 241

Apiru, *see* Habiru

Apocalypses and apocalyptic writings, I, 153; Baruch, II, 60; collection, V, 353; Daniel, III, 179, 183, 315; Elijah, III, 16, 19; and messianism, V, 139-50; and the supernatural, II, 17, 335

Apocrypha: biblical, I, 385, II, 145, VI, 159; contribution to mysticism, VIII, 5; glorification of martyrs, IV, 95 f.; messianic speculation, II, 59, 60, V,

139; parallels in Yosephon, VI, 419 f.; Pharisaic acceptance, II, 17, 44; Slavonic translations, III, 211; source of folk tales, VI, 186 f.

—— other: Falasha books, II, 212; *Megillat bene Hashmona'i,* VI, 269; midrashic, II, 296, 426; pseudo-Philo, VI, 421 f.

Apocryticus, II, 391

Apoios, I, 389

Apokatastasis, term, II, 360

Appollinopolis Magna (Edfu), Jewish quarter, I, 188, 380

Apollo, I, 61, 119

Apollonius Molon, I, 194, 195

Apollonius of Tyana, II, 175

Apologetics, Jewish, I, 195-99, V, 83 ff., 110 ff.; and Christian polemics, II, 130 ff., V, 109 ff., 114 f.; and Jewish philosophy, VIII, 135 ff.; major themes, V, 117

Apostasy, I, 172; departure from orthodoxy as, II, 292; from Islam, III, 132; and magic, VIII, 47 f.; and relapse of a convert, III, 14; *see also under* Convert

Apostates, treatment of, II, 253, 287

Apostolé (aurum coronarium), II, 194

Apostolic Constitutions, I, 186

Apothecaries, V, 96

Apries, king of Egypt, I, 110, 346

Aqabiah b. Mahallalel, II, 41, 346

'Aqedot, in Mayence, VI, 193, 218

'Aqiba, R., I, 231, II, 46, 116, 118, 125, 204, 220, 230, 287, 314, 319, VI, 181; Alphabet of, II, 426, V, 259, VIII, 11 ff., 191; buried in Caesarea, II, 371; compilation of tannaitic law, VI, 107; disciples of, I, 190, IV, 145; encounter with ghost, VI, 23, VII, 245 f.; fervor of prayer, VII, 74 f.; on free will, VIII, 109; intellectual leader, II, 98, 100, 121; letter symbolism, VIII, 15; on marriage relations, II, 221, 228, 409, 410; martyrdom, II, 100, IV, 96, 104; mishnah, unnamed, VI, 204; priestly blessing, II, 282; on the revelation of the Torah, V, 93; on transmigration of souls, VIII, 36

'Aqri'el, angel, VIII, 8 f.

Aquila, proselyte, II, 143, 147; Greek fragments, II, 17; literalness of, VI, 271; quoted, II, 153

Arabia: archaeological excavations, III, 256 ff.; cultural and economic contributions of Jews, III, 70, IV, 161; destruction of Jewish communities, VII, 191; Jewish inscriptions, III, 61, 66, 82, 258; Jewish refugees from, V, 180; Jews in, I, 169, 372, II, 211, III, 60 f., 63 ff.; messianic movements, V, 168; Mohammed's treaties with Christians and Jews, III, 163; a province of Rome, II, 369; role of kings, III, 61; urban settlements, III, 71

Arabia Felix, III, 71

Arabic alphabet: adopted in Persian language, VII, 5; Muslim view of use of, VII, 190; weak consonants in, VII, 43

Arabic classics, translations: Hebrew, IV, 3; Latin, IV, 32, 248

Arabic language: Aramaic displaced by, II, 387, VI, 255; borrowings from Hebrew and Aramaic, III, 81, VII, 10, 89; dialects, VI, 407, VII, 4 ff., 10, 221; diminutive forms and biblical parallels, VII, 16; glorification of, V, 330, VI, 168; grammarians and lexicographers, VII, 5 ff., 20; in Hebrew alphabet, V, 112, VIII, 75, 140 f.; influence on Hebrew speech, VI, 250; latitude in punctuation, VI, 243; like-sounding words, VII, 8; liturgical use, VII, 67; masoretic monograph, VII, 33; medical writings, VIII, 242 ff.; numerical values, VIII, 150; plant and animal names, VIII, 229; in poetry, VII, 150; refinement of, VII, 59; Saadiah's purism, VI, 268 f.; spread of use of, IV, 21, VII, 6 ff., 33, 45, 59 f.; translations of sacred writings into, VI, 263-72; transliteration of names and terms, VIII, 172, 174; unifying force in expansion of Judaism and Islam, III, 118 f.; use of, in explaining Hebrew terms, VII, 18; use of, by Jews, III, 118, 170, IV, 3, 36, V, 110, VII, 7, 59 f., 191 ff.

Arabic numerals, VIII, 150

Arab-Jewish relations, III, 60 ff.; and the Berbers, III, 90 f.; occasional violence in, III, 122 f.; in Spain, III, 157 f.; *see also* Judeo-Muslim relations

Arabs: ancient: Ammonites and Moabites overrun by, I, 190, VI, 308; Mesene occupied by, II, 405; penetration into Palestine and Babylonia, III, 60, 89 f.;

pressure upon Edomites, I, 106; relations with Jews and Romans, II, 92, 114, 369, 375, seminomadic southern, I, 57

—— medieval: alliance with Jews against Mohammed, III, 78 f.; attitude toward agriculture, IV, 152; conquest of Alexandria, III, 90; cultivation of self-esteem, III, 98; familiarity with Scripture, III, 82; ignorance of Hebrew, V, 328; rhyming technique, VII, 88; *see also* Berbers; Muslims; Muslim-Christian relations; Judeo-Muslim relations

—— modern: multiple marriages, II, 227

Aragon: *fueros*, IV, 13; rabbinic manuscripts, VII, 171; royal flour mills, IV, 318; *see also* Spain

Aramaeans, I, 55, 67, 322

Aramaic deeds, I, 111, VI, 66 f., 357; *see also* Deeds

Aramaic language: Abraham's, I, 20; areas of use, I, 121, 159, 185, II, 146 f., 405, VI, 27 ff., VII, 5; biblical, VII, 26, 39; biblical translations in, II, 146, 387, 411, III, 72 f., VI, 239 f., 255-63, 312 (*see also* Targum); decline in use, VI, 56, 63, VII, 20; eastern dialect, VII, 29; Hebrew and, II, 142, 147, VI, 240; of Jesus and disciples, II, 66, 67, 145, 355; loan words, III, 70, VI, 13; magic formulas in, VIII, 9; in Palestine, I, 187, V, 227; plant and animal names, VIII, 229; prayers in, VII, 66 f.; repudiated by some Jews, II, 145, 146; supplanted by Arabic, II, 387, III, 119, VII, 5, 101; transliterations, VI, 248; use by Hebrew authors, VII, 192 f., 195

Ararat, Mount, location of, VII, 18

ARB, ARD, number, III, 315

Arbitration, courts of, II, 266, 267

Arc, measurement of, VIII, 355

Arcadius, Roman emperor, II, 191; re Gaza, III, 8

Archaeology: Palestinian, II, 10 ff.; 'Ain Fashkha cave, II, 52; *see also* Dead Sea Scrolls; Qumran; and ancient art, II, 330; Bethshan, II, 28; Beth She'arim (*q.v.*), II, 398; coins, II, 28, 369; Gerasa, II, 174; lack of evidence for Christianity, II, 63, 74, 353, 361; ossuaries, II, 63; paucity of extant sculptures, II, 9; Philippopolis, II, 175; search for churches, II, 392; synagogues

discovered, II, 241, 284, 285, 423; Third Wall in Jerusalem, II, 108, 369, 377

—— other: Antioch, III, 230; Arabia, III, 256 ff.; Khwarizm, III, 326; magic bowls in Euphrates Valley, II, 23, VIII, 8 ff., 274 ff.; Russia, III, 213, 333 f.; and spread of Jews in Europe and the Orient, II, 210 f., 406 f.; at Vatican, II, 74; *see also* Inscriptions

Archelaus, king, I, 263, II, 21, 33; banishment to Vienne, III, 47

Archevolte, Samuel, VII, 207

Architecture: impact of Greek, II, 9; unimportant to synagogue, II, 284; Jewish, in England, IV, 281 f., VIII, 159

Archives: ancient, II, 265, 266; geonic, VI, 112 f., 383

Archontes, I, 274

"Arch Presbyter," in medieval English Jewry, V, 319

Ardashir I, Persian emperor, II, 174, 176, 317, III, 55; Mesene conquered by, II, 405

Ardea Viraz, II, 229

Areopagus in Athens, Paul's speech, II, 79 f., 362, 363, 389

Aretino, Pietro, VII, 149

Areus, king, I, 185

Argabadh, title, II, 196, 403

Arians, sect, II, 134, 188, III, 7, 25, 35, VI, 6 f.; *see also* Arius

Aribert, bishop of Narbonne, IV, 47

Aristarchus of Hippo, VIII, 163 f.

Aristeas, Letter of, *see Letter of Aristeas*

Aristobulus, philosopher, I, 196, 204, 207, 396

Aristobulus II, high priest, II, 13, 54, 349

Aristocracy: caste system of Persia and Rome, II, 176; lay, I, 73 f., 274; priestly, I, 149, 272, 274, *see also* Priests; sins and abuses, I, 126; *see also* Classes, social

Aristotle, I, 174, 283; basic concepts, VI, 146, 396, VIII, 76, 90 f., 92 f., 98, 114; commentaries on, VIII, 65 f.; division of sciences, VIII, 143, 146; ethical system, VIII, 117, 120 ff.; influence on Jewish philosophy, VIII, 63 ff., 324; and Judaism, VI, 230; legend of conversion, VIII, 77, 306; meeting with Jew of Coele-Syria, I, 377; quoted, I, 184; spurious "Theory" of, VIII, 91; translations of, VIII, 316

Arius, V, 379, VII, 128; *see also* Arians

Arks, built into synagogue, V, 247 f.

Ark of the Covenant, I, 49, 59, 314

Arles, France, III, 250, IV, 55 f.; corvée labor by Jews of, IV, 56; custumal, IV, 60 f.; defense of, II, 179, 398; Jewish community, IV, 59

Armenia: Christianity in, II, 165; deportees from, II, 204, 404; and Edessa, IV, 114, V, 203; families of Jewish descent, I, 169, 283; forced Jewish purchase of churches, III, 160; Jews in, I, 372, II, 405, III, 110, VIII, 288; Persian invasion, III, 18; and Syrians, III, 98

Armenian Code, VI, 4

Armillary sphere, VIII, 166 f.

Armilus, III, 19, V, 144 ff., 152, 160, 358 f., 364, VI, 481

Armoricus, William, IV, 62

Arms, *see* Weapons

Arms, Assize of, IV, 126, 141

Army, *see* Military service

Army camp, Jewish, *see* Elephantine

Arnulf, patriarch, IV, 114

Aroer, city, VI, 293

Arpad, Magyar chief, III, 211

Ar-Radi, Baghdad caliph, VI, 214

Arras, Flanders, IV, 57

Ar-Rashid, *see* Harun ar-Rashid

Ar-Rawandi, *see* Rawandi, ar-

Arrian (Flavius Arrianus), II, 157

Arroyo de los Judíos, Spain, IV, 33

Arsham, governor, I, 347

Arsinoe, city, II, 199

Arslan Tash, Syria, I, 329

Artabanus, Parthian king, II, 20, 177, 316

Artapanus, historian, I, 198 f., 207, 304, II, 16, 31, 334

Artaxerxes I, king of Persia, I, 130, 245, 349

Artaxerxes II, I, 130, 349, II, 229

Artaxerxes III (Ochus), I, 131

Artisan guilds, *see* Guilds

Arts: alien motifs and techniques assimilated, II, 11; Christian, II, 11, 84, 154 f., 165, 365; Graeco-Oriental music and, II, 6-15, 146, 154, 330-34, 402; representation of Jew in medieval, V, 132; "seven," VIII, 145; *see also* Architecture; Figurines; Mosaics; Music; Painting; Pottery; Sculptures

'Arukh, dictionary, VI, 28

Asa, king, I, 322

Asaph Judaeus, Jewish medical writer, III, 240, VIII, 235, 241 f., 256, 258, 393; on medical ethics, VIII, 238; on ritualistic ablutions, VIII, 262

Asarhaddon, king, I, 96

Asatir, Samaritan book, II, 29, 339, VI, 212

Ascalon, city: burning of St. Mary's Church, III, 137; Jewish captives in, IV, 110 f.; refuge of Jews from Palestine, IV, 111, 113, 296

Ascension: of human soul, VIII, 21 f., 23; of Mohammed, VIII, 284 f.; of Moses, VIII, 6

Asceticism, VIII, 119 f.; Christian, VIII, 53; of Essenes, II, 48, 49; and love of God, VIII, 116; and traditional Judaism, II, 256, 435, VIII, 53

Asclas, Gaius Julius, I, 404

Asenath, daughter of Potiphar, VI, 170

Ash'ariya (Ash'arites), school of Islamic theology, V, 90 f.; VIII, 103, 109, 113, 248; doctrine of divine Speech, VIII, 343

Ashdod, city, I, 361

Ashema, II, 28

Asher, "the great Sheikh," VI, 245

Asherah worship, I, 78, II, 13, 332

Asher b. David, VIII, 42

Asher b. Yeḥiel, VI, 55, 136 f.; on book lending, VII, 287 f.; laws of phylacteries, VI, 65; and tax exemption, V, 77

Asherites, generations of, VI, 446

Ashi, R., II, 14, 134, 179, 247, 261, III, 3, VI, 100; advocate of proselytism, II, 149; assumed title Rabbana, II, 198; date of death, VI, 202; as redactor of the Talmud, II, 295, 296, 425, VI, 17

Ashkenazi author of anonymous grammatical work, VII, 54 f., 241

Ashkenazi, Bezalel, VI, 348

Ashkenazim, III, 174, IV, 3 f., 345, V, 61, 275, VI, 75, 87, VII, 144; conversions to Christianity, VII, 304; dynamic approach of, VII, 123; ethical literature, VII, 180; formula for confession, VII, 80, 92; Hebrew pronunciation, VI, 250; influence of Tam, VI, 55; and Khazars, IV, 235, VII, 18; liturgy of, VII, 105, 175, 183, 282; poetry of, IV, 309, VI, 422, VII, 175, 199; and Saxony, IV, 4; and Sephardim, IV, 3 f., 43, 235, VI,

25 f.; talmudic commentary, VI, 344

Aṣhor, I, 113, 114

Ash-Shafi'i, *see* Shafi'i

Ashshur, V, 162; *see also* Assyria; Mosul

Ashur, province, I, 326

Ashurbanipal, king, I, 96

Asia Minor: Christian art in, II, 165; Crusaders in, IV, 106 f., 309; deportations to, I, 373; Jewish rights threatened, I, 401; Jews in, I, 169, 170, 216, 283, III, 182; Marcionism, VIII, 288; religious situation, II, 3, 166, 393; *see also* Near East

Asinaeus, principality, I, 168, II, 213, III, 63

Asklepios, god of healing, II, 336

Asma, poet, VII, 191

"Assassins" (*sicarii*), II, 47, 347

Assault and battery, IV, 70; punishment for, III, 49, IV, 69, 129 f., VIII, 231

Assi, R., II, 113, 208, 270, 275, 283

Assidaioi, I, 237; *see also* Ḥasidism

Assimilation: ancient, I, 118-21, 349; to culture of conquered population, I, 56 —— modern, I, 27; Aryan opposition to, I, 19; and survival, I, 30

Assize of Arms, IV, 126, 141

Associations, professional, I, 257; *see also* Guilds

Assumption of Moses, II, 47, 59, 346

Assyria: banking, I, 108; expansion, I, 67; fall, I, 96; imperialism, I, 95, 108, 345; interest rate, I, 69; Israelitic settlement, I, 107, II, 27; price fixing, I, 85; protection of masses by law, I, 84; revenge for conquest of Israel by, I, 210; "rod of God's anger," I, 90

Assyrian code, I, 327

Astafortis, Hungarian tax collector, III, 188; conversion, III, 319

Astarte, goddess, I, 49, 57, 146, 318, 374; figurines of, I, 59, 329

Astrabadh-Ardasher (Mesene), II, 405

Astrolabe, VIII, 166 f., 170, 173

Astrology, VIII, 175 ff.; alleged Jewish origins of, II, 16 f., 334 f., VIII, 176; appeal of, VIII, 225; and astronomy, VIII, 145, 181 f., 367; and biblical interpretation, VI, 298; computation of dates by, VI, 231, VIII, 25, 206 f.; and interpretations of history, V, 143, VIII, 62; Maimonides and, V, 384; and man's fate, VIII, 111; in messianic computations, V, 146, 162 f., 200 f.,

204 f., 384; and music, VII, 210 f.; natural and judicial, VIII, 169 f., 175, 182; and occult sciences, II, 15 f., 44, 334; parallels for seven "kings," VII, 241; and poetic themes, VII, 162; practical applications, VIII, 160
Astronomy: Aristotelian-Ptolemaic approach, VIII, 93; and astrology, VIII, 145, 181 f., 367; Babylonian, I, 6, II, 16; computations, II, 206, 209, V, 246, 279, VI, 269, VIII, 26 f., 160 ff.; Gentile writers, VIII, 175 ff., 366 f.; Latin translations of Arabic works, VIII, 167; opposing doctrines, VIII, 173 f.; research in, VIII, 166 ff., 359 ff.; tables, VIII, 139, 171 ff.; 362 ff.; talmudic age, II, 306; Yeraḥmeel's knowledge of, VI, 422
Asturlabi, al-, quoted, VIII, 139
Asylum, institution of, I, 145, 276, 360, 414
Asylums for homeless and aged, II, 285
'Atar, meaning, I, 124
Atheism and atheists, I, 179, 234, VI, 298, VIII, 72; attacks on Islam, V, 104
Athens: exclusion of Jews from, III, 232; Paul's work in, II, 79 f., 362; philosophic academy, III, 11, VIII, 241
Athinganoi, Judaizing sect, III, 178, 181
Athos, city, I, 304
Athos, Mount, III, 232
Athtar, god, I, 57, 318
Atlantic Ocean, VIII, 214 f.
Atmosphere, of earth, VIII, 213
Atomist hypothesis, VIII, 88, 222, 323
Aton, god, I, 46, 311
Atonement, V, 217; see also Day of Atonement
Atrocities, IV, 109 f., 133 ff.; see also Burning; Massacres; Murder
Attaleia, Byzantium, V, 413
Attalus III, king, II, 25
Attire, see Clothing
Attributes, divine: in Judaism, I, 312, VIII, 95 ff., 326 ff.
Auch, France, inscription, III, 251
Augustine, Saint, I, 191, II, 138, 166, 188; on Easter controversy, VIII, 195; on Jewish dispersion, II, 168 f., 395; on Jewish serfdom, V, 129; on Latin Bibles, VI, 292; on Roman law, II, 299; sermon on the prodigal son, III, 31 f., 244
Augustus, Roman emperor, I, 236, II, 57, 151, 175, 198, 237; complaints before,

against Herod's regime, I, 263; pro-Jewish attitude, I, 404; and Sebastes, I, 236; subsidized sacrifice, I, 245, 404; western orientation, I, 246, 404
Aurelian citizens, II, 109
Aurelius Dionysius, Tiberian Jew, III, 207
Aurum coronarium (apostolé), II, 194, III, 191
Authority, governmental, V, 77 f., see also State; Karaite doctrine of, V, 235; see also Power
Authorization, letters of, IV, 212 f., V, 27, 52 f., 303; re non-Muslim cemeteries, III, 137
Authors, Jewish, bilingual and trilingual, VII, 6 ff.; creative upsurge, VII, 39-46; influences on, VII, 193 ff.; and Arabic script, VII, 191 ff.; volume of production, VII, 138 f.; see also Literature; Poetry
Autobiography, VI, 219
Autonomy, see Self-government
Auxerre, bishop of, IV, 13
Avaris (Tanis), I, 35, 37, 38
Avars, tribe III, 239
Avempace, see Ibn Bajja
Avendeath, John (Johannes Hispalensis or Hispanus), V, 214, VIII, 61 f., 178 f.; apocalyptic vision, V, 146
Aven gilyon, term, II, 133
Averroës (Ibn Roshd), V, 85, VIII, 66; books banned, III, 133; on heretics, VIII, 310 f.; "Outline of the Almagest," VIII, 358
Averroists, "double truth" theory, VIII, 80
Avicebron (or Avicebrol), see Ibn Gabirol
Avicenna, VIII, 63, 387; Canon, VIII, 249
Avitus, bishop of Clermont, III, 52
Azariah, martyr, I, 116
Azariah de' Rossi, see Rossi, Azariah de'
'Aziz, al-, Faṭimid caliph, III, 154
Azizus of Emesa, king, II, 21
Azriel, Gerona mystic, VIII, 286
Azulai, biographer, VI, 50 f.

B

Baal, I, 13, 37, 48; Egyptian counterpart, I, 304; Elijah's struggle against priests of, I, 87; inscription to, III, 66; names

Baal (Continued)
compounded with, I, 78; temple, moneylending, I, 86; worship of, I, 57, 59, 146, 334 f.
Ba'alah, I, 43
Ba'ale batim, term, II, 276, 422
Baal Hammon, deity, I, 374
Ba'al marriage, I, 310
Baalshamem, I, 87, 374
Baal Zaphon, I, 347
Baalzebul, I, 63
Baal-Zeus, coins dedicated to, II, 28
Baba Raba (Rabbah), Samaritan leader, II, 33, 340, III, 9, 62, V, 170
Babel, I, 107, 134; see Babylonia; identification with Baghdad, III, 100; Tower of, VII, 15
Babli, see Talmud
Babylonia: ancient and Achaemenid, I, 108, 282, 355; conflicting influences in, I, 105, 118; deportations to Asia Minor, I, 373; and deported nations, I, 108; economic, ethnic, and religious structure, I, 282; economic changes, I, 68, 85, 108-11, 132, 346; festivals taken over from, I, 5; houses rented, I, 109, 346; Jewish population, I, 108, 115, 168, 170; a leader of house of David, I, 116; legal structures, I, 142; mythology, VIII, 10 f.; purity of family valued in, I, 125; religion, I, 44, 45, 105, 107, 197, 311, 373, VIII, 175, seven-day week, I, 360; ten genealogical classes returned from, I, 275; use of numerical principle, VIII, 284; see also Exile, Babylonian; Persia, Achaemenid
—— Hellenistic and Sassanian, VI, 402; agriculture, II, 244, 246, 257, 414; ancient traditions, II, 205 f., 207; astral and astrological influences, II, 15 f., 206; Christianity's slight advances, II, 164; class position of Jews, I, 281, II, 279, 320; compromises upset by religious fanatics, II, 213; exilarchate, II, 195 ff., 200 f., 205, 291, 403; family records, reliability of, II, 234; immigration to, II, 164, 173, 204, 208, 210, 404, 405; intergroup relations, II, 190; joyfulness, II, 113; Julian's Persian campaign, II, 179; leadership, economic and intellectual, II, 204 f., 206 f., 247, 320; leaders of Jews, II, 196, 204 f., 206 f., 247, 320 f., 403; learning, II, 205, 206, 207, 405; marriage customs,

II, 226, 232; Media's association with, II, 205; mortgages and interest, II, 251, 414; official control of Jewish settlements, II, 196, 403; Palestinian rivalry, II, 205, 207 f.; Parsiism checks other religions, II, 150; Pharisaism's dominance, II, 36; pilgrims sent to Jerusalem, I, 213; proselytism, II, 149, 150; ritualistic divergences, II, 7; supremacy, II, 204-9, 405; theocracy, II, 279; world-duration computations, II, 318; see also Persia, Sassanian; Talmud, Babylonian; and individual localities
—— medieval, IV, 161; academies (q.v.), V, 13 f., 25, 34, VI, 133 f., VIII, 76; Arab penetration, III, 62, 89 f.; Aramaic speech, VI, 255 f., see also Aramaic language; communal leadership, V, 5, 50, VI, 214; decline of state revenue, III, 311; exilarch's letter on intercalation, VIII, 194, see also Exilarchs and exilarchate; influence on Spanish Jews, V, 61; intellectual supremacy, VI, 262; Jewish agriculture in, IV, 151; Jewish population, III, 99, VI, 224; legal institutions, VI, 4 ff., 133 f., see also Judges; liturgy, VII, 100-105, 266; Karaites, V, 271; religious observances, V, 246; and Sefardim, IV, 4; sexagesimal system, VIII, 373; welfare of city dwellers and farmers, V, 304; see also individual localities
Bachelors, II, 225
Bacon, Roger, VIII, 215
Badges, III, 139 ff., 159, 298, V, 133, 202
Badis, Berber ruler of Granada, III, 157, V, 311 f.
Baghdad: academy, III, 195, VI, 105, 112, 224, VI, 17; 'Adhud Hospital, VIII, 389; 'Ananites, V, 221; bankers, III, 153 f., 167, IV, 202, V, 10 f., VI, 214; building of, III, 99 f., IV, 159, 170, VIII, 148, 159; burning of books, III, 133; cantorial family, VII, 80, 144; capital of caliphate, III, 120; center of philological learning, VII, 5, 19, 21; chief ḥazzan, VII, 80; delegation from Meshekh, III, 202; exilarchate, V, 43; and Fusṭaṭ, III, 105; influence of Ar-Rawandi, V, 103; Jewish community, III, 99, 159, V, 50; Jewish quarters, III, 100, 145; Jews in government employ, III, 151; messianic

movement, V, 202 ff.; musical accompaniment to psalms, VII, 129; Muslim riots, III, 133, 165; Nizamiya Academy, VI, 468; oppressive decrees, III, 141; philosophers' assemblies, VI, 198 f., VIII, 55 f.; physicians, VIII, 237; population, III, 276; public debates, V, 83; Rabbanite center, V, 269; seat of *catholicos* and exilarchs, V, 7; Shi'ites, III, 123, 133; synagogues, III, 135; taxation of Jews, III, 169; wedding ordinance, VI, 140; *see also* Exilarchs and exilarchate

Bagohi (Bagoas), Persian governor, I, 129, 353 f.

Bagratids (or Bagratuni), Armenian family, I, 169, III, 110; genealogy, III, 282

Bahir, Sefer, VIII, 32-37, 55, 289 ff.

Bahram I, king of Persia, VI, 428

Bahram Tshubin, Persian general, III, 17, 58

Bahrein Islands, III, 65

Bahya ibn Paquda, V, 366, VI, 95, VIII, 39, 224 f.; appeal to the masses, VIII, 71; on asceticism, VIII, 120; on biblical law, VI, 143, 148; biblical semantics, VI, 296; on creation *ex nihilo*, VIII, 89; dialogue between Soul and Intellect, VIII, 105 f.; on divine attributes, VIII, 97; "Duties of the Heart," VII, 10, 222, VIII, 62, 68 f.; duties of the "limbs" and "heart," VIII, 113; on emigration, IV, 221; evaluation of sciences, VIII, 143; on humility, VIII, 121; on love of God, VIII, 116; on necessity and justice, VIII, 109 f.; prayers, VI, 175; *see also* Pseudo-Bahya

Baihaqi, scholar, VII, 4

Bailiffs, Jews as, IV, 267

Bakhtawi, Abu Ya'qub (Joseph) al-, Karaite grammarian, VII, 16

Bakri, Abu 'Ubaid 'Abd Allah al-, geographer, III, 65, 217, VI, 221 f., 434

Balaam, I, 46, 312, V, 192, VIII, 133; oracles of, I, 320

Baladhuri, III, 168; re capture of Caesarea, III, 88; on Mohammed's statement of religious rights, III, 131; re Tripolis, III, 104

Baldicus, *see* Baudri

Baldwin, archbishop of Canterbury, IV, 125

Baldwin I, king of Jerusalem, IV, 112; biblical manuscript redeemed from, VI, 247, 447 f.

Balfour Declaration, I, 200

Bali Yama, I, 349

Balkans: civil law re Jews, V, 57; Crusaders in, V, 200; invasions of, III, 24 f.; Jewish communities, I, 169, 283, III, 189, 206 ff., IV, 173, V, 54 ff.; Jewish literature, VI, 187; Karaites in, VIII, 195; proselytes, I, 283; tax farmers, IV, 153; *see also* Byzantium

Balkh, Persia, Jewish community, III, 109

Balsam, I, 252, VIII, 253

Baluqiya, legend of, V, 367

Bamberg, bishop of, IV, 98

Bamot, I, 332, 353

Banco di San Giorgio, IV, 209

Banking and bankers, I, 132, 255, 261, 410, II, 431, IV, 197 ff., 338 ff., VI, 68 f.; in Assyria, I, 108; *dhimmis*, IV, 199; entry of Jews, I, 108 f., 346, IV, 197 ff., 338 f., V, 10; holdings in convertible commodities, VIII, 224; laws, IV, 198 f.; prominent Jewish family, III, 152 f., 158, 167, IV, 202, V, 10 f., VI, 214; ramifications, IV, 207-15, 344 ff.; and tax farming, IV, 201 f.; varied enterprises, IV, 349; wealth, IV, 214, *see also under* Merchants; Moneylenders and moneylending

Bannus, Essenian hermit, II, 49

Banu Hishna, tribe, III, 65

Banu Nadhir, tribe, III, 64, 79

Banu Qainuqa', tribe, III, 64, 78 f.

Banu Quraiza, tribe, III, 64, 79, 264, V, 179

Baptism, I, 179, II, 75, 361; of children with parental consent, III, 10; fees for, III, 249; freedom of slaves through, III, 14; inviolability of, IV, 6, 117; of Jews, III, 23, 182, IV, 100; Pope Nicholas I re, III, 209; and relapse of faith, III, 320; worldly inducements to, III, 28; *see also* Conversion; Converts

—— enforced, III, 20, 28, 38, 51, 52, 184, 240 f., 254, IV, 104 f.; Leo VII re, IV, 6; suicide as alternative to, IV, 96

Baptists, pre-Christian, II, 348

Baqillani, Abu Bakr al-, Asharite, V, 84

Barabbas, II, 72, 359

Baraita de-Niddah, VI, 181 f.

Baraita de-Shemu'el, VIII, 147, 171, 192 f., 253

Baradani, al-, family, VII, 144

Baradani, Nahum b. Joseph al-, cantor, V, 296

Baraitot, I, 270; compilation of, VI, 204

Barcelona, Spain, IV, 29; Jewish community, III, 281, IV, 34, 159; Montjuich cemetery, IV, 33, 249; ownership of land, IV, 161; population, III, 281, IV, 34; public baths, IV, 37; rights for Jewish litigants, IV, 41 f.

Bardeisan, heresiarch, VII, 128

Bards, I, 141

Barhebraeus, Gregory, Syrian scholar, I, 170, 372, III, 16, 177, V, 9, VIII, 249

Bar Ḥiyya, Abraham (Savasorda), Spanish-Jewish astronomer and mathematician, IV, 37, V, 146, 162 f., VI, 149, VIII, 69, 148 f.; ambivalence toward astrology, VIII, 169 f., 182 f.; astrological interpretation, VI, 231 f., 298, 440, VIII, 170, 176, 182; astronomic works, VIII, 158, 169 f., 183, 360 ff.; on biblical synonyms for sin, VI, 296; calendar computations, VIII, 204, 207 f., 209 f., 361; categories of man's souls, VIII, 110 f.; classification of sciences, VIII, 142 f., 347 f.; collaboration with Plato of Tivoli, VIII, 148 f., 266, 351 f.; on divine government of the universe, VIII, 86; doctrine of creation, VIII, 94; doctrine of repentance, VIII, 105; on ethical conduct and free will, VIII, 119; ethical works, VIII, 62, 304; on existence of time, VIII, 88; geographic observations, VIII, 214 ff.; on Hipparchus, VIII, 372; justification of scientific studies, VIII, 219; letter to Yehudah b. Barzillai, VI, 149, 439; mathematical works, VIII, 155 ff., 351 ff.; quoted in the book of the Bright Light, VIII, 33; on scriptural guidance, VIII, 119, 335 f.; sources, VIII, 356, 360 f.; style, VIII, 74; on superiority of Israel, VIII, 133; theological context of scientific data, VIII, 201 f.; *Yesode ha-tebunah,* VIII, 347 f., 352

Bari, Italy, III, 281, IV, 24, V, 46, 56, VI, 119, 421

Baridi, al-, emir, III, 165, IV, 208 f.

Bar Kocheba (Koziba), Simon, I, 231, V, 188, VI, 239, 241, 430, VII, 244; messiahship, II, 121, 126, 132; military measure against Christians, II, 132; rebellion led by, II, 97 f., 101, 102, 106, 107, 121, 371, 372; rebellion's aftermath, II, 130, 142, 169, 271

Barley, I, 251, 252

Barnabas, Saint, II, 86, 366; Epistle of, II, 137, 167, 382

Bar Qappara, VIII, 161

Bar Satia, Joseph b. Jacob, VI, 483

Bartenora, Obadiah, VII, 120

Bartholomew, bishop of Exeter, V, 136

Baruch, I, 334, 341; apocalypse of, II, 60

Baruch b. Samuel of Mayence, VII, 179

Bashyatchi, Elijah b. Moses, V, 229, 234, VII, 220; re candle lighting, V, 403; Code, V, 405 f.

Bashyatchi, Moses b. Elijah, V, 214, 390

Basil I, Byzantine emperor, III, 179; and conversion of Jews, III, 183, 193; *Epanagogé,* III, 186; *Procheiros Nomos* (Legal Handbook), III, 186

Basil II, Byzantine emperor, III, 184, IV, 24 f.; edict on Venetian shipping, IV, 24 f.

Basilika, Byzantine code of, III, 181, 186 ff., 190, 319

Basil the Great, Saint, VII, 65

Baṣra, VI, 245; commercial and intellectual center, VI, 81, 153, 364; contribution to Sura academy, V, 14; Jewish banker in, IV, 202; Jewish community, III, 90; local customs, VI, 124 f.; school of Arabic philology, VII, 11, 15, 19, 34, 58

Bastards, II, 218, 222, 276, 409, V, 267

Baths, public, II, 400; in Barcelona, IV, 37; decrees re, III, 142, 175, 194, 299

Bathsheba, I, 127

Baṭlanim, title, V, 50 f.

Battani, al-, VIII, 201, 360; astronomical tables, VIII, 139, 170, 376 f.

Baudri (Baldicus) of Bourgueil, IV, 107

Bavaria, IV, 65 f.

Bayyit, term, VII, 199

Bazaars, IV, 179 f.; *see also* Fairs

Becket, *see* Thomas à Becket

Bede, Venerable, VI, 279

Bedouins, I, 33, 71, 301, 335; assaults on Palestine, I, 57, II, 246

Beena marriage, I, 310

Beer, II, 249

Beersheba, I, 167, 344; pilgrimages to, I, 94, 338

Beggars, I, 275, 282, II, 272, 274
Behemoth, V, 148
Beirut, law school, III, 11
Beja, Spain, V, 298
Bekhor Shor, Joseph, VI, 295
Bel, Temple of, I, 168; *see also* Baal
Belgium, Jewish physicians in, VIII, 390; *see also* Flanders
Belisarius, Byzantine general: conquest of Naples, III, 25; suppressive measures, III, 230; trophies from the Temple of Jerusalem, III, 11; western campaigns, III, 7
Ben Asher, family chronology, VI, 445 f.
Ben Asher, Aaron, Tiberian Masorite, VI, 245 f., VII, 32 ff., 126; biblical manuscript, VI, 246 f.; effect of mysticism on, VIII, 15; masoretic monograph, VI, 252; punctuation, VI, 445; as Rabbanite, VI, 447
Ben Asher, Moses, VI, 246, 445, 446
Ben 'Azzai, Simon, II, 221
Ben Bag Bag, II, 220; re the Pentateuch, V, 212
Benedictions, II, 333, 361, VII, 66 ff., 96 f., 120, 244; deviations in, VII, 279; differences on, in ancient sources, VII, 109, improvisations for, VII, 86; the hundred, VII, 110 f.; at meals, VII, 81; Samuel b. Ḥofni's classification of, VI, 70; seven-word, VII, 244; *see also* '*Amidah;* Blessing
Benedict of York, IV, 125
Bene-Israel, in India, III, 115
Bene Moshe, V, 192
Benevento, Italy, IV, 236
Bene Yisrael, I, 41
Benjamin, tribe of, I, 65, 321
Benjamin b. Ḥiyya, Hebrew poet, IV, 288
Benjamin b. Jonah of Tudela, Jewish traveler, III, 185, VI, 222 ff., VIII, 379; reports on: Baghdad, III, 100; Bohemia, III, 214; Byzantine taxes, III, 192 ff.; communal officials, V, 50 f.; Damascus, III, 104; the exilarchate, V, 11 f.; Fusṭaṭ, III, 106; Jerusalem, IV, 113; Jewish communities in Germany, IV, 73; Jewish population, III, 113 f., 283 f.; Narbonne, IV, 47; Paris, IV, 60; Rome, IV, 13 f.; Samaritans, V, 176; sectarians in the Orient, VI, 475; Slavonia and Canaan, III, 214
Benjamin b. Moses Nahawendi, Karaite leader, V, 182, 223 ff., 227, 363, VIII, 58, 91, 297; biblical exegesis, V, 225, VI, 276, 283 f.; Book of Commandments, V, 231, 259, 401; calendar reform, V, 224; on double holiday, VIII, 374 f.; re Jesus, V, 344; theory of divine government of world, V, 259
Benjamin of Tiberias, III, 23
Ben Mashiaḥ, Karaite, V, 277, VIII, 204 f.
Ben Meir, Aaron, V, 32 f., 223; letter to Babylonian leaders, V, 49; month of creation, VIII, 197; struggle with Babylonian chiefs over calendar, V, 30 f., 212; *see also under* Saadiah Gaon
Ben Naphtali, Moses (b. David), Masorite, VI, 247
Ben Sira, alphabet of, VI, 159, 169; *see also* Sirach, Jesus
Ben Tabal, I, 155
Ben Zoma, Simon, II, 218, 248
Berakhiah b. Naṭronai the Punctuator, VII, 189 f.
Berbers, I, 176; antagonism to Arabs, III, 91, 107; attacks against Solomon, governor of Africa, III, 230; dialect, VII, 12; in Granada, III, 156 f.; IV, 29; and Judaism, II, 212, III, 7, 90 f., 272; mass conversion to Islam, III, 132
Berditshevski, Micah Joseph, I, 11
Berenice, Jewish princess, II, 92, 369
Berenice inscription, II, 202 f., 404
Bereshit rabbati, medieval midrash, V, 146; *see also* Moses the Preacher (ha-Darshan)
Bernard, hermit, IV, 61
Bernard of Clairvaux, Saint, IV, 11; injunction to Cistercian monks, IV, 299; on Jewish serfdom, V, 129; letter in behalf of Jews, IV, 121; on usury, IV, 206, V, 128
Beroea (Verria), city, II, 79
Berossos, historian, I, 197, 345
Beruriah, scholar, II, 239, 275, VI, 408, 415
Bet 'almin (house of eternity), II, 289; *see also* Cemeteries and catacombs
Beth-Alpha, synagogue, II, 138, 285, VIII, 367
Bethel: city, I, 129, 346; images erected, I, 66; excavations, I, 106
——— deity, I, 128; theophorous names connected with, I, 352
Bethlehem, V, 147, 153
Beth-shan (Scythopolis), I, 225, II, 27, 392

Beth She'arim, cemetery, II, 10, 14, 174, 272 f., 286, 333, 336; destruction of, II, 179, 398; inscriptions, I, 378, II, 289, 424; Palmyrene and Arabian Jews buried in, II, 211, III, 68, 258, 260

Beth-shemesh, pottery, I, 320

Beth-Zur, city, I, 184, 369

Betrothal, V, 29 f., 401 f., VI, 391; forms of, VI, 98; ring without stones, VI, 130; *see also* Marriage; Wedding

Bet-Zabdai, city, II, 52

Bezalel, I, 14, VIII, 7

Bezalel Ashkenazi, VI, 348

Béziers, France, IV, 55 f., 132

Bible: allegorical vs. literal interpretation, I, 202, II, 144, 386; in Arabia, III, 82, 265; authorship of books, VI, 159, 307 f.; books and manuscripts ransomed from the Crusaders, IV, 111 f., 296 f.; canonical recension by Jewish scholars, VI, 312; Catalan, with musical notation, VII, 282; Christian students, and Jewish scholars, VI, 272; contradictions in, V, 87, VI, 305 f., 474 f.; early versions of parts of, III, 82; exegesis, II, 141-47 *passim*, 385-87, *see also* Exegesis; fictional use of narratives, VII, 183 ff.; and history, I, 42, 295, VI, 306 ff.; Justinian's decree re versions of, III, 12 f., 233, V, 209, VII, 94 f., 263; Khazars and, III, 202 f.; loan on copy of, IV, 340; marriage relationships mentioned, II, 230, 411; masoretic accents, VII, 126; Masoretic text, III, 72, V, 176, 195 f., VI, 236 ff., 441 ff.; Mohammed's knowledge of, III, 81 ff.; Muslim criticisms of, V, 87 ff., 97, 174, 175 f., VI, 8 f., 242, 254, 274, 291 f., 307; narrative in sacred poetry, VII, 180 f.; new philological approaches, VI, 268; persecution for possession of, VII, 86; poetic allusions to, VII, 193 f., 201 f.; popularity of hermeneutical sermons, VI, 153; Porphyry's criticisms, II, 158, 391; preoccupation with each letter of, VIII, 14 f.; in Rabbanite community of Cairo, VII, 137; reading of, III, 12, 189, 253, V, 218, VI, 248 f.; references to God's love, VIII, 114; restudy of, VI, 235-313, 441-86; revealed word of God, VI, 294, 307 ff., VIII, 127; rules of cadence in reading, VI, 237; Samaritan, II, 30, 340, V, 262, VI, 236; scarcity of copies, III,

201; study of, III, 72 f., V, 229, VI, 11, 34 f., 123 f., 142 f., 234, VIII, 5, 84; tannaitic law on acquisition of, VII, 135; use of different texts in computing chronology, VIII, 206; use of historical data from, VI, 437; zoological and botanical names in, VIII, 226 f.;

—— translations, III, 211, V, 39, 83, 85; Arabic, III, 82, 265, V, 85, VI, 263-72, 459-61; Aramaic, II, 146, 387, 411, III, 72 f., VI, 239 f., 255-63, 312, 453-57; *see also* Targum; books other than the Pentateuch, VI, 260 f.; Christian, VI, 271; *see also* Vulgate; Greek, III, 189, 211, V, 39, 89; *see also* Aquila; Septuagint; Latin, VI, 272-74, 292, 462 f.; *see also* Jerome, Saint; *Vetus Latina;* Syriac, VI, 241; *see also* Peshitta; Western, VI, 272 ff., 462 f., VII, 222

—— *see also* Apocrypha; New Testament; Old Testament; *also under* names of sections, books, and ancient or medieval versions

Bida', Arabic term, VIII, 65

Bigvai, I, 119

Bilingualism, I, 19, VII, 4 ff., 222 f.

Bilshan, I, 119

Biography, VI, 203, VIII, 223

Biology, VIII, 225 ff.

Birth control, II, 209

Bitruji, al-, Arab astronomer, VIII, 162

Black clothing, III, 140, 153

Black Sea, III, 197

Blasphemy, I, 92, V, 335; against king, V, 237; of Mohammed, III, 94, 132; punishment for, III, 295; *see also* Curse

Blessing, priestly, II, 282, VI, 178, 182, 336; omission of, VII, 249; ritualistic, VI, 123 f., 359; *see also* Benedictions

Blessing of Moses, II, 31

Blois, France: blood accusation, IV, 137 f., 307 f., VII, 179; suffering of Jewish community, V, 131, VI, 219

Blood: circulation, VIII, 242; and soul, VIII, 107

Blood accusation, I, 193, IV, 80, 83, 135-39, 306 ff.; origin of myth of, I, 192, 382

Blood money, fine for murder, III, 132

"Blood of the covenant," V, 390

Blood ritual, I, 51; *see also* Ritual

Boaz, house of, V, 295

Bodleian Library, I, 347

Bodo (Botho), IV, 9, 52f., 264, V, 126

Body, human, VIII, 229 f.; "humors" of, VII, 210; and soul, VIII, 36 f., 226; well-being of, VI, 142; words as, VII, 51

Boethos, I, 221

Boethosians *or* Boethuseans, II, 342, V, 255, 280

Bogoljubov, duke of Kiev, III, 216

Bogomils, III, 209, IV, 132, VIII, 31, 56

Bohemia: Benjamin of Tudela re, III, 214; Jewish resistance to Crusaders, IV, 291; jurisdiction of local rulers, IV, 72

Bohemund I, Crusader in Macedonia, IV, 107

Bohemund III, of Antioch, IV, 114

Bologna, Italy: expulsion of Jews, IV, 27; university, VI, 54

Bondage, of debtors, I, 69

Bondage, Egyptian, V, 167, VI, 303, VII, 181, 290

Bones, number of, in human body, VIII, 230

Bonfils, Joseph, *see* Tob 'Elem

Bonn, Germany, IV, 306

Book of Adam, VI, 17, 197

Book of the Bright Light, *see Bahir*

Book of the Dead, I, 50

Books: acquisition of, VII, 135 f.; banned or burned, III, 133, IV, 32; in codices, II, 156, 390; collected at synagogue, VII, 139; decorated with signs of Zodiac, VIII, 184; introduction of paper, VI, 184; lists of, VII, 139; 287; production and distribution, VII, 136; reverence for, VII, 139; shortage of, VI, 181

Boppard, Germany, IV, 133, 143

Bordeaux, France, IV, 55

Borion, city, III, 8, 230

Bosporus, III, 197

Botany, VIII, 226 f.

Botho, *see* Bodo

Bowls, magical, II, 336, VIII, 8 f., 277

Boycott: of *dhimmi* physicians, V, 97; of Judeo-Christian trade, IV, 13

Boys, *see* Children

Bracteates, Hebrew, III, 218, 339

Bratislav, duke of Prague, IV, 100

Braulio, bishop of Saragossa, III, 40

Bray-sur-Seine, France, IV, 62, 128 f.

Bread: blessing of, VI, 123; thrown into the water, III, 241; unleavened, V, 217, 239, 247, 346

Brethren of Purity, VII, 206, VIII, 15, 112, 345, 347

Breviarium Alarici, III, 35, 49

Bribery, I, 263; *see also* Tribute

Bride: homecoming of, and moon's conjunction, VIII, 375; laws re, VI, 63; substitution for, VII, 188; *see also Kallah*

Bridegroom: astral forces and, VIII, 182; hymn for, VII, 143

Bristol, England, IV, 80

Bronze Age, I, 60

Brotherhood, II, 4

"Bryson," *Oikonomikos*, IV, 349 f.

Buddha, Gotama Siddhartha, I, 315

Bug, river, III, 333

Building industry: ancient, II, 334; medieval, IV, 170

Bukhari, al-, III, 87; compilation of traditions, VI, 78

Bulan, ruler of Khazars, III, 198, 199, 326

Bulgaria, II, 210, 406, III, 209, V, 210

Bun (or Abun), R., II, 13, VIII, 34

Bureaucracy, II, 186; *see also* Public office

Burghers: Caen charter, IV, 205; and the clergy, IV, 99; economic rivals of Jews, IV, 60, 65, 141 f.; Jews and, IV, 67 f., 69, 74 f., 85; and protection of Jews, IV, 100; status of, IV, 23, V, 319

Burgos, Spain, IV, 250

Burgus Judaicus, IV, 314

Burial, II, 287 ff.; body dressed for resurrection, II, 312; in Cave of Machpelah, III, 278; cremation replaced by, I, 382, II, 423; historical significance of, III, 335; Jewish practice of, III, 22, 297; in Khazaria, III, 202; in old graves, III, 138; Zoroastrians re, III, 22, 297; *see also* Cemeteries and catacombs

Burning: of books, III, 133, IV, 32; death by, IV, 22, 62, 138

Burnt-offering, I, 179, III, 29

Bury St. Edmunds, England, IV, 136 f.; expulsion of Jews, IV, 84; massacre of Jews, IV, 148; "Moyses Hall," IV, 282; synagogue, IV, 85

Businessmen: public discourses for, II, 275; scholars aided, II, 277

Business transactions, IV, 174; agents, IV, 180, 196; astrology and, VIII, 365; cessation of, in Alexandria, I, 266; competition, V, 68; currency ex-

Business transactions (*Continued*)
change, IV, 209 ff.; documentation,
II, 266; ethics, VIII, 48 f.; of Jewish
converts, III, 43; laws of, III, 45, IV,
185, VI, 71; local customs, VI, 122, 126;
mathematics for, VIII, 156; mosque
and synagogue as centers of, V, 67;
Muslim law re, IV, 186; partnerships,
IV, 37, 177, 185 f.; safeguards for
secrecy of, VI, 139; *see also* Industry;
Trade
Businesswomen, I, 113, II, 237, V, 243
Busrah, "house of the Jew," III, 296
Bustanai (Ḥaninai), exilarch, III, 89, V,
141 ff., VI, 19; controversy over marriage and legitimacy of offspring, III,
270, V, 8 ff., VI, 11, 200, 214 f.
Butchers, I, 275
Butter, IV, 315
Byblos, city, I, 318
Byzantine Church, VII, 68
Byzantine Empire: attitude toward
polygamy, VI, 137; calendar controversy, VIII, 195; campaigns against
Caliphate, III, 86 ff., 193; continuity
of Jewish communities, V, 54-58, 315-
17, VIII, 60; Crusaders in, IV, 107 f.,
130; division between civil and religious law, VI, 3; employment of
Jewish scholars, III, 184; enforced
conversion in, III, 182 f.; fiscal contributions of Jews, III, 190-95, 320 f.;
influence in Italy, III, 25; influence
on Visigothic life, III, 246; Jewish civil
judiciary, V, 57; Jewish cultural center, VI, 366; and Jewish migrations,
III, 210, 220, IV, 108; Jews in military forces, III, 236 f.; Karaites in, V,
272, 399; legal codes, III, 187 f.; list of
rulers, III, 317 f., VI, 211 f.; medical
literature, VIII, 235; minting monopoly, IV, 210 f.; mystic literature in,
VIII, 29 ff.; outlawry of Christian
apostasy, VII, 256; Persian invasions,
III, 17, 18, 74 f.; pig symbol, II, 152;
recapture of Asiatic provinces and
Egypt, III, 75; restrictions on Jewish
worship, VII, 83 f., 94 f.; revival of
Greek historical literature, VI, 199;
scope of laws of Justinian, III, 233 f.;
sectarianism and theological debates,
VIII, 31; separation between Muslim
and Christian worlds, IV, 44; sermons
by emperors, VI, 154; slave trade, IV,
337; Slavonic mercenaries, III, 98;
spread of Islam into, III, 4; status of
Jewry in, III, 173-90, 199, 313-20, IV,
153; Venetian shipping rights, IV, 24

C

Cade, William, IV, 207
Caen, France, IV, 205
Caesar, Julius, I, 190, 218, 238
Caesarea, I, 225, 236, 256, 280, III, 20;
academy, II, 175, VI, 248; captured
by Arabs, III, 88; congregation, II,
199; population, III, 270; Samaritan
stronghold, V, 171; synagogue, II, 423
Caesarea Mazaca, II, 177, 397
Caesarius of Arles, Saint, II, 398, III,
52, 244 f., IV, 265, V, 123; polemics
vs. Jews, III, 250
Caesarius of Heisterbach, V, 134
Caesaropapism, II, 401
Caesars, Jewish loyalties to, I, 191
Cahorsins, IV, 207
Cain: as symbol, II, 136, 382; meaning
of name, I, 60; sign of, I, 7; role in
religious controversy, VI, 481
Cainites, gnostic sect, II, 137, VI, 481
Cairo: decree re public baths, III, 142;
Fadhiliya mosque, VII, 138; Jewish
community of Fusṭāṭ, III, 105, 160,
see also Fusṭāṭ; Karaite community,
V, 257 f., 268, 272; Katai quarter, III,
137; Nasiri Hospital, VIII, 248; ob-
servatory, VIII, 161; riot against
Amalfitans, IV, 331 f.; Samaritan
population, V, 177; synagogues, III,
135, VI, 247; taxation of Jewish estates, III, 169; *see also* Genizah
Calatayud, Spain, V, 298; merchant
privilege, IV, 179
Calcarienses, congregation of, II, 261
Calebites, I, 57
Calendar: change in, in Mohammed's
time, III, 84, 266; coincidence of Easter
and Passover, II, 188, 209, 401; computation of date of Second Coming, III,
15; Gregorian, VIII, 190 f.; Jewish use
of Christian, VIII, 172; Julian, VIII,
191; Muslim, V, 153 f., 191
—— Jewish, VI, 103, 269; computations,
II, 306, 307; V, 404, VIII, 184; and
dates of religious holidays, VI, 203;
dispute over, V, 30 f., 94, VIII, 203 ff.,
see also under Saadiah Gaon; first

month of, I, 6, 294; Hebrew treatises on, VI, 307, VIII, 202-11, 377-80; inception of, VI, 227 f.; scholar Moses re, III, 184; Karaite vs. Rabbanite observances, V, 30 ff., 243 f., 273; Khazar, III, 201; lunar, I, 44; and mathematics, VIII, 147, 208; Mishawayh's approach to, V, 382; perpetual, V, 196, 212; and plant life cycles, V, 246 f.; proclamations concerning, II, 125, 198, 206, 209, VI, 216; purported Mosaic origin, V, 94, VIII, 373; reform, V, 224, 226 f., 305; sectarians and, V, 190, 195 f., 211 f., 382; stabilization, VIII, 192 ff.

—— see also Chronology; Year

Calf, talmudic tale of, VIII, 28

Caligula, Caius, I, 245, 284, 381, 404, II, 5, 57, 100, 368; attempt to force imperial worship on Jews, I, 218 f., 231

Caliphate, III, 75-119; concubinage with slaves, IV, 190 f.; customs duties, IV, 181 f.; expansion and dissolution of, IV, 86, V, 180; freedom of movement, VIII, 211 f.; influence of law, II, 264; international trade under, IV, 174, 178 ff.; and Jewish academies, V, 14; Judeo-Christian disputations, V, 110 f.; persecutions, III, 123; political influence of Jews, III, 154 f.; religious toleration, V, 82, 210, 264; restoration of exilarchs, VI, 200; reverence for law, VI, 11; role of Jewish communities, I, 30, IV, 225-27, VII, 107, VIII, 55; and scientific evolution, VIII, 261; Secret Profits Bureau, III, 139; sermons delivered by caliphs, VI, 153 f.; violent death of caliphs, III, 122; see also names of caliphs and dynasties

Calixtus II, pope, IV, 7 f., 235 f.

Calligraphy, Arabic, IV, 36 f.

Callinicum, synagogue, II, 189, III, 30

Callistus, bishop of Rome, II, 224

Cambyses, I, 129, 349

Camels, I, 301

Canaan, son of Ham, I, 335

Canaan: agriculture, I, 55; cities; I, 300; conquest and settlement, I, 16, 18, 32, 39, 308, VI, 230, 232; cult of the Sun and Moon, I, 45; figurines found in ruins of cities, I, 43, 310, 314, 318, 329; Israelitic festivals taken over from, I, 5, 72; migrations from, III, 91, 214 f.;

origin of name, I, 302; and palace of Mari, I, 300 f.; political disaster, I, 53; popular religion reasserted, I, 161; term, with reference to Slavs, III, 214 f.

Canaanites: and Carthage, III, 91; circumcision, I, 6; incense altars, I, 352; incest, II, 229; influences, I, 44 ff., 63, 105, 316; injunction against marriage with, I, 38; Israelites outnumbered by, I, 40; nomadic ideals, I, 61; in North Africa, III, 91, 271; outposts of ancient race, I, 175; religion, I, 45, 49, 58, 105, 301; in Slavonic lands, III, 335, VI, 437; see also Phoenicia; Ras Shamra (Ugarit)

Canals, construction of, VIII, 356

Canary Islands, VIII, 215

Candelabrum, II, 11, 12, 44, 285, 333, 346; five-branched, III, 48; seven-branched, III, 11; of Temple, VII, 78

Candle lighting: Bashyatchi re, V, 403; see also under Light

Candles, Ḥanukkah, I, 400

Canon law, I, 182, VI, 3, 153; attitude toward Jews, III, 26 f., 33 f., 212 f., IV, 241; basic toleration, IV, 53 f., 56, 121, 141; Carolingian rulers and, IV, 51 f.; codification of, IV, 6, 17 ff.; on conversion, III, 36, IV, 6 ff., 189; difficulty of enforcement, III, 44, IV, 16 f., 54; Johannes Scholasticus, III, 187; on physicians, VIII, 231; on usury, IV, 197 ff., 338 ff.

Canons, Apostolic, IV, 18

Canterbury, England, IV, 84

Canticles, see Song of Songs

Cantor, II, 283, VII, 41; assistants to, VII, 125; composition of piyyuṭ, VII, 89-93; composition of tunes, VII, 125 ff., 144; elegies dedicated to, VII, 145; function of, VII, 81 f.; hand signals for congregational singing, VII, 127; improvisations, VII, 86, VIII, 12; latitude permitted to, VII, 79-85; liturgical handbooks for, VII, 124; name used as acrostic, VII, 141; omission of divine name by, VIII, 294; as preacher, VII, 81; professionalization, VII, 80 ff.; qualifications of, VII, 58, 129 f.; and reading of Torah, II, 283; selection of, VII, 80; see also Chant

Capernaum, II, 164

Capital, accumulation of, IV, 211; see also Wealth

Capitalism, Jews' success in, I, 261, 264

Capital punishment, I, 82, 145, II, 267, 419, V, 57, 390, VIII, 310; for adulteress, II, 222, 409; for aliens entering Temple, I, 239, 402; biblical sanctions, VI, 91 f.; in Italy, V, 316; Karaites re, V, 240 f.; perpetual excommunication as substitute for, V, 17, 280 f.; Spanish Jewry and, V, 45 f., 312; violation of biblical law, V, 235

Capitation tax, *see* Poll tax

Capito and Labeo, controversies, II, 299

Capitolina, the "God-fearing," II, 338

Capitoline Temple, II, 13, 106, 373

Cappadocia, III, 17

Capsali, Moses, V, 406

Captives: amount of ransom, V, 315; Christian, of Persians, III, 22; communal ransom of, III, 78, IV, 118, 119, 177 f.; four, story of, VI, 325, 342; Karaites and Rabbanites, V, 413; scholars, V, 46 f.; slaves, IV, 110, 192; women, problem of legitimacy of children, V, 8 f.; *see also* Piracy and pirates; Slaves and slavery

Capua, Italy, IV, 23

Caracalla, emperor, I, 244, II, 109, 110, 190

Caravans, trade route, IV, 172

Cardinals, College of, IV, 10 f.

Care (*Sorge*), I, 16

Caritas, term, II, 330

Carmel, Baal cult, I, 334

Carolingian Empire, IV, 43-53, 256-64, VIII, 42; continuity of traditions, IV, 64 f.; dissolution of, and Jewish status, IV, 53 f.; influence in Spain and England, IV, 27 f., 79 f.; *see also under* individual emperors

Carpentras inscription, II, 203, 404

Carthage, city, III, 91; Jewish proselytism, I, 176, 183, 283, 374; religion, I, 43, 374

Cassiodorus, III, 25, VI, 241

Caste system, *see* Classes, social

Castile: Jewish status in, IV, 27 ff., 245 ff., 255; *see also under* individual cities and kings

Castles as refuge of Jews, IV, 35 f., 99, 119, 125 f.

Castra Judaeorum, IV, 35

Castration, I, 147, II, 107, 219; of animals, V, 174; of humans, IV, 191 f.

Castro, Jacob R., V, 274

Castrojeriz, Spain: anti-Jewish disturbance, IV, 251; privilege, IV, 35

Catacombs, *see* Cemeteries and catacombs

Catalonia, IV, 43; *see also* Aragon; *also under* individual cities and kings

Catastrophes, I, 68; *see also* End of days

Catchwords, in liturgical poems, VII, 88

Catechisms, I, 178

Catechumenate, and enforced conversion, III, 36, 245

Catharii and Catharism, VIII, 32, 42, 46, 288 f.

Catholicoi, charter from Al-Muktafi II, V, 6, 293 f.

Cato, Marcus Portius, I, 253

Cattle raising, I, 55, 57, 60, 72, 89, 253, 254, 301, 407; change in attitude toward, II, 263; communal ownership, II, 315

Caucasus, III, 199 ff., 208

"Cause of causes," VIII, 41 f.

Cautinus, bishop of Clermont, III, 51 f.

Cave Men (*Magharians*), V, 192, 379 f.

Caves: burial in, II, 287; Dead Sea, V, 188, 378; *see also* Dead Sea Scrolls; documents preserved in, V, 188, 255, 377 f.; Machpelah, III, 278; Murabba'at, V, 188; Petcherskii Monastery, III, 215 f.; use of, for religious purposes, III, 327 f., 378

Celestine III, pope, IV, 8

Celibacy, V, 134, 351; asceticism and, VIII, 53

Celsus, philosopher, II, 36, 111, 131; anti-Christian and anti-Jewish polemics, II, 157 f., 159, 163, 391; impressed by Egyptian magic, II, 21; quoted, II, 23

Cemeteries and catacombs, I, 378, II, 25, 109, 286-90, 423 f., III, 140, V, 258; in Barcelona, IV, 33; *bet 'almin*, or house of eternity, II, 289; community owned, II, 199; cremation and catacombs, II, 12; decorative motifs, epitaphs, I, 378, II, 10 ff., 146, 284, 330 ff., *see also* Inscriptions; in England, IV, 80; joint use by Jews and Christians, II, 188; location, II, 286; Muslim, in Jerusalem, III, 297; Muslim rulings re, III, 137 f.; papal injunction re vandalism, IV, 8

Censorship, of books, V, 207, VIII, 69; under the Caliphate, III, 133

Census of Jews, Roman, I, 263, 410

Cephas (Kaipha), II, 74, 361

Ceramics, I, 257

Cereals, I, 251

Ceremonial, Jewish: appeal of, II, 149, 189, 191; *see also* Ritual

Ceremonial law, *see under* Law

Cesarius of Arles, *see* Caesarius

Ceylon, I, 321

"Chain verses," VII, 179 f., 199

Chairemon, priest, II, 55

Chajes, Zvi, VI, 158

Chalcedon, city, III, 18, 236

Chalcedon, Council of, III, 5; John Rufus re, III, 229; and Monophysite churches, III, 240

Chaldaea and Chaldaeans, I, 33, 106, 141, 338; last king of, III, 63 f.; migrations before approaching armies of, I, 105, 106; priests and magicians, II, 22; religious propaganda, I, 159; *see also* Babylonia

Châlons, Council of, III, 252; and slave trade, IV, 335

Châlons sur Saône, town, III, 253

Champagne, region: fairs, IV, 183, 329; Jewish synod, V, 70 f.; viticulture, IV, 317

Chance, Epicurean doctrine of, VIII, 103

Chansons de geste, VI, 190

Chant, synagogue, VII, 125-31; accompaniment, VII, 127 f.; Gentiles attracted by, VII, 128; improvisation, VII, 128, VIII, 12 f.; modes of, VII, 127

Characteristics of Jews, I, 20 ff.; polarity in action and thought, I, 19

Chariot, divine, VIII, 5; descenders of, VIII, 12 ff., 17, 27 f., 37, 113; discussed in the *Guide,* VIII, 73; works concerning, VIII, 11 ff.

Chariots, I, 137, 332, 357

Charity, I, 86, 275, 281, II, 269-74, 420; communal and individual, II, 273, VI, 174 f.; dependence upon, II, 256; Gentile and Jewish, II, 270 f., 420; *heqdesh* as, VIII, 240; a religious duty, I, 175; synagogue exchequer, II, 285; *see also* Poor, the

Charlemagne, IV, 44; envoy to Harun ar-Rashid, IV, 45, 174, VI, 220; influence of, in Germany, IV, 64; second embassy to Baghdad, IV, 257; trade charters, IV, 48 f.

Charles II (Charles the Bald), emperor, IV, 18; letter to Barcelona, IV, 34

Charles II, king of Navarre, IV, 30

Charles III (Charles the Simple), king of France, IV, 13, 58 f., 239

Charles Martel, ruler of Franks, IV, 43

Charms, verbal, VIII, 234

Charters: Carolingian, IV, 48 ff.; English, IV, 79 f.; merchants', IV, 48, 50; moneylending, IV, 205 ff.; Seleucid, I, 216, 369, 393; trade, IV, 48 f.

Check, prototype of, IV, 213

Chenoboskion, gnostic library of, VIII, 274

Chess, game, VIII, 160, 356 f.

Chicken, prohibition re, V, 196

Childebert I, Frankish king, III, 51

Children: compensation for suffering, VIII, 103 f.; conversion of, IV, 55, 69, V, 113; of converts, III, 43, 126, 248; education, II, 274, 275, 276, 279, 280, 421; exposure of, I, 268, II, 219, 408; illegitimate, II, 218, *see also* Bastards; of Jews, reared as Gentiles, II, 102; Karaite injunctions, V, 223 f.; legal protection for, I, 361, II, 253; legends of Christian martyrdom, IV, 80, 135 f., *see also* Blood accusation; marriages, I, 265, II, 219, 238; sacrificed, I, 51, IV, 144; slavery for debt and taxes, II, 258, 303, III, 169, 312; of slaves, II, 223, 224, III, 45, IV, 195, V, 8 f.; training in poetic arts, VII, 150, 292; *see also* Girls

"Children of Light," II, 53

Chilperic I, Frankish king, III, 52

China, Jews in, II, 212, III, 115, 173, 285 f.

Chintila, Visigothic king, III, 42

Chios, monastery of Nea Moné, III, 192

Chirograph offices, in England, IV, 280, 304, VI, 357

Choirs, church, VII, 284; use of, VII, 125

Chosen people: concept of, I, 3, 7, 11, 19, 30, 62, 88, 97, 138, 164, II, 170, V, 125 ff., 137, 285, VIII, 123 ff., 340 ff.; enhanced by individualistic doctrines, I, 276; ethics, II, 10-16; *see also* Messiah and messianism

Christ: "logos Christology" of Paul, II, 81, 364; as title with name of Jesus, II, 357; vision of resurrected, II, 71; *see also* Jesus Christ; Messiah and messianism

Christian-Arab relations, *see* Muslim-Christian relations

Christian Church: abjuration formula
for converts, III, 41 f., 184, 194; aes-
thetic appeal, II, 154 ff., 389; antecedents, II, 86, 366; calendar, II, 125,
209, VIII, 206 f., 378 f.; collectivity of,
I, 226; concessions to popular religions,
II, 168; converts admitted, II, 388; decrees of anti-fraternization, III, 175;
dichotomy in position of, III, 242; formation of, II, 82-88, 364-67; founders'
ideal and beliefs, II, 73; growing sta-
bility and power, IV, 17, 19 f.; heir of
imperial Rome, II, 87; and Judeo-
Roman conflicts, II, 99, 107; language
difficulties, VII, 68; on moneylending
and usury, IV, 198 ff.; music, II, 155,
330, 389, VII, 130; and Nestorians, II,
164; ordination, II, 120; poetry in
Syriac and Greek, VII, 98; policy of
limited toleration, IV, 56, 121, 141;
property, acquired by Jews, III, 230 f.;
reform, IV, 10, 28; religions pre-
eminent in, II, 165, 393; revenue from
Jews, IV, 153 f., see also Tithes; sermons on special occasions, VI, 162;
see also Canon law; Clergy; Judeo-
Christian relations; Orthodox Eastern
Church; Papacy
Christian Druthmar of Aquitania, III,
205
Christian Empire, see Roman Empire
Christian era, VIII, 378 f.; system of dating, VIII, 172
Christian of Stavelot, V, 131
Christians and Christianity: ancient: account of rise of, II, 62-66, 352-55, VI,
191, 258; Arian heresy, II, 134; arts,
attitude toward, II, 11, 154 f.; codices
and their uses, II, 156, 390; concessions,
II, 168; conversion to, II, 150, 163 ff.,
392, 393, see also Converts; declared
illicit, II, 167; divorce, attitude toward,
I, 114, II, 228, 410; emigration to
Pella, II, 82, 99, 132; Essenes and
Sadducees, II, 51, 129 f., 348; the Eucharist, I, 193, II, 71, 75; evolution of
church, I, 226, II, 86 f., 366; exegetical
and linguistic effects of controversy, II,
141-47, 384; expectation of redeemer,
II, 57 ff., 73; fall of Jerusalem and, II,
82 ff., 364; first monarch, II, 165; and
gnosis, II, 315, 435; Gospel stories of
Jesus, II, 64 ff., 72, see also Gospels;
New Testament; historical controversies, I, 296, II, 136 ff., 161; Jewish expansion checked by, II, 87; Jewish
influences on worship, II, 26, 84, 365;
Jewish proselytism and, I, 373; Jewish
Scriptures, use of, II, 144, 145, see also
Bible; Jews' magic powers, belief in,
II, 189; Josephus' writings on, II, 131,
379; Judaism, separation from, II, 79,
82, 83, 85, 129-71 passim, 167, 169, 170,
183, 200, 378-95 passim, 399; Judaism's
aid in spread of, II, 122, III, 35, 208 f.;
Judaism's reaction to success in Diaspora, II, 147; Judeo-Christians, legal
concepts of, II, 303, 432; leadership
and community life, II, 74 f.; leadership of Hellenistic world, II, 83 ff.,
163 ff.; marriage, attitudes to, I, 114,
II, 224, 228, 408, 410; martyrdom, I,
400; Neoplatonists and, II, 159; pagan
counterattacks, II, 156 ff.; Pauline
schism, II, 76-81, 83-86, 361-67; Persia's
antagonism, II, 181; pessimism and
internal divisions, II, 57 f.; Pharisaism
criticized, II, 343; polemics against
oriental religions, II, 390; promoted by
Constantine and successors, II, 150,
152; ritualistic transformation, II, 84;
Roman view of, II, 86, 366; sectarian
currents, II, 111; Semitic flavor of early
writers, I, 187; slaves, II, 259; social
background and teachings, II, 67, 356;
spiritual acceptance of Roman Empire,
II, 152; state religion intolerant, II,
172 ff., 180; successes, II, 151-56, 169-71,
388-90; talmudic reticence about, II,
130; term, II, 86, 356, 366, V, 119; the
"third order," II, 366, 396; transformations in first century and a half, II, 25;
writings in Greek and Latin, II, 156;
see also Church; also under individual
names, e.g. Jesus; Paul
——— medieval, V, 108, VIII, 119; Al-
Ḥakim's persecution of, IV, 57; anthropomorphic beliefs, VIII, 30; Arabian,
early attitude toward Mohammed, III,
78; and atrocities of Crusades, IV,
139 f.; in Baghdad, III, 276 f.; biblical
laws observed, III, 83 f., V, 124; Byzantine protection of, III, 189; "Christian," as derogatory term, III, 147;
class status, IV, 87; and Code of
Justinian, III, 231; controversy over
Jewish era of Creation, VIII, 206 f.,
378 f.; conversion to, see Converts; in

Damascus, V, 96; debate over *filioque*, VII, 109; debate over redeemer as founder, V, 117 ff.; declaration of compliance to 'Umar I, III, 129; and divine attributes, VIII, 95 f.; eastern and western, III, 51, 176; employment by Jews, III, 30, 38, 140, IV, 15, 54, 269, 336; ethnic strains, III, 103; evacuated from Syria, III, 103 f.; excommunication for employment by Jews, IV, 269; and geographic studies, VIII, 216 f.; Hebraists, VIII, 384; icons used, VIII, 26, *see also* Iconoclastic movement; Images and symbols; intercession of Spanish Jews for, III, 156; on Jewish alliance with Satan, IV, 139 ff.; and Jewish homiletics, VI, 152 f.; on Jewish hostility, IV, 133 ff.; Jews as witnesses to, V, 135; and Judaism, III, 17, 208 f., 221, 243, V, 136, VI, 8, VIII, 51; and Karaites, V, 262; in Khazaria, III, 198, 203; Latin Bible used, VI, 292, *see also* Bible; liturgical music, VII, 128; loss of churches, III, 139; merchants, IV, 179 f.; minority status under Caliphate, III, 120; Mohammed and, III, 83 f.; moneylending, IV, 202 f.; New, III, 176 f.; as new Israel, V, 125 f., 137; and pagan practices, III, 252; and Palestine, III, 20, 103, IV, 109, *see also* Latin Kingdom; papal injunction re Jews, IV, 8 f.; penalty for murder of, IV, 39; persecutions by Almohades, III, 123 ff.; Persian captives sold to Jews, III, 22; Persian law code adapted, II, 430, VI, 4 f., 321 f.; political and religious pressures on Jews, VII, 181; religious drama, VII, 308; safety in pretending to be Jews, III, 160; sectarianism, III, 160 f., V, 189, VI, 5 f., *see also* Sectarianism; and synagogue, VII, 84, 128; Talmud condemned, II, 427

—— *see also* Judeo-Christian relations; Muslim-Christian relations

Chronica Adefonsi Imperatoris, exhortations re Jews, IV, 132

Chronicles, Books of, I, 104, 341, 343; number of verses, VI, 238; Qimḥi's commentary on, VI, 467

Chronicles, historical, VI, 212 ff., 430 ff.; Austrian, VI, 437; oral transmission, VI, 433; on persecutions of Jews in the Crusades, IV, 285 ff.

Chronology, I, 130, 294, 354, II, 73, 158; based on building of Jerusalem, V, 119, 130; biblical, II, 139, 307, VI, 307 ff., VIII, 209 f.; of book of Jubilees, V, 167 f.; computation of, VIII, 202 ff., 377 ff.; dating systems, II, 116, 118, 376; difference between Jews of East and West, VIII, 204; disregard of, in aggadic works, VI, 181 f.; increasing concern for, VI, 201 ff.; Jesus' ministry and death, II, 64, 353; of Jewish history, VI, 232; of Masorites, VI, 445 f.; misconceptions of, V, 119 ff.; Parsee and Jewish, II, 16; problems of, in Book of Daniel, V, 156 ff.; Saadiah's Book of, VI, 211; of *Seder 'Olam rabbah*, (*q.v.*), VII, 15; World Chronology (*Seder 'Olam*), II, 141, 376, 384, V, 147 ff., 256, 366, VIII, 203 f.; "World Orders," VI, 200, 233; *see also* Calendar

Chrysostom, John, Saint, II, 139, 140, 156, 188, 390, 401, V, 358, VI, 153; on Christian visitors to synagogues, VII, 84; sermons, VI, 157; and use of Syriac, VII, 68

Churches: Armenian, Jewish purchase of, III, 160; ban on building or repair, III, 129, 134, 139; built by Justinian, III, 232; conversion into synagogue, III, 136, 296; depositories of valuables, IV, 84, 208; Jews blamed for destruction of, IV, 57; Jews' possession of objects from, IV, 202, 301 f.; and land reclamation, IV, 161; pre-Constantine buildings in Holy Land, II, 392; protection of, under Byzantine law, III, 189; use of, to denounce Islam, III, 123

Church Fathers, I, 399, II, 33, 51, 309, 374, 401; method employed, II, 320; *see also under* names of Fathers, *e.g.*, Augustine

Cibetum, Asia Minor, IV, 107

Cicero, I, 174, 215, II, 5, 16; attack on Jewish plaintiffs, I, 188, 380; quoted, I, 192

Cid, The, IV, 29, 246

Cidello or Cidellus, *see* Ibn Ferrizuel, Joseph

Circle, computation of area of, VIII, 154

Circumcision, I, 6, 157, 168, 176, 179, II, 78 f., 86, 132; Aḥai on, VI, 39; Christians and, V, 122 f.; of converts, I, 183,

Circumcision (*Continued*)
V, 219; forcible, I, 235; as instituted
by Abraham, II, 137, 138, 383; of Itureans, I, 396; Karaite leaders on, V,
215, 217, 223; laws of, VI, 81, 103, V,
122 f.; poem on, VII, 267; Rome's
stand on, II, 97, 105, 107, 109, 374;
Samaritan, II, 29, 339; of slaves, III,
36, IV, 187 f., 193, 219; symbolism, I,
388
Cistercians: and the Crusades, IV, 300 f.;
nun, Jewish convert, V, 113
Cities: Greek: on Mediterranean coast, I,
255; in Palestine, I, 225, 280; in Transjordan and Galilee, I, 224
—— Israelitic: in Palestine, I, 72
—— medieval: centers of commerce and
culture, IV, 44; clerical and secular
jurisdiction, IV, 58; constitutions, V,
62; custumals, IV, 13, 22 f., 41 f., 60 f.;
government, VIII, 348; political role,
IV, 60; privileges, IV, 23, 35, 38, 42,
67 f., 71 f.; see also Urbanization
Cities of refuge, see Asylum
Citizenship, in Roman Empire, I, 240, II,
372; after Judeo-Roman wars, II,
108 ff.; Aurelian, II, 109, 374
City state, I, 55, 234, VIII, 348
Civil rights, ancient: public-office hold-
ing, II, 110, 180, 181, 375; under Persia,
II, 181; in Rome, II, 106, 108-10, 180,
374 f.; see also Self-government
Civil service, see under Public office
Civitas Dei and civitas terrena, VIII, 18
Clan, Israelitic, I, 51, 125, 351; cohesive
force in Diaspora, I, 125, 127; dissolution, I, 55, 58; religion, I, 43; ties,
cause of economic and social difficulties, I, 69
Clarendon, Constitution of, IV, 77
Classes, social: ancient distinctions, I, 75,
112, 160, 277 f.; antagonisms, II, 241,
244, 277; caste system in India, I, 297;
in communal charities, II, 272; and
Jesus, II, 67; misfits and outcasts, I,
275, II, 46; of Persia and Rome, II,
176; priestly hierarchy, I, 274; schol-
arly, and masses, II, 241; social level-
ing, II, 242, 279; solidarity of Jews, I,
281; stratification, I, 112, 271-76, 364,
413-14, II, 176; in talmudic Judaism,
II, 234; see also Poverty; Socioeconomic conditions; Wealth

Classics, ancient, translations of, V, 84,
VI, 264
Class struggle, see Social unrest
Claudius I, emperor, II, 91, 110, 198; cen-
sus of Jews, I, 170, 372; edicts concern-
ing Jews, I, 239, 240, 246, 248, 402, 403;
quoted, I, 189; son of a Jewess? I, 190
Claudius Tiberius Polycharmus, II, 11
Clearchus of Soli, I, 184, 377
Clement III, anti-pope, IV, 8, 98, 105, 116
Clement of Alexandria, I, 184, II, 81,
VIII, 133; Christian doctrine and theories, II, 161
Cleomedes, astronomer, I, 186
Cleopatra III, queen of Egypt, I, 215, 217,
381
Clergy: antisemitism, IV, 14 ff., 83 f.,
129 f.; celibacy, V, 134; corruption
among, III, 249; derelictions in enforc-
ing canon law, III, 44; disposal of
consecrated objects, IV, 301 f.; importance as preachers, VI, 155 ff.; mediation offered by elevated position, II,
168; and moneylenders, IV, 83 f., 204 f.;
proselytizing among Jews, IV, 54 f.;
relations with Jews, III, 50, 52, 175, IV,
37 f., 53, 84, see also Judeo-Christian
relations; tax privileges to, II, 243 f.,
V, 76; see also Jurisdiction, ecclesiastical; Priests and priesthood
Clermont, France, III, 52 f., 253 f.
Clermont, Council of, IV, 96
Climate: influence on man, VIII, 226;
"seven climates," VIII, 216
Clothar II, Frankish king, III, 47
Clothing: black, III, 140, 153; decrees
re, III, 96 f., 126 f., 139 f., 141, 170, 298,
VII, 145; yellow badges, III, 159
Cluny, monastery, IV, 10
Cochin, state, III, 114 f.
Cocks, sacrificed, V, 196
Codes, legal, VI, 4 ff.; Bashyatchi, V, 406;
Byzantine, III, 181, 186, 187 f., 319;
fundamental methods of, VI, 78;
Hebrew-Aramaic, VI, 94; Jewish op-
position to, VI, 107 f.; systematic, VI,
90-107, 371-81; Theodosian, III, 13,
25, 49, 187, 243, IV, 50 f.; see also
Priestly Code; and under names, e.g.,
Halakhot gedolot; Justinian; Maimoni-
des
Codices, II, 156, 390
Coele-Syria, I, 377

Cognition, theory of, VIII, 79, 318

Cohen, Hermann, VIII, 117, 121

Coimbra, Portugal, monastery of Santa Cruz, III, 160

Coins and coinage: ancient: Apamaean, I, 214, 393, II, 24; crown symbol, II, 332; early use, I, 318; of Flavian emperors, II, 92, 368; Hebrew, I, 130, 353; Jesus' "Render unto Caesar," II, 77; legends of Bar Kocheba, II, 98, 371; Maccabean, I, 225, 235, 369, 401, II, 36; metallic content, II, 245; Nerva's, on abrogation of fiscal tax, II, 106; Parthian, II, 174; priests' rights, I, 130, 166, 353; Roman, II, 175, 178, 368; Schechem's, II, 28

—— medieval, VIII, 255; Arabic, in Russia and Scandinavia, III, 339; Arabic, in Spain, IV, 210; of Cabillonum (Châlons sur Saône), III, 253; gold, IV, 29; Italian, mentioned in Spires privilege, IV, 273; metallic content, IV, 210 f.; Polish, with Hebrew inscriptions, III, 218, 338 f.

—— see also Currency; Money

Collectio legum Mosaicarum et Romanarum, II, 301, 431

Collectio veterum canonum ecclesiae hispanae, IV, 18

Collegia, Roman, I, 258, II, 260

Cologne, Germany, IV, 72, 117; burghers and Jews, IV, 100; burning of heretic, VIII, 46; fairs, IV, 175; Jewish community, III, 48 f., IV, 119

Coloman, king of Hungary, III, 212 f.

Colonate, Roman, I, 324, II, 258

Coloni: ancient (*ḥofshim*), I, 324, II, 257; medieval, III, 31, 38, IV, 153, 155

Colophon, Karaite, on scrolls of law, IV, 112

Colossus of Rhodes, III, 16, 235

Columbus, VIII, 215

Columella, Lucius Junius Moderatus, I, 251

Commandments, biblical, II, 308; adherence to, by the masses, VIII, 81; Aḥai's interpretation, VI, 38; 'Anan's Book of, V, 212, 219 f., 227; basic equality of, VI, 143 f., 396; clarified by Oral Law, VI, 300; concerning man's attitude toward God, VIII, 115; division of, I, 80, II, 421, VI, 90 ff., 102, 372, VII, 21, 276, VIII, 20; eternal validity of, VI, 98, VIII, 20; exemption from one in performance of another, VII, 135; in Genesis, V, 214; Maimonides' Book of, *see under* Maimonides; Nahawendi's Book of, V, 231, 259, 401; Noahide, VI, 5, 145; substantive import of, VI, 267; underlying reasons for, VI, 375, VIII, 118; *see also* Decalogue; Oral Law

Commandments, Ten, *see* Decalogue

Commenda, commercial contrast, IV, 200 f., 339

Commerce, *see* Trade

Commercial colonies, foreign, I, 175

Commercial instruments: check, IV, 213; dating of, VIII, 204; development of, IV, 209; letters of authorization, IV, 212 f., V, 27, 52 f., 303; letters of credit, IV, 348; letters of introduction, IV, 177; *see also* Contracts; Deeds

Commercialization, dangers inherent in, II, 254, 260

Commercial law, *see* Jurisprudence

Commodus, Roman emperor, II, 375

"Common sense," Aristotle re, VIII, 79

Commonwealth, First, V, 255; liturgical freedom, VII, 133; *see also under* Palestine; *also* Temple at Jerusalem, First

Commonwealth, Second, III, 19, 61, V, 255; apocalyptic visionaries, V, 140; apocryphal midrash, VII, 97; chronology of, V, 119; compilations relating to, VI, 159; dependent status of, VII, 290; and the exilarchate, VI, 200; history of, VI, 191, 210; hospices, VIII, 239; messianic statements related to, VI, 310; observation of new moon, VIII, 205; predictions of Daniel, V, 156; prophecy and, V, 158; restoration of Jubilee years, VIII, 210; rulers of, V, 9, 130; Sanhedrin (*q.v.*), VI, 24; sectarianism, V, 183; *see also under* Palestine; *also* Temple at Jerusalem, Second

Communal controls, IV, 146, V, 3-81, 178, 235, 293-325; academic independence, V, 13-20; adherence to V, 100; burials supervised, II, 287; Byzantine continuity, III, 190 ff., V, 54-58; central and local, II, 198-204, 403 f., V, 38-46, 49 ff., 199 f., VI, 18; collective leadership, V, 51; collective responsibility, IV, 39 f., 134 f., 137 f., 146, V, 66; and

Communal controls (*Continued*)
decline of academies, VIII, 4; economic controls, II, 252, 253 f., 261, IV, 185; elections to boards, V, 67 f.; exilarchate vs. gaonate, V, 20-25; vs. external interference, V, 69-78, 179; forces of integration and disintegration, V, 46-54; and the individual, IV, 222, V, 65, VII, 106, 133, VIII, 120 f.; and individual rise to power, IV, 38 f.; instruments of, V, 220; leadership supplied by, II, 204, 242, III, 119; loyalty and solidarity, I, 79, II, 291, III, 132, IV, 91, V, 80, VIII, 263; officials, V, 67 f., 71, 73 f.; Palestino-Babylonian conflict, V, 47 ff.; political and economic disintegration, I, 284; primacy of scholars, V, 32-38; residence permit, IV, 71, 185; responsibility for common welfare, II, 251, 269, 270, 271, 273, 291; self-government, III, 190 ff., V, 69-81, VI, 172, 213, VIII, 109; strengthening of traditional moorings, II, 290-92; Tannaim (*q.v.*), VI, 204; weakening of, V, 179, VI, 171; in Western democracies, V, 58-69; *see also* Excommunication

Communal property, *see* Property

Communion with God, *see under* God

Communism, I, 3, 30; Essenian, II, 49, 54; Mazdakite, II, 182, 222, 251

Communities, Jewish, I, 18, 124, 132-33, 241, 283, 351, 393; accretions through slavery, III, 111; Arab influence on modes of life, III, 283; attitude toward heretics, VIII, 69; biological strength, III, 110-14; bridge between East and West, IV, 3, 94, 149; centers of learning, III, 102, 104 (*see also* Academies); and congregations, I, 123, II, 199, 286; conservatism of leaders, VIII, 67 f.; and the Crusades, III, 102, 212, IV, 89 ff., 97 f., 103, 109 f., 119, 124-28, 147-49, V, 98 ff., 398; cultural contributions, III, 189, 209, IV, 24, 29, 32 f., 38, VII, 119, VIII, 220; delegations to pope, for redress, IV, 17, 97 f.; "democratic" life, II, 200-203, 288, 424, VI, 149; development into mercantile population, IV, 150 ff.; differences in structure and outlook, VII, 175 f.; dissolution into territorial units, V, 25; diversity in local observances, VII, 63, 107 ff.; economic success, V, 126 ff., *see also under* Wealth; effect of Christian proselytiz-

ing, IV, 55; effect of individual's behavior, VIII, 254; emergence in struggle between Byzantium and Islam, III, 220 ff.; environmental pressures, VIII, 5; expansion and influence in Western Europe, IV, 86-88; expansion under Islam, III, 99-110; and the Faṭimids, III, 105 f., 154 f., 171, 184; feudalistic restrictions on, VII, 176; fiscal contributions, II, 185 f., 243, III, 161 ff., 170 f., 190-95, IV, 12-20, 23, 81, *see also* Taxation; fortified quarters, IV, 35, *see also* Castle; funereal customs, III, 22, 297; *see also* Cemeteries and catacombs; hospitality to coreligionists, V, 53 f.; influence of foreign refugees, V, 68, 179 ff.; intellectual centers, IV, 7, 26, 34, 47 f., 112; intellectual life, III, 71, 173, 195, IV, 32 f., intercommunal cooperation, V, 63 ff.; intercommunal noninterference, VI, 393; international solidarity, IV, 176; intervention in monastic quarrels, IV, 84; Judeo-Christian communalism, II, 75; Karaite propagandists, V, 269 ff., *see also* Karaites; legal continuity, III, 185-90; linked by liturgical poems and responsa, VI, 111, VII, 144 f.; linked through travelers, VI, 219; location near church property, IV, 244, 266; and magic practices, VIII, 54 ff.; medical responsibility, VIII, 239, 404; Mediterranean, need for talmudic dictionary, VII, 13; Mediterranean, reunited under Great Caliphate, VII, 107; Monophysite charges of heresy, III, 5; Muslim belief in preordained poverty of, III, 159; ownership of property by non-Jew, III, 144; papal protection of rights, IV, 8 f.; payments to avert hostile acts, IV, 38 f., 55 f., 142 f.; persecution of, III, 123, 281; personal security under the Caliphate, III, 120 ff.; pioneering services, III, 197, 222, V, 62, 319; political basis of separation among, V, 47 ff.; powers of resistance, III, 74; preponderance of males, III, 252; prestige of Hebrew language, VII, 222; property rights, III, 143 f., 300 ff.; provisions in city custumals, IV, 60 f.; ransom of members, III, 78, IV, 119, 177 f.; refugees from Arabia, V, 373; resistance to serfdom, IV, 63 f.; on Roman trade routes,

IV, 175; and royal grants of transfer of persons and property, IV, 59 f.; royal protection, IV, 40, see also Protection; Royal alliance; rural, and religious observances, IV, 156 f.; and science, IV, 24, VIII, 171; scriptural guidance for, VIII, 119; and sectarianism, V, 178 ff., 194; secular music, VII, 284; separate quarters, III, 11, 232 f., 301, V, 79 ff., see also Segregation; sociopolitical security, IV, 7 f.; solidarity among, I, 175, V, 4, VIII, 122; status of synagogue reader, VII, 130; trade associations and guilds, IV, 171; trilingualism, VII, 5 ff.; use of Arabic language, III, 118, 170, VII, 6 f., VII, 8; vitality of, in Western Europe, IV, 20; in Western democracies, V, 68 f.; world-wide leadership, V, 5-13; see also Communal controls; also under respective countries, cities, institutions, and officials

Community of women, II, 183, 222, 251

Comparative religion, VI, 301, VIII, 68 f.

Competition, communal attitude toward, V, 68

Conat, Abraham, VI, 191

Concordance, talmudic, VII, 28 f.

Concubines and concubinage, II, 224, 409, 410; Christian, of Jews, IV, 269; combated by rabbis, I, 269; and slaves, I, 71, III, 111, IV, 190, 190 f.; see also Harem; Slaves and slavery

Condotta, treaty, IV, 27

Condottieri, groups of, I, 34

Confession of sin: in Musaf service, VII, 249; liturgical formulas, VII, 79 f., 92

Congregations, see Communities

Conrad III, king of Germany, IV, 119, 120 f.

Conscience, II, 78, 362, V, 66

Consonants, Hebrew, VI, 242, 448; in divine name, VI, 249; double pronunciation, VI, 250 f.; Semitic, VI, 242; weak, VII, 33 f., 41 ff.

Constantine I, Roman emperor, II, 172, 181, 187, 243; anti-Jewish laws, II, 399, 401; edicts concerning Cologne Jewry, II, 210, III, 48 f.; legislation on concubinage, II, 409; as pontifex maximus of state religion, II, 398; promotion of Christianity, II, 150, 152

Constantine VII, (Constantine Porphyrogenitus), Byzantine emperor, III, 155 f., 183, 211, IV, 238; biography of

Basil I, III, 179 f.; edict on Venetian shipping rights, IV, 24 f.

Constantine IX, Byzantine emperor, III, 192

Constantine (Cyril), see Cyril (Constantine)

Constantine Africanus: a founder of Salerno medical school, VIII, 245; Latin translations, VIII, 243 f.

Constantinople (Istanbul), II, 151; in the age of the Crusades, IV, 107, 130 f.; Arab assault on, III, 97, 175 f.; "Book of the Prefect," IV, 170, 321 f.; custom duties, III, 192; earthquake, III, 16; Greeks' hatred of Jews, IV, 166; Hagia Sophia, III, 174, 232, 314, V, 343; Jewish community, III, 11, 175, 195, V, 55 f., 406; Jewish quarter, III, 232; Karaite community, III, 221, V, 234, 237, 272, VI, 173; Latin Empire, IV, 130; law school, III, 11; manuscripts, VI, 7; non-Muslim cemeteries, III, 137; riot of Jews in, III, 24; sectarians, V, 267; sieges, III, 199, 239; strategos of the Stenon, V, 57; threat of conquest by Persia, III, 18; early use of paper, IV, 320

Constantius II, Roman emperor, II, 172, 179, 259, 398, 399; missionary efforts in Arabia and Ethiopia, III, 66

Constitutio Antoniniana de civitate, II, 109, 374

Constitutio pro Judaeis, IV, 8

Constitutio Tanta, II, 425

Contracts, I, 332, II, 258, 304; commenda, IV, 200 f.; fisqa, IV, 201; labor, IV, 170; legal, and moneylending, IV, 200 f., 205; marriage, IV, 195 f., V, 265 f.; suftaja, IV, 213; trade, IV, 48 f.; witnesses to, V, 56; see also Covenant; Deeds

Controversies, socioreligious, II, 133, V, 82-137, 326-52; antisemitism, IV, 84, V, 125-34; arguments from Scripture, V, 86-94, VI, 298 ff., VII, 223 f.; and biblical anthropomorphisms, VI, 258; in Cairo, III, 160, V, 268 f.; calendar issue, VIII, 184 ff.; Catholic-Protestant, VI, 306; over Chosen People, VIII, 123; Christology and trinitarian dogma, V, 117-22; and conversion, V, 102; gnostic-Jewish, V, 106; interfaith, III, 133, IV, 77, V, 83 ff.; Jewish law, V, 123-25; Judaic, III, 175, 179 f.; Judeo-

Controversies (*Continued*)
Christian, II, 136 ff., III, 83, 215, 336, IV, 57, 117, V, 108-22, VI, 171, 481, VIII, 29 f.; Judeo-Muslim, III, 123, 133 f., V, 172 f.; 209, 374, VI, 254, VIII, 29 f.; Karaite-Rabbanite, V, 269 ff., 277 ff.; in Khazaria, III, 198; over liturgical phrases, VII, 109; on Mazdakism, III, 255; messianism in, V, 119 f., 138 ff., VII, 178 f., VIII, 295; among philosophers, VIII, 66 ff.; polemics and apologias, V, 83-94; political and economic issues, V, 95-102; predestination and free will, VIII, 333; the rebel, V, 135-37; religious liberals and Zoroastrians, V, 103-8; sectarian, V, 186; on sex ethics, VIII, 52; street brawls and riots, V, 84 f.; talmudic, III, 233, V, 180 f.; theme in Hebrew poetry, VII, 177 f.; tradition vs. innovation in, V, 109 ff.

Converts and conversion: attitude of the Church toward, III, 44, 247, IV, 5-12; baptism, III, 41 (*see also* Baptism); Catechumenate, III, 36, 245; to Christianity, III, 10, 18, 19, 23, 32, 52, 176 ff., 182 ff., 193, 203, 220 f., 230, 241, 253 f., 313, 320 f., IV, 15 ff., 93, 189, V, 112 f., 126, VI, 257, VIII, 246, 249, 295; communal condemnation of, IV, 146; communities, loss of members through, III, 182, IV, 148, V, 135; denunciation of former faith, V, 97, 115, VI, 12; disposition of property, III, 143 f., IV, 279; exclusion from public office, V, 74; fees for, IV, 42; inheritance rights, III, 10, 158, V, 18, 299; to Islam, III, 95, 112, 113, 123, 125, 126, 132, 179, 272 f., 281, 300, IV, 152, V, 88, 102, 105, 179, VII, 304, VIII, 342; Jewish resistance to, IV, 92, V, 108, VI, 193 f.; of Karaites, V, 266 f.; martyrdom, in Spain, III, 39; among minority faiths under the Caliphate, III, 131; physicians among, VIII, 246, 249; reasons for, V, 113 f.; relapsed from, III, 14, 41 ff., 123, 127, 132, 248, 259, 295, IV, 5, 61, 77, 117 f.; religious discussions, V, 116; rights, III, 144, IV, 255 f.; Samaritan, III, 14, V, 171; scientific contributions, VIII, 141, 173 ff.; of slaves, IV, 187 f., 195; suicide preferable to, VI, 193 f.; tax concessions and, III, 96, 164, 242; use of olive press, III, 180,

315; in "Vision of Daniel," III, 179
—— conversions to Judaism, I, 171-79, 181, 373-75; III, 196, VIII, 77; of Alans, III, 208; of Arabs, III, 65; of Christians, III, 10, 22, 189 f., 238, IV, 9, 47, 52 f., 66, 116, 154 f., V, 113 f., VII, 256; circumcision, V, 219; instruction, VIII, 124; Jewish attitude toward, VIII, 123 f.; *see also* Proselytes and proselytism
—— forced conversions: III, 179 f., IV, 99, 104 f., 138, 189, VII, 177; acts of retribution, IV, 291 f.; Gregory I on, III, 28; inducements to, III, 14, 158, 179 f., 193, 242, 295; inefficacy of, III, 14, 291 f.

Convocation of "all the people," I, 73, 325

Convocations, academic, V, 19 f.; *see also* Kallah

Coponius, I, 263

Copper, I, 64, 256, 321

Copts, V, 95 f.; black garments, III, 140; church in Alexandria, III, 9; conversion to Islam, III, 123

Copyists, economic condition, II, 422

Corbett, William John, IV, 77

Cordova, Spain: Caliphate, III, 98, 160, 183, IV, 27, 194; delegation from king of "Gebalim," III, 210 f.; Jewish intercession for Christians of, III, 156; Jews of, III, 198; library, IV, 28, VII, 138; messianic movement, V, 200 f., 384; rabbinate, V, 54; redemption of captive scholar, V, 47

Corn trade, monopoly of, I, 261

Coronation, ceremonies, VI, 420

Corporal punishment, *see* Flogging

Corporate affairs, rabbinic regulation, II, 187, 261; *see also* Communal controls; Communities

Corporate personality, sense of, I, 135

Corporate responsibility, decline of, I, 135, 136, 146

Corpses: on battlefields, V, 346; wonder-working, IV, 299 f.

Correspondence: diplomatic, VII, 149; literary quality, VII, 165; privacy of, VI, 139

Corvée labor, I, 324, III, 192, 236, IV, 56

Cosmas, bishop of Prague, IV, 100

Cosmas Indicopleustes, III, 67, 259, IV, 167 f.

Cosmas of Jerusalem, Christian poet, VII, 142
Cosmic cataclysm, II, 59, 60
Cosmic Intellect, I, 174
Cosmocrator, term, II, 394, 435
Cosmogony and Cosmology, I, 48, 358, II, 310, 311; biblical and Babylonian stories, I, 47; Jewish story, I, 138; mystic, VIII, 22 f., 35 f.; Platonic, VIII, 318; restrictions on teaching of, II, 315; sublunary and superlunary worlds, VIII, 82; *see also* Creation
"Council of all of Africa," III, 230
Council of Nicaea, *see* Nicaea, Council of
Council of the Four Lands, I, 302
Councils, ecclesiastical, IV, 10 ff., 18, V, 64 f.; Agde, III, 36, 245, IV, 241; in France, III, 50 ff.; local character of, III, 253; provincial, IV, 17; Trullan, V, 109
Councils, communal, II, 199, 201, 404
Counter Reformation, Catholic, VI, 306
Counting devices, VIII, 353
Courtiers, III, 171, 216
Court poets, of Spain, VII, 146 ff.
Courts: ecclesiastical, II, 267, IV, 17, *see also* Jurisdiction, ecclesiastical
—— Jewish, II, 137, 265 ff., 419 f., V, 56, 317; 'Anan's rules, V, 220; Aramaic formula of edict, V, 5; exilarchic, V, 16, 115 f., 300 f.; geonic, V, 16 ff.; international rulings, IV, 176 f.; *see also* Judges and Judiciary; Litigation
—— Muslim, V, 293, VI, 324
—— Western, and clerical litigants, IV, 16 f.
Covenant, between God and Israel, I, 16, 48, 89, 90, 313
Covenant, Book of the, I, 80, 85, VIII, 231
Coyanza, *see* Oviedo
"Crab poems," VII, 197 f.
Crafts and craftsmen, I, 60, 256, 257, 260, IV, 170; hereditary, I, 69, II, 260; local concentration of, IV, 171; pre-Israelitic, I, 323; prestige of, IV, 167 f.; priestly, I, 258; ratio to other occupations, IV, 171; role in industry, II, 248, 249, 408; *see also* Industry
Cranmer, Thomas, I, 9
Crassus, I, 215
Creation, V, 357; biblical story of, VI, 227, 283 f., 470, 479, VIII, 6, 226 f.; chronology of, VIII, 86, 185, 201 ff.,

375 f.; continuing, VI, 268; era of, II, 376, VIII, 202 ff., 207, 380; *ex nihilo*, VI, 146, VIII, 59, 69, 73, 87 ff., 99; imperfect, and perfect Creator, VIII, 91 f., 102; month of, VIII, 197, 204, 377; of numbers, VIII, 151; principles of, VIII, 15; purpose of, VIII, 101 f., 105 f.; questions concerning, VI, 303 f.; ten elements and ten instrumentalities, VIII, 7; theories of, VIII, 78 f.; things preexistent to, VIII, 22 f., 273; through emanation, VIII, 91; works of, VIII, 11 ff.; *see also* Cosmogony and Cosmology
Creation, Book of, II, 21, VI, 241 f., VIII, 11 ff., 24, 58, 61, 147, 185, 191 f., 280, 342; attitude toward numbers, VIII, 151; authorship, VIII, 25; "book, number, and word," VIII, 15; ideas of the earth, VIII, 212
Credit, letters of, IV, 348
Creditors: debt collection, II, 262, 417 f.; right to service as payment, I, 69; treatment of, II, 303
Credit transactions, II, 302; *see also* Banking; Moneylending
Credo, Jewish, VI, 60, 102; Muslim, VII, 85
Cremation, I, 382, II, 12, 423
Crescas, Ḥisdai b. Abraham, VIII, 63, 316
Crete, messianic movement, V, 167 f.
Crime: assault, III, 49, IV, 69 f., 129 f.; blasphemy, III, 132, 295; capital, V, 17, 134, *see also* Capital punishment; heresy, III, 9; Karaite decrees re, V, 240 f.; murder, III, 132, IV, 39, 50, 127 f., 133; religious, penalties for, III, 186, 193; sexual, III, 111 f., 143, 300; tax default, III, 309 f., 312; town's responsibility for unsolved, I, 79, 327
Crimea: Byzantine invasion of, III, 198 f.; inscription, VIII, 203; Karaite communities, V, 237, 247; Khazar assaults, III, 203; sectarians in, V, 271
Crispin, Gilbert, abbot of Westminster, V, 347; *Disputatio Judaei cum Christiano*, V, 114 f., 341 f.
Criticism, biblical, new approaches, VI, 291-311, 474-86
Crops, as tribute to conquerors, III, 79; *see also* Sharecropping
Cross, ban on display of, III, 103, 140, 142, IV, 183; ban on sign of, IV, 25;

Cross (Continued)
Christian worship of, V, 125; "True,"
in Ctesiphon, III, 22 f., 238
Crowns, mystic, VII, 78; adorning letters
of the Torah, VIII, 29; symbols, II, 12,
14, 332; three, doctrine of, II, 45, 346
Crucifixion of Jesus, II, 64, 70, 71 f., 358;
alleged contumely of Jews for, III, 34,
47, IV, 92, 103, 257, V, 108, 118, VII,
177; belief in Jewish reenactment of,
IV, 102, 139; Karaites and, IV, 112
Crusades and crusaders, age of, IV, 89-
149, 283-311; attacks on Jews, IV, 101,
119, 124-29, 139 f., 212, VII, 179; background of, IV, 94 f., 102; financing of,
IV, 121, 123; as holy war against Islam,
IV, 95; Flemish crusaders in Constantinople, IV, 130; glorification of death
in, VI, 194; Hebrew chronicles, IV,
285 ff., VI, 217 f., 433; Jewish sources
of food and supplies, IV, 102 f.; Jews
and Muslims vs., III, 102; Karaites
and, V, 398; marauding bands, IV,
106 ff., 126 f.; meaning of, to Judaism,
IV, 147; and messianic hopes, V, 199 f.,
VIII, 295; portent of, VIII, 46; proselytizing, V, 135 f.; psychological after-
effects, IV, 139-47, 308-11; Saladin's appeal to Almohades, IV, 298; and Saladin tithe, IV, 81, 279; Saracen victories
in Syria, IV, 309; secularization of, IV,
123 ff., 131; self-sacrifice in, VIII, 44;
in Spain, III, 125 f., IV, 132; spread of
mysticism, VIII, 31 f.; treaties with
conquered cities, IV, 30 f.
—— First, IV, 94-106, 289-93, V, 199 f.
—— Second, IV, 7, 116-23, 299-302
—— Third, IV, 123-30, 302-5
—— Fourth, IV, 130 f., 305
Ctesiphon, Persian capital, II, 196, 204,
III, 99; anti-Jewish violence in suburbs
of, III, 58; complex of cities, III, 255;
Cross carried to, III, 22; fall of, III, 18;
see also Madaïn
Cuenca, Spain, fuero, IV, 41
Cultic prophets, I, 153, 365
Cults: of the dead, I, 148; local, I, 347;
primitive, I, 44 f., 311
Cultural exchanges, I, 183-87, 228, 376-79
Cummian, Saint, V, 346 f.
Currency: depreciation, II, 245; of Pales-
tine, I, 184; see also Coins and coinage;
Money

Curse, biblical prohibition, V, 72, see
also Blasphemy; protective, II, 336
Cush, Noah's grandson, I, 335
Cush, city, traveler's report of population, VI, 224; see also Abyssinia and
Ethiopia
Custom houses, Jewish officials of, IV,
182
Customs, local: adaptation to, VI, 10;
binding force of, VI, 63 ff., 121-30,
389-92; contrary to talmudic law, VI,
391; on death of a traveler, VI, 436;
differences of, in Babylonia and Palestine, V, 179; Gentile, imitation of,
VI, 123; halakhic miscellanies, VI, 75;
historical reinterpretation, I, 4-10;
legal adjustments to, VI, 121-30; and
liturgy, VII, 106, 121, 273; origin in
innovations, VI, 131; records of, VI,
129 ff.; and tradition, VIII, 5
Customs duties, IV, 65 f.; ancient Roman, I, 279, 415; under Caliphate, IV,
18 ff.; in Constantinople, III, 192; discriminatory, IV, 181 f.; exemptions
from, IV, 78
Custumals, city, IV, 13, 22f., 41 f., 60 f.;
European, VI, 129; French, IV, 268; "of
Good Conduct," IV, 310; Italian, IV,
22; Sepulveda, IV, 253 f.; see also
Fueros
Cutheans, II, 127, V, 173, 369, 372; see
also Samaritans
Cycles, astronomic, VIII, 188 f.; of jubilee
years, VIII, 191 f., 209; Sabbatical,
VIII, 208 f.
Cyprian of Palermo, III, 242
Cyprus: Christianity in, II, 165; copper
mines, I, 256; Jewish settlement, I, 375,
II, 102, 371, III, 19 f.; Roman war, II,
94, 95, 96, 97, 102
Cyrenaica, I, 169, III, 108; Jews in, I, 262,
375; Roman war, II, 94, 95, 96
Cyril, bishop of Alexandria, II, 189 f.,
391, 402, III, 90; action against Jews,
III, 9, 24, IV, 5
Cyril (Constantine), brother of Metho-
dius, III, 198; apostle to the Slavs,
III, 208; controversial tract, III, 215;
conversion of Russians, III, 221; jour-
ney to Kherson, III, 209; knowledge of
Jewish letters, III, 209 f.; name, III,
209
Cyrillic alphabet, II, 208 f.

Cyrillonas, Syriac poet, VII, 92

Cyrus I, the Great, I, 102, 324, 355, II, 160, 213, III, 19; decree of, I, 130 f., 161, 353 ff.; Isaiah's reference to, V, 157 f.; professions of toleration, I, 117

Cyrus (Artaxerxes), legendary king of Persia, III, 19

D

Dagobert, decree on baptism of Jews, III, 47, 53 f.

Dagon, god, I, 63

Dahriya, Muslim school of atheists, VI, 298, 311, VIII, 72, 90; attacks on Islam, V, 104

Dahya (Dehiyya) bint Tatit al-Kahina, Jewish "priestess," III, 91, 271

Dairy products, ritualist requirements on, IV, 138

Daiva temple, destruction of, I, 348

Dajjal, Muslim Antichrist, III, 109; myths, V, 358, 386; see also Armilus

Dalata, Palestine, burial place of Elijah Gaon, V, 37

"Dalimil," Czech chronicle, IV, 103

Dalmatia, Jewish settlement, III, 210

Damascus: ancient: antisemitism, I, 177; and Aramaean monarchy, I, 67, 322; dating of documents, II, 376; proselytes, I, 182; Samaritans in, II, 34

—— medieval, III, 20; good will of religious minorities, III, 161; Grand Mosque, III, 134; Isaiah's prophecies, VI, 293; Jewish community, III, 104, IV, 108 f., V, 103; Muslim charges vs. Christians and Jews, V, 96; Nuri Hospital, VIII, 236; sacked by 'Abd Allah ibn 'Ali, III, 121 f.; sectarian communities, V, 177, 182, 193, 266 f., 271 f.; synagogues, V, 28; traditional tomb of Moses, III, 308; treaty of surrender, III, 165; 'Umayyad capital, III, 88, 97

Damascus sect (New Covenanters), II, 52-54, 62, 130, 223, 228, 348, 351

Damietta, Egypt, III, 155; Byzantine raid on, III, 315, IV, 334

Damwah, Egypt, synagogue, III, 106, 280

Dan, city, I, 64; images erected in, I, 66

Dan, tribe, I, 95, III, 116 f.

Danel, I, 307

Daniel, prophet, I, 116, 354; apocalyptic visions, VI, 309, VII, 169

Daniel, exilarchic pretender, V, 222

Daniel, Book of, III, 179, 183, 315, V, 140, 225, VIII, 132; exegesis, V, 156 ff.; four evil beasts, II, 59; Hereafter, II, 39; messianic computations, II, 61, V, 87, 119 f., VI, 308, VIII, 206

Daniel al-Qumisi, see Qumisi

Daniel b. Azariah, exilarch, V, 33, VI, 215 f.; elected gaon, V, 34 ff.; sons of, V, 36

Daniel b. Ḥisdai, exilarch, V, 8, 11, 310; on calendar regulation, V, 305; on priestly leaders, V, 36

Daniel the Babylonian, VI, 279

Danube, Jewish settlers in Roman communities, III, 207

Daphne-Taḥpanḥes, I, 111, 184, 347

Dara-Izdadwar, Persian princess, III, 89

Dar al-Babunnaj, Khazaria, III, 203

Dar al-Islam, and dar al-ḥarb, III, 95, 119, 130

Darazi, prophet of the Druses, III, 123

Dar'i, Moses, al-, V, 201 ff., 207

Darius I, king of Persia, I, 130, 349, 353, II, 213; and local theocracies, I, 131, 149

Darius II, king of Persia, I, 131, 349, 354; decrees, I, 148, 344, 361

Darius the Mede, I, 354

Darkness and light, VI, 305 f., VIII, 22, 34

Daroca, Spain, privilege, IV, 42

Dating systems, II, 116, 118, 376

David, Hebrew king, I, 22, 63, 127, III, 63; apocalyptic vision, V, 355; devotion to religion of Moses, I, 65; and Egypt's central administration, I, 74, 326; and Goliath, I, 332; harp, VI, 343; injunction to Solomon, VII, 174; Israelitic unity made permanent by, I, 61; Jerusalem as royal capital, I, 65, 312; Melchizedek's successor, I, 322; population under, I, 29, 84, 139, 320; as prophet, VIII, 132; Psalms attributed to, I, 322, VI, 307 f.; shield of, III, 204; snake symbol, I, 66, 322; violation of tomb, I, 410

—— House of, I, 93, 130, 158, V, 35, 38; 'Anan's descent from, V, 220 f.; calendar computations and, VIII, 373; descendants of, II, 196, 205, 403, VI, 200, 207, see also Exilarchs and exilarchate; dual line, V, 305 f.; and exilar-

David (*Continued*)
chate, V, 7, 141, 236, VI, 200; genealogical records, VI, 423; Hillel, II, 140, *see also* Patriarchate; Messiah as scion of, I, 99, 101, II, 59, 69, V, 147, 168, 184, 202, *see also* Messiah; Moabite branch, V, 90; non-Jewish wives, I, 321; and priesthood, VI, 215, 432

David, exilarch: penitential poems, VII, 145

David, son of Daniel b. Azariah: establishment of exilarchate in Fusṭaṭ, V, 36, 38, 41; marriage to Karaite, V, 38

David al-'Adeni: *Midrash Hagadol*, VI, 401

David al-Muqammiṣ, *see* Al-Muqammiṣ

David Alroy, *see* Alroy, David

David b. Abraham al-Fasi, Karaite scholar, VI, 28, V, 233, VII, 18, 38; on prophecy of Isaiah, VI, 308 f.; use of Masorah, VI, 252

David b. Boaz, V, 231; on marriage and inheritance rights, V, 242 f.

David b. Jacob, IV, 29

David b. Maimon, brother of Maimonides, III, 115

David b. Solomon (As-Sadid ibn abi al-Bayan), Karaite physician in Cairo, VIII, 247 f.

David b. Yehudah, exilarch, V, 10, 226; controversy with brother Daniel, V, 9, 15

David b. Zakkai, exilarch, V, 11, VII, 277; conflict with Saadiah, V, 21 ff., VI, 214; Ibn Daud on, V, 178; line of descent, V, 295

David ibn abi Zimra, VI, 15

David ibn Merwan al-Muqammiṣ, *see* Al-Muqammiṣ

David of Baghdad, IV, 46 f.

Day, "cosmic," VI, 232; planetary movements and, VIII, 185

Day of Atonement, I, 5, 144, 256, II, 256, 283, III, 315, V, 30, 195 f., 245 f., VI, 86, 125; date of, VIII, 188, 195; *Kapparot* ceremony, VII, 78; and liturgy, VII, 79; *Musaf* prayer, VII, 86, 91; prayers and *piyyuṭ* for, VI, 368, VII, 90, 92, 146, 178, 245, 271, 273; recitation of "Royal Crown," VII, 171 f.; self-mortification and, VII, 122; Temple worship on, VI, 390, VII, 271; traditionally adopted by Mohammed, III, 81

Day of judgment, annual, I, 5, 144

Day of rest, *see* Sabbath

Day of the Lord, I, 94, 96, II, 58, VIII, 191; *see also* Kingdom of God

Day of Vengeance and Recompense, II, 31, 341

Dead, the: public lamentation for, VI, 14; punishment for communication with, I, 82; *see also* Burial; Funerals; Mourning

Dead Sea, I, 257; caves, V, 188

Dead Sea Scrolls, I, 331, II, 52, 349, V, 192, VI, 158, 409, VIII, 368; biblical recensions, VI, 442; Isaiah Scroll, VI, 238; Jubilee cycles, VIII, 372; liturgical poems, VII, 270; Manual of Discipline, VI, 78; phylacteries, VII, 244; *see also* Qumran sectarians

Death, I, 9; and origins of sin, I, 139; poems on, VII, 267; unnatural, for sanctuary desecration, II, 93, 369; views of cause of, VIII, 259; *see also* Immortality of the soul; Resurrection

Debates, talmudic, III, 233; VI, 141 ff.; at *kallah* gatherings, VI, 111; Alfasi's method, VI, 85; rules governing settlement of, VI, 30 f.; Tam and, VI, 55; Yehudai's summary of, VI, 80; *see also* Controversies

Debir, population, I, 321

Deborah, prophetess, I, 64, III, 91; Song of, I, 141, 317, 318

Debtors: protection of, IV, 83; treatment of, IV, 62

Debts: bondage for default, I, 69, 268, II, 303, V, 224; cancellation of, VIII, 209; of clergy, IV, 83 f., 204 f.; destruction of records of, in York, IV, 126; of foreigners, I, 156; laws of, II, 301 f., 132; owed moneylenders by Crusaders, IV, 121, 123; payment of, IV, 200, 202, 204, 206; registration of deeds of, IV, 304; sabbatical cancellation, I, 261, II, 262, 417; seizure of property for, I, 412, II, 303; transferral of, IV, 204

Decalogue: ethical, I, 49, 186, 227; abrogation of, VI, 145; Christians' view of, II, 381; elaboration of, V, 229; on inscriptions, V, 370; in Jewish theology, I, 25; Mosaic origin, I, 50, 314; oral and written transmission, VI, 427; prohibition of imagery (*q.v.*), I, 314; public recitation, II, 134, 381, V, 28, VI, 127, VII, 66; Rabbanite expositors,

VI, 289; revealed character of, VI, 144 f.; Saadiah on, VI, 296, VII, 141; *see also* Commandments

——— ritual, I, 50, 314

Decapolis, I, 225

Decimus Valerius Dionysius, II, 203, 404

Decorative arts, Graeco-Oriental, 10 ff.; *see also* Arts

Decurionate, III, 187 f.

Dediticii, the "stateless" class, II, 103, 109, 372

Deeds, of debts, II, 304, IV, 304; *dioqni*, IV, 212; formulas, II, 302, VI, 66 f.; Hebrew, IV, 320 f., IV, 34; use of Greek, II, 266; *see also* Contracts; Divorce

Deeds, Book of, IV, 34; agricultural transactions, IV, 316; *prosbol*, IV, 200, VIII, 209

Deir Qunna, scribes of, III, 151

Deities, *see* Goddesses; Gods

Delos, I, 377

Delphi, manumissions, I, 259

Deluge, year of, VIII, 203 f., 378

Demetrius I, king of Syria, I, 216; promise to free captive Jews, I, 259

Demetrius II, king of Syria, I, 216

Demetrius III, king of Syria, I, 217

Demetrius, alabarch, I, 261, 265

Demetrius, Alexandrian Jewish historian, VIII, 208

Demiurge, V, 380; and "cause of causes," VIII, 41 f.; equated with "prince of the world," VIII, 19; as "little Lord," VIII, 16

Democracy, I, 75, 209; ancient Hebrew, I, 48, 325

Demography, *see* Population

Demonology, I, 139, 358, II, 17, 32, 42 ff., 436; Babylonian-Persian, in Arabia, III, 82; in German pietism, VIII, 45 f.; *see also* Exorcisms; Incantations; Magic arts

Demons, VI, 103; disguised as black dogs, VIII, 368; female, VIII, 10; as intermediaries, VIII, 3 ff.; magic formulas vs., VIII, 233; in messianism, V, 142; obsession by, III, 180; tale of, VII, 311; talmudic characterization of, VI, 342; in Testament of Solomon, VIII, 283

Dental research, VIII, 262

Denys of Tell-Mahré, V, 9

Deportations: Assyrian, I, 95; Babylonian, I, 105-6, 115, 159; expulsion from

Alexandria, II, 189, 402; to Hyrcania, I, 131, 354; Samarian, I, 95, 159

Deposits, business in, IV, 208 f., VI, 68 f.

Derekh Ereṣ, tractate, VI, 63

Dervishes, VIII, 83

Descartes, and Jewish formulas of doubt, VIII, 80, 318 f.

Descriptio orbis terrae, II, 246, 414

Desert, God of the, I, 48

Determinism, II, 41, VIII, 109 ff., 333 ff.; astral, VIII, 111

Deutero-Isaiah, I, 22, 152, V, 158; God of, I, 137-40 *passim;* life and work, I, 103, 107, 135, 342; on the Sabbath, I, 144, 145, 360; on sacrifice, I, 126; "Servant of the Lord," I, 231; universalism of, I, 157

Deuteronomic reformation, I, 83, 330, 332; fugitive slave, I, 71, 85, 324; Josiah's acceptance, I, 84 ff.

Deuteronomy, Book of, VI, 302; alleged copy in Moses' handwriting, VI, 243 f.; author, I, 153; date, I, 330, 332; and history, I, 15, 25; homiletical exposition, VI, 165; on image worship, V, 125; litany of curses, VII, 179; source of *Shema'*, VII, 95

Deuterosis, see Oral Law

Dew, prayer for, VII, 98, VIII, 202

Dhaḥḥak, adh-, Arab poet, III, 264

Dhimmis: in Baghdad, III, 277; discrimination against, III, 139-40, 298-303; distinguishing marks, III, 140, 159 f., 170; economic role, III, 140, 150 ff., IV, 199, 225, V, 95 f.; mutual antagonisms, III, 160, 297; physicians among, VIII, 236, 253; physique of, V, 334; property rights, III, 146; status of, III, 97, 120-72, 149, 174, 288-312, V, 200; taxation of, III, 161-70, 308-12, IV, 152; treaties with, III, 123

Dhu an-Nun, alchemy and ṣufism, VIII, 225

Dhu'l-Nun al-Misri, Muslim mystic, VIII, 116

Dhu Nuwas (Marthad-ilan Ahsan?), Jewish king, II, 211, III, 66 f., 198, V, 111, 349

Diabetes, VIII, 262

Dialectics, in talmudic commentaries, VI, 54

Dialects: local, liturgical pieces in, VII, 67; West-Semitic, I, 36; *see also* Languages

Dialogues: between God and Israel, V, 154 f.; in religious debates, V, 114 f.

Diaspora, ancient, I, 16, 18, 24, 95-96, 112, 161, 225, II, 110; and antisemitism (q.v.), I, 188, 285; beginnings, I, 94, 105-8, 338; Christian, I, 29, II, 62, 82, 169, 366; community, I, 121-29, 350-53, II, 198-204, 215, see also Communities; divisions within, I, 281; economy, I, 259-62, 409-10; effects on tradition, VI, 100 f., VIII, 5; ethnic homogeneity, I, 131, 183; freedmen, I, 269; as galut, I, 30, 199; Graeco-Roman, I, 170, 282, 388, VII, 84, VIII, 57; growing dispersion, I, 105-8, 168 ff., 344-45, VII, 62, 245; growth of synagogue, VII, 62; intermarriage, II, 233; Israel's unity in lands of, I, 162; and Jewish role in cultural expansion, VIII, 256; and Jewish survival, I, 118; law and the, II, 77; linguistic assimilation, I, 185 f., 196, 212; little-known Jewries, I, 165; local autonomy, II, 198-204, 403 f.; and Maccabean uprising, I, 231; migratory movements, I, 172; neglect of Hebrew in, VII, 15; and Palestine, I, 215 ff., II, 82; and pariah caste, I, 297; under Persia, I, 372; and Pharisaism, II, 56; and Phoenicians, I, 374; pilgrimages to Jerusalem, I, 213, 258, 392, II, 108, 117, 118, 374, see also Pilgrimages; political inactivity, I, 217, 247; population, I, 170, 371, 372; prayers for rulers, VII, 265; rationale of, I, 135, 200; and rebellions against Rome, I, 217, II, 89, 96, 102; and religion, I, 100-101; Samaritan, II, 34 f., 341, 342; slaughtering, private, I, 148; statelike features, I, 18, II, 366; and ultimate ingathering, V, 176; see also Exile

"Diaspora nationalists," V, 221

Dicaearchia, see Puteoli

Dictionaries, Hebrew, VII, 20; earliest, VII, 29; rhyming, VII, 89; to the Talmud, VI, 28; of technical terms, VIII, 227

Didaché, I, 178, IV, 18

Didrachmon, I, 215; see also Temple, Second, tax

Dietary laws, V, 93; breach of, V, 279 f.; Karaite, V, 249

Dietetics, VIII, 243; treatises on, VIII, 226

Diocletian, emperor, II, 151, 178, 185, 260;

Dimi of Nehardea, R., II, 249

Dinawari, Abu Ḥanifa ad-, VIII, 386

Diocaesarea, name for Sepphoris (q.v.), II, 108

Dio Cassius, II, 98, 101, 102, 371 f., VIII, 185

Diocletian, decree on idolatrous worship, V, 172; price edict, I, 257, II, 250, 255, 415; prohibition of polygamy, II, 226; tax system, II, 263

Diodorus Siculus, II, 16, 410

Diogenes, I, 178

Dionysius, identification with Sabbazius, II, 24

Dionysius, head of Jacobite Church, V, 9

Dionysius b. Salibi, V, 345

Dioqni, commercial deed, IV, 212

Dioscorides, VIII, 65; "Book on Simples," VIII, 393; materia medica, VIII, 246; popularity of work, VIII, 246

Diplostoön, I, 257

Dirges, VII, 167; for apostasy, VII, 177; in Hebrew poetry, VII, 159 ff.; on Yequtiel's assassination, VII, 163

Disasters, natural, as messianic portents, III, 15 f., V, 143 ff.

Discourses, public: by scholars, II, 275; see also Sermons

Discrimination, anti-Jewish, II, 216, 241; see also Antisemitism; Public office

Diseases, VIII, 231; communicable, quarantining for, VIII, 239; psychogenic factors, VIII, 260; see also Medicine

Disinherited class exalted, I, 152; see also Poor, The

Disloyalty, see Loyalty

Dispersion, see Diaspora

Disputations, religious, see Controversies, socioreligious

Disputes, extra-legal settlement of, I, 329

Disraeli, Benjamin, III, 204, V, 202

Dissection, Jewish law on, VIII, 230 f.

Dithmar (Volkmar?), count, IV, 103

Divine grace, prayer for, VII, 244 f.

Divine mediation, II, 318; prayers for, VII, 66

Divine names, see Names, divine

Divine right of kings, VI, 10; and authority of Church, IV, 53 f.

Divine voice, II, 139, 383

Divorce, I, 112, 113, 114, 146, II, 221, 238, 291; 'Anan on, V, 221 f.; of child-

less wife, VI, 469; compulsory, II, 222, 411; of converts to Islam, III, 142; freedom of, V, 242; Karaite, V, 266, 281; laws on, III, 112, IV, 20, V, 18, VI, 64, 132 f., 390 f.; material restraints, II, 228; of merchants, IV, 184; movement against, I, 114; of tanners, IV, 167; writs, I, 395, II, 230, VI, 133, 139, 357, 394 f.

Doctors, see Physicians

Documents, II, 266; dating of, II, 116, 376; see also Deeds

Dodona, countess of Toulouse, IV, 202

Doggerel, VII, 315

Domesday Book, IV, 277

Domination, foreign, in messianism, V, 148

Domitian, emperor, II, 92, 104, 110, 121, 368, 372; in Melitene, III, 18; taxation by, II, 105 f.

Domninus, Jewish philosopher and mathematician, VIII, 57, 241

Donkey drivers, II, 261, 417

Donkey's load, measure for manuscripts, VII, 13 f.

Donkey worship, I, 193, 383

Donnolo, Shabbetai b. Abraham, Jewish scientist in Italy, VI, 470, VIII, 60, 253; Commentary on Yeṣirah, VIII, 30, 185; copies of writings of sages, VIII, 171; doctrine of Microcosm, VIII, 103; medical writings, IV, 44, VIII, 243, 244 f., 258

Dosa b. Saadiah Gaon, V, 14, VI, 23, 446, VII, 116

Dositheans, sect, II, 221, V, 173, 262, 369

Dositheus, priest, I, 220

Dositheus, Samaritan messiah, II, 33, 221

"Double faith" theory, VIII, 80

"Double truth" theory, VIII, 80

Doubt, religious, justification of, VIII, 80 f.

Dove cult, II, 30, 341

Dowry, II, 221, 236; return of, IV, 47 f.

Dramas: Greek, I, 189, II, 9; Hebrew, VII, 308; historical, V, 343; religious, VII, 308

Dreams: distinguished from prophetic visions, VIII, 129; interpretation, V, 260, VIII, 46; method of securing visions in, VIII, 28

Drivers' organization, II, 261, 417

Drugs: glossary, VIII, 252; international trade, VIII, 257; names of, VIII, 253; study of, VIII, 245

Drug store, treatise on management, VIII, 257

Druses, and Al-Ḥakim, III, 123

Drusilla, Herodian princess, II, 21

"Dual allegiance," I, 19

Du'ali, al-Aswad ad-, grammarian, VII, 18

Dualism, religious, V, 105 f., VIII, 296, 318; and light and darkness, VIII, 34; in magic arts, VIII, 11; vs. monotheism, VIII, 16; among Paulicians, VIII, 288; Zoroastrian, VI, 302, 305 f.; see also Gnosticism; Zoroaster

Dueling, IV, 40

Dukhifat, bird, V, 390

Dulebs, tribal union, III, 333

Du'l Qarnayim, designation of Alexander the Great, V, 329

Dumah, kingdom of, VII, 97

Dunash (Adonim) b. Labraṭ, Jewish settler in Spain, V, 46, VI, 220, 277 f.; accused by Ibn Ezra of blasphemy, VII, 51 f.; criticism of Menaḥem's dictionary, VII, 21 f.; criticisms of Saadiah, VI, 270, VII, 41; linguistic riddles, VII, 219; poems, VII, 22, 236; principle of triliterality, VII, 41 f.; synagogue reader and poet, VII, 146 f.; use of Arabic meter, VII, 22, 195; on verb forms, VII, 36

Dunash ibn Tamim, see Ibn Tamim

Dura-Europos, III, 296; church excavated at, II, 393; frescoes, II, 11, 14, 331, 346; inscription, VII, 128; synagogue, I, 14, II, 241, 346

Duran, Profiat, on Ibn Ezra, VI, 280

Duran, Simon b. Ṣemaḥ, V, 283; on mishnaic commentaries, VI, 61; on physician's responsibility, VIII, 238; polemics, V, 85

Duration of the world, computations, II, 16

Dyeing industry, II, 249, 261, IV, 166, 168; Jewish monopoly in Jerusalem, IV, 113

Dyes, durability of, IV, 168; production of, IV, 163

E

Eagle, golden: placed over Temple gate, I, 238, 402

Earth: division of surface, VIII, 214; habitable area, VI, 469, VIII, 215 f.; influence of heavenly bodies on, VIII, 175; measurements, VIII, 168, 213 ff.; rotation, VIII, 163 f.; shape, VIII, 212 f.; size, VI, 46, VIII, 162 f., 215 f., 360

Earthquake: at Antioch, III, 234 f.; churches and synagogues and, III, 232; Ḥananel on, VI, 45 f.; hazard to farming, IV, 153; at Laodicaea, III, 10; Palestinian, VII, 167

Easter: anti-Jewish outbreaks, IV, 55 f.; date, II, 188, 209, 401, VIII, 195, 369; and Passover, III, 11, 248, V, 303, 346, 410; "R. Eliezer" formula for, VIII, 190; see also Passover

'Ebedjesu, see 'Abd Isho b. Berikha

Eber, descendants of, I, 56

"Ebionite Acts of the Apostles," II, 75

Ebionite sect, II, 74, 348

Ecclesia, term, II, 394

Ecclesiastes, Book of, V, 225 f.; authorship of, VI, 160, 308; commentaries on, V, 231, VI, 270, 469, 477

Eclipse, lunar and solar, IV, 107

Economic conditions: adaptation of talmudic law, II, 262, 264, 291; of Alexandrian Jewry, I, 411; of ancient Israel, I, 67-72, 85 ff., 322-25; changing trends, II, 241-51, 413 f., IV, 150-227, 312-52; competition of burghers and Jews, IV, 60; decrees vs. Jews in Spain, III, 45; effects of Jew-baiting, I, 281; exilic period, I, 108-11, 115, 346-47; inflationary and fiscal pressures, II, 245, 414; Israelites' denunciation of system, I, 88; levies on populace, I, 272 ff., II, 82; and merchants and craftsmen, II, 204; position of women, I, 111, II, 236; procreation and, II, 220, 409; pursuit of goods glorified, II, 256; rabbis' psychological-ethical approach, II, 255, 415; religion and, IV, 221; social outcasts, II, 46 f.; talmudic policies, II, 251-55, 415-18; varied attitudes toward growth of poverty, II, 46; see also Agriculture; Banking; Business Transactions; Crafts; Poverty; Taxation; Trade; Wealth; also under Political; Social

Economic man, IV, 224-27

Economic theory, IV, 216-24

Ecstasy, prophetic, I, 334; revulsion against, II, 315; as source of knowledge, VIII, 113

Edessa, Christianity in, II, 165; III, 19, 239; elimination of minority groups, III, 57; Jews of, III, 23, IV, 114, V, 203

Edfu, ghetto in, I, 188, 380, 392

Edom and Edomites, I, 55, 56, 156, 162, 224, 307, V, 200; endogamous exclusion, II, 232; enemy of Israel, V, 161 f.; equated with Rome and Byzantium, II, 152, V, 134, VI, 309; expansion into southern Palestine, I, 106, 344; forcibly incorporated into Jewish body politic, I, 189; identified with Jews, V, 126; and Ishmael, VI, 407; list of kings of, VI, 309; messianic war on king of, V, 144 f.; world dominion, V, 143; see also Idumaea and Idumaeans

Edrei, Jewish tribesmen from Medina, III, 87

Education, II, 274-79, 421 f.; among Babylonian Jews, VI, 224 f.; communal ordinance, VI, 140 f.; curriculum, VIII, 146; Greek influence, II, 433; Jewish level of, VIII, 220; jurisdiction over, I, 150; for the masses, II, 279; medical, VIII, 236, 255; Muslim, VIII, 222; and "new" Torah, VI, 302; in poetry and language, VII, 150, 191, 223, 292; in preexilic Palestine, I, 323; prestige of learning, II, 201, 235, 276, 279; "reproofs of instruction," VIII, 37; for resisting propaganda, II, 133; responsibility of the academies, V, 18 f.; story of R. Kahana's son, VI, 183 f.; talmudic scheme, VI, 235; and talmudic study, VI, 34 f.; teacher-pupil relationship, II, 422; teacher's compensation, II, 278; universal for men, II, 279; women's, II, 239; see also Academies; Scholars and scholarship; Schools; Students; Study

Edward the Confessor, Laws of, IV, 79

Effigy, and sympathetic magic, IV, 92

Eggs, consumption of, V, 249

Egibi, House of, I, 109; pagan names, I, 346

Egica, king of Visigoths, III, 43; decree on converts to Christianity, III, 126; decrees vs. Jewish economic power, III, 45, IV, 156

Egilbert, archbishop of Treves, IV, 99, 290

Egypt and Egyptians: ancient: circumcision, I, 6; conquest by Asarhaddon and Ashurbanipal, I, 96; conscription of free laborers, I, 324; and consumption of sacred animals, I, 309; credit, I, 323; economic conditions, I, 110-11, 346-47; exilic or postexilic period, I, 111, 116, 118, 121, 165; exodus from, I, 308, V, 133, see also Exodus; group segregation, I, 117; interaction with Asia, I, 35, 67, 303, 322; Israelites in, I, 35-39, 96, 303-8, V, 167, VI, 303, VII, 181, 290; and Philistines, I, 320; property accumulation by small minority, I, 68; religion, I, 14, 45 f., 52, 199, 207, 311, 373; ritual, I, 40 f., II, 7; Semitic localities, I, 304; treatment of enslaved population, I, 35; see also Elephantine
—— Hellenistic and Roman, I, 165, 213, 282, III, 24; antisemitism, I, 188 ff., 381, 383, II, 89, 159; Christianity's slow advance, II, 164, 393; cultural influences, I, 165, 213, 282, 350; economic conditions, I, 251, 260, 266, 382; ethnarch, II, 198; incest, I, 146, II, 229; Jewish group life, I, 247, 281, 283; Jewish population, I, 168, 170, 172, 371, II, 102, 371; Jewish sanctuary, I, 14, 200; Jewish soldiers, II, 93, 94; Jews in semipublic occupations, I, 243; Judeo-Roman war, II, 94 f., 96, 97, 102, 370; language, II, 147; law and judiciary, II, 266, 418 f.; marriage, I, 146, II, 219, 233, 236, 408, 410, 412; nationalism, I, 381; and Palestine, I, 213, II, 94; Samaritans, II, 34, 341; sorcery and magic, II, 16, 21, 22; taxes, II, 105, 106, 373, 399, 413; see also Alexandria; Edfu
—— medieval: anti-Jewish riots, VII, 167; Arab penetration, III, 90 ff.; controversies over regional leadership, VI, 214; desertion of land by farmers, III, 168; employment of Jews in public office, III, 155; exilarchic office in, VI, 215; funds for Palestinian poor, V, 37; ideas of size of, VIII, 215; Jewish communities, III, 105 f., IV, 171, VI, 150; Jewish liturgy, VII, 119; Jewish places of worship, III, 296; Jewish refugees from Palestine, IV, 110 f., 113; Karaites in, V, 271 f.; Monophysitism, III, 239, 268; Muslim charges vs. dhimmis, V, 95 f.; negidim, V, 39 f.; "Palestinian"

congregations, V, 49 f.; philological studies, VII, 19; poll tax and passport, III, 166 f.; purchase of church property by Jews, III, 136; rabbinic ordinances, VI, 134 f., 138 f.; ransom of victims of Crusaders by Jewish community, VI, 447; ritual, VII, 276; Samaritan communities, V, 177; scarcity of doctors and drugs, VIII, 257; trade controls, IV, 351 f.
Ehyeh, divine name, VII, 21, VIII, 28, 152 f.
Einlager, IV, 62
Eiovdea Isdraelites, I, 182
'Eis Theos (One God), II, 406
Eklogé, of Leo III, III, 185 f.; recodification of Byzantine law, III, 177
El, Semitic deity, I, 36, 44, 46, 158, 312, III, 93, VI, 409; worship of, I, 37; YW son of, I, 309; see also Names, divine
El-Amarna age, I, 55, VIII, 385; decline of commerce after, I, 60; letters, I, 34, 40, 309, 350
El berit, I, 61
Elchasai and the Elkasites, II, 348
Eldad ha-Dani, III, 286, 329, VI, 122; Book of, VIII, 179; genealogy, VI, 433 f.; itinerant storyteller, VI, 220 f.; on the Jewish tribes, III, 116 f., 208; on laws of slaughtering, VIII, 228
Elders, I, 73, 125, 274, II, 201
Elders, Jewish: appointment of, V, 75; authority of, V, 63; communal, V, 50, 54 f., 60, 322; Palestinian, proclamation of leap year, VIII, 194; titles, V, 55, 59
Eleazar, high priest, I, 197
Eleazar, scribe-martyr, quoted, I, 232
Eleazar b. Abina, R., II, 214
Eleazar b. 'Arakh, Tanna, II, 121, 314, VI, 181
Eleazar b. Asher ha-Levi, compilation of Yerahmeel's works, VI, 197
Eleazar b. Azariah, Tanna, II, 104, 134, 256, 346, 351, VI, 164; quoted, I, 254
Eleazar b. Pedat, R., I, 180, II, 119, 122, 127, 162, 175, 198, 208, 242, 312, 389, 435, V, 163, VIII, 6; on agriculture, II, 245; historical records left by, II, 113; on Pentateuch, VIII, 20; quoted, II, 153
Eleazar b. Perata, R., I, 265
Eleazar b. Samuel, responsum from Natronai, VI, 389

Eleazar b. Shammua', R., II, 126
Eleazar b. Yehudah of Worms, German pietist, VI, 140, VIII, 42; against innovations in prayers, VII, 101; on carrying of weapons, IV, 70; on struggle between God and Satan, VIII, 46; tribute to Abu Aaron, VIII, 43
Eleazar b. Zadok, R., II, 289
Eleazar ha-Qalir, see Qalir
Eleazar of Adiabene, I, 183
Eleazar of Bartotha, R., II, 271
Eleazar of Modein, I, 231, 399, II, 16, 98, 122, 271, 317, 435
Elections, to communal boards, II, 201, V, 67 f., 74
Elegies, Zionide, VII, 168 f., 197
Elements: basic cosmic, VIII, 23 f.; created on first day, VIII, 7; Hypocratic doctrine of, VIII, 318; philosophic discussions of, VIII, 222 f.; transmutation of, VIII, 224
Elephantine, Jewish military colony, I, 14, 110, 113, 121, 346, 350, 352; economic conditions, I, 110-11; ghetto life, I, 117; interest rates, I, 323; names, I, 121; papyri, I, 121, 345, 347 f., 351, 352, 360, VI, 66, VIII, 371; prayer and sacrifice, I, 350, 362; relations of Jews and Egyptians, I, 116; support Persian rulers, I, 190; temple, I, 128, 129, 351; women in, I, 113, 114, 340, 348, II, 228
Elephants, I, 77
Elesboas (Kaleb Ella Asbaha), Ethiopian king, III, 68
Eleusian mysteries, I, 181
Elhanan, legendary Jewish pope, VII, 177
Eli, I, 351
Eliakim, see Jehoiakim
"Eliezer, R.," author of Pirqe: on Arab treatment of cemeteries, III, 138; formula for Easter, VIII, 190; on Gentiles, VI, 397; Mishnah of, VI, 406 f., 412; see also Pirqe de-R. Eliezer
Eliezer, R., poet, identified with Eleazar Qalir (q.v.), VII, 104, 264
Eliezer, R., son of R. Jose, II, 267; hermeneutic rules formulated by, II, 142, VI, 295
Eliezer b. Hyrcanus, the Great, R., I, 179, 181, 294, II, 9, 37, 104, 114, 116, 117, 121, 139, 148, 222, 227, 228, 237, 239, 296, 377, 408, VIII, 19; alleged pro-

Christian leanings, II, 383; alphabet acrostics, VII, 257; controversies with Joshua b. Hananiah, II, 276; marital life, II, 221, 230, 409; prayer by, II, 120, 377; quoted, II, 315; a rich landowner, II, 276
Eliezer (b. Jacob?), R., II, 275
Eliezer b. Joel ha-Levi, IV, 36, 70, VI, 118, 138, 371; re Baraita, VI, 182; on communal representatives, V, 60
Eliezer b. Nathan, halakhist, III, 219, V, 320, VI, 118, VIII, 262; chronicle, VI, 217 f.; on disposition of land, IV, 158; Eben ha-'Ezer, IV, 288; on ordinance against polygamy, VI, 137
Eliezer ha-Qalir, R., see Qalir
Eliezer of Touques, VI, 350
Eliezer the Great, R., on the Midrash Sar Torah, VIII, 19; see also Eliezer b. Hyrcanus
Elijah, prophet, I, 61, 66, 78, 89, 314, II, 68, V, 140; alleged appearances of, III, 153, IV, 107 f., V, 167; Al-'Ukbari's allusion to, V, 195; apocalypse of, III, 16, 19; in folklore, VI, 186 f.; and Joseph b. Yehudah, VIII, 7; in liturgical poems, V, 155; in messianic visions, I, 99, 339, V, 147, 153, 202, 353, 384; and mysticism, VIII, 39; as "one head," V, 159; purism, I, 334; struggle against priests of Baal, I, 87; on Torah, V, 130
Elijah, Palestinian gaon, V, 36, 37
Elijah, unknown author of Seder Eliyahu, VI, 160
Elijah b. Abraham, V, 227 f., 388
Elijah Bashyatchi, see Bashyatchi, Elijah
Elijah b. Solomon, V, 33
Elijah Gaon, of Vilna, battle against Hasidism, VII, 183
Elijah ha-Kohen, V, 35 f.
Elijah-Phineas, eschatological role, V, 153
Elioenai, I, 119
Elisha, prophet, I, 66; and the poor widow, VI, 168; supports Jehu's rebellion, I, 89
Elisha b. Abuyah, II, 155; on injustice, VIII, 102; on Metatron, VIII, 280
Elisha b. Shinaya, III, 184
Elkasites, II, 51, 348
Ells, Palestinian, V, 27, 303, VII, 63
Eloah, I, 158

Elohim (God), I, 46, 312, II, 162, 311, 335; *see also* El

Elohist, I, 42, 309

Eloi, V, 120

El Shaddai, II, 311

Elvira, Council of, II, 188, 210, III, 35, 50, 196, IV, 42 f.

Elyon, divine name, I, 312

Emanation, doctrine of, V, 226, VIII, 22, 82 f., 91 ff., 101, 113, 318

Emancipation: from state and territory, I, 16-25; Jewish effects of, I, 3; revaluation, I, 21

Emblems: in catacombs and tombs, II, 11; over temple gate, I, 238, 402, II, 13; significance, II, 12 ff.; *see also* Images and symbols

Embroidery, gold, IV, 168

Emesa, revolt in, III, 140

Emicho, count of Mayence, IV, 102 f., 106 f.; defeat at Wieselburg, IV, 106 f.; in German folklore, IV, 140

Emigration: from Germany to England, IV, 80; from Khazaria, III, 206 ff., 215 f.; from Khiva, III, 197; from Nablus, V, 176; from Palestine, III, 48, IV, 113, 221; from Spain, IV, 21; *see also* Migratory movements

Emmanuel, I, 340

Emmaus inscriptions, II, 29

Emmeh, Mar, patriarch, V, 184

Empedocles, VIII, 91; *see also* Pseudo-Empedocles

Emperors, Roman: donations to synagogues, II, 187, 191, 402; imperial worship, I, 244, 404, II, 5, 99, 109; lists of, V, 354, VI, 212; *see also* Rulers

Employment: of Christians by Jews, III, 30, 38, IV, 15, 42, 62, 69, 155, V, 133, 240; of *dhimmis*, III, 140, 150 ff., V, 95 ff.; gainful, rabbinic theory of, IV, 220 f.; of Jews in official capacities, III, 150-61, 302-8, IV, 15, 26, 36-43, 251 ff.; and study, IV, 223 f.; *see also* Occupations

End of days, II, 58, 61, 73, 312 f., 318, 435, V, 160 f., VI, 309; cosmic cataclysm and redemption, II, 59, 60; date, V, 162, 167 f.; envisaged in terms of Temple's destruction, II, 83, 364; portents of, III, 15, 97, 176, V, 142 f., VII, 61; supremacy of Israel, V, 138 ff.

Endogamy, tribal, I, 146, 147, II, 231 f., 411

Endor, Saul at, VIII, 130

Engelbert, archbishop of Cologne, V, 113

England: blood accusation against Jews, IV, 135 ff.; debate on episcopacy, II, 366; effect of Crusades, IV, 148; Jewish architecture, VIII, 159; Jewish communities, IV, 75-86, 276-82; Josephus read, II, 379; landholding and inheritance rights, IV, 156, 163 ff.; massacres of Jews, IV, 124 ff., 302 ff.; population of, III, 100; royal control over Jews, IV, 203 f., V, 63

Enlightenment, era of, VIII, 262 ff.

Enoch, prophet, VI, 437; astrological teachings attributed to, VIII, 176, 178 f.; identification with Idris and Hermes, VIII, 10, 134, 366; Muslim name for, VI, 449; piety, I, 44; roles attributed to, VIII, 282

—— Book of, II, 335, III, 211, VIII, 11, 178, 189; excerpt, II, 39; messianic prophecy, II, 59; speculations on angels, II, 18, 335

Environment: communal adjustment to, V, 3 ff.; effect on aggadic studies, VI, 152 ff.; influence on Jewish philosophy, VIII, 301 f.; Muslim, effect of, V, 371

Epaphroditus, II, 157

Epelytos, I, 375

Ephesus, Third Council of, III, 5

"Ephetics," VIII, 79

Ephraem, Saint, VII, 93, 136; liturgical poems, VII, 84 f., 196; sermons in hymn form, VII, 82

Ephraim, disciple of Alfasi, VI, 87

Ephraim, tribe, I, 65

Ephraim b. Azariah ibn Sahalun, V, 203

Ephraim b. Isaac of Ratisbon, VI, 391

Ephraim b. Jacob, of Bonn, VI, 218; "Book of Remembrance," IV, 119, 124, 307; chronicler of massacres, VII, 179

Epictetus, II, 157

Epicureans, I, 208; defined, II, 278; world outlook, II, 310, 434

"Epicuros," I, 208

Epicurus, VIII, 323

Epicycles, VIII, 164 f.

Epigrams: ascribed to Sirach, VI, 408 f.; on grammar, VII, 242; of Ibn Nagrela, VII, 138; use of, in poetry, VII, 164 ff.

Epigraphy, II, 11-15, 331-34; early Arabic, III, 61; *see also* Inscriptions

Epiphanius, Saint, II, 29, 123, 393

Episcopacy, II, 366
Episcopus, Jewish office, *see* Presbyter
Epistemology, VIII, 78 ff.
Epistle of Barnabas, II, 137
Epistle of Jeremy, I, 197
Epitaphs, *see* Inscriptions
Equality of rights, I, 243; *see also* Emancipation; Rights, legal
Equator, measurement, VIII, 213
Equinox, vernal, VIII, 368
Equity, II, 304
Eratosthenes, VIII, 168
Erech, III, 64
Erfurt, Council of, III, 182
Erfurt, Diet of, IV, 25, 66
Erigena, John Scotus, VI, 273
Erwig, king of Visigoths, III, 43; appeal to Toledan Council, III, 44; and negligent clergy, III, 45
Esau, V, 90; and Edom, V, 129; equation with Christendom, V, 93; Gregory I on, III, 29; Rome's ancestor, VI, 437
Esau, Mount of, I, 344
Eschatology, II, 313; divergent, I, 207-9, 390-91; in German Ḥasidism, VIII, 47; and messianic age, V, 147 ff.; Near Eastern, V, 358; Parsee computations, II, 435 f.; in Pharisaic and Persian philosophies, II, 318; in prophetic writings, I, 99; Samaritan, V, 371; *see also* End of days; Hereafter; Immortality of the soul; Punishments; Resurrection
Eshmunazar, king of Sidon, I, 162, 367
Eshnunna, I, 327
Eshtemo'a, II, 332
Esoteric movements, II, 314, 315, 435
Essenes, VIII, 109; and Cave Men, V, 379 f.; determinism, II, 41; elements that survived, II, 51, 130, 348; heroism, I, 233; ideology and way of life, II, 48-51, 347 f.; influence of 'Anan, V, 391; meat consumption forbidden? I, 407; name, II, 347; oaths, II, 48, 347; pacifism, II, 50; pregnant wife safeguarded, II, 221; sexual abstinence, II, 218; Therapeutae, an analogous order, II, 51, 347; wing of Pharisaic movement, II, 48, 342, 349 f.; writings about, II, 49
Estates: confiscated from Jews, II, 244; increase in number and size, I, 277; *post mortem* distribution of, VI, 85, VIII, 153 f.; settlement of, V, 300 f.

Estates, the, in European feudalism, IV, 87
Estella, IV, 35
Esther, Book of, I, 169, 345, 394, 411, IV, 92, VI, 188; Scroll of, VI, 185, 403, 431; Targum on, VI, 403
Etamps, France, expulsion of Jews, IV, 269
"Eternal" life of the nation, I, 9, 12
Eternity, II, 311; of Israel, II, 153, 389, 396; of Jewish law, II, 161; *see also* Immortality of the soul
Ethical monotheism, I, 10, II, 5
Ethics, I, 10-16, 47, 294-97; contribution of Judaism, I, 294; and human conduct, VIII, 62 ff.; individual and social, VIII, 117 ff.; Jewish, adopted by non-Jews, I, 294; in Jewish medical writings, VIII, 257 f.; in Jewish pietism, VIII, 48 ff.; and law, I, 227, II, 308; in mystic literature, VIII, 21 f.; and reason, VIII, 113 f.; and sex behavior, II, 221, VIII, 53; theme in poetry, VII, 163 ff.; 187 f.; *see also* Moral law
Ethiopia (Abyssinia), I, 169, 372; Falashas in, III, 116; ideas of size of, VIII, 215; Jews in, II, 211 f., 407; native land of Prester John, VI, 434; raids in Arabia, III, 68; slave girls, II, 238
Ethnarch, office of, II, 198, V, 39
Ethnic groups, I, 24, 52; Jewish, in Egypt, I, 117, 283; partition of Palestine among, I, 37, 55; *see also* Ghettos; Segregation
Ethnic unity, I, 39-43, 97, 163, 180, 308-10, 338, 339, 383; conditions in Exile, I, 134; controlling significance, I, 4, 31, 61, 94, 132, II, 227; dual allegiance and, I, 19; exclusivism, I, 155-58, 365-66; marriage as foundation of, II, 217; a positive principle, I, 98, 181; religious vs. territorial principle, II, 290; weakened at times, I, 54, 58, 212
Ethnology, Yosephon's efforts in, VI, 226
Ethnos, I, 168
Etiquette, court, under Fāṭimids, III, 171
Etymology: Arabic, VII, 232; in biblical exegesis, VI, 166; Greek, VII, 232
Eucharist, I, 193, II, 71, 75; Saadiah's allusion to, VI, 303
Euclid, teachings preserved by Bar Ḥiyya, VIII, 157
Eudaemonistic progress, I, 21

Eudes, see Odo

Eudoxios, II, 12

Eugenics, talmudic, II, 229-37, 411-12

Eugenius III, pope, IV, 7, 59

Eulogy, VII, 98 f.

Eunuchs, II, 219; trade in, IV, 191 f.

Euphrates Valley, II, 261; biblical punctuation in, VI, 238, 241; olive trees, II, 247; settlements, II, 206, 405; see also Babylonia

Eupolemus, I, 185, 207, 234, 378

Europe: Continental crusades, IV, 131 f.; influence of Jews, II, 264; travels in, VI, 221 f.

—— Eastern, III, 171-222, 313-40; Crusaders in, IV, 106; effect of clash with West, IV, 91 ff.; importation of labor, IV, 172

—— Southeastern: Jewish settlements in, I, 283

—— Western, III, 24-54, 240-54, IV, 3-88, 235-82; contribution of Jewry to, IV, 86 f.; difficulties of book production, VII, 136 f.; establishment of rabbinate, V, 63; exegetical tradition, VI, 48 ff.; expansion of Oriental trade, IV, 172; feudalism, VII, 176; gravitation of eastern Jewry to, IV, 147 ff.; halakhic miscellanies, VI, 72 ff.; isolation from East, VIII, 43; Italo-Byzantine influences on, VIII, 31 f.; Jewish communal democracies, V, 58-69; Jewish settlement in, IV, 90 f., VI, 437; liturgical compilations, VII, 121 ff.; moneylending, IV, 205 ff.; pioneering agricultural services to, IV, 161; political implication of the Crusades, IV, 124; slavery in, IV, 188 ff., 333; slave trade, IV, 194 ff., 335 f.; written Hebrew in, VII, 47 f., 54

Eusebius of Alexandria, VI, 160

Eusebius of Caesarea, I, 196, 246, 354, II, 27, 94, 131, 144, 161, 372, 379, 389, 401; on language of the Gospels, II, 66, 355

Eustratios, Saint, IV, 192

Euthinos, priestly family, I, 270

Euthymios Zigabenos, V, 338, 348

Eutychius, III, 22

Eve, allegorical meaning of, VIII, 86, 338

Evidence, rules of, IV, 277, 281, VI, 66

Evil, I, 7, VIII, 102

Evil spirits, belief in, VIII, 45 f.; and

disease, VIII, 234, 262; magical control of, VIII, 8 ff.; see also Demons

Evil-Merodach, king of Babylonia, I, 115

Evreos, Thomas, silentiarius, III, 235

Exaltation, mystic, VIII, 279

Excavations, see Archaeology

Excommunication: Christian: for employment by Jews, IV, 269; for preferring Jewish witnesses, IV, 16; threat of, to quell riots, IV, 290; for violation of protected rights, IV, 8 f.

—— Jewish, II, 192, IV, 39, V, 17, 65, 207, 220, VI, 134 f.; 'Anan's use of, V, 220; for changes in pattern of prayers, VII, 102; exemption through a hundred men, VI, 136, 138, 394; of Karaites, V, 275 f.; for litigation, V, 5; by a nasi, V, 47 f.; for opposing a gaon, V, 53; for recourse to Gentile courts, V, 223; of Samaritans, V, 172; for violation of dietary laws, V, 279; and violation of loyalty oath, V, 36; see also Curse

Exegetes and exegesis: biblical, II, 141-47, 385-87, VI, 274-311, 463-86; Benjamin b. Moses and, V, 225; contradictory interpretations, VI, 471 f.; eastern, VI, 281; harmonization, VI, 304 f.; historical, VI, 306-11, 484 ff.; individualistic, VI, 471; Judeo-Christian, VI, 274 f., 304; Karaite, V, 389; legal safeguards of works of, VI, 313; methodology, VI, 286 f.; Muslim, VI, 282 f., VII, 219; Palestino-Babylonian, VI, 305; and philology, VII, 37 f., 43, 52, 219; prolixity, VI, 282; and scientific exploration, VIII, 218; see also Bible; Interpretation, biblical; Talmud

Exhortations, VI, 165

Exilarchs and exilarchate, II, 195 ff., 200 f., III, 288; and the academies, II, 291, V, 14, 20 ff., VI, 116; appointment of local judges, V, 50; Arab superstition and, V, 297; authority of, V, 8, 12, 198, VI, 18, 199, 216; Bustanai, V, 141; and the Caliphate, V, 5 ff., 11 f.; establishment in Egypt, V, 36, 38, VI, 215; hereditary principle vs. election, V, 6, 21, 211, 222, 237, VI, 36; installation, VI, 214, VII, 284; Karaites vs., V, 210, 230 ff., 236; omission of, in prayer, VII, 245; religious disputations before caliphs, V, 85; revenues, V, 12 f.,

Exilarchs and exilarchate (*Continued*) 236 f.; rivalry with "dynasty" of patriarchs, II, 198 ff., 205, 403; weaknesses of, V, 8 ff., 179

Exile: Babylonian, I, 18, 22, 106, 345, II, 320, VII, 290, VIII, 125, 205; and assimilation, I, 105, 118; as crucial test, I, 102-33, 341-55; holiness on national scale, I, 154; insecurity, I, 158; leaders' tenacity, I, 160; legislation during, I, 115, 348 f.; as penalty for sins, I, 135, 199, 399; resemblance to age of Moses, I, 143; return to Palestine, I, 158 ff.; social transformations in, I, 112; surplus of men, I, 113; survival in, I, 104, 105, 134

—— Second, III, 195; computations of duration of, V, 153 f., 167 f., 363; connotations of name *galut,* III, 171, 195; effect of, VI, 230 f., VII, 290; as Jewish mission, V, 100 f.; life in, V, 129 f., VI, 438; and messianic ingathering, V, 203; priestly dues in, V, 236; problem of, V, 99 ff., VII, 177, VIII, 126; and repatriation, IV, 62 f.; as retribution, V, 130, VI, 233 f.; in sacred poetry, VII, 181; and sexual transgression, III, 291 f., 300; *see also* Diaspora

Existence, conceptual vs. real, VIII, 88

Exodus: from Egypt, I, 5, 16, 32, 39; Christian charges and, V, 133; creation displaced by, I, 47; date, I, 307; in Hellenistic literature, I, 189; in Jewish chronology, VIII, 205; and later conceptions of God, I, 46; national holiday commemorating, I, 148; non-Israelitic Hebrews among refugees, I, 57; and population under David, I, 320; work of Moses, I, 46-53

—— Book of, commentaries on, VI, 51, 296

Exorcisms and incantations, I, 139, 329, 359, II, 19 ff., 189, 336, 401; by Jesus, II, 67; validity of, II, 316

Expansion of Judaism: natural increase and conversions, I, 171-79, 373-75; *see also* Population

Expectoration, during prayer, VII, 251

Expositio totius mundi et gentium, II, 414

Expropriation, I, 68; of private property, IV, 13, 34, 82, V, 320; right of, II, 252

Expulsion of Jews, IV, 5, 148, 156; from Alexandria, II, 189, 402; as alternative to forced conversion, IV, 6, 57; from Baghdad, III, 100; from Bologna, IV, 27; from England, IV, 76, 84; from France, IV, 61, 80, 156; from Italy, IV, 25 ff., 26; from Khaibar, III, 80; in messianic rationale, V, 162; from parts of Germany, IV, 26, 66, 73, 92, 271; from Sens, IV, 56; *see also* Deportations

Extradition, treaties of, IV, 80

Extramarital relations, II, 225

Eye, diseases of, VIII, 243, 405

Eye doctor, fees, VIII, 254 f.

Ezechielos, I, 189, 197, 381, 385, II, 9

Ezekiel, prophet, I, 103, 342, II, 117; concept of God, I, 134 f., 137 f.; individualism, I, 136, 138, 357; against Israel's claim to special treatment, I, 138; law for the restoration, I, 143; leadership, I, 122, 135; personality, I, 356; recollection of the Temple, I, 122, 350; ritualistic injunctions at variance with the Torah, I, 154; sages mentioned by, I, 307; on segregation of aliens, I, 156; vision of, I, 335, 356, II, 315; wrath provoked by "idols," I, 335

—— Book of, I, 341, II, 436; Pope Gregory's homilies on, III, 29; and proclamation of leap year, VIII, 194; vision of the Chariot, VI, 161, VIII, 5

Ezion Geber, I, 64, 321, 326

Ezra, scribe, I, 106, 114, 116, 125, 142, 160, 162, 180, II, 117; association with Babylonia, II, 206; first scribe, I, 397; historicity, I, 341; no new law, VI, 145; Pentateuch known through, I, 345; racialist extremism, I, 147, 163; on reading the Torah, VI, 256; recension of Torah, VI, 254; restoration under, I, 103; 161; service to mankind, I, 158

—— Books of, II, 60, 351, III, 61; authenticity, I, 104, 343

F

Fables, collections of, VII, 189 f.

Fadl ibn Yaḥya al-, 'Abassid courtier, III, 149

Fadus, Cuspius, I, 239

Fairs, IV, 182 f.; Jewish merchants and, IV, 175; moneylending at, IV, 344; money transfers, IV, 213; and religious holidays, IV, 175, 220

Faith: biblical synonyms, VI, 296; a

democratic possession, I, 154; history
and, I, 296; law and, II, 78, 79; and
reason, VI, 108 f., VIII, 55-137, 296-
346; *see also* Religion
Falasha Jews, I, 169, II, 211, 407, III,
116
Fallowness, Jewish year of, I, 333, 382,
II, 263, VI, 307, VIII, 208 f.
Family life, ancient, I, 31, 50 f., 328, 361;
in Diaspora, I, 125, 127; halakhic
works on, VI, 64; household management, IV, 218; importance in community, I, 361, II, 219, 291, V, 133 f.;
and local customs, VI, 122; marriages within family, II, 229 ff., 411;
Palestino-Babylonian differences in,
V, 29 ff.; position of children, I, 361;
position of father, I, 310, II, 309; position of mother, I, 43, 310; procreation,
I, 31, II, 210, 218, 219; purity, II, 234;
regulation of, I, 145 ff., II, 217 ff.,
408 ff., VI, 68, 74; rituals, I, 148, 353;
sectarian deviations from law of, V,
190; and sex, VIII, 53; and slaves, IV,
193, 196; taxation, IV, 154; and tribe,
I, 317
Famine, in Jerusalem, I, 414; transpor-
tation difficulties, II, 245
Fanaticism, religious, in the Crusades,
IV, 90, 133 ff.
Farabi, VIII, 65, 122; commentaries on
Plato, VIII, 61; influence on Ibn
Gabirol, VIII, 325; on theology and
politics, VIII, 348
Faraj ibn Salim, *see* Farragut
Far East: early penetration by Jews? II,
212; Jewish trade with, IV, 175; *see
also* China; India
Farghani, al-, VIII, 360; comparative
sizes of fixed stars, VIII, 162 ff.
Farḥi, Estori, V, 262
Farmers: ancient, I, 71, 277 ff.; compliance with law, II, 242; education of, I,
68, 323; poverty, I, 277, II, 250, 257;
public discourses for, II, 275; tithes
and heave-offering, I, 277, 279, II,
262
—— medieval: desertion of land, III,
168; and expansion of Islam, IV, 151 f.;
land tax, III, 168; and length of
synagogue service, VII, 69; migration,
III, 168, V, 176 f.; tithes, V, 236; *see
also* Agriculture; Fruit culture; Land;
Landlords; Landownership

Farm laborers, *see under* Agriculture;
Peasants
Farragut (Faraj ibn Salim), Sicilian Jew,
VIII, 242
Fars, Persia, mixed population, III, 109
Fast days and fasting, I, 123, 294, II,
134, 140, 143, 182, 380, 385, V, 214, 216,
245, VI, 330 f.; attitude of German
rabbis toward, IV, 145; of Heraclius,
III, 23; merits of, VIII, 119; Muslims
and, VI, 14; Ninth of Ab, IV, 145;
Nisan, V, 216, 392; purposes of, IV,
103 f., 109, VI, 16, 86; scriptural readings, VII, 73; self-mortification
through, VI, 331; Sivan 20, IV, 138,
145; Yehudah's observance of, VIII, 49
Fatalism, in Muslim theology, VI, 151
Fate, human, astrology on, VIII, 178 f.
Father: creator known as, II, 309; in
family relationship, I, 310, II, 309;
see also Family life
Fatherhood of God, *see* God
"Fathers, merit of the," doctrine, II, 42,
346
Faṭima, daughter of Mohammed, III,
107, 305
Faṭimids, and descent from Faṭima, III,
107, 305; in Egypt, III, 289; emphasis
on court etiquette, III, 171; flight of
Jews to Byzantium, III, 184; and Jews,
III, 105, 154 f., 170, V, 40 f.; Pales-
tinian academies and, V, 33; royal ser-
mons, VI, 153 f.
Fatwa, term, VI, 110
Faustus, the Manichaean, II, 154
Fayyum, I, 266, VII, 19
Fayyumites, V, 197
"Fear of the Lord," I, 11
Feast of Tabernacles, I, 5, 73, 235, 254,
V, 217, 279; agricultural labor and, IV,
315; Canaanite origins, I, 72; date of,
VIII, 185 f., 188; names referring to, I,
120; poems for, VII, 101, 170
Feast of Unleavened Bread, I, 131, 148;
see also Passover
Feasts, I, 220; *see also* Festivals
Fees, medical, VIII, 232 ff.
Feet, washing of, VI, 14
Feivish, name, I, 119
Felix, Roman procurator, II, 21
Female deities, *see* Goddesses
Ferdinand III, king of Spain, IV, 28
Fermosa (Raquel), IV, 37
Ferreolus, bishop in Uzès, III, 253

Ferruziel, Solomon: assassination of, IV, 253; journey to Aragon, IV, 252

Fertile Crescent, I, 350; *see also under* Assyria; Babylonia

Fertility cults, I, 361; Canaanite, I, 137, 357; repudiated by prophets, I, 87

Festival of Heracles, I, 229

Festival of the Rejoicing in the Torah, poem for, VII, 282

Festival of Weeks, III, 106, V, 195, 215, 376, 404, VI, 267, VII, 172; *Musaf* services, VII, 276; Saadiah's prayer for, VII, 257

Festivals, I, 5, 58, 125, 220, 395, II, 45; clan and family religious, I, 55; mating, I, 294; *see also* Feast; *also under* respective holidays

Festive seasons, Parsee, II, 317

Feudalism: and agriculture, IV, 153 ff.; Carolingian institutions, IV, 49; vs. centralized controls, III, 185, IV, 65; decline of slave trade and, IV, 187; lack of personal security, IV, 35; and landownership, II, 257, IV, 163 f.; mixture of ecclesiastical and secular jurisdiction, IV, 58 f.; in Persia and Rome, II, 186, 191; separation of the "estates," IV, 87; status of Jews under, IV, 27 f., 41, 53, VII, 175; villein labor and, IV, 155; *see also* Serfdom

Fevers, VIII, 244

Fez, Morocco: academy, VI, 84; center of Jewish culture, III, 108; foundation by Idris II, VII, 225; Ibn Quraish in, VII, 17; Karaite community, VII, 226; Maimonides at, III, 291 f.; massacre of Jews, III, 108; messianic movement, V, 201; religious minorities, III, 124 f., 144 f., V, 79; repercussions of Mohammed's marriage to Ṣafiya, III, 262; use of Onkelos, VII, 5 f.

Fideles, *see* Vassals

Fidelity, oath of, IV, 49, 163

Fig tree, identification with tree of knowledge, I, 253

Figurines, Canaanite: female, I, 43, 310, 318, 329; male, I, 314

Finance, *see* Banking and bankers; Business transactions; Taxation; Trade

Fines: imposition of, VI, 10; for murder, IV, 39, 50, 127 f., 133

Fiqh, Muslim, VI, 24; *see also* Law, Muslim

Firdausi, VI, 271 f., 439

Fire: cosmic principle, VIII, 22; sacred element, I, 353; worshipers of, Zoroastrian, I, 400

Firkovitch, Abraham, III, 197, 202, V, 408, VI, 245

First-aid manual, VIII, 249

First-born, slaying of Egypt's, I, 197

First Cause, VIII, 93, 98

First fruits, I, 279

Firuz Shabur, academy of, III, 99

Fiscus, royal, IV, 41

Fiscus judaicus, I, 411, II, 104, 105 f., 186, 373, 399, III, 191; *see also* Taxation

Fish, consumption of, V, 405

Fishermen, I, 254

Fish-salting industry, I, 255

Flaccus, Avilius, I, 404

Flaccus, Lucius Valerius, I, 188, 380; effort to appropriate temple funds, I, 215

Flag, Jewish, III, 204

Flagellation, *see* Flogging

Flanders, Jewish settlers in, IV, 57

Flavia Neapolis (Nablus), Shechem renamed, II, 123

Flavius Zeuxis, I, 172

Flax, I, 257

Flight, miraculous, in messianic movements, V, 184, 203, 385 f.

Flogging, public, II, 218, IV, 49, V, 224; biblical sanctions for, VI, 91 f.; for cursing, V, 72; for insubordination, VI, 42; rabbis on, IV, 261, V, 16 f.

Florus, French churchman, IV, 54

Florus, L. Annaeus, II, 156

Flour mills, royal, IV, 318

Folklore, II, 4, 316; and apocalyptic visions, V, 152; Arabic prototypes, VI, 187; dating of, VII, 310 f.; on death of Qalir, VII, 270; expanding literature of, VI, 181 ff., 414 ff.; halakhic, VIII, 50 ff.; historical, VI, 188-98, 416-23; literary use of, VII, 76 ff., 187 f.; and messianism, V, 164 ff., 168 f.; Muslim and Jewish, V, 115 f.; and mysticism, VIII, 43; and oral tradition, V, 188; ritual and, V, 249; superstition, V, 258, 348

Folk plays, religious themes, V, 116

Folksongs, VII, 204 f.

Food: Christian and Jewish, III, 50; consumption of, and local customs, VI, 122; decrees governing Jewish con-

verts, III, 42; ritualistic requirements, III, 83 f., IV, 157 f., 188, V, 123, 131; *see also* Dietary laws

Foreigners, attitude of exilic Jewry toward, I, 156

Forgiveness, flogging as means of, V, 17

Form: connected with numbers, VIII, 353; primordial, VIII, 87 f.

"Four ells," V, 303; and private devotions, VII, 63

Four Martyrs, VIII, 19

Fowl: creation of, VIII, 226; prohibitions on, V, 249

France, I, 169, III, 47-54, 250-54, IV, 43-64, 256-70; anti-Maimonidean controversy, V, 47; Arab occupation of, III, 91; blood accusation, IV, 137 f., 307 f.; communal distribution of property, VIII, 156; and Crusades, IV, 128 f., 131 f., 289, VIII, 31 f.; halakhic miscellanies, VI, 74 ff., 362 f.; Jewish mystics in, VIII, 32; Jewish physicians in, VIII, 390; liturgical treatises, VII, 121 f.; moneylending, IV, 205 f.; *produit de Juif*, IV, 62; state organization of Frankish Jewry, V, 62; warned by Maimonides against astrology, VIII, 180; *see also* Gaul

Franconia, Germany, peace proclamation, IV, 71

Frankincense, cost of transporting, I, 250

Franks: Jewish status under, III, 50; *see also* Carolingian Empire; France

Frederick, archbishop of Mayence: compilation of canon law on Jews, IV, 73 f., 241; query on forced conversion and expulsion, IV, 6, 26, 66, 73 f.

Frederick I (Frederick Barbarossa), emperor: on clerical rights over Jews, IV, 59; Crusade led by, IV, 130; intercession for Jews of Münzenberg, IV, 304; policy toward Jews, IV, 68, 71 f., 129, 133, 176

Frederick II, emperor, IV, 22; establishment of government monopolies in Sicily, IV, 168; investigation of blood accusation, IV, 306; privilege of Worms, IV, 68

Freedmen, I, 269, II, 416

Freedom: of movement, IV, 32 f., 63 f., 78, V, 68, 78, VIII, 211 f.; thanksgiving for, VII, 109

Free love, II, 218

Free will, II, 41, V, 196, 228, VII, 22,

VIII, 119; foreknowledge of God and, VIII, 128; and influence of stars, VIII, 181; and predestination, VIII, 108 ff., 333 ff.

Freising, Otto von, IV, 120

French language: Rashi's use of, VI, 52, VII, 31; technical terms translated into, VIII, 227

Frescoes, *see* Painting

Friends, Society of, VII, 80

Friendship, poems of, VII, 160 ff.

Frisians, international traders, IV, 327

Friuli, Council of, IV, 26

Frontlets, V, 215, VII, 21

Fruit culture, I, 251, 407

Fueros, IV, 13, 30, 41, 43; *see also* Custumals

Fulbert of Chartres, V, 344

Fulvia, Roman lady, I, 405

Funerals: arts and rituals, II, 287 ff., 424; of rich and poor, II, 287 f.; meals, wine, II, 288; as source of hostility, III, 297; *see also* Burial

Furat b. Shahnata, Jewish physician, VIII, 243

Furqan ibn Asad, *see* Abu'l Faraj Harun

Fustat, Egypt: academy, V, 42; "Babylonian" congregation, V, 300 ff.; establishment of exilarchate, V, 36, 38; geonic copies of responsa, VI, 111; Jewish community, III, 105 f., 289; Jewish refugees, III, 294; Maimonides and VI, 11; persecutions of Christians, III, 123; riots against Jews, III, 122; slave market, IV, 191; synagogues, III, 134 f., V, 28

Future life, *see* Immortality of the soul; Resurrection

G

Gadara, Palestine, II, 65, 174

Gaelic, VII, 222 f.

Gaius, Roman jurist, I, 268, II, 103

Gaius Julius Alexander Berenicianus, II, 4

Galen, Claudius, II, 159, 432, VIII, 250; on cause of death, VIII, 259; on diabetes, VIII, 262; equation with Gamaliel, VIII, 388; on Jewish and Christian doctors, II, 159, VIII, 234 f.; on number of bones, VIII, 230

Galilee, I, 168, II, 105, III, 20, VII, 3; center of Jewish life and learning, II,

Galilee (*Continued*)
123, 164; Christians and churches in, II, 164, 392; cities, I, 224, II, 123; Jesus' teachings in synagogues, II, 67, 69, 355; linen industry, I, 408; under Maccabeans, I, 167-68, 278; population, I, 167, 370, 372, II, 123; social conflicts, I, 224, 278, II, 47, 179

Gallus, jurist, VI, 55

Gallus, ruler, II, 179

Galut, II, 135, 381; *see also* Exile

Gamaliel, ancient sage, equated with Galen, VIII, 388

Gamaliel, Rabban, VIII, 190

Gamaliel I, R., II, 135, 145; astronomer, VIII, 193; quoted, II, 70; teacher of Paul, II, 76

Gamaliel II, R., I, 265, II, 10, 104, 105, 119, 131, 135, 202, 311, 351; address to dispersion, II, 205; apology to R. Eliezer, II, 115; astronomic formula, VIII, 193; burial, II, 273, 288, 290; chairmanship of academy, II, 197, 403; degree of Hellenization, II, 141; descendants, II, 197, 227; lending losses, II, 250; Romans who studied under, II, 300, 430

Gamaliel IV, patriarch, II, 197

Gamaliel V, (Gamaliel b. Hillel), patriarch, II, 188, 193

Games and sports, II, 421

Gans, David, IV, 105

Gaon, title, V, 59; *see also* Geonim and gaonate

Garcia Fernandez, count, IV, 35

Garden of Eden, V, 86, 146, 149, VIII, 273; expulsion from, VIII, 329

Gardens, aesthetic-therapeutic value, VIII, 229

Garmo, priestly family, I, 270

Gates, temple, I, 122, 350

Gaul, I, 169, II, 106; restive tribes in Germany and, II, 106, 373; Visigothic, Jews in, III, 250

Gautier de Chatillon, V, 356

Gaza, I, 225, 255, III, 8; Arab assault on, III, 87; center of learning, III, 102

"Gebalim," king of, III, 210, 331

Geber, *see* Jabir

Gedaliah b. Ahikam, I, 104, 105, 344

Gedaliah ibn Yaḥya, III, 236, IV, 105, 130

Gehenna, V, 149, VIII, 273

Gelasian Sacramentary, II, 169

Gelasius, pope, II, 169, III, 27

Gemara, Babylonian, VI, 57; Ḥananel and, VI, 343; term, VI, 77; *see also* Talmud

Gemaṭrias, V, 86, 89, 157, 167, VI, 166, VII, 290, VIII, 14

Genders: masculine and feminine, VII, 242; monograph on, VII, 48

Genealogical records, I, 125, 272; fifteen generations list, II, 195

Genealogy, in Hebrew Enoch, VIII, 20 f.

Generalissimo, title, II, 196, 403

Generations of Man, The, VI, 197

Generative forces, I, 146

Genesis, Book of, V, 106, 214; commentaries on, VI, 38 f., 282 ff., 467, 479; cosmogony, VI, 228; erotic passages, II, 275; Ḥivi's questions, VI, 301; Muslim controversialists on, V, 89; Rashi on, VI, 51; six seasons, VIII, 201; story of creation, VI, 161; *see also* Creation

Geniba of Babylonia, II, 198

Genizah, Cairo-Fusṭaṭ, II, 297, 428, IV, 173, 175, 177; archives of responsa, VI, 111; method of collection, VII, 139; poetical material, VII, 167

Genizah fragment: on Fusṭaṭ, III, 106; letters from Ḥisdai, III, 156; on 'Umar I's agreement re Jews of Jerusalem, III, 101

Genoa, Italy: Jewish community, IV, 26; merchant-mariners, IV, 332; role of fleet in the Crusades, IV, 332; synagogue, III, 26

Gentiles, II, 187-91, 400-402, V, 100, 187, 265, VIII, 265; 'Anan's attitude toward, V, 218 f.; attracted to synagogues, VII, 128; circumcision of, V, 390; and the commandments, VI, 145, 397, 440; conversion to Christianity, II, 163, 166, 392, 393 f.; discriminations against, II, 124 f., 301, 418, 430, IV, 183; "eighteen laws," I, 180; equality for converts to Judaism, VIII, 125; exclusion from Temple, I, 157, 258; incestuous unions among, II, 230, 231, 411; influence of mystics on Jews, VIII, 15; intergroup relations, I, 6, 141, 155, 157, 159, 179, 193, 319, II, 148, 167, III, 139 ff., 298 ff.; intermarriage with, I, 147, 163, 361, II, 223, 232 f., 401 f., 411 f.; in Jerusalem, III, 101; Jewish prohibition of music of, VII, 205; loans to, IV, 199, V, 128; outlawry of syna-

gogue services, VII, 247; and prophetic gifts, VI, 229, VIII, 133; reference to, in Jewish prayer of thanksgiving, VII, 109; religious disparity, I, 145, 297, II, 170; renting of Jewish houses to, V, 79; sale of slaves to, IV, 193; and study of the Torah, V, 393, VI, 11; trade with, IV, 219 f.; *see also* Antisemitism; Christians and Christianity; Islam; Paganism; *and under* peoples, *e.g.,* Greeks

Geoffroi de Ville-Hardouin, IV, 130 f.

Geography: Hellenistic, VIII, 213; knowledge of, II, 306, 433; VI, 226; study of, VIII, 211 ff.

Geometry, VIII, 153 ff., 354 ff.

Geonim and gaonate: and the academies, V, 14, 48; appeals for funds, V, 23 f.; attitude toward *piyyuṭim,* VII, 103 ff., 132 f.; attitude toward preaching, VI, 155 f.; authority of, V, 16 f., 22 f., 63, 198, VI, 26; chronology, VI, 7, 208, 446; debate on miracles, VIII, 128; and decisions of exilarchic court, V, 16; differences of opinion among, VII, 43; election, V, 24; hereditary succession, V, 14; investiture, V, 24; legal monographs, VI, 65 ff., 362 ff.; liturgical works, VII, 63 ff., 78, 111 ff., 274 ff.; and local customs, VI, 122, 131; ordinances, VI, 131 ff.; Palestino-Babylonian rivalry, V, 37 f., 48, 303; vs. the priestly leaders, V, 36; responsa, V, 52, VI, 29 ff., 339, VIII, 229; and *rishonim,* VI, 334; in Sherira's Epistle, VI, 205; sources for period of, VI, 208; and the Talmud, VI, 21 ff., 77 ff., 242 ff., 363 ff., VII, 14; title, V, 13, 33; transition from Saboraim to, VI, 18 f.; use of vernacular Aramaic, VII, 220; *see also* Scholars and scholarship; *also under* individual geonim, *e.g.,* Saadiah

George, Saint, at battle of Antioch, IV, 96

Georgios, prefect of Phokas, III, 19

Georgius Syncellus, VI, 273

Ger, term, I, 155, 375

Gerard of Cremona, VIII, 158

Gerasa (Jerash), excavators' finds, I, 396, II, 174, 285; renaming of, I, 229, 398

Gerizim, Mount, I, 220, 229, II, 26 ff., 339, III, 9, V, 170, 236

Germany, IV, 64-75, 270-76; aid of Jews to Crusaders, IV, 98; ancient, II, 106,

210, 373, 406; biblical commentary, VI, 278; blood accusation, IV, 138 f.; communal ordinances on polygamy, VI, 385; effect on Jews of Saladin's conquest of Jerusalem, IV, 305; emigration of Jews to England, IV, 80; expeditions against Wends, IV, 131; Fichte on problem of, I, 18; hostility toward Jewish communities, and the clergy, IV, 91 ff.; identification with Ashkenaz, IV, 4; Jewish communities during the Crusades, IV, 98 ff., 116 f., 129 ff., 148, 289 ff., 304 ff.; Jewish folk literature, VI, 187; moneylending, IV, 205 f.; mysticism in, VIII, 32 f.; nationalists appealed to by John's Gospel, II, 359; Nazi historiography, IV, 270; and reforming tendencies among Jews, I, 131; salt mine, IV, 169; sources of Yeraḥmeel's work, VI, 422; upsurge of Jewish learning, VI, 48; *see also* Nazis and Nazism; *also under* individual cities, *e.g.,* Mayence

Gerona, Council of, IV, 43

Gerousiarches, title, II, 404

Gershom b. Yehudah of Mayence, R., IV, 65, 213, V, 62, 64, VI, 27, 48 f., VII, 30; date of death, VI, 345; identification of talmudic terms, VIII, 227; on messianic hopes, VII, 179; mourning for son's apostasy, VII, 177; ordinance vs. polygamy, VI, 135 ff.; penitential poem, IV, 93, VII, 179 f.; on reason for supplying biblical names, VI, 281 f.; recension of Babylonian Talmud, VII, 28; on residence permit, V, 68 f.; responsa, VI, 120, 138; transcript of Yosephon, VI, 191

Gersonides, VIII, 99; on seven pillars of wisdom, VIII, 349

Ger toshab, I, 179, 375

Gervase of Canterbury, IV, 80

Gesta Treverorum, IV, 105 f.

Gezer, city, I, 64, 323

Ghassanids, Christians, III, 66, 68, V, 180

Ghazzali, al-, Muslim mystic, VIII, 15; "anti-rationalism" of, VIII, 320 f.; attitude toward Arabic script, VII, 191; books banned, III, 32, 133; on conversion, III, 131; "Incoherence of the Philosophers," VIII, 84, 113; on jurisprudence, VIII, 70; spokesman for Asha'rite movement, VIII, 248

Ghettos, Graeco-Oriental, I, 188, 380; in

Ghettos (*Continued*)
Elephantine colony, I, 117; Phoenician, I, 176; voluntary, II, 149; *see also* Segregation
Ghosts, belief in, VIII, 45 f.; R. 'Aqiba's encounter with, VII, 245
Gibeon, miracle at, VI, 311
Gibeonites, I, 40
Gigen, *see* Oescus
Gilyonim, term, II, 380
Girard, duke of Lyons, IV, 55
Giudecca, Venice, IV, 25
Glagolitic alphabet, III, 209, 218; characters of Hebraic pattern, III, 330
Glassblowing, IV, 168; in Tyre, IV, 113
Glassware, II, 249, 338, 414
Gleanings left on fields, I, 279
Glebae adscripti, IV, 63
Glory, divine, VIII, 345
Glossary, Mishnaic-Greek, VI, 333
"Glossators," Tosafist, VI, 54 ff.
Glosses: on Prophets, VII, 23, 43; in geonic commentary, VI, 28
Gloucester, England, IV, 136
Gnomon, VIII, 157
Gnosticism, II, 26; VII, 181, VIII, 6 ff., 31; of Bogomils, III, 209; Christian, VIII, 52; criticism of Old Testament, VI, 298; on cyclical changes in history, VI, 438; and dualism, VIII, 34; fountainhead of, II, 335; Jewish ethical, VIII, 118 f.; main traits, II, 315; opposition to, II, 314-18, 434-36; principles of emanation and light, VIII, 22; transition to Neoplatonism, VIII, 39
Goat raising, II, 263
God: ancient Judaism's doctrines of, I, 13, 93, 337, 366, II, 311; and angels, II, 317; attributes, II, 314, 434 f., V, 120 f., VII, 178, VIII, 42, 95-101, 279, 326-29; and Caligula, I, 404; changeability of, VI, 482; commandments concerning, VI, 95, 97, 98 f.; communion with, I, 124, 202, VII, 73 f., 87, 106, 132, 168, 179, VIII, 3 f., 83, 113, 116; covenant with Israel, I, 16, 90, *see also* Covenant; Creator, I, 138, VIII, 91; cult of the "highest," II, 25; and destruction of the Temple, II, 112, 114; direct intervention, II, 141; divine name, appellations and circumlocutions, I, 46, 229, 244, 312, 352, II, 17 f., 162, 311, 314, 335, 357, 361, 394, 434, 435, VIII, 8 ff.,
see also under Names; divine presence, VIII, 27; divine voice, II, 139, 383; "enemies of," IV, 107; eternality and immanence, II, 311; ethical, I, 136, VI, 303, VII, 92, VIII, 290; existence of, VIII, 90 ff., 324; fatherhood, I, 13, 43, 310, 337, 366; foreknowledge, VIII, 110 ff., 128, 259, 334 f.; God formula, "of Abraham, Isaac, and Jacob," II, 23, 337; glorification of, VIII, 23, 345; as God of War, I, 46, 61; Ḥananel on, VI, 45 f.; Ḥivi's questions concerning, VI, 300 f.; holiness, I, 138; identified with local deities, II, 23, 24; incorporeality, I, 13, II, 310, VI, 267 f., 302, VIII, 26 f., 29, 35, 40, 81 f., 97, 100, 284, 286; Israel as "man who sees" Him, I, 182; kingdom of, in prophecy, VIII, 18; likenesses of, prohibited, I, 49, *see also* Imagery; love of, VIII, 114 ff., 337; magic power of name, II, 22 f., 314, 434; Maimonides on essence of, V, 47; martyrdom as "sanctification of the name of," IV, 144; might of, and influence on rain, II, 40, 345; Mosaic, I, 43, 46; Muslim concept of, VI, 6 ff., 151; nature, VIII, 45, 50 f.; observes all laws, II, 135; omnipotence, VII, 182 f., VIII, 18; of patriarchs, I, 46 f.; praised by Jews and angels, VII, 131, 171; quest for knowledge of, VIII, 81 ff., 117, 319 ff.; references to, in *piyyuṭim*, VII, 102; as shepherd, I, 254; sign from, VIII, 361; and sins of Jews, I, 297, II, 112; transcendence, I, 13, 137, 138, 140, 295, II, 42, 311; triune, VII, 264; *see also* Trinity; unity, I, 43, II, 311, III, 93, 292, VII, 85, 95, 172, 179, 182, 250, VIII, 56 ff., 97 f., 152, 290; and the universe, VIII, 87 ff., 112 f., 322 ff.; unknowable, I, 389; will of, VI, 145, 482, VIII, 91 f., 324 f.; *see also* Kingdom of God
Goddesses: mother, I, 43, 318; of fertility and generation, I, 57; *see also* names, *e.g.*, Astarte
Godfrey of Bouillon, IV, 102, 105; on Crusaders' capture of Jerusalem, IV, 295 f.
Gods: belief in deities secondary to God, I, 128; Moon god, I, 44, 45, 311; Phoenician and Punic, I, 374; of primitives, I, 46; rebirth, I, 294; Sumerian-Babylonian, I, 376; worshiped in sec-

ond millennium B.C., I, 308; *see also
under* names of gods, *e.g.*, Baal

Goethe: on detached critical analyses,
VI, 232 f.; on learning a foreign language, VII, 9

Gog and Magog, II, 60, 83, V, 145, 160,
200, VII, 97

Gold, I, 256; assaying of, VIII, 385; coins,
IV, 29, 210 f.; standard, IV, 209 f.;
transmutation into, VIII, 224

Golden Age, I, 98, 99, 101, 209; *see also*
Messiahs and messianism

Golden Bull, enacted by Andrew II, III,
213

Golden Calf, representations of, III, 140

Golden mean, VIII, 120 f.

Golem, of Yehudah the Pious, VIII, 47

Golgotha, IV, 102

Goliath, I, 332

Gontram, Frankish king, III, 53; welcomed by Orléans, III, 53

Good and evil, balance of, VIII, 119

Good Friday, anti-Jewish outbreaks on,
IV, 56

Goose, Mayence woman and, IV, 96

Gordian III, emperor, II, 177

Gorgippia (Anapa), Caucasus, III, 200

Gorni, Isaac, Provençal Jewish troubadour, VII, 151, 204, 292, 319

Goshen, Egypt, I, 37, 40, 304

Gospels, II, 64 ff., 70, 353 ff.; archaeological documentation lacking, II, 63,
74, 353, 361; burning of, II, 132; charge
of misquotations in, V, 126; chronological sequence, II, 72, 131, 359, 361,
VI, 210; critical problems of texts,
sources, etc., II, 360; geographic data,
II, 353; Ibn Daud on value of, VI, 207;
increasingly anti-Jewish, II, 72; language, translations, II, 65 f., 355, VI,
263, 457; terms for, II, 133; underlying oral formations, II, 66; *see also
under* names, *e.g.*, Mark, Saint

Gossip, penalty for, VI, 179

Government, *see* Self-government; State;
Theocracy

Governors, provincial, in ancient Israel,
I, 75

Gozan, biblical, I, 323, 345

Graeco-Arabic loan words, VI, 422

Graeco-Byzantine world, continuing Jewish contacts with, VIII, 299; *see also*
Byzantine Empire

Graeco-Oriental art and music, II, 6-15,

330-34, 402; as distinguished from
Greek, II, 334

Graeco-Roman civilization: Arab rule
superimposed upon, VII, 30, 32; heritage in science, VIII, 147; hospitals,
VIII, 392; interest in Jewish question,
I, 183; magic gemmas, VIII, 8; monogamy, II, 227; and Near East, Jews as
intermediaries between, VIII, 255 f.;
and Phoenician colonies, I, 175; rhetoric, VII, 3, 283; unprepared for
monotheism and imageless worship, I,
193; *see also* Hellenism; Roman Empire; *also under* names of respective
countries

Graeco-Roman loan words, VII, 141

Graeco-Syrian *Testamentum Domini*,
VII, 125

Grain, Palestinian, II, 246

Grain speculators, I, 277

Grammar: Arab, VII, 219, 224; biblical
accents, VII, 284; biblical and *pay-
yeṭanic*, VII, 57; development of basic
rules, VII, 32-39; as exegetical aid,
VII, 40; independent research, VII,
3 ff., 37; parts of speech, VII, 50; rules
of, applied to poetry, VI, 40 ff.; *see
also* Verbs

Gran, Hungary, III, 207; Council of,
III, 212

Granada: Berbers in, III, 156 f., IV, 29;
Beza bath, III, 299; destruction of
Jewish community, III, 123, 158; influence of scribe, III, 156 f.; Jewish
influence, III, 109, IV, 29, V, 45

Grape culture, I, 251, IV, 324

Gratian, *Decretum*, IV, 6, 18 f.

Graves: leveled with ground, III, 140;
pilgrimages to, V, 258; *see also* Cemeteries and catacombs

Great Mystery (*Raza rabba*), VIII, 32 f.

"Great Synagogue, Men of the," I, 162,
367, 397

Great War, II, 90-93, 96, 368 f., 372; Essenes in, II, 50; oracle on, I, 210; rebellions following, II, 94 ff.; strength and
type of Jewish forces, II, 90 f., 93, 368;
sufferings in Antioch community, II,
3; Zealots in, II, 101, 372

Greece: Jewish sources of science and
philosophy, VI, 230; Jews transported
to Italy by Roger II, IV, 21; philosophy of history, VI, 227; refugees in
southern Italy, III, 25; revival of his-

Greece (*Continued*)
torical literature, VI, 199; taxation, III, 192

Greek church, II, 166; *see also* Orthodox Eastern Church

Greek language: Aquila's translation of Scripture, VI, 256; education in, II, 133, 141 f.; Gospels, II, 65, 66, 142 f., 355; Jews' knowledge of, I, 185 ff., 378, II, 133, 141 ff., 147, 385, 387, III, 260; letters and formulas on epitaphs, II, 332; mystics' use of, VIII, 9 f., 16; reading of Scripture in, III, 189; in Sicily, IV, 21; terms used in Talmud, II, 300, 302, VI, 407; "translation Greek," VII, 4; translators of classics, V, 84

Greek law, borrowings from, VI, 5

Greek literature, Arabic translations of, VI, 264

Greeks, achievements in science, VIII, 138 ff., 219; adulation of, I, 228, 399; antisemitism, I, 190, 193, 195, 236, 401, IV, 166; athletics, I, 397; deeds, II, 266; and differences in cultures and creeds, I, 173; early contacts with Jews, I, 184, 283; influence on Christian ceremonies and arts, II, 84; influence on education in Palestine, II, 433; influence of Graeco-Oriental art and music, II, 6-15, 330 ff., 402; Judeo-Greek legal controversy, I, 190, 241; proselytism and, I, 176 ff., 374 f.; wisdom derived from Mosaic antecedents, I, 198; *see also* Hellenism

Greeting ceremony, III, 123, 276, IV, 10, 12, 238, V, 39, 41

Gregentius, bishop of Zafar, V, 111

Gregorios Asbestas, III, 193; treatise on forced conversion, III, 181

Gregory the Great (Gregory I), pope, II, 154, 282, III, 25; aversion to secular songs, VII, 203; distrust of medicine, VIII, 231; exegetical and homiletical works, III, 242 f., VI, 279; reaction to *vox psallentium*, VII, 283; on Jewish question, III, 27 f., 32, 53, IV, 5, 155

Gregory IV, pope, on forced conversion, IV, 6

Gregory VII, pope, IV, 237; warning to Alphonso VI, IV, 37

Gregory IX, pope, Decretals, IV, 240

Gregory X, pope, IV, 12

Gregory of Tathew, Armenian polemist, V, 123

Gregory of Tours, Saint, III, 251; on Cautinus and the Jews, III, 51 f.; debate with Priscus, V, 114; on Gontram's welcome by Orléans, III, 53; veracity of, III, 253

Grimoaldo, duke of Benevento, IV, 20

Grotius, Hugo, VI, 397

Groups, ethnic, *see* Ethnic groups; Ghettos; Segregation

Guadalajara, Jewish community, IV, 251 f.

Guaranties and sureties, VI, 70

Guarnerius, VI, 55

"Guest house," II, 285

Guildford, England, Jewish impost, IV, 81

Guilds: and clan organization, I, 69; discriminatory policies, IV, 170 f.; Jewish, I, 257, 258, 260, II, 249, IV, 199; mercantile, IV, 184 f.; mutual support, II, 260, 417; silk merchants', IV, 183; types, usages, II, 261

Gulgolet, capitation tax, III, 192

Gundissalinus (or Gundisalvus), Dominicus, VIII, 61, 174 f.

Guy of Dampierre, IV, 62

Guzana, interest rates in, in 7th century, I, 323

Gymnasium in Jerusalem, I, 228

Gynarchy, in Egypt, I, 112

H

Habakkuk, Dead Sea Scroll of, II, 53, 349, VI, 158

Ḥabbus, Berber ruler of Granada, III, 157

Habdalah, ceremony, VII, 168; prayer, V, 153, 155

Ḥaberim, I, 375

Ḥabiru (Ḥapiru), I, 34, 40, 44; identified with *'Ibrim,* I, 302, V, 219; non-Israelitic, I, 56

Hadad I, I, 322

Hadassi, Yehudah, V, 191 f., 229, 234, 272; on biblical interpretation, V, 252 f.; *Eshkol ha-kofer,* V, 399; mystical elements in work of, VIII, 30; opponent of astrology, VIII, 180; on rich and poor, V, 239; on study of Hebrew, VIII, 4

Ḥadhramaut, Jewish community, III, 260; prophets of, III, 82; temple of Sin, III, 64, 257

Ḥadith, V, 83, 88; biographical coloring, VI, 24; evolution of, III, 92; Jewish ingredients of, III, 273; on prayer, VI, 15

Hadrian, Roman emperor, II, 97, 108-9; dejudaizing efforts, I, 7, II, 106 ff., 118, 120, 266, 371, 374, VI, 241, VII, 95; places renamed by, II, 107, 380; quoted, II, 22; revolt against, *see* Bar Kocheba

Hadrian I, pope, IV, 18; on relapse of converts, IV, 5

Haduta (or Ḥaduta), priestly poet, VII, 90, 259

Ḥafiz, Persian poet, VIII, 15

Hafṭarah, prophetic lesson, VI, 355, 405

Haga (Haggai), name, I, 120

Haggadah of Passover, I, 189, 197, 381, II, 119, III, 289, V, 392, VI, 15

Haggai, name, I, 120, 121, 349

Haggai, prophet, I, 130, 161, VI, 23; question to the priests of Jerusalem, VI, 483

Hagia Sophia, Constantinople, III, 174, 232, 314, V, 343, VI, 212

Hagiographa, I, 345; 'Anan's attitude toward, V, 212; Aramaic version, VI, 260, 262; number of verses, VIII, 149; as source of Jewish law, VI, 244; textual transmission, VI, 237

Hagiography, V, 116; use of, in sermons, VI, 167 f.

Hai b. David Gaon, VII, 91; on Karaism, V, 276

Hai b. Sherira, Babylonian gaon, V, 48; advice on "things of merit," VII, 137; on appointment of judges, VI, 9; attitude toward Aggadah, VI, 176 ff., 412; attitude toward science, VIII, 68; at Baghdad academy, III, 195; on chronology of *Seder 'Olam*, VIII, 378; commentaries on tractates, VI, 43, 114; vs. corrupt judges, V, 178; death of, VI, 208; defense of Bustanai, VI, 11; on emending Mishnah or Talmud, VII, 347; explanation of King David's harp, VI, 343; and geonic "secret scroll," VI, 23; halakhic monographs, VI, 70 ff., 359 ff.; on letters of authorization, IV, 212; lexicographical work, VII, 26 f.; on local customs, VI, 122 ff.; and messianism, V, 161 f., 200, 206 f.; methodological work on the Talmud, VI, 205 f.; on miracles, VIII, 128; on mystic prac-

tices, VIII, 15 f.; on mystic writings, VIII, 27; on observance of New Year's day, VII, 107; poems by, VII, 105, 145 f., 166, 290; on prophet and magician, VIII, 130; at Pumbedita, V, 14, 24; quoted in Nathan's dictionary, VII, 30; on recitation of the *'Abodah*, VII, 90; responsa, VI, 29 ff., 115, 385; on synagogue "messenger," VII, 127; on Talmudim, VI, 17, 176 f.; on Targumim, VI, 260 ff.; volume of correspondence, VI, 113; on words and their context, VII, 68

Haifa, Palestine: defense of, IV, 111; "fortress," III, 102

Hajek, Czech chronicler, III, 216 f.

Ḥakim, al-, Fatimid caliph, III, 105, 173; on "distinguishing marks," III, 140; persecution of Christians and Jews, III, 111, 184, 289, 298, IV, 57, 271 f.; prohibition of synagogues, III, 135; and the riots in Fusṭaṭ, III, 122

Ha-Kohen, Mordecai b. Hillel, *see* Mordecai b. Hillel ha-Kohen

Ha-kohen ha-levi, Samaritan priests, V, 174

Ha-kohen ha-mashiaḥ, I, 152

Halakhah, II, 293, V, 125; academic differences on principles of, V, 22; Aggadah a handmaid of, II, 298, 429; evolution of, II, 305, 316 f., VI, 36; and local customs, VI, 128; monographs and miscellanies, VI, 62-76, 112, 354-63; Philonic, V, 216; practice, III, 111 f.; and Roman law, II, 299; scholars of, and mysticism, VIII, 37; sectarian deviations from, V, 189; and *shari'ah*, VI, 7, 12 f.; use of Arabic in, VII, 6; written, VIII, 38 f.; *see also* Law

Halakhah ke-batrai, II, 320

Halakhic midrashim, *see* Midrash

Halakhot, VI, 41; "adjudicated," VI, 108

Halakhot gedolot, IV, 195, VI, 23, 81 f., 98, 121, 364 ff.

Halakhot qeṣubot (Adjudicated Laws), VI, 108, 356, 366

Ḥaleb, *see* Aleppo

Halevi, Yehudah b. Samuel, Spanish Jewish poet, I, 5, 20, 295, III, 98, 258, IV, 32, VI, 231, VII, 152, 154; on Adam, VI, 228 f.; anti-Karaism, V, 407; apocryphal poems, VII, 308; on Arabic and Hebrew meters, VII, 200, 202 f., 313; bilingualism, VII, 9; birthplace, IV,

Halevi, Yehudah b. Samuel (*Continued*)
248; on conflict between history and
nature, I, 295, VIII, 111 f.; definition
of pious individual, VIII, 121; dialogue
before the Khazar king, VIII, 3, 22, 62,
67, 84 ff., 125 ff.; on divine origin of
Torah, VI, 142; on fast-day, VI, 16;
historical rationale of Hebrew, VII,
27; historical theory of prophecy, VIII,
134; on the individual and society,
VIII, 120; influenced by Saadiah, VII,
294; on influence of heavenly spheres,
VIII, 181 f.; on knowledge and revelation, VIII, 113 ff.; messianic belief, V,
163 f., 365; on movements of the sun,
VIII, 166; mystic philosophy, VIII, 39;
on natural law, VI, 144 f.; octocentennial anniversary, VII, 295; opinion
of Masorah, VI, 247; on origin of all
science, VIII, 77; poem on divine government, VII, 174; poems honoring individuals, IV, 251 f., VI, 84, 149, VII,
154; prayers, VIII, 260, 391; on predestination and free will, VIII, 109 f.;
on preexistent things, quoted, VIII,
126; problem of the Exile, V, 101; on
quest for knowledge, VIII, 84 f.; rationale of Israel's selection and sufferings, IV, 146 f., VIII, 125 f., 127, 133;
rationalism of, VIII, 320 f.; on the
revelation of Sinai, V, 92; riddle in
verse, VII, 162; on role of martyrs and
scholars, VI, 439; on sacrifices, VI, 148;
on Sadducees, V, 255; on *Sefer
Yeṣirah*, VIII, 22; ship as symbol, V,
361; on the soul, VIII, 107; spiritualization of love in poetry, VII,
212 f.; on study of the Torah, VI, 144;
on talmudic law codes and natural
sciences, VIII, 228; verses in Castilian,
VII, 192; on wealth vs. intellectual
achievement, IV, 349; wedding poem,
VII, 314; Zionide poems, V, 155, VII,
168 f., 197, 300
Ḥalfon b. Nethanel, VII, 295
Halicz, Karaite settlement, V, 285
Ḥalil, Arabic lexicon, VII, 27
Ḥaliṣah, ceremony of, II, 231
Ḥallah, offerings, VI, 10, VII, 274
Hallaj, Ḥussain ibn Manṣur al-, mystic
and martyr, III, 133, VIII, 15, 112
Halleluyah, congregational chant, VII,
125
"Hall of reckonings," I, 393

Ḥaluqqah funds, V, 37
Ḥaluṣ, pioneer, III, 212
Haly Rodoam, *see* Ibn Ridhwan
Ham, son of Noah, I, 335, VI, 192; de-
scendants of, VII, 256
Ḥama, R. (Babylonian), II, 290
Ḥama b. Ḥanina, R., I, 254, II, 213, 284
Hamadani, Arab writer, VII, 183
Haman, I, 5, 132, 136; denunciations of
Jewish separatism, I, 131; effigy of, IV,
139
Ḥamma b. Tobiah, II, 222, 409
Ḥammanim, I, 352
Hammath: inscriptions, II, 142; syna-
gogue, II, 174
Hammurabi, and Amraphel, I, 301
Hammurabi, Code of, I, 79, 324, 327
Hamnuna, R., II, 221, 283, 289, III, 61,
VI, 340; on Mosaic commandments,
VI, 9
Ḥanafites, III, 132, VI, 16
Ḥananel b. Ḥushiel, VI, 26, 108, V, 366;
commentaries, VI, 45 f., 342, 343; on
equality of oral and written laws, VI,
427; influence in southern France,
VIII, 292; legal compilations at-
tributed to, VI, 83 f.; quoted in
Nathan's dictionary, VII, 30; reply to
charges of talmudic anthropomor-
phism, VIII, 100; transcript of Eldad's
Halakhot, VI, 221
Ḥananel b. Palṭiel, V, 317
Hanani, I, 322
Hananiah, prophet, I, 116
Ḥananiah, R., II, 46, 125, 206, 225
Ḥananiah, brother of 'Anan b. David,
V, 210
Ḥananiah b. 'Aqashia, R., II, 308
Ḥananiah b. Hezekiah, I, 154, II, 436
Hanbalites, III, 132, VI, 16
Handicrafts, *see* Crafts and craftsmen;
Industry
Hands, washing of, VI, 14, *see also* Ablu-
tion
Hangchow, III, 286
Ḥanina, R., Palestinian Amora, II, 21,
278, 403, VI, 200; on birth under a par-
ticular planet, VIII, 178; on days and
hours, VIII, 185; objections to poly-
logy, VIII, 14; riots against ordina-
tion of, II, 243, 277
Ḥanina, priest, II, 115, 117, 121
Ḥanina b. Dosa, V, 21
Ḥanina b. Isaac, II, 20

Ḥanina b. Teradyon, martyrdom, II, 100, 371

Ḥaninah Gaon, VII, 259 f.

Ḥaninai, see Bustanai

Hannah, martyr, story of, VI, 417

Hannah, Samuel's mother, prayer of, I, 123, 351

Ḥanokh Gaon, VII, 78

Ḥanokh b. Moses, R., V, 45

Hanseatic league, IV, 332

Ḥanukkah, festival of, I, 5, 169, 220, 235, 395, III, 202, V, 284, 407, VI, 167, 269; Karaite rejection of, V, 246, 255; lights, I, 400, VI, 80 f.; Palestinian poem for, VII, 268; Sabbath of week of observance, VI, 162 f.; and Scroll of Antiochus, VI, 189

Hapax legomena, VI, 267, VII, 15, 226

Ḥapiru, see Ḥabiru

Hapki'el, angel, VIII, 8 f.

Har, I, 36

Haran, city, I, 33; moon goddess of, I, 44, 311

Haran b. Teraḥ, VI, 437

Harem: as instrument of imperial policy, III, 201; rivalry in, II, 225; for safeguarding women, III, 283; slaves for, I, 324

Hariri, al-, Arab writer, VII, 183, 184 ff.

Harlot's quarters, II, 225

Harmilos, communal titles in, V, 316

Ḥarran: destruction of synagogues and churches, III, 135 f.; religious toleration toward Sabian community, III, 130, VI, 437

Ḥarta de-Argiz, burial place of Hamnuna, VI, 340

Harun ar-Rashid, caliph, III, 160, VI, 107, 220; appeals to Jewish farmers, IV, 151 f.; Charlemagne's embassies to, IV, 45, 174, 257 f., VI, 220; delight in public religious debates, V, 83, 85; destruction of synagogues, III, 135; land tax, III, 168

Harun ibn al-Haik al-Dharir, Arab grammarian, VII, 222

Harun ibn Musa al-Asdi, Arab philologist, VII, 11; critical work on Qur'anic text, VI, 243

Ḥarut, fallen angel, III, 265

Ḥasan b. Mar-Ḥasan, Spanish astronomer, VIII, 376

Ḥasidism, I, 6, 11, 237; ancient, and Pharisaism, II, 342; Franco-German, VI, 46, VII, 183, VIII, 42 ff., 262 f., 293 ff.

Haskalah movement, VIII, 262 f.

Hasmonean Children, Book of, VI, 188 f.

Hasmonean dynasty, V, 256; see also Maccabeans

Hasmoneans (or Antiochus), Scroll of, VI, 159, 167, 185, 485; date, VI, 416; use in synagogue services, VI, 167

Hatshepsut, queen of Egypt, I, 36, 304

"Havilah," region, Africa, III, 116

Ḥayyuj, Yehudah b. David (Abu Zakariya Yaḥya ibn Daud), Hebrew grammarian, III, 180, VI, 290, VII, 23, 44; Book of Glosses on Prophets, VII, 23, 43; contributions to grammar and philology, VI, 290 f., VII, 60; disciple of Menaḥem b. Saruq, VII, 22, 23 f.; influence of, VII, 44; theory of triliterality, VII, 42 ff.

Ḥazzan, communal official, II, 367, V, 53, 316, VII, 80 ff., 254 f.

Ḥazzan, Israel Moses, R., of Smyrna, VII, 84

Healing: Greek God of, II, 336; by Jesus, II, 67; magic, II, 21, 22, 336, VI, 178, VIII, 21; see also Medicine

Heart, and soul, VIII, 107

Heaven, Kingdom of, see Kingdom of God

Heavenly bodies, motion of, VIII, 142, 164 ff.

Heavenly family, Zoroastrian concept, II, 317

Heavenly hosts: musical rationale of, VII, 210; participation in prayers, VII, 181 f.; praise, with Israel, to God, VIII, 4, 12 f.; prayers for, VII, 76 ff.

Heavens, seven, guardians of, VIII, 23

Heave-offerings, V, 313 f.

Ḥeber, I, 236, 401

Ḥeber ha-'ir, II, 201, 404

Ḥebrah qadisha, II, 289

Hebraisms, in Arabic, VII, 8 f.

Hebrew, term, as distinguished from Israelite and Jew, V, 126 f.

Hebrew alphabet, III, 209; in Arabic writings, VII, 8, 60, 190 f.; compared to Arabic, VII, 185; and Phoenician alphabet, I, 307; poems on, VII, 91 f., 142, 219; rhymes in order of, VII, 142; and sefirot, VIII, 22 f.; and sentence divisions, VI, 239

—— Letters of: classification, VII, 34 ff.;

Hebrew alphabet (*Continued*)
components of verb, VII, 41 f.; double,
VII, 38, VIII, 23 f., 25, 150; errors in
distinguishing between, VI, 240, 248;
final, VIII, 150; and Metatonic cycle,
VIII, 192; "mothers," VII, 34; mystic
approach to, VIII, 14 f., 284; as
numerals, VIII, 150; of the Pentateuch,
VIII, 29; permutation of, VII, 21, 38;
pronunciation, VI, 250 f.; radical and
functional, VII, 32 f., 39, 42, 49 f.; riddles, VIII, 357; role in the Creation,
VIII, 282; significance in study of the
Torah, VIII, 19 f.; square characters,
V, 175, VII, 56 f., VIII, 152; symbolism, VI, 247, VIII, 13, 35 f.
"Hebrewisms," VII, 10
Hebrew language: Abraham's use of, I,
20; antiquity and sanctity of, VII, 14,
27, 55 ff., 60, 158 f., 186, VIII, 77; and
Arabic, III, 81, VII, 8, 18, 48, 184 f.;
Arabs' lack of knowledge of, V, 89;
Babylonian pronunciation, VII, 235;
biblical and mishnaic, VII, 5, 56 f.;
blend of Aramaic and, II, 142, 147; and
Christian scholars, V, 121, VI, 272 f.,
462 f.; cultivated by the intelligentsia,
VII, 222 f.; development of accents, VI,
237; development of linguistic parallels, VII, 11; dialects, V, 175, VI, 250;
diminutive forms, VII, 16 f.; excel-
lence of, VI, 291 f., VII, 158 f., 186,
VIII, 217; Gospels, II, 66, 355; Hebrew-
Greek interrelations, I, 184, 376; historic evolution, VII, 242; in international trade, IV, 173 f.; Italian pronunciation, VII, 235; Jewish apologias
written in, V, 112; literary continuity,
VII, 68 f.; medical works in, VIII,
244 ff.; modern Palestinian, VI, 250 f.;
neglect of, VII, 45; Palestinian, VII,
235; philosophic tracts in, VIII, 75 ff.;
plural forms, VII, 197; prayers (*q.v.*),
VII, 68; premasoretic, VII, 233; in
religious affairs of Egyptian Jewry, I,
186, 395; religious ingredients, I, 27;
in Sicily, IV, 21; stimuli from other
languages, VII, 9; study of, II, 145 f.,
III, 102, VI, 290, VII, 3-61, 219-43;
translations from Aramaic into, VI, 56;
transliterated into Greek alphabet, I,
187; writing of, in Khazaria, III, 197;
see also Pronunciation; Roots; Spelling; Verbs

Hebrews: appearance of first, I, 32 ff.,
301; Israelitic and non-Israelitic, I,
37 f., 56, 225, 336
Hebron, I, 106, 344; Cave of Machpelah,
III, 278; export of grapes, IV, 324
Hecataeus of Abdera, I, 168, 189, 192,
200, 370, 373, 377, 386
Hecataeus of Miletus, I, 184
Ḥedvata, liturgical poet, VI, 248; *see also*
Haduta
Ḥefeṣ b. Yaṣliaḥ, VI, 59; reformulation
of Jewish laws, VI, 93 ff.
Hefqer, II, 252
Ḥefzibah, in apocalyptic messianism, V,
141, 152
Hegesippus, II, 121, 131, VI, 437; Yose-
phon's use of, VI, 418 f.
Heifer, red, and purification rites, V,
173
Hejaz, and Mt. Paran, V, 86, 89
Hejira, to Medina, III, 77
Hekhal, I, 332
Hekhalot, VIII, 11 ff.; mystical midrash-
im, VI, 162, 175, VII, 181; *rabbati*,
VIII, 13, 17 ff., 281 ff.; praise of Torah
and Talmud, VIII, 17
Ḥelbo, R., II, 148, 238, 388
Helena, empress of Byzantium, III, 156,
183; and the Cross, V, 125
Helena of Adiabene, queen, II, 14
Helgo-Oleg, *see* Igor
Heliopolis, city, I, 304
Helios, zodiacal representation of, VIII,
367
Hell, for evildoers, VIII, 104; *see also*
Gehenna
Hellenism: and antisemitism, I, 195;
decided in favor of Christianity, II,
251; decline, II, 173-75, 396; hellenization of Jewry, I, 165, 185, 188, 212,
219, II, 142; Jewish heritage of, VIII,
4; and Jewish law, II, 299; Judaism's
contribution to, I, 174; and Maccabean
revolt, I, 166; paucity of Jewish records, I, 199; Paul as intellectual
spokesman, II, 76, 80, 84 f.; Philo as
spokesman, I, 201, 388; regional divisions, I, 208, 210, 282; religious propaganda, I, 173, 177, II, 36; Sadducee reaction against, II, 36; Semitic resistance
to, I, 370; *see also under* Graeco-;
Greek
Hellenistic influences, I, 283; on Christianity, II, 163 ff., 392 ff.; in the Orient,

II, 3, 4, 54; in Palestine, I, 229, II,
299 f., 430; on Persia, I, 131
Hellenistic world: and Christian leader-
ship, II, 83; every fifth inhabitant a
Jew, I, 171; growing independence of
cities, II, 369; Jews attracted to cities,
I, 170; and Palestinian Jewry, II, 89;
and sacrilege in a sanctuary, I, 192;
self-governing municipalities, I, 167
Hemerobaptists, sect, II, 348, V, 250
Hemorrhoids, treatment of, VIII, 260
"Henotheism," I, 311
Henry I (Henry the Fowler), German
emperor, IV, 25; and Diet of Erfurt,
IV, 66
Henry II, German emperor, IV, 65 f.;
anti-Jewish policy, IV, 92 f.; expulsion
of Jews, IV, 66, 271
Henry III, German emperor, IV, 164
Henry IV, German emperor: break with
the episcopate, IV, 67, 99; negation
of forced conversion, IV, 106; peace
treaty, IV, 70; pro-Jewish decrees, IV,
67 f., 71, 102 f., 116 f., 272 ff., V, 62
Henry V, German emperor, IV, 117
Henry VI, German emperor, IV, 134
Henry I, king of England, IV, 78 f.
Henry II, king of England, IV, 80, 124 f.
Henry III, king of England, IV, 311
Heqqesh, V, 213 f., 243, VIII, 240
Heracles, I, 376; festival of, I, 229
Heraclius, Byzantine emperor, II, 179,
III, 16, IV, 151, V, 302; attempts to
reestablish religious uniformity, III,
24; defeat of Persian armies, III, 18;
dream of danger to Christendom, III,
54; "fast" of, III, 23; and Khazars, III,
198; suppression of Judaism, III, 23,
32, 40, 174 f., 220
Herban, debate with Gregentius, V, 111
Herbert of Bosham, VI, 273
Herbs, in magic therapy, VIII, 234
Hereafter, the, V, 166, 228, VIII, 81;
animals in, VIII, 230; compensation
for suffering, VIII, 126; Maimonides
on, V, 164 f.; in messianism, V, 147 ff.,
358 ff.; punishment and reward, VIII,
103 ff., 330 f.; see also Immortality of
the soul; Resurrection
Hereditary principle, in election of officials, II, 202, V, 73 ff.; see also under
Exilarchs and exilarchate; Geonim and
gaonate
Heredity, Mendelian theory, VIII, 242

Ḥerem, see Excommunication; Residence
permit
Heretics and heresies: Jewish, III, 233,
VIII, 66 ff.; belief in corporeality of
God as, VIII, 100; fostered by indi-
vidualistic exegesis, VI, 471; incor-
porated in sermons, VI, 171; and litur-
gical disunity, VII, 64; logic and, VIII,
68; punishment for, III, 9, V, 45 f.;
see also Apostasy
—— Christian, III, 194, VII, 128, VIII,
32, 46; Manichaean, V, 105 f.; Muslim,
V, 375, VI, 235
Hermann, bishop of Prague, IV, 118
Hermann, Premonstratensian monk, V,
112 f., 340 f.
Hermann III, archbishop of Cologne,
IV, 99 f.
Hermann of Dalmatia, VIII, 167
Hermeneutics, talmudic, II, 427, 429
Hermes: identified with Enoch (q.v.),
VIII, 366; invoked in magic formulas,
VIII, 9 f.
Hermes Trismegistos, magician, VIII, 10
Hermetic writings, VII, 174
Hermopolis papyri, I, 347, 352
Herod Antipas, tetrarch, I, 238, 401, II,
62, 352; banishment to Lyons, III, 47;
palace in Tiberias, II, 15
Herod dynasty, I, 225, II, 90, 91, VI,
192 f.; in Armenia and Chalcis, II, 3 f.;
bigamy among, II, 226; despotism of,
I, 223; messianism, II, 61, 352; Ro-
manization of, I, 243, 401; social conditions under, I, 217, 281
Herodotus, I, 25, 162, 177, 353, II, 104,
410
Herod's Temple, see Temple at Jerusalem, Second
Herod the Great, king of Judaea, I,
220, 223, 225, II, 24; building, I, 236,
237; coins, I, 236; copper mines, I,
256; fiscal reign of terror, I, 262, 280,
410; Greeks attracted to Caesarea by,
I, 256; and high priest's office, I, 216;
"Idumaean slave," I, 397; and imperial
worship, I, 218; Jewish majority in
kingdom, I, 167; Jewish soldiers used
by, II, 91; and oath of fidelity, II, 36;
sale of insolvent Jews, II, 257; Samaria
as a "Greek" municipality, II, 27; settlement of Babylonian Jews by, I, 172,
214; Temple rebuilt by, I, 238, 258,
402, II, 9, 213

Heroes, biblical: aggadic works associated with, VI, 159 f.; association of places with, VI, 228; benedictions ascribed to, VII, 66; foreign domination, VI, 192; in historical folklore, VI, 188 ff., 416 ff.; interfaith approach to, VI, 408; role of, in mysticism, VIII, 20 ff.; in storytelling, VI, 168, 186 f.

Heronian formula, VIII, 158

Hero worship, II, 5

Ḥesed Abu Nasr, Jewish banker, III, 158

Hesiod, I, 196

Ḥesna Ebraya, see Mosul

Hesperia, and Sefarad, IV, 4

Hexagram of David, II, 11

Hexateuch, I, 330; Samaritan, V, 176

Hezekiah, king of Judah, I, 66, 79, 126

Hezekiah b. David, exilarch, V, 11 f., 40; correspondence, VI, 116

Hezekiah b. Samuel, VI, 27, VII, 13

Hibbat Allah (Nathaniel?) ibn Jumay‘, see Ibn Jumay‘

Ḥiddushim (novellae), VI, 353 f.

Hierapolis: guilds, II, 261, 417; temple plundered, I, 398

Hierarchy, I, 149-55, 362-65; see also Priests and priesthood

Hierocles, II, 159

Hierodules, I, 146

High Holidays, VII, 72; ‘Alenu prayer, IV, 138; length of services, VII, 79 f.; poems for, VII, 93; ritual, VIII, 279

High priest, title, I, 152

Hilai b. Naṭronai, VI, 446

Hilarion, Russian metropolitan, III, 215

Hilary, bishop, III, 52

Hilderic, governor of Nîmes, III, 46

Hillel, I, 180, 221, 265, 269, II, 206, 220, 236, 272, 421, V, 213; authority on law and traditions, II, 37; controversies with Shammai, V, 255; pronunciation, VI, 248; Prosbol enacted by, II, 262, 417

—— House of, II, 117, 140, 205; attitude on divorce, II, 228, 410

Hillel II, V, 196; calendar reform, V, 212, VIII, 186, 369

Hillel b. Jacob, IV, 138

Hillukh, Samaritan law, II, 32

Ḥimyara, Jewish community in, III, 65 f., 258 f.; contacts with Tiberian Jewry, V, 180

Hin, pronunciation of, VI, 248 f.

Hipparchus, VIII, 139, 187 f.; list of fixed stars, VIII, 162

Hippocrates, Aphorisms, VIII, 238, 250, 261; on number of bones, VIII, 230

Hippocratic oath, VIII, 238, 242

Hippodrome, Solomon's, VIII, 18 f.

Hippolytus, II, 50, 347

Ḥira, Lakhmid capital, III, 61, 163, VI, 340

Hiram I, I, 64

Ḥisda, R., II, 14, 221, 249, 258, 264, 268; on poverty of cantor, VII, 129 f.

Ḥisdai, Egyptian leader, V, 8

Hisdai b. David, exilarch, VI, 336

Ḥisdai ibn Shapruṭ, Jewish physician, III, 155 f., 183, 198, 201, IV, 29, V, 44, 47, 161, VI, 27; copy of Yosephon, VI, 195; correspondence with king of Khazaria, III, 156, 204 f., 210, 305 f., 324, VI, 219 f., VII, 273; and Ibrahim ibn Ya‘qub, III, 217; patron of learning, VII, 20, 22, 146; VIII, 245 f.; translation by, VIII, 65; on use of caves, V, 378

Hisham, caliph, III, 103, VI, 324

Hisham I, Spanish ruler, III, 169 f.

Historical literature, I, 25-26, 100, 340, VI, 198-219, 416-33; Arab, VI, 192, 199, VIII, 77; folkloristic, VI, 188 ff., 217, 232 ff., 416 ff.; Jews' loss of interest in writing, I, 26; medieval, contents, VI, 190; Western, and dominant Jewish historical outlook, VI, 437; see also under individual historians, e.g., Ibn Daud; Sherira

History: concepts, I, 8, 47, 293 ff., II, 363, V, 102 f., VI, 218, 232 ff., 404, VIII, 62, 78 ff.; chronology of, VI, 202, VIII, 205 ff., 378 ff.; common, among Israelitic tribes, I, 41; and Hellenistic Jewry, I, 208; historic continuity in new order, I, 135; "lachrymose conception of Jewish history," I, 297, VI, 218, 234, 404; and messianism, II, 99; mystics' outlook on, VIII, 20; nadir of, VI, 230; and nature, I, 5 ff., 12, 18, 101, II, 81, VIII, 111 f.; sources, I, 298-99, 369; significance of biblical, VII, 167 f., 306-11, 484-86, VIII, 86 ff.; supreme religious experience, I, 8, 100 f., 295 f.; synchronization of, with Roman history, VI, 422; theme in poetry, VII, 134, 163, 167 f.; transition

to legend, VI, 233; use in Judeo-Christian controversies, II, 80 f., 136-41, 170, 381-85, V, 119 f., 128 ff.; view of divine guidance, VI, 234; waning interest in totality of, I, 26, 165, 199, 293

Hittite code, I, 327

Hittites: incestuous marriage, I, 146; religious ideas, I, 45

Ḥivi ha-Balkhi, exegetical extremist, III, 134, V, 105, 107, VI, 272, 298-306, 478-84; alleged convert, VI, 302, 303, 482; date of literary activity, VI, 478; new Torah, VI, 302; questions concerning the Bible, VI, 299 ff., VIII, 58; replies to, VI, 303-4, 480 ff.; sources, VI, 299; use of rhymed Arabic prose, VI, 478

Ḥiyya, R., II, 197, 206, 270, 422; mispronunciations of Scripture, VI, 240; "secret scroll," VI, 41

Ḥiyya b. Abba, R., II, 194, 208

Ḥiyya of Sepphoris, R., II, 112, 375

Hodayah Nasi, V, 47

Ḥofshim (coloni), I, 324

Hohenstaufen, in Sicily, IV, 22 f.

Holidays, I, 5, 220, II, 209, III, 50; Christian observance of, IV, 60 f.; computation of dates, V, 279, VII, 203, VIII, 187 ff., 200, 208; disturbance of, IV, 236; double, VIII, 374 f.; Hoshaʻnah, III, 101; Karaite observances, V, 245 ff.; laws of, VI, 80; observance of, V, 270; prayers for, VII, 124, 180; retelling of biblical narratives, VII, 180 f.; and rise of antisemitism, V, 108 f.; scriptural readings, VII, 72 f.; sectarians and, V, 191 f., 195 f.; Sefirah season, V, 283, VII, 67; sermons, VI, 162; trade restrictions on, IV, 219 f.; tunes for prayers, VII, 127; two-day observance, V, 28 f.; see also Festivals; High holidays

Holiness, doctrine of, I, 138, 358; of God, VIII, 99; incommunicable nature of, VI, 483

Holophernes, story of, VI, 187

Holy Land, see Palestine

Holy Roman Empire: German leadership, IV, 64 ff.; see also Germany; also under names of emperors

Holy War, Muslim concept of, IV, 90, 291

Holy Week, anti-Jewish assaults, V, 108

Homer, I, 196, VI, 406; papyri, II, 393

Ḥomesh, double tithe, V, 14

Homicide, I, 145

Homilists and homiletics, II, 144, 280, 294, 316, 320, 422, VIII, 30; see also Aggadah; Midrash; Sermons

Homonyms, biblical, VII, 12; in Maimonidean system, VIII, 82

Homosexuality, as poetic theme, VII, 158 ff., 308

Honey, I, 252

Ḥoni ha-meʻaggel, prayers for rain, II, 349

Honorius, Roman emperor, II, 191, 192

Honorius I, pope, III, 24; on Jewish converts, III, 40

Horaʼah, amoraic age, VI, 17

Hormizd, king of Persia, III, 57

Horn: blowing of, on New Year's day, II, 120, 138, 383, VII, 76, 107; "little horn," V, 87; ram's horn, II, 256, 333, 416; symbol II, 11

Horoscopes, VIII, 178, 183, 366

Horseback riding, ban on, III, 141, 149, 152, 298 f.

Horses, I, 332

Hosea, prophet, I, 89, 91, 99, 336; condemns animal sacrifices, I, 124

—— Book of, V, 163, 239; commentaries on, VI, 165, 289, VII, 38; Karaites on, VI, 473

Hosea, king of Israel, I, 348

Hoshaiah, R., II, 225; mystic speculations, VIII, 6

Hoshaiah II, R., II, 284

Hoshaʻnah, III, 101

Hospice, communal, VIII, 239 f.

Hospitals: in East and West, VIII, 240; noted, VIII, 236, 389; use of music, VII, 321

Hours: division of, VIII, 373 f.; planetary movements and, VIII, 185

Houses: in Babylonia, I, 109, 346; construction of, VIII, 356; door-post inscriptions, V, 59; figures of devils on doors, III, 140; near mosque, III, 138, 145; ownership and right of preemption, III, 145 f.; renting of, to Gentiles, IV, 158; stone, I, 257, IV, 85, 170, 281 f.

Howden, Richard, on moneylending, IV, 83

Ḥubaysh, Arabic translation of Greek writings, VI, 264

Hud, III, 82
Huesca, Spain, IV, 39
Hugo of Flavigny, IV, 100 f.
Hulaju, conqueror of Baghdad, VI, 11
Huldah, prophetess, II, 286
Hullin, tractate, VI, 86
Human and animal figures in art, II, 9, 10, 13, 15, 154, 402
Humanitarianism, I, 22, 155-58, 365-66, II, 3-6, 329, VIII, 124 f.; and belief in "chosenness," II, 170
Humanitas, Graeco-Roman concept, II, 6, 329 f., VIII, 263
Human nature, transformation in, on advent of the Messiah, V, 165, 175
Humility, biblical synonyms for, VI, 296; Jewish ideal of, VIII, 121
Humor, in exegesis, VI, 288
"Humors," physiological, VIII, 260
Huna, exilarch, VI, 17; conflict with R. Hanina, VI, 200
Huna, R., Amora, II, 221, 231, 237, 240, 249
Huna, Mar Rab, gaon, VI, 132 f.
Huna b. Joshua, R., VIII, 379
Huna Mari, II, 182, 196
Hunayn ibn Ishaq al-'Ibadi, Syriac Christian translator, III, 80, VI, 264, 271, VIII, 250; on music, VII, 207
Hundred men, in suspending Gershom's excommunication, VI, 136, 138, 394
Hungary, Jews in, II, 210, 406, III, 206 f., 211 ff., 330, 332 f.
Huqqe ha-Torah, VI, 140, 395
Hurrians, I, 36, 313
Husain, grandson of Mohammed, V, 7; wife of, III, 89
Husband: and divorce (q.v.), V, 241 f., VI, 394 f.; duties, I, 237; supremacy of, I, 114, 146
Hushiel, captive scholar, V, 46; father of Hananel, VI, 46, 213; two Hushiels?, V, 312 f., VI, 342
Hussain ibn Mansur al-Hallaj, see Hallaj
Hydatius, chronicle, VI, 429
Hyderabad, I, 321
Hygiene, ritualistic ablution and, VIII, 262
Hyksos: in Egypt, I, 35 ff., 303; and Exodus, I, 195; feudal cleavages under, I, 54; worship of Seth, I, 304
Hymns: accompanying sacrificial worship, I, 123, 395; alphabetic, VIII, 13;

Amun, I, 52; mystic, VIII, 12; numinous, VIII, 23; see also Psalms
Hyperetes, communal factotum, II, 367; see also Hazzan
Hypocrisy, VI, 143
Hypsistos, supreme god, I, 23, III, 62
Hyrcania, I, 131
Hyrcanus II, high priest, I, 218, II, 206
Hyrcanus, John, see John Hyrcanus

I

Iamblichus, II, 401
"I am that I am," see Ehyeh
Iberia, Armenian, Persian conquest of, III, 22
Iberian Peninsula, center of Jewish intellectual life, VIII, 61; Karaites in, V, 271; medical writings, VIII, 245 f.; see also Portugal; Spain; also under individual kingdoms and cities
Ibn 'Abbas, 'Abdallah, "the Arab rabbi," VI, 275; on Jewish biblical interpretation, V, 88; warning against "people of the book," V, 88, VI, 444
Ibn 'Abbas, Yehudah b. Samuel, VI, 56, VII, 155
Ibn 'Abd Rabbihi, V, 194
Ibn 'Abdun, of Seville, V, 97; on clothing of dhimmis, III, 139 f.; disparagement of dhimmi doctors, VIII, 254; on social distinctions between Muslims and non-Muslims, III, 146
Ibn abi ad-Dunya al-Quarashi, VII, 203
Ibn abi al-Bayan, As-Sadid, see David b. Solomon
Ibn Abihi, Ziyad, IV, 226
Ibn abi'l Thanna, see Yehudah b. Joseph
Ibn Abitur (or Ibn Satanas), Joseph b. Isaac, Spanish scholar, V, 45, VI, 220, VII, 75, 155; Arabic translation of the Talmud, VI, 264; excommunication and exile, VII, 149; liturgical poems, VII, 170 f.; talmudic exegesis, VI, 61
Ibn abi Usaibi'a, Arab physician and medical historian, VII, 8, VIII, 236, 240, 247 f., 249; story of physician's fee, VIII, 254
Ibn Abu'l Husain, Abu Sa'id, Samaritan scholiast, V, 89, 175, VI, 271
Ibn 'Adi, al-Haitham, VI, 143
Ibn Adret, Solomon, VI, 136, 390; on animal sacrifice, VII, 79; on communal authority, V, 63

Ibn Aflaḥ, Jabir, *see* Jabir
Ibn al-'Arabi, Muslim mystic, VIII, 15
Ibn al-Ashraf, K'ab, VII, 191
Ibn al-Bazyar, "Book of Conjunctions,"
  VIII, 207
Ibn al-Faqih, III, 205
Ibn al-Furat, vizier, III, 153, 158, V, 10,
  11
Ibn al-Hajj al-Abdari, V, 96
Ibn al-Jasus (or al-Gasum), VII, 118,
  278 f.
Ibn al-Jauzi, Sibt, IV, 110, VI, 298
Ibn al-Jazzar, Abu Jafar, Muslim med-
  ical author, VIII, 236, 396
Ibn al-Kaziruni, Jewish banker of Cairo,
  III, 160
Ibn al-Latif, scholar of Damascus, VIII,
  249 f.
Ibn al-Masarra, Arab mystic, III, 124,
  VIII, 124, 135
Ibn al-Mu'tazz, Abu'l 'Abbas 'Abdullah,
  VII, 142
Ibn al-Muthanna, Abu 'Ubaida Ma'mar,
  Arab philologist, VII, 11
Ibn al-Qalanisi, Muslim historian, IV,
  109 f., 295
Ibn al-Qama, IV, 31
Ibn al-Qifṭi, historian of science, VIII,
  240
Ibn al-Taras, Sa'id, VI, 206, VII, 228
Ibn al-Waḥshiya, VIII, 217
Ibn al-Wasiti, Muslim sage, III, 128
Ibn 'Allan al-Yahudi, Jewish banker, IV,
  202
Ibn an-Nadim, Abu Isḥaq, Arab bibliog-
  rapher, III, 197, VII, 317, VIII, 167,
  224, 240; *Fihrist*, VI, 265, VIII, 148
Ibn an-Naqqash, III, 128, 152; *fatwa*, III,
  167 f.
Ibn 'Aqnin, Joseph b. Yehudah, pupil of
  Maimonides, VIII, 259, 340; alleged
  Maimonidean letter to, VIII, 3; on
  denunciations of converts, III, 126;
  educational program, VIII, 146; identified with Ibn Shime'on, V, 296 (*q.v.*);
  on Maimonides, VIII, 250; music and
  mental hygiene, VII, 208 f.; on relapsed converts, III, 127; on useful
  sciences, VIII, 159; on voluntary exile,
  III, 291
Ibn ar-Rawandi, Muslim heretic, VI,
  298 f.; *Destroyer of the Brain*, VI, 301;
  Emerald, VI, 301
Ibn Aryeh, false messiah, V, 201

Ibn Asad, Abu'l Faraj Furqan, *see*
  Yeshu'a b. Yehudah
Ibn ash-Shuwaikh, head of Baghdad
  academy, III, 167
Ibn as-Saffan, Ephraim, court physician,
  VIII, 248 f.
Ibn Bajja, Abu-Bekr ibn aṣ-Ṣaij (Avem-
  pace), VIII, 162
Ibn Bal'am, Yehudah b. Samuel (Abu
  Zakariya Yaḥya), VI, 95, VI, 277, VII,
  201; on Aramaic and Arabic parallels,
  VII, 230; attack on Ibn Chiquitilla,
  VI, 311 ff., 485 f.; attack on Saadiah,
  VI, 277; collection of biblical passages
  relating to miracles, VII, 201; com-
  mentary on Genesis, VI, 282 f.; gram-
  matical monographs, VII, 49; use of
  methodological innovations, VI, 291
Ibn Baron, Isaac (Abu Ibrahim b. Joseph
  ibn Benveniste): lexicographic treatise,
  VII, 27; on verb forms, VII, 49
Ibn Baṭṭuṭa, III, 161
Ibn Buklarish (Beklaresh), Junus (Jonah
  ibn Isḥaq), medical author, VIII, 248
Ibn Butlan, VIII, 388
Ibn Chiquitilla, Isaac: disciple of Menaḥem, VII, 22; ascription of poems by,
  VII, 302 f.; influenced by Saadiah, VII,
  301
Ibn Chiquitilla, Joseph b. Abraham,
  kabbalist, VIII, 287
Ibn Chiquitilla, Moses, V, 158; biblical
  critic and poet, VI, 310 ff., 485 f., VII,
  155; Hebrew translations, VII, 7, 23,
  47; use of methodological innovations,
  VI, 291 f.
Ibn Danan, Saadiah, of Granada, VII,
  225
Ibn Daud, Abraham, III, 203, IV, 214,
  VIII, 137; on Aḥai's *She'elot*, VI, 339;
  on aims of philosophy, VIII, 78, 135,
  218; on alleged Jewish tampering with
  biblical text, VI, 254; anti-Christian
  apologetic purpose, VI, 210; on the
  attainment of happiness, VIII, 121;
  biological discussion, VIII, 225 f.; Book
  or Order of Tradition, III, 156, VI, 30,
  131, 206 ff., 233; choice of words, VI,
  481; on the commandments, VI, 142 f.,
  VIII, 118; on David b. Zakkai and
  Saadiah, V, 178, VI, 356; on dreams
  and prophetic visions, VIII, 133; editions and translations, VI, 209; enumeration of generations of Saboraim,

Ibn Daud, Abraham (*Continued*)
VI, 328; on exilarchs, V, 301; on the existence of God, VIII, 90 f.; on free will, VIII, 110; on Ḥayyuj and Ibn Janaḥ, VII, 44; on Ibn Gabirol, VIII, 75, 84, 92; influence of Aristotle on, VIII, 63; on Karaites, V, 272, VI, 453; on man's love of God, VIII, 115; on matter and form, VIII, 87 f.; organization of material, VI, 208 f.; potential readers, VIII, 71; on preoccupation with science, VIII, 143; sources, VI, 210, 429 f.

Ibn Eleazar (Abenalazar), Jacob, Spanish liturgical poet and translator, VII, 189

Ibn Ezra, Abraham, biblical commentator and poet, IV, 26, V, 152, VII, 155; and astrology, VII, 210 f., VIII, 170 f., 176 ff., 183 f., 365 ff.; astronomic works, VIII, 161, 171 f., 362 f.; attack on Karaites, VI, 290; attitude toward *piyyuṭim*, VII, 104; concerning Balaam, VIII, 133; and Bar Ḥiyya, VIII, 169 f.; on biblical substitute words, VI, 293 f.; birthplace, IV, 248; on the commandments, VI, 396; criticism of verbose commentators, VI, 284 f.; dependence on Rabbanite linguists, VI, 291; on deviations from linguistic rules, VII, 58; dirge over his son's apostasy, VII, 160; on divisions of earth's surface, VIII, 214; on eternality of matter, VIII, 94; on Enoch, VIII, 178 f.; on *Ehyeh*, VIII, 152 f.; *ge'ulahs*, V, 362; grammatical treatises, VII, 50 ff.; on headings for Psalms, VII, 203; Hebrew work on meters, VII, 196, 317; horoscopes, VIII, 178, 366; on Ibn Tamim, VII, 16 f.; on Ibn Yashush, VI, 309 f.; on identification of biblical names and anonyms, VI, 281; on identity of Job, VI, 308; legend on death of, VIII, 368; linguistic riddles, VII, 4; on man's soul, VIII, 106 f.; on Mar Samuel's formula for solar year, VIII, 198 f.; and Masha'allah, VIII, 166; mathematical discussions, VIII, 352; medical writings, VIII, 248; on messianic problem, V, 156; on musicology, VII, 209; observations on human anatomy, VIII, 229 f.; philosophic-ethical treatise, VII, 52; praise of Ibn Chiquitilla, VII, 49; prohibition of lights, V, 403; and proverb on wisdom, VIII, 145; on

psalm tunes, VII, 283; puns, VIII, 192; quoted by authorities, VIII, 172; revision of his works, VIII, 171; on Saadiah, VI, 266, 270, VII, 16, 50 f., 141; scientific tracts, VI, 422; on square characters, VII, 56 f.; student's comment on, VI, 467; translations, VII, 7, 23, 47, VIII, 65; on types of poetry, VII, 203 f.; use of *gemaṭrias*, VIII, 152; versatility and prestige, VIII, 160; world-wide influence, VII, 173 f.
—— works, VIII, 62 f.; "Astrolabe," VIII, 177; "Beginning of Wisdom," VIII, 176 f.; "Book of Nativities," VIII, 178 f.; Commentary on Genesis, VI, 175; Commentary on Job, VI, 277, 291; Epistle on the Sabbath, VI, 475 f.; Fundamentals of Astronomic Tables, VIII, 171; "Pisan Tables," VIII, 171

Ibn Ezra, Isaac, son of Abraham, VII, 155, 160

Ibn Ezra, Moses, Jewish poet of Granada, III, 158, IV, 31 f., 159, V, 389; admiration for Arabic poetry, VII, 194; Arabic work on Hebrew poetic arts, VII, 191, 198 f.; attitude toward *piyyuṭim*, VII, 103; on biblical language, VII, 57 f.; bilingualism, VII, 9; career, VII, 153 f., 293 f.; on charges of Jewish anthropomorphism, VIII, 101; on Dunash, VII, 42; on Hermes, VIII, 10; on immortalization through poetry, VII, 147; liturgical poems, V, 362; on "mixture of doubt with certainty" in figure of speech, VII, 315; penitential prayer, VII, 173; poems on the mysteries of existence, VII, 172 f.; survey of Spanish Hebrew poetry, VII, 146 ff., 155; on term for nature, VIII, 112, 335; on worship by men and angels, VII, 210; youthful indiscretions, VII, 291

Ibn Fadhlan, Arab envoy, III, 201, 325
Ibn Fadhlan, Baghdad vizier, VIII, 237
Ibn Fadhlan, Abu 'Ali, Jewish banker of Baghdad, III, 159, 196
Ibn Falaquera, Shem Ṭob b. Joseph, VIII, 137; on effects of liturgical music, VII, 209; epitome of "Fountain of Life," VIII, 74; poem on mental and physical health, VIII, 405; on reading Maimonides' *Guide*, VIII, 312; on Solomon's knowledge of natural sciences, VIII, 387

Ibn Ferrizuel, Joseph (Cidellus): against Karaites, V, 45; Halevi's poem to, IV, 251, VII, 192; service to Alphonso VI, IV, 36

Ibn Ferrizuel, Solomon, IV, 36

Ibn Gabirol, Solomon b. Yehudah (Avicebron or Avicebrol), V, 49, 152 ff., VIII, 61 f., 69, 322; astronomic themes, VIII, 168 f.; bilingualism, VII, 9; career, VII, 152 f., 292 f.; on division of earth's surface, VIII, 214; doctrine of sin, VIII, 119; on the First Cause, VIII, 98; on goal of human soul, VIII, 113 f.; on good and evil, VIII, 119; influences on, VIII, 324 f.; intermediary position of nature, VIII, 335; legend of, VIII, 47; on love of God, VIII, 114 f.; messianic teachings, V, 153 ff., 162 f., 361 f.; poem on a sunset, VII, 163 f.; potential readers, VIII, 73 f.; on purpose of creation, VIII, 106; religious poems, V, 99, VI, 92, VIII, 84, 134; on the senses, VIII, 108; sources, VIII, 324 f.; on sources of knowledge, VIII, 82 ff.; theme of exile, V, 99, VIII, 126; theory of mediation between God and man, VIII, 91 f.; use of allegory, VI, 297, VII, 167 f., VIII, 77 f.; "voluntaristic" doctrine, VIII, 322; wedding poem, VII, 314
—— works, VIII, 302; "Fountain of Life," VIII, 61 f., 74, 92, 112, 135; "Necklace," VII, 49 f., 162; "On the Improvement of Moral Qualities," VIII, 62; "Royal Crown," VII, 151, 153, 171 f., 194, VIII, 62, 92, 106, 168

Ibn Gaon, Shem Ṭob b. Abraham, VIII, 38 f.

Ibn Garcia, III, 98

Ibn Gayyat, Isaac b. Yehudah, jurist and poet, VI, 61, 84, 113, VII, 155; and Alfasi, VI, 87; decision on recitation of Musaf 'Amidah, VII, 107; on Ecclesiastes, VI, 270; halakhic works, VI, 73, 354, 360 f.; sacred poetry, VII, 171, 246; support of local customs, VI, 126

Ibn Ḥabib, Moses b. Shem Ṭob, III, 244 f.

Ibn Ḥalfon, Isaac, Hebrew poet, VII, 146

Ibn Ḥamdin, Cordovan qadi, III, 124

Ibn Ḥanbal, Aḥmad, VI, 26; see also Ḥanbalites

Ibn Ḥasan, Sa'id, of Alexandria, convert to Islam, V, 97 f., 102; on image worship, V, 125; prediction, V, 201

Ibn Ḥawqal, Muslim traveler, VI, 220

Ibn Ḥazm, Muslim theologian, V, 327, VIII, 136; antisemitism, V, 95; biblical criticism, V, 85, 88; on conversion to Islam, V, 102; on the exilarchate, V, 13; on the Karaites, V, 271; religious studies, VIII, 11, 301; and Yosephon, VI, 191

Ibn Ḥisdai, Abraham b. Samuel: attitude toward Arabic script, VII, 191; "Prince and Dervish," VII, 189

Ibn Ḥisdai, Abu Ja'far Yusuf, VIII, 357

Ibn Ḥisdai, Abu'l Fadhl: Jewish convert to Islam, III, 158; adviser of Al-Muqtadir and Al-Mu'tamin, III, 158; musicologist of Saragossa, VII, 206

Ibn Ḥisdai, Joseph b. Aḥmad, VIII, 248

Ibn Hisham, III, 163

Ibn Hud, Muslim mystic, V, 103

Ibn Hudail, Mu'tazilite leader, VIII, 96

Ibn 'Imram, Isḥaq, Muslim physician and teacher, VIII, 236

Ibn Jaḥiz, III, 98

Ibn Janaḥ, Jonah (Abu'l Walid ibn Merwan), Spanish Hebrew grammarian, III, 102, 148, VII, 24 ff., 44 f., 229, 237; accused of plagiarism, VII, 229; on alteration of text by copyists, VII, 150; contributions to grammar and lexicography, VI, 291 f., VII, 7, 24 ff., 44 ff., 229; and David Qimḥi, VIII, 386; medical dictionary, VIII, 248; on neglect of Arabic, VII, 8; on philological debates among Spanish Jews, VII, 3 f.; praise of Masorites, VI, 252; quotations from Yose, VII, 261; Rabbanite scholar, VI, 28, 270; use of multilingual like-sounding words, VII, 223; on word substitutions in biblical text, VI, 293

Ibn Jau, Jacob, Cordovan silk manufacturer, V, 44 f.

Ibn Jumay', Hibbat Allah (Nathaniel?), medical treatises, VIII, 226, 247, 249

Ibn Kafron, Ephraim, disciple of Menaḥem, VII, 22

Ibn Kammuna, Sa'd ibn Manṣur, V, 90, 274; on conversion to Islam, V, 102

Ibn Kaspi, Joseph, VI, 376

Ibn Khaldun, Arab historian, VI, 192, VIII, 122; on the Kahina, III, 91

Ibn Khurdadhbah, VIII, 212; Book of

Ibn Khurdadhbah (*Continued*)
Routes, IV, 180 f.; on Byzantine taxation, III, 191, 193
Ibn Kusin, physician in Mosul, VIII, 246
Ibn Lahi'a, exilarch, V, 7
Ibn Megas, Joseph b. Meir ha-Levi, V, 68, 76 f., 168, VI, 58, 61 f., 84, 108, 367; on authority of responsa, VI, 115 f.; on authorship of responsa, VI, 114; *Hiddushim*, VI, 353; responsa, VI, 117
Ibn Mubarak, physician and teacher in Cairo, VIII, 236
Ibn Muqlah, vizier, III, 154
Ibn Musa al-Asdi, *see* Harun ibn Musa
Ibn Nagrela, Joseph b. Samuel: Arab revolt against, III, 123, 219; succeeds father as nagid, III, 158
Ibn Nagrela, Samuel b. Joseph, nagid of Granada, III, 156 f., IV, 29, 36, 179, V, 45, 48 f., VI, 113, 215, VII, 26, 30, VIII, 69; acclaimed as patron of learning, VI, 21; aphorisms, VII, 164 f.; controversy with Ibn Janah, VI, 474, VII, 25; correspondence, VII, 165; critique of Qur'an, V, 330; dirge on death of brother, VII, 159 f.; disappearance of writings, VII, 286; epitome of Yosephon, VI, 191; explanation of divine name, VIII, 179 f.; halakhic miscellanies, VI, 72 f., 360 f.; Ibn Hazm's attack on, V, 95; *Introduction to the Talmud*, VI, 33, 333 f.; philological work, VII, 45 f., 237 f.; poetic achievement, VII, 151 ff., 296 ff.; on royal patrons, VII, 148 f.; source of rise to power in Granada, VII, 149 f.; sources for geonic period, VI, 208, VII, 45 f.; on Spanish Jewry, V, 58; supply of books to students, VII, 137 f.; on Targumim, VI, 262, VII, 82, 193, 249, 262; use of Arabic, VII, 191; use of Arabic meter, VII, 195 f.; use of personal experiences as themes, VII, 156
Ibn Nuh, Joseph, grammatical work, VII, 38 f.
Ibn Paquda, Bahya, *see* Bahya
Ibn Parhon, Solomon, lexicographer, VII, 26, 27 f., 52; on Saadiah, VI, 276; on the use of Hebrew, IV, 173; on veiling of women, III, 142
Ibn Qayyim al-Jauziya, V, 86, 96
Ibn Quraish, Yehudah, of Tahort, Algeria, VI, 264, VII, 17 f.; interest in

Berber dialects, VII, 11 f.; on Onkelos, VII, 5, 17; pioneer in comparative linguistics, VII, 11
Ibn Qurra, Tabit, Sabean mathematician, VIII, 243; theory of "trepidation" of the stars, VIII, 164
Ibn Qutaiba, poet, III, 148; on interest in history, VI, 198 f.; on the savant, VI, 72
Ibn Rahamun, Salama (Solomon) ibn Mubarak (Meborakh), Egyptian Jewish physician, VIII, 226
Ibn Ridhwan, 'Ali (Haly Rodoam), of Cairo, VIII, 249, 250; debate with Ibn Butlan, VIII, 388
Ibn Riyahin, Arab admiral, V, 46 f.
Ibn Sa'd, 'Abdallah, treaty with Nubians, IV, 181
Ibn Saddiq, Joseph, VIII, 67, 69, 137; on knowledge of God, VIII, 118; on man as microcosm, VIII, 62, 103; messianic problem, V, 366; potential readers, VIII, 71
Ibn Sahl, Abraham, of Seville, VII, 191 f.
Ibn Sahula, Isaac b. Solomon, VII, 189 f.
Ibn Sahula, Meir, VIII, 42
Ibn Sa'id, Abu Qasim, Toledan judge: "Categories of Nations," IV, 31, VIII, 264; on Hisdai ibn Shaprut, V, 47; on Jewish preoccupation with law and biographies of prophets, VIII, 135, 264
Ibn Sa'id, Abu 'Umar Ahmad, V, 83, VIII, 56
Ibn Salam, Ahmad ibn 'Abdallah, VI, 265, 275; commentaries on the Qur'an, VI, 282 f.
Ibn Salim, Faraj, *see* Farragut
Ibn Saqawaihi, VIII, 100; Book of Shameful Things, V, 253 f.; identified with Salmon b. Yeruhim, V, 406
Ibn Sarjado, Aaron, V, 23, 24, 295
Ibn Satanas, *see* Ibn Abitur
Ibn Shahin, Muslim exegete, *tafsir*, VI, 468
Ibn Shahin, Nissim, *see* Nissim b. Jacob
Ibn Shaprut, *see* Hisdai ibn Shaprut
Ibn Shime'on, Joseph b. Yehudah, disciple of Maimonides, VI, 380; identity of, V, 296; *see also* Ibn 'Aqnin
Ibn Sim'an, Isaac, Jewish composer, of Cordova, VII, 206
Ibn Siqbal, Solomon, VII, 188

Ibn Sosan, Yehudah, III, 291
Ibn Suleiman, Yaḥya, *see* Zechariah b. Solomon
Ibn Tamim, Abu Sahl Dunash (Adonim), of Kairuwan, VII, 34, VIII, 24, 59, 236, 246; alleged conversion, VII, 225; lexicographic works, VII, 16 f.
Ibn Tibbon, Moses, VIII, 384
Ibn Tibbon, Samuel, translator, VI, 11, VIII, 64, 306 f.; Maimonides' epistle to, VIII, 72, 232; translation of the *Guide*, VI, 11, VIII, 315
Ibn Tibbon, Yehudah, "father of translators," VI, 270, VIII, 60, 65; apologia for use of Arabic, VII, 6 f.; attitude toward Arabic script, IV, 36 f., VII, 191; censure of Ibn Parḥon, VII, 231; "Ethical Will," VIII, 235, 258; library, VII, 138 f.; translations, VII, 7, 47, 166, VIII, 39
Ibn Tulun, Aḥmad, Egyptian ruler, III, 136, 161; on non-Muslim tombs in Cairo, III, 137
Ibn Tumart, VIII, 98, 326; on the unity of God, III, 292
Ibn 'Ubayya, III, 128; treatise of 1474, III, 135
Ibn Verga, Joseph, IV, 238
Ibn Waqar, Joseph, Spanish kabbalist, VII, 182
Ibn Wallad, Aḥmad, Egyptian philologist, VII, 19
Ibn Yaḥya, Tam b. David, VI, 191
Ibn Yaḥya al-Maghribi, Samau'al, *see* Samau'al ibn Yaḥya
Ibn Ya'qub, Ibrahim, Spanish Jew, III, 214, IV, 169, 174, 194, VI, 434 f.; and Ḥisdai, III, 217, VI, 435; report on journey to central Europe, VI, 221 f., 434 f.; on Slavs, III, 217 f.
Ibn Ya'qub, Solomon b. Joseph, VI, 61
Ibn Yashush, Isaac (Abu Ibrahim): historical biblical criticism, VI, 309 f.; identification of Jobab with Job, VI, 293; monograph on inflections, VII, 49
Ibn Yunus, Egyptian astronomer, VIII, 167; length of solar year, VIII, 198
Ibn Zabara, Joseph b. Meir, poet of Barcelona, VII, 187 f.; Book of Delight, VII, 308 f., VIII, 237
Ibn Zaid al-Ḥasan, III, 115
Ibn Zeraḥ, Menaḥem, VI, 50
Ibrahim, *see* Ibn Ya'qub

Ibrahim (Isaac), son of Neṭira, III, 153
'Ibrim, identity of, with Ḥabiru, I, 302
Iconoclastic movement, III, 178, 193, VIII, 31; alleged Jewish influences on, III, 178; in Near East, VIII, 26
Iconodulism, III, 193 f.
Icons and iconography, V, 125; *see also* Imagery; Images and symbols
Idalius, bishop of Barcelona, III, 250
Ideas, development of, I, 52
Idjma', Muslim principle, V, 169, VI, 145 f., VIII, 324; against individual analogy in linguistics, VII, 58
Idolatry: condemnation of, I, 177, 179, II, 217, V, 347, VIII, 10; Diocletian and, V, 172; at Temple of Jerusalem, I, 335
Idris, identified with Enoch (*q.v.*), VIII, 366
Idris I, forced conversions, III, 281
Idris II, founder of Fez, VII, 225
Idrisi, al-, Muslim geographer, IV, 243, VIII, 214 f.; Book of King Roger, VIII, 212; and Dioscorides' work, VIII, 246; on Tarragona and Lucena Jewries, III, 109, 170
Idumaea and Idumaeans, I, 106, 167, 224, 382, VI, 192 f.; prisoners liberated by, I, 412; protagonists of political principle, II, 48; *see also* Edom and Edomites
"Idumaean slave" (Herod), I, 397
Ifran, Africa, tombstone inscriptions, III, 230
Ifriqiya, province, Africa, III, 107; Spanish immigrants to, VII, 273
Ignatius, Saint, II, 136, 167, III, 243
Ignoramus, reference to, in Jewish prayer of thanksgiving, VII, 109 f.
Igor (Helgo-Oleg), Russian prince, III, 203
Illegitimacy, II, 218, 253; *see also* Bastards
Illiteracy: attitude toward, IV, 167, V, 75, VIII, 295; of witnesses, VI, 255; *see also* '*Am ha-areṣ*
Imagery: prohibition of, I, 13, 14, 48, 49, 59, 314, 335, II, 15, 284, 285, 330; departure from prohibition, I, 66; and iconoclasm, III, 178
Images and symbols: in decorative arts, II, 9 ff., 13, 15, 154, 330, 322 f., 402; destruction of statues and, II, 400;

Images and symbols (*Continued*)
    emblem over Temple gate, I, 238, 402,
    II, 13; found in catacombs and tombs,
    II, 11; in Jerusalem, I, 322; signifi-
    cance, II, 12 ff.; vine symbol, I, 253, II,
    13; *see also* Sculptures
Imagination: as "internal" sense, VIII,
    79; of prophet, VIII, 131; in storytell-
    ing, VI, 168 ff.
Imam, Muslim official, V, 315, VI, 13;
    descendant of Mohammed, III, 304 f.
Immaculate Conception, VIII, 30
"Immanuel," interpretation of, V, 157
Immanuel of Rome, Hebrew poet, IV,
    238, VIII, 48, 176; books copied by,
    VII, 139; on cantors, VII, 130
Imma Shalom, II, 227
Immigration, *see* Migratory movements
Immolation, self-, *see* Suicide
Immortality, literary, VII, 147 f.
Immortality of the nation, I, 12
Immortality of the soul, I, 9, 12, 137,
    207-8, 357, 358, II, 14, 215, 312, 333,
    V, 166; and funeral rites, II, 289; posi-
    tion of Pharisees and Sadducees, II,
    38 f., 344 f.; *see also* Resurrection; Soul
Imperial worship, I, 244, 404, II, 5, 99,
    109
Import trade, Jewish role in, IV, 165
"Impostors, three," V, 104, VI, 301
Impurities, physical, I, 81; communica-
    ble nature of, VI, 483
'Imram b. Sedaqa, Jewish physician in
    Damascus, VIII, 236
Imru al-Qais, Lakhmid king, epitaph,
    III, 61
Inbreeding, I, 146, 360; *see also* Incest;
    Marriage
Incantations and exorcisms, I, 139, 359,
    II, 19 ff., 67, 189, 316, 336, 401, VIII,
    8 ff., 45 f., 274 ff.; Aramaic texts, VIII,
    7 f., 274 f.; divine name in, VIII, 281;
    eclecticism, VIII, 10; erotic, VIII, 283;
    magic formulas, VIII, 8 ff., 274 ff.;
    repetition of, VIII, 284; used during
    childbirth, I, 329; use of great names
    in, VIII, 233
Incarnation, doctrine of, I, 13, V, 115, VI,
    103, VIII, 30
Incense, I, 127, 129, 352, II, 333
Incest, I, 146, II, 229 ff., 411, V, 221 f.,
    242 f., 325, VI, 69
Independence, Karaite doctrine of loss
    of, V, 260

India, VIII, 217; Christians in, III, 285;
    confused with Ethiopia, VI, 434; im-
    pact of science, VIII, 148, 172, 193,
    360; influence of Hebrew language,
    VII, 222; international trade, I, 64,
    III, 284, IV, 175; and Jewish origins,
    I, 377; Jews in, II, 212, 407, III, 114 f.,
    173, 285, IV, 174; numbering, VIII,
    150; pariah caste, I, 297; religion, I,
    373, *see also* Parsees and Parsiism; reli-
    gious toleration, III, 130 f.
Indian Ocean, VIII, 214 f.
Indian sages, Jews as descendants of, I,
    184
Individual and individualism, I, 8, 136,
    138, 357; 'Anan's view of, V, 221; in
    biblical interpretation, V, 230; com-
    munal responsibility for, IV, 40, 134 f.,
    137 f., V, 4, 100 ff.; and free will, VIII,
    109; and Judaism, I, 11, 12, 29, V, 225,
    VIII, 263; Karaite, V, 234 f., 261; and
    society, IV, 222 f., V, 4, 100 ff., VIII,
    120 ff.; *see also* Responsibility
Indo-European peoples, I, 36; Yosephon
    re, VI, 226
Indo-Iranian cultures, I, 102
Industry, I, 64, 69, 255-58, 407-8, II,
    247 ff.; intensification of, IV, 164-71,
    318-22; refined methods of production,
    IV, 168; reserve labor army, I, 270;
    sociopolitical strife in Hellenistic cen-
    ters, I, 271; urban Jews turning to, II,
    123
Infants, souls of, VIII, 108
Inferiority, Jewish, Church emphasis on,
    IV, 10, 12, 16
Infidel, VIII, 66; tax receipt as mark of,
    III, 168; term, III, 149; *see also* Dhim-
    mis
Inflationary pressures, I, 277, 414, II, 245,
    250, 414
Inflection, biblical, principles of, VII, 35
Influence, divine, Muslim concept of,
    VIII, 134
Informers among Jews, II, 142, 385; fu-
    neral of, 287; hatred of, V, 46, 241;
    punishment of, VI, 134
Inheritance, laws of, III, 158, IV, 16, VI,
    4, 67 f.; of converts, III, 10, 158, V, 18,
    299; of daughter and son, V, 243; of
    husband, V, 223, 373; interfaith, III,
    301; of land, IV, 162; and mathematics,
    VIII, 147, 153 f.; moneylenders and,
    IV, 205; Muslim, III, 143 f., V, 18, VI,

436; under "Ordinances of the Jews," IV, 204; and settlement of estate, V, 300 f.

Injustice, divine, VIII, 103 ff.

Innkeeping, IV, 165

Innocent II, pope: ecumenical council, IV, 11 f.; greeted in Rome by Jewish deputation, IV, 10; struggle with Anacletus II, IV, 10 f.

Innocent III, pope, IV, 227; advice on delinquent Jewish tithe payers, IV, 13; codification of canon law, IV, 19 f.; *Constitutio pro Judaeis*, IV, 8; on employment of Jews, IV, 42; on Jewish slaveholders, IV, 188 f.; protest against disregard of canon law, IV, 16 f.; on usury, IV, 206

Innocent IV, pope, IV, 306

Inscriptions: Afghanistan, III, 282; Africa, III, 230, 335; Arabia, III, 61, 64, 66, 82, 258; Behistun, I, 353; Crimea, VIII, 203; Cyrenaica, III, 108; doorpost, V, 59; Dura-Europos, II, 331, VII, 128; eastern Europe, III, 206 f.; France, III, 48, 251, IV, 260; funerary, I, 378, II, 10 ff., 146, 331 ff.; Fusṭaṭ synagogue, III, 134 f.; grave of Adoniram, III, 244; and Jewish chronology, II, 376; Khazaria, III, 200 f.; Khirbet Mafjar, III, 103; Latin, I, 378; Mesha, I, 336; Monotheistic, III, 66; Nabatean, III, 64; with name of Iao, VIII, 275; on Polish coins, III, 218, 338 f.; preponderance relating to males, III, 252; Samaritan, V, 370; of Shapur I, II, 380, 396 f.; showing spread of Jews, II, 210 f., 406 f.; Sinaitic, I, 35, 314; Spain, III, 34, 244, IV, 33, VII, 313; symbolic, II, 11 ff.; synagogue of Theodotos in Jerusalem, VIII, 239; Ten Commandments, V, 370 f.; Thamudic, III, 258; Venosa, Sicily, IV, 20, VIII, 204

Institute of Research and Study in Medieval Canon Law, IV, 242

Insurance association, II, 261

Intellect, "knowledge of," VIII, 79

Intellectual life, academic, V, 33 f., *see also* Academies; under Byzantine domination, VIII, 30; centers of, IV, 7, 45, 47 f., 112; *see also under* Learning; and disappearance of ancient writings, VI, 438 f.; freedom of, under authority, VII, 211 ff.; of northern European Jewry, VI, 422

Intelligences, intermediary, VIII, 93 ff., 111 ff.; and spheres, VIII, 82, 114, 128, 168 f., 180

Intelligentsia, Spanish, and poetry, VII, 150 ff.

Intention, Judaism's stress upon, II, 307

Intercalation, VIII, 186 ff., 193 ff.; Palestinian-Babylonian dispute, VIII, 194 ff.

Interest, legal restraints, II, 250, 414; rates, I, 69, 261, 323, 409, IV, 198 ff., 214, 338, 342; *see also* Usury

Intermarriage, between Egyptian Jewess and foreign Jew, VI, 138 f.; Karaite and Rabbanite, VI, 135; *see also* Marriage, interfaith

Intermediaries: between God and man, I, 139, 140, II, 42; doctrine of, V, 226, 228, 259, VIII, 91 ff.; protective, II, 17 ff., 42 ff.; *see also* Amulets; Angels; Talismans

International relations, II, 4

Interpretation, biblical: allegorical, II, 320, V, 215, VI, 273, 297, VIII, 77 f., 81, 84, 100, 110, *see also* Allegory; alternative meanings, VI, 287 f., 292 f.; of anthropomorphisms, VI, 258 f.; based on philological evidence, VI, 291 ff.; by common consent, V, 252; disputes over, V, 126; ethical or juristic approaches, VI, 35; geonic rules, VI, 333; Gregory I on, III, 29; hermeneutic elaboration of, VI, 155-63, 294 f., 400-405; hidden vs. ordinary meaning, VI, 166, 175, 275, 286, 290, 294 f., 463 f., VIII, 73; importance of grammar to, VII, 4, 6; independent, V, 221, 235; Innocent II on Jewish, IV, 10; Karaite, V, 213, 278 f.; literal, V, 213 f., 287, VIII, 81 f.; logical, V, 259; masoretic aid to, VI, 252; metaphorical, VI, 279; modes of, VI, 32 f., 166, 177, 412; Mohammed on Jewish, III, 84 f.; Mosaic law extended by, II, 319, 436; Muslim, V, 99 f., VI, 170; sectarian, V, 84 ff., 195 f., VII, 223 f.; talmudic, VI, 35-44, 336-41; traditional, VI, 274 ff.; Trullan synod on, V, 109; *see also* Bible; Exegesis

Interpreters: Jews' linguistic ability as, IV, 173 f., 322; of sermons, II, 280

Intolerance, *see* Antisemitism; Religious liberty

Introduction, letters of, in international trade, IV, 177

Intuition, prophetic, VIII, 131
Iran and Iranian Plateau, see Persia
Iraq: Arabic philology, VII, 19; Aramaic proverbs, VII, 220; claims to prophecies, VIII, 134; Muslim conquest of, III, 95; Syriac idiom of Jews in, VI, 453; tax payment and receipt, III, 168; see also Babylonia, also under cities, e.g., Baghdad
Ireland: Gaelic in, VII, 222 f.; Jewish settlement, IV, 280; Richard Strongbow's expedition, IV, 82
Irenaeus, Saint, II, 145, 168, 408
Irene, Byzantine empress, III, 177
Iron, I, 256, 320
Iron Age, I, 316; relapse into semi-primitive conditions, I, 53; seal cylinders, I, 323
Irrigation, I, 252, 407
'Isa, Jewish physician, VIII, 243
Isaac, patriarch, I, 22, 37, 341, V, 90, 93; age of, VI, 480; and Esau, V, 129; Mohammed on, III, 85; sacrifice of, II, 138, 383, VI, 144, 300
Isaac, Charlemagne's interpreter, IV, 45, 174, 257, 322 f.
Isaac, head of academy of Firuz Shabur, III, 99
Isaac II, Byzantine emperor, III, 188
Isaac al-Lucena, chief reader, VI, 113
Isaac b. Abba Mari of Marseilles, VI, 83, 132, 361 f.; commentary on Alfasi, VI, 88; juridical miscellany, VI, 74
Isaac b. Abraham of Narbonne, VI, 89
Isaac b. Abraham, R., of Sens, IV, 193
Isaac b. Asher ha-Levi, IV, 134
Isaac b. Baruch ibn al-Balia, Spanish astronomer, VI, 61, 354, VIII, 376; and Alfasi, VI, 87
Isaac b. Dorbello, IV, 58
Isaac b. Melchizedek of Siponto, VI, 62
Isaac b. Moses Or Zaru'a, III, 219, IV, 36, 70, VI, 50, 118
Isaac b. Nathan, III, 198
Isaac b. Reuben al-Barceloni, VI, 368
Isaac b. Samuel, Tosafist of Dampierre, IV, 63 f.; on Alfasi, VI, 90
Isaac b. Saul, poet: Ibn Janah's teacher, VII, 44; use of trick word, VII, 150
Isaac b. Sheshet, VI, 55
Isaac b. Solomon ha-Nasi, VII, 238
Isaac b. Solomon Israeli, see Israeli
Isaac b. Yehudah, German rabbi, VI, 75, 124

Isaac b. Yehudah ibn Gayyat, see Ibn Gayyat
Isaac (Nappaḥa), R., II, 5, 153, 162, 202, 238, 283, 316, VI, 152, 161; on investments, II, 260; on Moses' building of the tabernacle, VI, 163; on pronunciation, VI, 249
'Isa b. Nestorius, Christian vizier, III, 154
Isaiah, prophet, I, 86, 89, 138, 335, II, 173, 397; on animal sacrifices, I, 124; on darkness and light, VIII, 34; death, I, 79; grave, II, 423; prophecy on Aroer, VI, 293; Qumran Scroll, I, 103 f., 342 f., II, 349, VI, 238; religious teaching, I, 99, 339 f.; Trishagion, VIII, 13; vision of the watchman, V, 265; warning to rich landowners, I, 68
—— Book of, I, 103 f., 342, II, 349, VI, 238; break in continuity, VI, 310, 311; comment on, VIII, 155; Rashi's interpretation of, V, 157 f.; ratio of vowels to consonants, VII, 314
Isaiah, Second, see Deutero-Isaiah
Isaiah b. Mali of Trani, VI, 167
Isaiah ha-Kohen b. Maṣliaḥ ha-Maskil, IV, 110; ransom of scroll of law, IV, 112
'Isawites, V, 182, 193
Isfahan, Persia, II, 204; anti-Jewish riots, III, 55; Jewish community, III, 109; legend of Armilus, V, 359; messianic movement, V, 386; occupations of Jews, IV, 167, 318 f.; Yudghanites in, V, 193
Isfahani, Abu'l Faraj al-, VII, 207; preexistence of, VIII, 125 f.; redemption, VII, 115; relationship between the Lord and, I, 140, II, 134, 145, 386; reunification of, VII, 113 f., 117, 136; song and chant, VIII, 13; as source of all human wisdom, VIII, 77, 387; tribulations, V, 101 f., 144, 160, 355, VIII, 121
Ishmael, V, 137, 162; designation, V, 126; and Hagar, Arabs as descendants of, V, 93, 99, VI, 309; meaning of name, III, 274; Mohammed on, III, 85 f.; promised "dominion," V, 335; and Se'ir, VI, 407
Ishmael, R., II, 133, 230, 232, 237, 238, 251, 270, 282, 289, 430; modes of interpretation, V, 213, 218, VI, 177,

295, 304; as mystic, V, 142, VIII, 6, 179, 279; Rashi on, VI, 51; warning to biblical scribe, VI, 237

Ishmael b. Eleazar, R., II, 286

Ishmael b. Elisha, R., V, 140

Ishmael b. Jose, R., II, 247

Ishobokht, metropolitan, II, 430

Ishoyabh, Nestorian *catholicos*, III, 58, 90, 171

Ishshut, see Marriage

Ishtar, goddess, I, 57, VIII, 10

Ishtar-Sirius festival, I, 294

Isidore of Seville, Saint, III, 37, V, 8, 114; cosmic week, VI, 440; description of psalmody, VII, 283; on enforced conversion, III, 38 f., 247; on Israel and Judah, V, 126; on kingdom of Jews, III, 204 f., V, 130 f.; on laudation, VII, 282

Isidorus, I, 190

Islam: as apocalyptic beast, V, 153 f.; assimilatory trends in, VII, 59; attitude toward Mohammed, VIII, 127 f.; on attributes of God, VIII, 99; and biblical patriarchs, III, 85 f., 266 f., V, 93, VI, 8 f.; and Christendom, Jewish intermediary position, VIII, 255 f.; combination of religion and state, III, 94 f., V, 82; concept of soul's ascent to heaven, VIII, 284; continuity of traditions in Spain, IV, 28; controversies over tradition, V, 209; converts to, V, 105, *see also* Converts; creative syncretism, III, 80-86, 92, 265-68, VII, 11, VIII, 263; *dajjal* myths, III, 109, V, 358, 386; *dar al-Islam* and *dar al-ḥarb*, III, 95, 119, 130; development into world religion, III, 94; effect on Christian countries, III, 46; effect on Jewish farmers, IV, 151 f.; equation with Ishmael, V, 93, *see also* Ishmael; exegesis by Jewish converts, VI, 275; expansion, III, 4, 86-114, 168, 268-84, V, 3 ff., 99; fatalism (*q.v.*), VIII, 109; gold and silver mines, IV, 211 f.; Graeco-Roman and Persian influences on, V, 3 f.; growth of banking, IV, 198 f., 339 f.; *idjma'*, principle, V, 169, VI, 145 f., VII, 58, VIII, 324; industrial production, IV, 164 f.; Jewish influence in rise of, II, 211, 433, III, 80 ff., 264 ff., VIII, 255 f., 262 f.; Karaites and, V, 410 f.; methods of acquiring slaves, IV, 332; missionary

efforts, III, 94; Muslim traders and, IV, 181; mysticism, VII, 78; nomism, VI, 6 f.; number of daily prayers, III, 266; official creed, VI, 8; oral traditions, III, 273; outlawry of, in Hungary, III, 212 f.; plural marriage, VI, 137; policy of religious toleration, V, 82, 97, 103, 210, 264; preachment of racial equality, III, 98; prohibition of wine drinking, IV, 164 f.; as protector of Judaism, III, 93, VII, 136; religion and state, III, 75, VI, 150 f.; religious orders, VI, 10; Renaissance of, III, 117-21, V, 83, 103, 170, 197, 231, VII, 3 ff., 60 f., 176, VIII, 147, 255 f., 262 f.; on resurrection, VI, 8; rule in Sicily, IV, 20 f.; Samaritans and, V, 368; sectarianism, III, 123, 133, 148 f., V, 136, 169, 183, 189 ff.; segregation of faithful from infidels, III, 97 ff.; standards of education, VIII, 222; term, III, 85, 267, VI, 12 ff., 151; theological conservatism, VIII, 72; theory of prophecy, VIII, 134

Isma'ili, sect, VIII, 325; controversies over great imams, VIII, 134

Isolationism, *see* Segregation

Isonomia, see Rights, legal

Isopoliteia, see Rights, legal

'*Isqa,* contract, IV, 201

Israel (people): Chosen People, II, 383, V, 125 ff., 137, 285; eternity of, II, 39 f., 396, III, 17, V, 101 f., VI, 146; focal position in world history, I, 47, VI, 227 ff., 438 ff.; and influence of the stars, VIII, 175 f.; ingathering of, VIII, 217; and Judah, V, 126, 264, 285; mission of, VIII, 134 f.; political impotence, VII, 177 f., VIII, 19; precedence over angels, VIII, 279

Israel (state): ancient: corporate responsibility, II, 42; and Damascus, I, 322; divided kingdoms, I, 93 f.; education, II, 274; governmental diffusion, I, 63, 73-77, 325-27; international position, I, 63, 67; interplay with history of many nations, I, 16; kings' reverence for the men of God, I, 78; on Merneptah stele, I, 307; name, I, 41, 182, 309; origins, I, 32-62, 298-319; sepulchres of kings, III, 286, 423; towns, I, 72; *see also* Judah

—— Northern: aliens in, I, 107; divi-

Israel *(Continued)*
   sion into new districts, I, 77, 326;
   fiscal structure, I, 326; government, I,
   73 ff.; relations with Judah, I, 29, 325,
   II, 61; Samaritans as survival of, II,
   28; *see also* Samaria
Israel, republic, I, 3, 18, 29, II, 296
Israel al-Naqawa, VII, 149
Israel b. Samuel ha-Ma'arabi, V, 261
Israel b. Simḥah of Baṣra, acquisition
   of biblical manuscript, VI, 447 f.;
   gift to Karaite synagogue, VI, 246 f.
Israeli, Isaac b. Solomon, Jewish physician and philosopher, III, 157; "Book
   of Elements," VIII, 222 f., 298 f.; commentary on Genesis, VI, 226 f., 282;
   definitions of memory, VIII, 80;
   eschatological doctrine, VIII, 105;
   "Guide for the Physician," VIII, 258;
   Ibn Tamim on, VII, 16; "internal"
   senses, VIII, 79 f.; on matter and
   space, VIII, 88; medical training,
   VIII, 236; medical works in Latin
   translation, VIII, 394 f.; on nature as
   healer, VIII, 260; on philosophic interpretation, VIII, 73; quoted, VIII,
   234; works, VIII, 59, 65, 137, 243 f.,
   298 f., 394 f.
Israeli, Isaac, the Second, VIII, 371, 376
Israelites, ancient: absolute obligation
   of righteous living, I, 83; in Babylonia,
   I, 106, 275, *see also* Exile, Babylonian;
   brotherhood of all Jews, I, 41, 63, 94,
   274, 330; clan structure, I, 54; creative
   artists, I, 14; in Egypt, I, 35-39, 305;
   Falasha descent from, II, 212; rabbinic
   adage, VIII, 66; relations with other
   Hebrews, I, 38; settlement abroad, I,
   39, 94; tribal divisions, I, 55
Issachar, tribe, III, 208; children of, VI,
   269, VIII, 199; division of hours, VIII,
   373
Isserles, Moses, VI, 26
Istanbul, *see* Constantinople
Italy: ancient: agriculture, I, 251; anti-
   Jewish feeling, I, 246, 248, II, 103;
   Christianity in Northern, II, 165;
   fatherland of all races, II, 151; Jewish
   captives of Titus, VI, 216; proselytes
   and descendants in, I, 283
—— medieval: awakening of scientific
   interests, VIII, 171, 245; Byzantine
   influence in, III, 25; capital punishment, V, 316; dating of records,

   VIII, 204; dependence on sharecrop-
   pers, III, 244; development of religious philosophy, VIII, 60; folk tales,
   VIII, 43; foreign domination, VII,
   304; foreign trade, IV, 4 f., 186; homiletical learning, VIII, 30 f.; influence
   of Abu Aaron, VIII, 44; influence of
   Palestinian customs, VI, 47; inquiries
   to scholars, VI, 119; introduction of
   dyeing and silk industry, IV, 168 f.;
   Jewish communities, III, 24-33, 109,
   180, 189, 240-44, IV, 20-27, 242-45,
   VI, 217; Jewish martyrs in the Crusades, IV, 106; Jewish ownership of
   Christian slaves, III, 243; Jewish population, IV, 24 f.; Judeo-Christian relations, IV, 20-27, 242-45; mishnaic
   commentaries, VI, 62; opposition to
   science, VIII, 171; origin of Yosephon,
   VI, 195; Renaissance, VIII, 147; spread
   of Jewish communal development
   from, V, 60 f.; suicide of Jew in
   Saracen raid, VI, 194; synagogue tunes,
   VII, 130; talmudic lexicon for Jews of,
   VII, 29 f.; *see also under* individual
   cities, e.g. Rome
Ittobaal, king, I, 322
Itureans, I, 224, 396
Ius gentium, II, 300, 303
Izates, king, I, 168

J

Jabariya, school of Islamic philosophy,
   VIII, 109
Jabir (Geber or Jebir) ibn Aflaḥ, VIII,
   162, 163 f., 201; alchemistic treatises,
   VIII, 225
Jaca, Spain, IV, 318; voluntary segrega-
   tion, IV, 35
Jacob, patriarch, I, 22, 37, 41, V, 90,
   93 f.; blessing of Reuben, VI, 259;
   Gregory I on, III, 29; image of,
   VIII, 13; ladder, VI, 297, VIII, 84; and
   proclamation of leap year, VIII, 194
Jacob, R., in Palmyra, III, 63
Jacob, (French?) traveler, III, 104
Jacob b. Ahron, I, 340
Jacob b. Amram, Kairuwan leader, V,
   40
Jacob b. Asher, VII, 206; on Psalm 91,
   VII, 283
Jacob b. Ephraim the Syrian, VII, 223 f.

Jacob b. Ḥayyim, *Biblia Rabbinica*, VI, 255

Jacob b. Mordecai Gaon, VI, 31

Jacob b. Moses ibn Abbasi, VI, 353

Jacob b. Nathaniel al-Fayyumi, V, 204

Jacob b. Nathaniel ha-Kohen, traveler, VI, 225

Jacob b. Nissim, of Kairuwan, V, 52; inquiry to Sherira, VI, 204, 329

Jacob b. Reuben, V, 230

Jacob b. R. Naṭronai, R., V, 74

Jacob b. Tanumas (Tanḥuma), III, 21, 237, V, 116

Jacob b. Yagar, R., VI, 52

Jacob b. Yequtiel, IV, 17, 77, 92, V, 59; appeal for papal intervention, IV, 57, 66, 97, VI, 219; on titles of Jewish leaders, III, 233

Jacob ibn Eleazar, *see* Ibn Eleazar

Jacobite Church, V, 9

Jacob of Orléans, IV, 205

Jaffa, I, 255, II, 91; congregation in, II, 199; forcibly Judaized, I, 256; inscriptions, I, 378; necropolis, II, 14, 174, 286

Jaffe, Mordecai, R., VII, 125; on Rashi's commentaries, VI, 50

Jafia b. David of Monzon, IV, 37

Jahmiya, Muslim theologians, VIII, 343

Jalutiyites, sect, V, 197

James, Saint, apostle, II, 70, 74, 75, 82, 131, 361; liturgy, VII, 65

James II, king of England, III, 94

James of Edessa, Syriac scholar, VI, 241

Jamnia, *see* Yabneh

Januarius, bishop of Sardinia, III, 242

Jao, god, I, 382, II, 22

Jaoel, angel, II, 22; *see also* Yehoel

Japheth, descendants of, VI, 192, VII, 256

Jason, high priest, I, 185, 229, 398

Jason of Cyrene, I, 198, 207, 217, 232

Jativa Spain, paper manufacture, IV, 169

Jaubari, Zain ad-Din al-, V, 96

Jauhar, Faṭimid general, III, 154

Jebir, *see* Jabir

Jebusites, I, 72; Jerusalem taken from, I, 65

Jeconiah, Jewish king, III, 90

Jehoiachin, king of Judah, I, 119, 343, II, 195, 206, 435; in Babylonian captivity, I, 115, 116, 348; cycle of, V, 247

Jehoiakim (Eliakim), king of Judah, I, 78, 115, 327

Jehoshaphat, king of Judah, I, 141; VI, 309 f.; reforms, I, 75, 328

Jehovah: name of God, I, 13, V, 120, VI, 449; *see also* God; Tetragrammaton

Jehu, king of Israel, I, 73, 89, 325, 335

Jenghiz Khan, III, 206

Jephet b. 'Ali, Karaite exegete, V, 159, 196, 237, 389, VI, 78, 308 f., VIII, 60; on chronology of Creation, VIII, 203; comment on books by Gentiles, VIII, 247; grammar as exegetical aid, VII, 38; influence of Saadiah on, VI, 473; messianic interpretations, V, 260; on prophecies addressed to Hosea, VI, 289; on social justice, V, 238 f.; translation of Old Testament, VI, 270 f.

Jephet b. Sa'id, V, 256

Jerash, *see* Gerasa

Jeraua, North African tribe, III, 91

Jeremiah, prophet, I, 86, 89, 104, 112, 117, 136, 153, 331, II, 20, III, 61, VI, 174; categories of sciences, VIII, 142; condemns soothsayers, I, 87; employs scribe, I, 334; on individual conscience, I, 84; injunction to build and plant, I, 109; messianic prediction, IV, 96; on Sabbath, I, 360; and Scythian invasions, I, 96, 338; on supremacy of worship in the heart, I, 83; on universalism and peace, I, 122; uses term Torah, I, 331

Jeremiah, R., amora, II, 20; expectation of resurrection, II, 312; on foolish Babylonians, II, 208

Jerez de la Frontera, VIII, 240

Jericho, I, 354; conquest of, I, 307; fertility of region, I, 252; Khaibar Jews in, III, 87; ritualistic customs, II, 7, VII, 66; traditional tomb of Moses, III, 308

Jeroboam I, king of Northern Israel, I, 327, V, 254; images erected by, I, 66; followers of, VIII, 311; revolt, I, 75; schism of, VI, 207

Jeroboam II, king of Israel, I, 67, 95

Jerome, Saint, II, 108, 144, 168, 189, 192, 240, 256, 373, 377, III, 196 f., V, 114, VI, 248, 272; on fall of Rome, III, 14, 234; *Hebraica*, VI, 273; quoted, II, 210, 269

Jerusalem: Israelitic: altars prohibited,

Jerusalem (Continued)

I, 128, 140; animal sacrifices, V, 123; David's conquest of, I, 65, 312; fall of, and Jubilee years, VIII, 210; governed by Viceroy, I, 75; as heart of country, I, 72; high ecclesiastical officers, I, 81; Judean public life centered in, I, 83; king of Salem, I, 45; population, I, 168; preexistence of, VIII, 126

—— postexilic and after: archives, II, 99; Christians in, II, 82, 164; Cicero on conquest of, I, 192; a city state, I, 160, 221; collections for the poor, II, 82; emigration from, I, 345; fall of, II, 131, 341, 374, 377, III, 238, V, 199, 354; "Foundation Stone," III, 269; as "God's sanctuary" V, 49; graves and tombstones, II, 286, 333, 423; Greek structures in, I, 228, 401; Hellenistic party and the Jews, I, 193, 398; Jewish congregations, II, 199; "metropolis" of scattered Jewish settlements, I, 66, 218 f., 250, 284, 348, II, 55; metropolitan economy, I, 276; name, I, 229, 321, 398, II, 107; Persian imperialism, I, 129-32, 353-55; pilgrimages to, I, 213 f., 258, 392, II, 108, 118, 374; priestly schools, VIII, 228; rivalry with Gerizim, II, 27; synagogue of Theodotos, VIII, 239 f.; tanners exempted from pilgrimages to, IV, 166; under the Seleucids, I, 216, 229, 369, 393; walls, I, 130, II, 369; see also Temple at Jerusalem

—— Roman and medieval, III, 22; Arab conquest, III, 87 f., 101 f.; Arabic and Hebrew names of, III, 87 f., 269; "Babylonian" congregation, V, 37, VII, 65; captured by Crusaders, III, 102, IV, 109 f., 295 f.; Christian patriarchate, III, 20; chronology based on, V, 119, 130; Church of the Holy Sepulcher, III, 103, 279, IV, 57, 58, 257; expansion of Jewish community, III, 101, 277 f.; "Jewish market," IV, 180; Judeo-Christian relations, III, 38, 101, 160, 316 f.; Karaites in, IV, 112, 296 f., V, 222 f., 233 f., 237, VI, 246 f., VII, 226; Latin kingdom of, IV, 106-16, 294-99; mass conversion of Jews, III, 182; Mongolian siege, V, 368; Mosque of the Rock, III, 101, 134, 269, 272; "Mourners for Zion,"

(q.v.), V, 185; Muslim cemetery, III, 297; Muslim discrimination against Jews, III, 147; Muslim respect for holiness of, III, 269; "on high," V, 142, 146, 148; orientation toward, VI, 14, VIII, 211; Palmyrenes and destruction of Temple, III, 62; period after second fall, VI, 230; period of Jewish control, III, 73; Persian capture of, III, 21 f.; pilgrimages to, IV, 94 f., 166; prohibition of Jewish residence in, IV, 296 f.; Rabbanite academy, III, 104, IV, 24 ff., 302 ff., V, 233 f., 237, VI, 215, 245; removal of crosses from, III, 102; Seljuk rule, III, 104, IV, 94, 115 f.; Talmud of, VI, 331, see also Talmud, Palestinian; 'Umar's treaty with Christians of, III, 97, 269; under Hadrian, II, 97, 107 f., 123; Wailing Wall, III, 278, V, 236

Jesse, stock of, V, 157

Jesuits, Spanish, scientia media of God, VIII, 128

Jesus Barabbas (Bar Abba-the Father's Son), II, 72

Jesus Christ, II, 148, 357, 387, VIII, 134; alleged statement on vengeance, IV, 102; called disciple of Joshua b. Perahiah, II, 148, 387 f., V, 119; called impostor, V, 104; Chalcedonian formula re nature of, III, 5; contemporary treatment of, II, 63, 353; date of birth, II, 353, VI, 207, VIII, 206; dates of crucifixion and resurrection, VIII, 187; debates on, V, 118 ff., 343 ff.; descent, II, 65, 136, 140; disciples and their beliefs, II, 70, 71, 73, 74 f., 83; early references to, II, 131; expectations before coming of, II, 31, 58-62; foretold destruction of Temple, II, 74, 83; Gregory on reversion to the Jews, III, 243; and the high priesthood, V, 343; historicity of, and sources about, II, 63 ff., 353 ff.; homage of Moses, V, 138; Jewish repudiation of, II, 130 ff., 379 ff., V, 118 ff., 343 ff., VII, 177 f., VIII, 133; Josephus on, II, 131, 379, VI, 418; and Judaism, I, 180, II, 63, 65, 67, 70, 356; Karaites on, V, 263 f., 344; "kingdom of God" gospel, II, 68 ff., 73, 77, 357; language, II, 65 f.; last words, II, 358, V, 120; link with John the Baptist, II, 62, 65, 68; as Messiah, II, 64, 65, 67-75, 357, III, 15,

249 f., IV, 91 f., V, 117 ff., 343 ff., VI, 171, VIII, 127; Mohammed and, III, 81; and money-changers, I, 258; mystic body of, VIII, 277; name in Thamudic inscription, III, 258; recognized as prophet, V, 186, 192, 219; Roman opposition, II, 70, 134, 358; "sonship" and timelessness of, II, 81, 364; teachings, II, 67 ff., 77, 358; trial and execution, II, 70, 71 f., 358; visions of, II, 71, III, 229; see also Christians and Christianity; Cross; Crucifixion of Jesus; Messiah

Jethro-Hobeb, I, 38; legend, V, 129

"Jew," as derogatory term, III, 5, 147, IV, 9, 307, V, 126, 136

Jew-baiting, see Antisemitism

Jewelers, IV, 170, 214 f.

"Jewry Wall," Leicester, England, IV, 281

Jezebel, queen, I, 78, 322, 334

Jibal, Spain, III, 109

Jindibu, Arabian king, III, 61

Jinns, VIII, 10; see also Demonology

Jizya (poll tax), III, 163 f., 170; see also Taxation

Joash, king of Israel, I, 73, 91

Job, I, 136, 307, II, 227, V, 167; cited as authority for scientific studies, VIII, 219; identity of, VI, 293, 308; Tobiah b. Eliezer on, VI, 174

—— Book of, I, 151, 364, VIII, 344; commentaries on, VI, 460, VII, 186; priestly influence, I, 150; Saadiah's version of, VI, 266, 270, 460

Jobab, king of Edom, identification with Job, VI, 293

Joce de Brakelond, IV, 84

Joel, prophet: date of, VI, 310; ideal of, I, 154 f.

—— Book of, V, 201

Joel b. Isaac ha-Levi of Bonn, VI, 391

Joel b. Pethuel, III, 63

Johanan b. Matya, R., II, 257

Johanan (b. Nappaha), R., II, 13, 110, 133, 146, 148, 175, 194, 197, 203, 207, 221, 234, 235, 249, 264, 286, 305, 307, 315, 317, 392, 400, 409, VI, 11, 167, 336, VII, 62; on astronomical computations, VIII, 161; compunctions about informer, II, 142, 385; condemnation of pleonasms, VIII, 14; on the divine Chariot, VIII, 6; on fast days, II, 134, 380; on Men of the Great Synagogue,

VII, 65 f.; on Mishnah, II, 294; on prayers, VI, 44, VII, 66; quoted, II, 245, 246, 256, 268, VIII, 19; removed barrier between groups, II, 242; sentiments toward Rome, II, 152 f., 414; on synagogue attendance, II, 283; on Torah and the poor, II, 277; views disputed by R. Simon, II, 161; on "younger teachers," II, 262, 417

Johanan b. Nuri, R., II, 205

Johanan b. Toreta, R., II, 87

Johanan b. Zakkai, R., I, 262, 279, II, 101, 121, 128, 132, 197, 205, 220, 314, 396; on charities, II, 270; demand upon Vespasian II, 120, 377; leadership, II, 111, 117, 197, 403; on Nebukadrezzar, VIII, 26; rebuilder of national life, II, 277; teachings, II, 113-19 passim, 375, 376

Johanna, countess of Flanders, IV, 344

Johannes, Norman proselyte, see Obadiah (Johannes)

Johannes Hispalensis (or Hispanus), see Avendeath

Johannes Scholasticus, III, 187

John, Saint, II, 75, 82

—— Gospel of, II, 64, 66, 71, 72, 75, 83, 359, 361, 364

John bishop of Spires, IV, 74; protection of Jews, IV, 98 f., 101 f., 142

John I, Monophysite patriarch, VI, 263

John I (John Tsimiskes), Byzantine emperor, III, 193, 317, V, 162

John I, king of England, IV, 77, 204; appointment of first Jewish presbyter, V, 63; privilege to Jews, IV, 164, 170

John Cinnamus, Byzantine historian, III, 212

John Hyrcanus, Jewish ruler, I, 189, 223, 225, 235, 236, 276, 369, 400, 410, II, 27, 29, 339; appeal for restoration of Joppa, I, 255; conquests, I, 167, 224; slur on genealogical purity of, I, 227, V, 9

John of Capua, translations by, VII, 189

John of Damascus, V, 109; Christian writer, VII, 142; polemics vs. Islam, V, 84

John of Ephesus, III, 231

John of Gischala, II, 347

John of Nikiu, II, 402, III, 18, 235

John of Saxony, VIII, 175

John Rufus, bishop of Mayuma, III, 229

John Rylands Library, Manchester, V, 372

John the Baptist, Saint, I, 402, II, 62, 352; association with Jesus, II, 62, 65, 68; and Damascus sect, II, 52, 348; sacraments connected with, II, 75, 361

John the Essene, II, 51

Jonadab, son of Rechab, I, 89

Jonah, prophet, II, 20, 336

—— Book of, I, 158

Jonah, R., Amora, VIII, 213

Jonah (b. Abraham Gerondi) the Pious, R., VI, 61

"Jonathan," Targum, VI, 258 ff., 455 ff., VIII, 203

Jonathan b. David ha-Kohen of Lunel, VI, 88, 106, 119, 369 f.; correspondence, VI, 119, 380

Jonathan b. 'Uzziel, II, 386; see also "Jonathan," Targum

Jordan, river, I, 55

Josce of Gloucester, IV, 82

Jose b. 'Aqabiah, R., II, 145

Jose b. Ḥalafta, R., I, 251, II, 112 f., 125, 273, 310, 311, 319, 434; burial place, V, 37; chronology compiled, II, 141, 376, 384, VI, 200, 231, VIII, 208; on the Hallel, VII, 69; quoted, II, 250

Jose b. Netanel, II, 117

Jose b. Qisma, R., II, 100

Jose of Ma'on, II, 193

Joseph, patriarch, I, 37, 40, 304; marriage, I, 39; Messiah of house of, I, 99; as prophet, VIII, 132; and the wolf, VI, 170

Joseph, Khazar king, III, 196, 201; correspondence with Ḥisdai, III, 156, 210, 305 f., 324, VI, 219 f., VII, 273; Halevi's dialogue, VIII, 3, 22, 62, 84 ff., 125 ff.; importation of Jewish scholars, III, 203

Joseph, R., Amora, II, 74, 308; against Aramaic, VII, 6; defined "Epicurean," II, 278; on division of biblical verses, VI, 238; expert in viticulture, II, 414

Joseph, son of Tobiah, II, 349

Joseph (b. Jacob?), R., of Sura, chronological computations, VIII, 202

Joseph b. Abraham al-Baṣir, V, 233, 242 f., VII, 220, VIII, 60

Joseph b. Asher, of Chartres, IV, 124

Joseph b. Gershom, Jewish judge in Alexandria, V, 47 f.

Joseph b. Gurion, see Yosephon

Joseph b. Ḥanina, R., II, 115, 312, 376

Joseph b. Ḥiyya, gaon, V, 15

Joseph b. Isaac, poet, VII, 294

Joseph b. Isaac of Orléans, Tosafist, VI, 388

Joseph b. Isaac Sambari, see Sambari

Joseph b. Jacob b. 'Ali, booklist, VI, 360 f.

Joseph b. Jacob bar Satia, see Bar Satia

Joseph b. Meir ha-Levi, see Ibn Megas

Joseph b. Meir ibn Zabara, see Ibn Zabara

Joseph b. Moses the Elder, R., VI, 120

Joseph b. Nuḥ, V, 233; translation of Old Testament, VI, 270

Joseph b. Phineas, Jewish banker of Baghdad, III, 152 f., V, 10

Joseph b. Samuel, editor of Sefer ha-Yashar, VI, 198

Joseph b. Shemariah, V, 35 f.

Joseph b. Yehudah of Babylonia: benediction before Shema', VI, 131; mystic experience, VIII, 7

Joseph b. Zedekiah, V, 311

Joseph Bonfils, see Tob 'Elem

Joseph ha-Arukh (il Lungo), VIII, 285

Joseph (b. Joshua) ha-Kohen, Jewish chronicler, III, 39, 92, IV, 130

Joseph ha-Ma'arabi, VI, 380

Joseph ibn Abitur, see Ibn Abitur

Joseph ibn Abulmana, sheikh, III, 115

"Joseph's Prayer," I, 182

Josephus, Flavius, I, 35, 168, 174, 177, 184, 185, 190, 231, 255, 257, II, 9, 15, 20, 75, 83, 104, 120, 157, 195, 205, 280, 314, 349, 409, 423, III, 61, 62, 211, VIII, 253; on antisemitism, I, 177, 194, 382, 383; documents in, I, 242, 377; and era of Creation, VIII, 208; on Essenes, I, 233, II, 48, 49, 50, 347; genealogy, I, 272; Greek influence upon, I, 186, II, 38; on Herod, I, 236; on Jewish law, II, 117, 279; on Jewish magician, II, 21; on Jewish marriage, II, 223, 234; on Jewish race, I, 198; on messianic impostors, II, 61; and Pharisaism, II, 38, 342, 343, 344; on pilgrimages, I, 214; quoted, I, 223, 402, II, 47, 147; on rise of Christianity, II, 131, 379, VI, 418; on Roman wars, II, 90, 92, 93, 94, 99, 102, 368, 372; on Sadducee individualism, II, 41; on Samaritans, II, 26, 29, 30, 36, 37, 339, 341, 342; Slavonic version, II, 379, VI,

191 f., 417 f.; speech before fall of Jerusalem, VI, 192 f.; on suicide, VI, 193; term "theocracy" coined by, I, 152, 223, 271; wealth in Temple treasury, I, 215; widely read, II, 379; and Yosephon, VI, 190; on Zealots, II, 47

Jose the Galilean, R., II, 133, 142, 230; computations of, VIII, 6; son of, II, 267

Joshua b. Gamala, II, 421

Joshua b. Ḥananiah, R., I, 179, 221, 265, 294, II, 8, 21, 116 f., 119, 125, 139, 218, 275, VI, 35, 107; alphabet acrostics, VII, 257; on loss of the Temple, II, 112, 375; on rich and poor, II, 270; rise to leadership, II, 276; student of Greek, II, 142

Joshua b. 'Ilan, Rabbanite, on era of Creation, VIII, 204

Joshua b. Levi, R., I, 376, II, 122, 276, 295; on books of Aggadah, VI, 157; on confession, VII, 79 f.; mystic sayings, VIII, 6; quoted, II, 422

Joshua b. Nun, biblical leader, I, 53, 307, 308, 325, 354; miracle at Gibeon, VI, 311

Joshua, Book of, II, 30, 340

Joshua b. Peraḥiah R., II, 20, 148, 262, 336, 388, 421, V, 119, VI, 207

Joshua b. Qarḥa, R., II, 267

Josiah, king of Judah, I, 73, 91, 126, 183, 345; destruction of Bethel, I, 346; effort to revive militia, I, 84; reformation under, I, 79, 83 ff., 330, 331, 332, see also Reformation, Deuteronomic; tragic end of, I, 339

Josiah (Ḥasan) b. Zakkai, counterexilarch, V, 11 f.

Jotapata, siege of, VI, 193 f.

Jotham, parable of, I, 93

Jubilees, Book of, II, 344, 383, V, 167, VIII, 191, 208, 368; on coming of the Kingdom, II, 59; excerpt, II, 43; on intermarriage, II, 232; on the Law, II, 73

Jubilee year, I, 85, 332, V, 199 f., 404; effect on land ownership, IV, 160; first, VIII, 209

Judaea and Judaeans, VII, 3; agriculture, I, 251; aristocracy's contempt for masses, I, 224; education, II, 274; Jewishness of the people, II, 123, 277; and Jews of Galilee and Arbatta, I, 167; name changed, II, 123, 132, 380; political downfall, I, 247, II, 92, 132, 151; relations with Rome, I, 218, II, 90; variety of balsam, VIII, 253; wool industry, I, 408; see also Judah; Palestine

Judaei, term, IV, 271, V, 126

Judah, kingdom, I, 57, 73, 224; boundaries, I, 94, 345; depopulation in sixth century, I, 105; diffusion of government, I, 72-77, 325-27; exiles in Babylonia, I, 106, see also Exile, Babylonian; and prophetic literature, II, 28; scepter of, V, 118, 130, 313, VI, 193; Sennacherib's campaign against, II, 95; towns, I, 72; unity with Israel, I, 29, 94, II, 61, V, 126, 264, 285; in western Asiatic affairs, I, 67; see also Israel; Judaea and Judaeans; Palestine

Judah, son of Jacob, I, 61; descent from, II, 351, VI, 200; marriage, I, 39

Judah, Jewish doctor in Salerno, VIII, 245

Judah, R., Hindu, II, 212

Judah, R., son of R. Shalom, on Aramaic prayers, VII, 66; on the Mishnah, VI, 257 f.

Judah I, R., II, 20, 135, 146, 187, 193, 197, 205, 227, 248, 272, 280, 316, 400, 403, 408, 436, V, 167, 256, 359, VI, 17, 24, 181; against Aramaic, VII, 6; Amoraim in academy of, VIII, 6; authority of opinions of, VI, 31; editorship of Mishnah, II, 206 f., 294, 295, 426, VI, 99, 201, 205; on Ḥiyya's speech habits, VI, 240; Maimonides' study of, VI, 102; proclamation of defective months, VIII, 187; Saadiah's biography of, VI, 203; shipowner, II, 249; on destruction of the Temple, VI, 167

Judah II, II, 193, 194, 197, 276, 281

Judah al-Barceloni, see Yehudah b. Barzillai al-Barceloni

Judah-Aristobulus, I, 224

Judah b. Baba, R., II, 120, 126

Judah b. Batira, II, 36, 227, 262; adherence to Pharisaism, II, 56

Judah b. Ezekiel, II, 146, 208, VII, 129

Judah b. 'Ila'i, R., II, 153, 176, 224, 248, 250, 251, 257, 283, 376, 378, VI, 31; epigram on physicians, VIII, 233

Judah b. Naḥmani, R., VI, 178

Judah b. Ṭabbai, V, 255

Judah b. Tema, II, 421

Judah Maccabee, I, 185, 231, 369
"Judah's rod," V, 8
Judaica perditio, III, 29
Judaica perfidia, III, 31
Judaicus, title, II, 92
Judaism: and Aristotelianism, VIII,
63 ff., 305 ff.; Christians' lack of knowledge of, V, 114; continuity of, VI, 3;
contributions to Christianity, III,
208 f., 221, 243, V, 136, VI, 8, VIII, 51,
see also under Christians and Christianity; Judeo-Christian relations;
contributions to magical lore, VIII,
10 f.; controversies within and without, VIII, 66-75, 310-15; evolution of
aggadic lore, VI, 36; heterodoxy vs.
Oral Law, V, 104 f., VI, 22, VIII, 51 ff.;
history as prime element in, I, 4-16,
294-97, VI, 204 ff., 227 ff., 438 ff., VIII,
86 ff., 125 ff.; *see also* History; importance of synagogue, VII, 62; influence
on Islam, III, 80 ff., 265 ff., VI, 7 ff.;
and medical studies, VIII, 265; messianic hope in, V, 206 f., 366; Mohammed on, III, 83 f.; natural and social
factors in expansion of, III, 110 f.;
number of sects, V, 183, 197, *see also*
Sectarianism; outlawry of, III, 177, 220,
see also under Outlawry; papal charge
of inferiority of, III, 31 f.; religio-
juridical evolution, VI, 3-151, 321-98;
religious conflict between masses and
philosophers, VIII, 57 ff.; restoration
of Sanhedrin (*q.v.*) for calendar reform, VIII, 191; and self-realization,
VII, 59 f.; and study of Hebrew, VII,
4; synthesis with Hellenism, VIII, 32,
76; unity within diversity, V, 205 ff.;
universalism and particularism, VIII,
123 ff., 345; *see also* Converts and conversion; Proselytes and proselytism
Judaizanti, Russian sect, III, 216
Judan, R., on Gentiles and synagogue
sermons, VII, 128; homily on Canticles 1:1, VI, 155
Judas Iscariot, II, 71, 359
Judas of Galilee, I, 263, II, 47, 101; leadership in family of, II, 48
Judeo-Arabic language, IV, 197, V, 227,
VII, 60, 221; linguistic peculiarities,
VII, 8
Judeo-Christian relations, II, 188 f., 427;
affected by local conditions, IV, 14;
and Anacletus II, IV, 10 ff., 237; *Ba-*

silika and, III, 187; in biblical studies,
VI, 240 f., 272; blood accusations (*q.v.*),
IV, 80; canon law on, III, 194, 212,
IV, 9 ff., 18 f., 241 f.; charge of Jewish
disloyalty, IV, 37 f., 55 f.; complicated
by burghers, IV, 65, *see also* Burghers; controversy over Messiah (*q.v.*),
VII, 178 f.; cooperation among physicians, VIII, 236, 265; during the Crusades, IV, 89 ff., 116 ff.; Cyril's controversial tract, III, 210; denunciations
of Jews, V, 131 ff.; effect of Almohade
regime on, IV, 31; effect of, on Rashi
and Tobiah, VI, 173; fiscal pressures,
IV, 12 ff., *see also* Taxation; in France,
III, 50 f.; fraternization, IV, 21 f., 52;
growing animosity, IV, 132-39, 306-8,
VI, 230; and inheritance rights, V,
299; intellectual contacts, VI, 272 ff.,
279, VII, 173 f., VIII, 364 ff.; in Italy,
III, 26 f., 241; Karaite attitudes, V,
263 f.; lack of unity in common cause
vs. Muslims, III, 57, 137, 159; in Latin
Kingdom of Jerusalem, IV, 113 ff.; legal debates, VI, 141 f.; linguistic reci-
procity, VII, 10; litigation, III, 190,
IV, 15 f., 41 f., 49, 69, 78; and local
customs, VI, 128; monastic quarrels
and, IV, 84; moneylending and, IV,
202 f.; and Mosaic law, VI, 4; outlawry
of sex relationships, IV, 9, V, 133 f.,
see also Intermarriage; pietism and,
VIII, 48 ff.; in Portugal, III, 160;
precedent set by Sisebut, III, 38; pro-
Jewish intervention, IV, 142 f.; protection against alleged Jewish attacks,
IV, 9 ff.; public disputations in Cairo,
III, 160; rabbinic law on, V, 100; religious debates, V, 108 ff., VII, 84, *see
also* Controversies; religious holidays
and trade, IV, 219 f.; and religious
observances, V, 122 ff.; resentment over
royal favoritism, IV, 40, 50 f., 77, 80 f.;
role of religion in, VII, 176 ff.; sectarian controversies, III, 57, *see also*
Sectarianism; and sexual morality,
III, 300; socioeconomic factors, IV,
60, 65, 121 ff., 141 f., V, 126 f.; in Spain,
III, 160, IV, 158 f.; violence in, III,
38, 241, IV, 89 ff., 139 ff.; and voluntary segregation, III, 144 f.; in western Europe, III, 173 f.
Judeo-Christians, *see* Christians and
Christianity

Judeo-Greek language, I, 186
Judeo-Muslim relations, III, 102, 145, 166, 171 ff., 302, IV, 30 f., 225 ff., V, 108, 134; and biblical interpretation, VI, 274 f.; and communal control, V, 47 ff.; and consumption of wine, IV, 164 f.; controversies, V, 83 ff., 326 ff.; see also Controversies; and the Crusades, IV, 91; Faṭimid persecution, IV, 58; and language, VII, 9; legal evolution and, VI, 7 ff.; sectarianism and, V, 169; socioeconomic issues, V, 96 ff., 334 ff.
Judeo-Roman wars, I, 212, II, 89-102, 106, 121, 368-71; see also Bar Kocheba; Great War; Hadrian; Roman Empire; Trajan
Judeo-Samaritan relations, V, 172 f., 177
Judeo-Slav relations, III, 213 ff.
Judges and the judiciary, I, 68, 75, 80, 328, II, 137, 265-69, 418 ff., IV, 215, V, 395; appointment of, V, 20, 50, 71, 75, VI, 9, 122; compensation, II, 278; corruption of, V, 178; eminence of, VI, 325; exilarchic, V, 14 f.; influence on evolution of law, VI, 13; ordination, titles, II, 419; personal responsibility for errors, II, 268; preexilic, I, 80, 328; preservation of the law, IV, 222; proceedings at city gate, I, 80; Rabbanite, and illiterates, IV, 167; rules governing decisions by, V, 237 f., VI, 30 f., 46; status in Islam and Judaism, VI, 9; see also Jurists
Judges, Book of, I, 340; period, I, 32, 39
"Judges in the gate," VII, 245
Judgment, day of, I, 5, 144, V, 149
Judgment and retribution after death, II, 31, 38, 40, 41; see also Punishments
Judith, Book of, VI, 186 f.
Judith, queen of Poland, III, 219
Julian, Samaritan king, V, 170
Julian of Toledo, Saint, IV, 47, V, 114, 130 f.; Liber Responsionum, III, 45; on messianic character of Jesus, III, 249 f.; relations with Jews, III, 250
Julian the Apostate, Roman emperor, I, 282, II, 151, 154, 179, 186, 187, 194, 274, 374, 376, 391, 392, 398, 399, 403; adversary of Christian rule, II, 159 ff., 391; Jewish reaction to advances by, II, 160, 392; legendary visit of Tiberian rabbis, V, 350; request to Jews

for prayers, VII, 265; and the Temple of Jerusalem, II, 155, 160, V, 144
Julianus, revolutionary, II, 96, 370
Julianus, Marcus Antonius, II, 93, 369, 372
Julia Severa, II, 24, 338
Julius Africanus, III, 15, VIII, 189, 206
Julius Capitolinus, II, 400
Jumièges, monastery of, IV, 59
Jundeshapur, medical academy, VIII, 236, 241
Juno, goddess, I, 374
Jupiter, god, I, 374
Jupiter Capitolinus, Temple of, II, 13, 106, 373
Jurisdiction: capital, V, 45; civil, IV, 101, V, 57 f.; communal, V, 64, 317; of local rulers, IV, 72 f.
—— ecclesiastical, IV, 73 f.; difficulties of, IV, 98 ff.; in England, IV, 77 f.; in France, IV, 53-64; and Jewish quarter, IV, 266; over monarchs and princes, IV, 54; secular resistance to, IV, 13; transfer of control over Jews to, IV, 65 f., 274
—— royal: of Carolingians, IV, 48 ff.; and the clergy, IV, 59, 68; decentralization, IV, 72 ff.; expansion, IV, 72; of Frederick Barbarossa, IV, 71; local resistance to, IV, 22 f.; and moneylending, IV, 82 f.; weakness of, IV, 95
Jurisprudence: English, IV, 78 f.; economic theory, IV, 200 f., 216-24
—— Jewish, II, 298-309, 429-33, VI, 3-151, 321-98; based on equity, II, 304; Byzantine, halakhic works, VIII, 31; and Christianity, II, 134; commercial law, II, 302, 304, 431, IV, 179, 186; ethics and, II, 308; enforcement of, II, 265, 291; independent from Roman and Sassanian, II, 299; influence on Jewish economy, II, 251 ff., 264, 415 ff.; Judeo-Christian concepts, II, 303, 432; judiciary, I, 80, II, 137, 265-69, 418 ff., see also Judges and judiciary; legal fiction, II, 304, 432; legal principles, I, 327; legal status of Jews in Rome and Persia, II, 104, 180-87 passim, 398 f.; "natural law" in, II, 432; and non-Jews, II, 265, 301, 430; Philo's work on legal practice, II, 418; tenacity of customs, II, 302
Jurists, IV, 215; leadership of, VI, 149;

Jurists (Continued)
  Muslim, and literary style, VI, 94;
  need for biological data, VIII, 227;
  poets among, VII, 151; Spanish-
  Provençal, VI, 56
Jus divinum, V, 78
Jus gentium, II, 300, 303, VI, 5
Just, the, preexistence of, VIII, 125 f.
Just, Book of the, V, 353, VI, 233, VIII,
  43; biblical story, VI, 197
Justice: appeal to public conscience for,
  V, 66 f.; attribute of God, VIII, 42;
  ideal of, I, 25, 45 f.; and mercy, II,
  433; and necessity, VIII, 109 f.; public
  administration of, VI, 122; social,
  Karaite and Rabbanite, V, 238 f.; see
  also Judges and Judiciary
Justice, Book of, VIII, 265
Justin I, Byzantine emperor, III, 68
Justin II, Byzantine emperor, III, 17
Justinian I, Byzantine emperor, II, 178,
  181, 243, 267, 304, 401, 409, 413; age
  of, III, 4-15, 229-35; Code of, II, 178,
  303, 375, 397, 425, 432, III, 185, 191,
  231, 233 f., VI, 322, VI, 54; interest
  rates set by, IV, 198; on Nestorians
  and Jews, III, 229; Novella 131, III,
  8 f.; Novella 146, III, 11, 85, 189, 233,
  V, 26, 55, 209, VII, 94 f.; ordinance
  on Scripture reading, III, 12, 189; outlawry of study of Oral Law, III, 12,
  V, 26, VI, 153, 261, VII, 83, 94; peace
  with Kavadh I, III, 17; reprisals
  against Jewish ecclesiastical sanctions,
  V, 56; and Samaritans, II, 33, V, 170 f.;
  support of Western vs. Eastern
  Church, III, 7
Justinian II, Byzantine emperor, III, 198
Justin Martyr, Saint, II, 132, 138, 139,
  145, 151, 223, 380, 382; V, 115, VIII,
  133; quoted, II, 163, 167; on Simon
  Magus, II, 32, 341
Justus, Samaritan king, V, 170
Juvenal, bishop of Jerusalem, III, 20
Juvenal, poet, I, 179, 194

K

Ka'aba stone, III, 86, V, 86
Ka'b al-Aḥbar (Al-Ḥabr), III, 92, 272,
  VI, 275
Ka'b ibn al-Ashraf, Medinese poet, III,
  72, 76
Kabbalah, VI, 297, VII, 182, 306, VIII,

8, 55, 277; classification of souls, VIII,
  338; doctrine of creation, VIII, 94;
  doctrine of emanation, VIII, 22;
  transition to Neoplatonism, VIII, 39;
  see also Mystics and mysticism; rise
  of, VIII, 11-53, 277-95; in Spain, VIII,
  14; and the Torah, VIII, 282
Kadesh, I, 42
Kahana, R.: on destruction of Tadmor,
  III, 62; story of, VI, 183 f.
Kairuwan: academies, V, 40, VI, 9, 213 f.;
  center of Jewish medical learning,
  VIII, 396; Copts and Jews from Egypt,
  III, 90; exegetical works, VI, 45; group
  from, in Fez, III, 145; Ḥushiel (q.v.)
  in, VI, 342; inquiry re Eldad, VI, 241;
  interest in history of Judaism, VI,
  204; Jacob b. Nissim (q.v.) in, VI,
  426; Jewish community, III, 107, V,
  39 f., 306; legality of local customs,
  VI, 122; letters of authorization, IV,
  212 f.; liturgical compilations, VII,
  116 f.; moneylending in, IV, 339;
  mosque, III, 280; negidim, V, 51, 312,
  VI, 213 f.; proponents of written transmission of tradition, VI, 427; scholars,
  VI, 28, see also under individual
  scholars, e.g., Ḥananel; transcripts of
  geonic responsa, VI, 113
Kalam and Mutakallimun, V, 121, VIII,
  61, 89, 129, 136, 311; Arabic definition
  of, VIII, 136; arguments re creation,
  VIII, 89; doctrine of divine attributes,
  VIII, 97, 326; on predetermined life
  span and medical treatment, VIII,
  259
Kalat al-Hammad, Algeria, VI, 84, 367
Kaleb Ella Asbaha, see Elesboas
Kallah assemblies, II, 245, 247, 276, 277,
  V, 20, VII, 13; months of, II, 422
Kallah, tractate, VI, 183
Kalonymide family, IV, 46, VI, 117,
  VIII, 50; and Otto II, IV, 273; trans-
  planted from Lucca, V, 60 f.
Kalonymos b. Meshullam, defender of
  Mayence, IV, 103
Kalonymos b. Shabbetai, of Rome, IV,
  105
Kalonymos b. Ṭodros, Jewish leader in
  Narbonne, IV, 47
Kalonymos b. Yehudah, of Mayence, IV,
  145; lamentations, VII, 181
Kankah (or Mankah), Indian mathe-
  matician, VIII, 148

Kapparot ceremony, V, 249, VI, 125

"Karaimic tongue," V, 247

Karaites and Karaism, I, 30, II, 130, III, 161, 189, 221, IV, 38, V, 181 ff., 209-85, 388-416; analogistic method, VII, 236; and 'Ananites, V, 222-26, 395 f.; on anthropomorphic passages in the Aggadah, VI, 268; appeals to history, V, 251; Arabic works translated into Hebrew, VII, 7; attitude toward magic practices, VIII, 28; attitude toward synagogue, VII, 274; biblical research and interpretation, V, 159, 278 f., VI, 244 f., 275 f., 278 f., 287 ff., 305 ff., 445, 471 ff., VII, 36 f., 51; in Byzantium, IV, 294, V, 56, 272, 399, VI, 173, 366; and calendar controversies, VIII, 184, 194 f., 203; conversion to Islam, III, 112; designation, V, 232; determined minority, V, 257-67, 408-11; and divine attributes, VIII, 100; doctrine concerning loss of independence, V, 260; in Egypt, V, 257 f., 268, 272, VI, 134 f.; exilarchs, VI, 200 f.; Ibn Daud on, VI, 206; on Jesus, V, 344; and Khazar Judaism, III, 202 f.; laws and regulations, V, 240-51, VI, 108; on levirate, V, 332; linguistic superiority, VI, 290, VII, 6, 36 f., 51; linguistic use of rabbinic literature, VII, 56; liturgy, VII, 43, 64, 70, 110 ff., 244, 248; Muslim conversions to, V, 412; in northwest Africa, VII, 226; opposition to secular learning, VIII, 246 ff.; on oral tradition, VI, 427, VII, 78, 223, VIII, 58 ff.; origin of, V, 187, 405, 407 f.; in Palestine, IV, 111 f., VI, 118, 245 f.; proselytizing, V, 267-75, 412-14; pseudo-messiah, V, 202; reaction to Saadiah's translation, VI, 270 f.; recitation from vocalized scrolls, VI, 244; reestablishment of patriarchate, V, 32; religious philosophy, VIII, 60 ff.; reverence for the law, VIII, 312; Saadiah on, V, 94; Samau'al on, V, 335 f.; in Spain, VII, 228; studies of Arabic science and grammar, VII, 38; on substitute words, VI, 294; survivors of conquest of Jerusalem, IV, 111 f.; on true and false prophets, VIII, 130; view of David's injunction to Solomon, VII, 174 f.

Karbala, battle, V, 7

Karet, premature death, V, 241

Karkara, battle, III, 61

Karo, Joseph, VIII, 292 f.; on animal sacrifice, VII, 79; law code, VI, 26, 115; on medical fees, VIII, 233

Kartir, statesman, II, 317, 435

Kaspi, Joseph, of Provence: charges against local rabbis, VIII, 68; "Ethical Will," VIII, 361

Kavadh I, king of Persia, II, 183, 213, III, 68 f.; and the Mazdakite movement, III, 56; peace with Justinian, III, 17; prohibition of burying the dead, III, 22; and the Samaritans, III, 56

Kavvanah (intention), II, 307

Kemosh, god, I, 90

Keneset Israel, II, 285

Kenites, tribe, I, 46, 57, 60, 313

Kenizzites, I, 57

Kephaleiton, capitation tax, III, 191 f.

Keret legend, I, 301, 401

Kertsh (Panticapaeum; Samkartsh), III, 205

Kessan, city, I, 304

Ketubah, see Marriage contracts

Keturah, Abraham's wife, I, 39

Khabaroi, III, 212

Khaibar, Arabia, III, 163; derivation of names, III, 64; expulsion of Jews, III, 80, 86; Jews vs. Mohammed, III, 79; Mohammed's treaty with, III, 96, 262, 264, 274; refugees from, V, 179 f.; 'Umar and, III, 262

Khalid ibn Yazid, 'Umayyad prince, VIII, 224

Khalisioi, III, 212, 332

Khanfu, China, III, 115

Khaqani, Al-, vizier, III, 152

Kharaj, land tax, III, 162 f., 274 f., IV, 214

Kharijites, Muslim sect, V, 180, 186 f.

Khazars and Khazaria, III, 173, 196-206, 323-30, V, 130 f.; and Ashkenaz, IV, 235; Christians and Muslims, III, 199; conversion, III, 196-99, 323 ff.; and the gaonate, V, 23; Ḥisdai ibn Shapruṭ on, V, 161; influence of Jews of, III, 221; instruction in Judaism, VIII, 273; invasion of Adharbaijan, III, 199; and Karaites, III, 202 f.; migrants from, III, 206 ff., 215 f.; migrants to, III, 177, 183, 196 f.; military campaigns, III, 199; and neighboring Slavs, III, 203, 208; religious syncretism, III,

Khazars and Khazaria (Continued)
200-206, 327-30; rice cultivation, IV,
161; role in Jewish history, III, 110;
trade, IV, 181; Ugro-Finnic stock, III,
204
Kherson, Cyril's journey to, III, 209
Khirbet Kerak ware, I, 323
Khirbet Mafjar, inscription, III, 103
Khiva (Khwarizm), III, 212, 326; emi-
gration from, III, 197
Khorasan, Persia, III, 109; Karaites, V,
229; messianic movement, V, 200; wed-
ding custom, VI, 122, 395
Khosroe I, king of Persia, II, 178, 183 f.,
III, 18, VIII, 241; fiscal reform, III,
162; treatment of Jews, III, 56
Khosroe II, king of Persia, II, 185, 399;
letter to Emperor Maurice, III, 235;
reign of, III, 58; uprising vs., III, 17
Khozran, mosque destroyed by Khazars,
III, 203
Khwalisi, III, 212, 332
Khwarizm, see Khiva
Khwarizmi, Muhammed b. Musa al-,
II, 307, VIII, 153, 158, 355 f.
Kidenas, II, 16
Kiev (city and state), Ukraine, III, 217;
archaeological investigations, III, 213;
Jewish quarter, III, 217, 222, 337 f.;
Petcherskii (Cave) Monastery, III,
215 f.; trade center, IV, 176
Kilayim, I, 253
Kilwa, Africa, III, 116
Kindi, al-, V, 124, 347
Kingdom of God, I, 337, II, 68, 318, 357;
coming of, on earth, II, 58 ff., 73 f.,
351, 361 (see also End of days); teach-
ings of Jesus, II, 68, 69, 73, 77, 357
"Kingdom of wickedness" (Rome), II,
153
Kings, ancient, I, 63-101, 320-40; Anilaeus, I, 168, III, 63; Asinaeus, I, 168,
II, 213, III, 63; divine qualities, I, 336;
effort to remedy social wrongs, I, 84;
graves, II, 286, 423; and the Great
Sanhedrin, V, 75; Herodian, I, 225, see
also Herod, dynasty; Herod the Great;
Jeconiah, III, 90; obligations of, I, 92;
ritualistic functions, I, 271, 337; status
"under the law," II, 200, VI, 10 f.; and
study of Scripture, VI, 143; weakening
of power, I, 75, 91, 328; see also
Adiabene; Monarchy; Ruler
—— medieval: Arab, III, 61; Bulan,
III, 198, 199, 326; Dhu Nuwas, III,
66 ff.; divine right of, IV, 53 f.; Jewish
V, 130 f.; parable of slaves and, VIII,
36; Samaritan, V, 170 f., 367 f.; Nehardea, III, 62 f.; see also Caliphs;
Emperors; Monarchy; also under
names of individual rulers
"Kings," seven, vowels as, VII, 53, 241
King Solomon's Throne and Hippo-
dromes, mystical midrash, VIII, 18 f.
Kirmanshah, Persia, V, 10
Kislev, month, V, 31, 227
Kitchen, public, II, 273
Knights Templars: employment of Jew-
ish officials, IV, 37; land grants to
Jews, IV, 159
Knowledge: and action, VIII, 345; basis
of, VIII, 79; and love of God, VIII,
114 ff., 337; and revelation, VIII,
113 ff.; see also Gnosticism
Kofer, term, V, 375
Kohelet, see Ecclesiastes
Kohen and Kohanim, I, 149, 272, 274,
413; see also Priests
Kohen Zedek, on ablution, V, 30
Koiné, I, 187, VI, 240
Kol Nidre, prayer, V, 248 f., VI, 125,
389, VII, 78, 131
Kozari, Poland, III, 218
Kozarzów, Poland, III, 218
Koziba, see Bar Kocheba
Kresimir II, king of Croatia, III, 210
Kronos, I, 374
Krum, czar, III, 209
Kufa, Babylonia: Jewish community,
III, 89 f.; mosque, III, 148; Najran
Jews transplanted to, III, 271; school
of Arabic philology, VII, 15, 19, 58,
222; synagogue, III, 134
Kurdistan: Jews in, II, 210; Kurds ex-
cluded from Judaism, II, 222; mes-
sianic movement, V, 202
Kuta, I, 107
Kyrios, divine name, II, 18, 335
Kyrios Christos, cult of, II, 62

L

Labi, Solomon, VIII, 34
Lachish, garrison, I, 327; ostraca, I, 334
Ladino, language, I, 186, VII, 9; litera-
ture, VI, 187
Ladislas Herrmann, king of Poland, III,
219

Labor: free (hired), I, 70, 71, 267-71, 325, 412, IV, 170; breaches of contracts, II, 304; *corvée*, I, 65, III, 192, 236, IV, 56; cost of, and book production, VII, 137; Jewish attitudes toward, I, 9 f., 412, II, 256-60, 416, V, 74; Karaite attitude toward, V, 239 f.; laws, IV, 155, 170; names of workers, I, 408, 409; prestige of skilled workers, IV, 167 f.; ratio between slaves and, I, 325, IV, 154 f.; shortage, II, 263; social status, I, 88; wages, I, 270, 276, 325, II, 257, IV, 170, 321; see also Landlords; Proletariat; Slaves

Lag be-'omer, IV, 145

Lakhmids, dynasty, V, 180; and Ḥimyarites vs. Christians, III, 68; Jewish communities, III, 61

Lamentations, Book of, I, 134, 343, V, 357; commentaries on, VI, 174, 472, VII, 22, 37; midrash on, VI, 164, VII, 82; use of compilations on, VI, 167; use in rituals for Ninth of Ab, VII, 168

Lanciano, Italy, IV, 27

Land: claim of individual Jew to Palestine soil, V, 27, 303; Jewish alienation from, IV, 151-58, 168, 312-14; measurement, III, 163, VIII, 155; Palestinian, conferred by God upon Israelites, I, 88; Persian control, II, 184; purchase of, VI, 147; reclamation, IV, 161 f.; redistribution of, I, 333, II, 104 f., 373; taxation, II, 118, 242, 245, IV, 152, see also Land tax; tenure, IV, 163 f.; see also Agriculture

Landlords: absentee, I, 72, 277, II, 246; Isaiah's warning, I, 68; and landless groups, I, 280, II, 343; and tenants, I, 280, II, 105, 247, 257 f., 416; under Vespasian, I, 265

"Land of Israel," II, 261; see also Palestine

"Land of Onias," I, 394

Landownership: accumulation, III, 182; continuity, III, 31; division into ever-smaller parcels, I, 280; expansion, IV, 13; expropriation, I, 68 ff., 85, 265, II, 343; Gregory's attitude toward, III, 244; by individual or clan, I, 74; law of *siqariqon,* II, 104, 372; real estate mortgages, I, 109; responsibilities of, IV, 222; sales and leases to non-Jews, II, 124 f., 261; as source of political

power, IV, 163 f.; of Spanish Jewry, IV, 159 f.

Landscapes, VIII, 229

Landsmannschaften, I, 125

Land tax, III, 162 f.; burdensome effect of, III, 168; imposed by Muslims, III, 96

Land tenure, I, 277; see also Landlords

Langobards, III, 243 f.; and Jewish law, III, 244; persecution of Jews, III, 32

Language: approaches to study of, VII, 34; in international trade, IV, 173 f.; basic laws of, VII, 40; Bible translations, II, 142 ff., 386 f., see also Bible; classification of, VI, 226; historical grammar of biblical, VII, 242; Jews' use of various, I, 4, 19, II, 141 ff., 145 ff., 385; legal, in Talmud, II, 300, 302; Neo-Punic and Hebrew, I, 374; of Samaritans, II, 340; "seventy languages," VIII, 217; tablets inscribed in six different, I, 52; talmudic, VII, 28-32, 231 f.; see also Philology; also under respective languages, e.g., Hebrew

Laodicaea, VIII, 241; Council of, II, 188, VII, 128; earthquake, III, 10

Laographia, I, 190

La Palloza, Spain, inscriptions, IV, 33

Last Supper, II, 71, 359

Lateran Council: First, IV, 7, 235 f., 238
—— Second, IV, 7, 238
—— Third, IV, 8, 10, 236, 240; on employment of Christian servants, IV, 15; and Philip II Augustus, IV, 62; on testimony of Christians and Jews, IV, 16
—— Fourth, IV, 13; on practice of physicians, VIII, 231; imposition of tithes, IV, 154

Latin Kingdom of Jerusalem, IV, 106-16, 294-99, VI, 434; armed pilgrims, IV, 131; dissolution of, V, 203; new institutional forms, IV, 114 ff.; status of Jews, IV, 114 ff.

Latin language: Bible, VI, 272, 292; in Eastern provinces, II, 300; in scientific literature, VIII, 171, 243 f., 364, 403; in Sicily, IV, 21

Law: Ancient: Byzantine, III, 11, 177, 185-90, 318 f.
—— Egyptian: codified, II, 300
—— Graeco-Roman: and Jewish legal adjustments, II, 415; sanctions im-

Law (*Continued*)
posed on temple robbery, I, 215, 393
—— Hellenistic: codified, II, 300; influence upon Roman law, II, 303; Jewish indebtedness to, II, 302, 431
—— Jewish, I, 82; binding force of every detail, II, 138; bridging irreconcilable contradictions, I, 181; Canaanite origin of the "casuistic," I, 80; ceremonial or ritualistic, I, 81, 142, 196 f., 227, 359, II, 307-9, 433; Christian attack on, II, 134; commandment to "ransom captives," I, 259; controversy under John Hyrcanus, I, 227; Diaspora Jewry governed by Palestinian, I, 201, 221, 245, II, 320; divine origin, I, 7, II, 319; and egalitarian trends, I, 48, 83, 313; eternity of, II, 161; exilic ideals, I, 163; forgotten and restored, II, 37, 206; formulated partly outside Palestine, I, 162; Halakhah, II, 293, 298, 299, 305, 316, 429; idealistic slant of biblical, I, 76; impact of the, I, 10, 140-48, 359-62; influence on Roman codes, III, 231 f.; invalidated in messianic age? II, 73, 161, 298, 360, 365, V, 124, 347, 358; "is not in heaven," II, 139; Jesus came to fulfill, II, 67, 69; Jesus' disciples' adherence to, II, 74, 78, 361; on just prices, II, 255; Karaite expansion of, V, 224; moral, I, 80, 81, 227, II, 307-9, 328, 433; needed in exile, I, 140, 143; of Pharisees, II, 37 f., 45; Philo's restatement, II, 253, 415; preexistence of, VI, 8; pre-Mosaic, II, 136, 382; proselytism, I, 181; protection of basic prayers, VII, 101; recodification, VI, 76-84; recognized no special privileges, I, 75; reinterpretation of, V, 54, 61; religion and, I, 77-84, 327-32, II, 78 f.; of Sadducees, II, 36, 37; Samaritan *ḥillukh*, II, 32; sanctified daily pursuits, I, 9; study of, imperative, II, 120, 121, 251, 269, 275, 279; talmudic religion and, II, 215-321, 408-36; teaching to Gentiles forbidden, II, 430; term Torah in Jeremiah, I, 331; universality, I, 204; *see also* Moses; Pentateuch; Religion
—— Roman: VI, 4, III, 35, 49, 174, 231, *see also* Justinian; Hellenistic and Jewish influence, II, 303; Jewish independence of, II, 299, 429 f.; on usury, IV, 199 f.
—— Sassanian, II, 181, 299, 301, 303, 429 f.
—— Medieval: civil, V, 57 f., 224 f., VIII, 144; feudal, in Spain, IV, 41; Frankish and Langobard, influenced by Jewish, III, 244, 252; local, settlement of disputes by ordeal, IV, 40 f.; on segregation, V, 79 f.
—— Jewish: and agriculture, IV, 156 ff.; applied by pietists, VIII, 52; on attending houses of worship, III, 302; attitude of mystics toward, VIII, 17 ff.; business, IV, 185, VI, 71, *see also* Trade; on castration, IV, 192; Christian repudiation of, V, 122 ff.; codes, V, 212, 261, VI, 25 f., *see also* Codes, legal; compendia of, as source of responsa, VI, 118; conflict for control over, V, 211 ff.; consolidation of traditions, VI, 16-27, 327-32; on corporal punishment, IV, 261; on disposition of land, IV, 158; on divorce (*q.v.*), IV, 20; early Western books, VI, 48 ff., 66, 72 ff., 84 ff., 113 ff.; equation of Oral and Scriptural, V, 181; on family, VI, 321; formulation of, VI, 212; geonim and, V, 52, *see also* Geonim and gaonate; immutability of, VI, 144 f., 371; international uniformity of, IV, 174, 176; Karaites and, V, 230 ff., 240-51; of the kingdom (state), IV, 270, V, 77 f., 332; on land ownership, IV, 160 f.; and Langobard law, III, 244; Maimonides on study of, V, 76; on marriage to captive woman, III, 89, V, 8; and mathematics, VIII, 149, 153 ff.; and medicine, VIII, 238 f., 253; method of analogy, VII, 236; and occult practices, VIII, 55; philosophy of, VI, 141-51, VIII, 70 ff., 123 ff.; and *piyyuṭim*, VII, 103; preoccupation with, VIII, 143 f.; and prophecy, VIII, 132; rational, V, 325, VI, 142 ff., VIII, 117; reign of, VI, 3-151, 321-98; respect of German pietists for, VIII, 49 f.; and ritual, VII, 122; Samau'al on, V, 100; and scientific fact, VIII, 139 f.; sectarian deviations from, V, 189 ff.; and segregation, V, 79; sources of, VI, 244; support of, in the Aggadah, VI, 178 f.; unbroken con-

tinuity of, V, 3, *see also* Tradition; uniformity, VI, 108, 117 ff., 148 ff.; *see also* Judges; Jurisprudence; Jurists; Oral Law; Rabbis and Rabbinate; Talmud
—— Muslim, V, 18, 210, 213, VI, 63 ff., 78, 94; analogy in, VII, 236; biographical material, VI, 24; on business transactions, IV, 185 f., 351; civil and religious equality of minorities, III, 132, IV, 225; codification, VI, 107, 363; concubinage and, IV, 195; on *dar as-sulḥ*, III, 130; effect of Church and Roman law on, III, 174; foreign elements in, VI, 324; on interfaith partnerships, IV, 331; interpretation of, VI, 6-16; and Jewish *heqqesh*, V, 213; on public office, IV, 226; reign of, VI, 149 ff.; and religious persecution, III, 124; schools of, VI, 16 ff.; on slaves, IV, 195; on synagogues, III, 135; system of responsa, VI, 110; on usury, IV, 197
—— Ostrogothic, III, 25 f.
—— Syro-Christian, II, 303 f., 432, VI, 4 ff., 322 ff.
—— Visigothic, III, 36, 245 f.; on Christian servants of Jews, IV, 314 f.; *see also Leges Visigothorum; Lex Romana Visigothorum*
"Law of the kingdom," V, 77 f.
Laws, adjudicated, *see Halakhot qeṣubot*
Lawyers, *see* Jurists
Laziness, charge of, against Jews, V, 132 f.
Leadership: centered in Palestine, I, 247; Jewish, of Semitic world, I, 210; revolutionary, I, 86
—— communal, V, 3-81, 293-325; attitude toward magic practices, VIII, 54; conservatism of, VIII, 67; dilemma of philosophers among, VIII, 68 ff.; Karaite, V, 237 f., 261; poetic laudation of, VII, 147; scholars, II, 120, 197, 204-8 *passim*, 291, 403, V, 179, VIII, 263 f.; *see also* Elders; Geonim and gaonate; Rabbanites; Rabbis and rabbinate; Scholars and scholarship
Leah, and Rachel, VII, 188
Leander, archbishop, III, 36
Leap year, V, 246; cycles, VIII, 204 f.; proclamation of, VIII, 187, 193 f., 200

Learning: centers of, III, 102, 104, VII, 30; lack of, and sectarianism, V, 373; professionalization of, IV, 221, V, 76; rabbinic, IV, 215 f.; specialization of, VI, 72; transmission of aggadic, VI, 173; upsurge of, VI, 48; *see also* Academies; Education; Scholars and scholarship
Lease, Hebrew-Arabic, IV, 320
Leeds fragment, II, 29, 339
Legal problems: meaning of words involving, VII, 13; sermons instigated by, VI, 169
Legal status of Jews, *see* Rights, legal
Leges Visigothorum (*Liber judicum*), III, 36; lack of clarity, III, 44; regulations re Jews, III, 42
Leicester, England, "Jewry Wall," IV, 281
Leningrad fragment of Palestinian Talmud, II, 13, 333
Leo I, pope, III, 5
Leo IV, pope, IV, 90
Leo VII, pope, IV, 6
Leo, Roman emperor, II, 304
Leo III (the Isaurian), Byzantine emperor, III, 175 f.; *Basilika*, III, 186; *Eklogé*, III, 177, 185 f.; suppression of Judaism, III, 220
Leo VI (the Wise), Byzantine emperor, VI, 154; *Basilika*, III, 181; "Book of the Prefect," IV, 170, 183, 321 f.; *Epanagogé*, III, 186, 318; *Novella* 55, III, 180 f., 186, 318; ordinance re Scripture reading, III, 189
Leo Mung, patriarch of Ochrida, III, 210
Leon, Spain, IV, 28; false Messiah, V, 199
Leonardo Fibonacci of Pisa, VIII, 156, 158, 352
Leontopolis, Egypt: district, II, 12; temple, I, 14, 219, 220, 350, 394, V, 123
Leo of Naples, VI, 418
Leopold V, duke of Austria, IV, 72
Lepers and leprosy, I, 275, II, 249, V, 133, 250; Maimonides on, VI, 179
Lerida Spain, IV, 37, 247
Lèse majesté, I, 92, 336
Letter of Aristeas, I, 172, 185, 196, 251, 261, 384
Letters, Lachish, I, 334; *see also* El-Amarna; Responsa

Levi, house or tribe of, I, 274, 318, V, 202; genealogies, I, 329; redeemer from, II, 351

Levi, R., II, 138, 254, 312

Leviathan, V, 148, VIII, 10

Levi b. Ḥamma, R., VI, 407

Levi b. Ḥayta, R., II, 424

Levi b. Jephet, V, 233, 241 f., VI, 248

Levi b. Sissai, R., II, 268, 281, VI, 36

Levirate marriage, I, 79, II, 231, 411, V, 93, 216, 224, 332, VI, 65, 81, 138

Levites: ancient, I, 413, VI, 10, VII, 259; adherents to Mosaic religion, I, 59, 414; modern, I, 414; numbers of, in Palestine, I, 272 f., 413; in Pharisaic leadership, II, 117; relations with priests, I, 329, 362; tithe for, I, 280; see also Priests and priesthood

Leviticus, Book of: explanation, VII, 22; fragment, I, 331; as text for priests, II, 275

Lexicography, VII, 12-32, 223-33; Arabic, VII, 26; biblical, VII, 229 f.; see also Dictionaries

Lex Romana Burgundionum, III, 49

Lex Romana Visigothorum (Breviarium Alarici), III, 35, 49

Libanius, II, 188, 414

Liberalism: departure from traditional Judaism, I, 27; and nationalism, I, 28, 361

Liber judicum, see Leges Visigothorum

Libraries: Canaanite, I, 306, see also Ras Shamra; Christian and Muslim, compared, IV, 28; mosque, VII, 138, VIII, 246; school and congregational, VII, 138

Licentiousness, fought by rabbis, II, 217

Life: attachment to, I, 12; divine attribute, VIII, 96 ff.; Jewish way of, I, 174, II, 216, 217; and kindling of fire, V, 283

Life after death, see Immortality of the soul; Resurrection

Life span, II, 220, 408, VIII, 259, 336; Maimonidean responsum on, VI, 112

Light: creation of, VIII, 94 f.; and darkness, V, 106 f., VI, 305 f., VIII, 34 f.; divine Glory, VIII, 129; kindling and burning, V, 216 f., 223, 244, 283; prayer, VI, 126; principle of, VIII, 22; Sabbath, V, 269, VI, 16, 389, VII, 72; on Zion, VII, 115 f.

Lilith, II, 19, VIII, 10

Limoges, France: burning of ruler's effigy, IV, 92; sufferings of Jewish community, VI, 219

Lincoln, England, "Jews' court," IV, 281

Linen industry, I, 257, 408, II, 248

Linguistics, see Philology

"Linon," false Messiah of, V, 199

Lipit-Ishtar, code, I, 327

Lisbon, Portugal, IV, 132, 305

Literature: Jewish, I, 178; Al-Ḥarizi's literary criticism, VII, 186; apologetical, I, 195-99; historical, I, 25-26, 100, 340, VI, 29 f., 188-219, 416-33; Musiv style, VII, 202; poetry and belles-lettres, VII, 135-213, 286-321; popularization of, I, 141; proverbial, I, 141; in Renaissance of Islam, VII, 60 f.; sayings of Jesus traced in, II, 67; scientific, VI, 169; talmudic, II, 294-98, 425-29; translation of major works, I, 52, 187; see also Midrash; Old Testament; Talmud; also under respective branches, e.g., Poetry

—— Muslim: isra'iliyat, VI, 168; Kalilah ve-Dimnah, VII, 189; works on poetic art, VII, 316 f.

Litigation: business, settlement by compromise, IV, 176 f.; Byzantine laws on, III, 190; excommunication for, V, 5; exilarchic judges, V, 14 f.; Jewish, formula for, III, 195; Judeo-Christian, III, 190, IV, 15 f., 41 f., 49, 69, 78; oath in, IV, 41 f., 253, 255; rights of Jews in Barcelona IV, 41 f.; rules of evidence, IV, 277, 281; and state courts, V, 5; see also Courts; Judges; Oaths; Witnesses

"Little Lord," VIII, 16

Liturgy: Christian, VII, 68, 84 f.; anti-semitism in, V, 352; Jewish influences on, VII, 84 f.; political overtones, VII, 266; written transmission, VII, 258

—— Hebrew, II, 282, VI, 244; accuracy of halakhic contents, VII, 274; adjustments, II, 182; blame for changes in, VI, 42; compilation and crystallization of, VII, 63 ff., 245 ff.; disparities in ancient sources, VII, 109; dynamic approach to, VII, 131 ff.; efforts at unification, VII, 68 ff., 87, 279; incorporation of improvised prayers, VII, 86; Judeo-Christian interrelations, II, 134, VII, 84 f., 252; juristic-liturgical treatises, VII, 105-24, 271-81; Karaite,

V, 247 f., 392, 404 f.; linguistic difficulties, VII, 66 ff.; Maimonides' codification of, V, 28, VII, 118-21, 279 f.; memorizers, VII, 85 ff.; messianic theme in, V, 150 ff.; music, II, 8, 155, 330, VII, 125-31, 281-85; and mystical literature, VIII, 12; Ninth of Ab, V, 152; opponents of standardization, VII, 106 ff.; Samaritan modifications, II, 340; talmudic latitude on, VII, 108 f.; traditional, preservation of, VII, 106 ff.; see also Piyyuṭim; Poetry, liturgical; Prayers; Psalms; Ritual

Lives of the Prophets, II, 20

Loans, I, 109; contracts, I, 261; foreclosure and bondage, I, 161; see also Moneylending; Usury

Loan words, Greek, VI, 355, VII, 141, VIII, 229; Latin, VI, 355, VII, 141; Persian, VII, 141, VIII, 229; see also under the respective languages

Logic: and faith, VIII, 83 f.; and religious philosophy, VIII, 67 f.

Logos: doctrine of, I, 202, 392, V, 121, VIII, 101, 129; mediation through, VIII, 91; Philonic, V, 380; "shadow" equated with, VIII, 273; "son," VIII, 96

"Logos Christology" of Paul, II, 81, 364

Lombards, derogatory term, IV, 207

London, riot involving Jews, IV, 124

Longchamp, William, bishop of Ely, IV, 127 f.

Lord of Hosts, I, 61, 128; old concept of, I, 137

Lord's Prayer, II, 84, 138; and prayer for mourners, VII, 67; see also Qaddish

Lost tribes, see Ten Tribes

Lot, patriarch, VI, 39; names of wife and daughter, VI, 170; story of, V, 90

Lothar II, emperor, IV, 11

Lotharingia, VI, 48, 344

Louis I (the Pious), emperor, IV, 18, 44; and Church leaders, IV, 51; controversy over succession, IV, 52; and Jewish slave trade, IV, 193 f.; privileges to Jews, IV, 48-53, 260 ff., V, 62; trade charters, IV, 48 f.

Louis II, emperor, IV, 25 f., 61

Louis VI, king of France, IV, 59

Louis VII, king of France, IV, 61; outlawry of relapse to Judaism, IV, 61

Louis the Child, emperor, IV, 65 f.

Love, Canaanite goddess of, I, 363

Love poems, VII, 157 ff., 212 f.

Loving-kindness, religious duty, I, 175

Loyalty: aspersions on Jewish, II, 398, IV, 37 f., 55, 265, V, 131 f.; to the community, V, 4, 162, VIII, 263; division of, V, 162; oath of, IV, 49, 163, V, 35 f.; political, V, 293 f.

Lucca, Italy, IV, 26

Lucena, Spain, III, 34, V, 298; academy, V, 49, VI, 84; Book of Deeds, IV, 316; the hundred benedictions, VII, 110; Jewish community, III, 109, 124, 170; scholars, VI, 84 f., 149

Lucian of Samosata, II, 21

Lucifer, V, 132

Lucretia, VI, 232

Luke, Saint, I, 170, II, 23, 362

—— Gospel of, II, 66, 72, 73, 86, 355, 357

Lukuas-Andreas, Cyrenian king, II, 95, 370

Lulab ritual, II, 119

Lull, Raymond, V, 89

Lunar calendar, II, 125, 206; accepted by Jews, I, 44; see also Calendar; Moon

Lunel: academy, VI, 87 ff., 106, VII, 54; Jewish population, IV, 48

Lusius Quietus, II, 96, 371

Lute, VII, 210

Luther, Martin, I, 9, VIII, 83

Luxury items: of gold and silver, IV, 212; growing demand for, IV, 172; trade in, IV, 214

Lydia, I, 102, 216

Lynching, II, 85, V, 57; legalized, I, 239, 402; as punishment for sexual transgression, I, 402, II, 365, III, 143, 300

Lyons, France: charter for merchants of, IV, 48, 50; under Duke Girard, IV, 55; fairs, IV, 175; false Messiah, V, 199

Lysias, I, 217, 394

Lysimachus of Jerusalem, I, 185

M

Maacah, I, 66

Ma'arri, Abu'l Ala al-, Arab poet and

Ma'arri, Abu'l Ala al- (*Continued*)
skeptic, V, 103 f., VIII, 124; on unity
of mankind, VIII, 263

Ma'arufiah, term, IV, 185, 331

Ma'aseh ha-geonim, IV, 183, VI, 65

Ma'aser, biblical tithe, IV, 13

Macarius Magnus, II, 391

"Maccabean" martyrs, I, 230, 232, VI, 167

Maccabee, name, I, 369

Maccabees, house of: archaizing efforts, I, 225; coins, I, 225, 235, 369, 401, II, 36; conquests, I, 224, 250; corruption, I, 284; despotism, I, 223; drive for access to Mediterranean, I, 255; funerary monuments, II, 14; Hasmonean letter, I, 395; internal conflicts, I, 217, 237, 397, 401; Jewish vitality enhanced by, I, 166; Karaite condemnation of, V, 256; and lamp for Ḥanukkah, I, 235; priestly family, I, 271; priestly messiah, V, 356; in rabbinic literature, II, 139; significance in sociopolitical controversies, I, 399; zealots, I, 165

—— revolt by, I, 201, 216 f., 229 ff.; chronology, I, 394; first "war of religion," I, 233, II, 38, IV, 95 f.; and Hellenism, I, 166, 167; Jewish soldiers, II, 42, 94, 98; manumissions resulting from, I, 259; miracle tales, V, 407; objectives, II, 38; and possession of Bibles, VII, 86

—— Books of, I, 197, 232, 377; Book of the Hasmonean Children, VI, 188 f., 416 f., 484 f.

Macedon, I, 190, 234

Macedonia, III, 186, IV, 107

Macedonius, patriarch of Constantinople, III, 6

Mâcon, First Council of, IV, 188

Madaïn (Ctesiphon), III, 136

Madda', term, VI, 378

Magdalos, Egypt, I, 111

Magdeburg, Germany: merchants' guild, IV, 184 f.; monastic privilege over Jews, IV, 65

Maghariya, V, 192

Maghribi, Samuel b. Moses al-, V, 234; on duties of priests and judges, V, 237 f.; laws of incest, V, 243; liturgical poems, V, 249; on profanation of women, V, 240

Magi, I, 141, II, 181, 183, 190, 317, 347, VI, 302, VIII, 46

Magic arts, VI, 103; charges re, V, 96, 132; Christians' belief in Jewish powers, II, 189, 401; connection with alchemy, VIII, 224; distinguished from miracles, VIII, 130; and medicine, V, 334, VIII, 233 ff.; and mysticism, VIII, 27 ff., 46; opposition to, I, 82, 87, 139, II, 17, VIII, 234; popular beliefs and practices, I, 329, II, 15-23, 336 f., 390; protection from supernatural forces, VIII, 4; and science, VIII, 274; square, VIII, 354; sympathetic, IV, 92; texts, I, 139, 358, II, 156, 390, VIII, 233, 394; and women, I, 347, II, 21; *see also* Incantations and exorcisms

Magister judaeorum, official, IV, 49, V, 63

Magna Graecia, II, 392

Magna Mater, cult of, II, 168

Magyars: "black Ugrians," III, 204; Jewish settlements among, III, 206 ff.; and Khazars, III, 211 f.; *see also* Hungary

Mahbub, *see* Agapius

Mahdi, Muslim concept, V, 163, 185

Maḥoza, Babylonian city, II, 199, 205, 242, III, 58 f.; upper classes, II, 277

Maimon b. Joseph, father of Maimonides, III, 291 f., VI, 58; interpretation of Psalm 90, VIII, 126

Maimonides, *see* Abraham Maimonides; Moses b. Maimon

Maimuni, Abraham b. Moses, *see* Abraham Maimonides

Maimuni, Moses, *see* Moses b. Maimon

Majus, taxation of, III, 191

Makhir, Babylonian scholar, IV, 45, 47

Makhir b. Abba Mari, *Yalqut ha-Makhiri,* VI, 404

Makhir b. Yehudah: law collection, VI, 74 f.; lexicographical work, VI, 362, VII, 30

Makkot, tractate, VI, 53

Malabar spices, I, 321

Malachi, Book of, I, 114, 127, 151, 154, 158, 367; rejection of divorce, I, 114

Malalas, Byzantine chronicler: legend of Solomon and Tadmor, III, 62; on Samaritan delegation to king of Persia,

III, 17; on uprising of Antioch Jewry, III, 6

Malchiah, I, 352

Malchus Kleodemus, II, 31

Maledictions: in liturgical poetry, VII, 179; *see also* Curses

Males, preponderance over females in Jewish settlements, III, 252

Malik ar-Ramli, V, 182, 196

Malikians, *see* Ramlites

Malik ibn Ajlan, III, 65

Malik ibn 'Anas, jurist, VI, 94; on intermarriage, III, 142, on vocalized Qur'an texts, VI, 244

Malix ibn Dinar, Muslim mystic, VIII, 112

Malikites, III, 123, VI, 11, 16

Malka, R., V, 15

Malko of Palmyra, II, 407

Malvern, England, VIII, 174

Mameluks, III, 172

Ma'mun, al-, *see* Al-Ma'mun

Ma'mun al-Amiri, Egyptian vizier, VIII, 248

Mamzer: exclusion of, I, 147; term, II, 409

Man: dignity of, as created in God's image, I, 49; influence of stars on, VIII, 175 ff.; love of God, VIII, 115 ff.; microcosm, VIII, 103; relation to God and the universe, VIII, 108 ff.; *see also* Individuals and Individualism; Mankind

Manasseh, king of Judah, I, 78, 79, VI, 122, 143

Mancosi, term, IV, 212

Mandaeans and Mandaism, II, 26, 51, 348, 433, III, 160, VIII, 276

Manethon priest, I, 36, 195, 304, III, 149

Mani, prophet, II, 178; Ibn Daud re, VI, 208

Manichaeans and Manichaeism, II, 26, 178, III, 82, 177, 186, 242, V, 344, VIII, 31, 296; as "heresy," V, 107 f., VI, 171; strictures on the Old Testament, VI, 298, 303; survivals of dualism, V, 105 f., VIII, 46

Mankah, *see* Kankah

Mankind: early history of, VI, 192; emergence of concept of, VIII, 263; history in terms of spiritual evolution, VI, 228; liturgical poems on

nature of, VII, 180; poets' concern with problems of, VII, 176

Manna, miracle of, VI, 269, 300

"Man of War," God as, I, 46, 61

Manṣur b. Sahlan, VIII, 246

Manuel I (Comnenus), Byzantine emperor, III, 184, VI, 434; *Novella* 55, III, 195

Manufactures and trades, II, 248 ff.; *see also* Industry

Manuscripts: illuminated, VIII, 246; mutilation of, VII, 137; Samaritan, V, 372

Ma'onite synagogue in Tiberias, II, 199, 404

Maqna, Mohammed's treaty with the Jews of, III, 79

Maqqari, al-, III, 148

Maqrizi, VI, 243, VIII, 161; on 'Anan, V, 219; on conversion of Copts to Islam, III, 123; on Muslim libraries, VII, 138; on synagogues, III, 106, 135

Mar Abba, *see* Abba, Mar

"Mar" b. Rabina, VII, 75

Marcella, wife of Porphyry, II, 159

Marcian, Roman emperor of the East: Monophysites' petition to, III, 5; rescript of 452, III, 234

Marciana, Saint, III, 8

Marcion, heresiarch, II, 73, 167, 394, V, 107

Marcionites and Marcionism, II, 408, III, 209, VI, 298, VIII, 16, 31, 42; *see also* Gnosticism

Marcus Rutilius Lupus, II, 95

Marcus Tittius, II, 202

Mardan Farukh, Pehlevi author, V, 105 f., 121, VI, 271; biblical criticism, VI, 303 ff.; *The Decisive Solution of Doubts*, VI, 301 ff.

Marduk, god, I, 93, 105, 327, 349

Marḥeshvan, month, V, 31, 227

Mari, palace of, I, 77, 300

Mari ha-Levi, gaon, VI, 446

Marinus, Jewish thinker at Athenian academy, VIII, 241

Marisa, Palestine, I, 224

Marissa, Sidonian colony of, I, 374

Mark, Saint, II, 68; identification with Syriac Marcus, VI, 458

—— Gospel of, II, 64, 66, 70, 71, 72, 73, 357, 359, 364

Marqa, Samaritan poet, II, 340 f., VII,
64; quoted, II, 31
Mar Rab Huna, see Huna, Mar Rab
Mar Rab Raba, see Rab Raba, Mar
Marrakesh, Morocco, III, 108
Marranos and Marranism, III, 44, IV,
6, 293
Marriage: abstention from, II, 209; 'Anan's rules, V, 217 f., 221 f.; bridal sheet,
V, 242; of converts, III, 112, IV, 255 f.;
customs, II, 218, VI, 122 f., 130, 391;
of divorcées, V, 18; during mourning,
VI, 120; early, I, 265, II, 219, 238, 408;
economic considerations, II, 220, 409;
good luck sign, VIII, 184; incest, I,
146, II, 229 ff., 411; Karaite and Rabbanite, V, 265 f., 413; levirate, I, 79,
II, 231, 411, V, 93, 216, 224, 332;
Maimonides on, VI, 179; matriarchal
forms, I, 310; monogamy or polygamy,
I, 112, 347, II, 223-29, 409 f., VI, 135 f.,
393 f.; morality demanded, II, 221 ff.,
228; presentation of ring, V, 283;
priestly, I, 376, II, 235, V, 240; prohibited degrees in, I, 146, 275, V, 92 f.;
promotion of, II, 127; with proselytes
and with heathens, I, 376, II, 232;
rabbinic law, V, 134, 190, VI, 81 f.,
134 ff., 393 f.; scholar's eligibility, II,
235; sectarianism and laws of, II, 408,
V, 190; settlement, II, 220, 303; with
a slave, III, 89; substitute, II, 231; in
Talmud, I, 275, II, 217-23, 408 f.;
within tribe, I, 146, 147, 360; see also
Bride; Bridegroom; Divorce; Levirate
marriage; Wedding
—— interfaith, I, 114, 147, 163, 189,
361, 376, II, 223, 232 f., 401 f., 411 f.,
III, 10, IV, 9, 52, 114, 241, V, 100;
Byzantine law on, III, 189; in France,
III, 50; Jewish attitude toward, III,
143; legislation on, III, 36 f., 42, 143,
189; Muslim attitude toward, III,
299 f.; and preponderance of males,
III, 252; religious laws vs., III, 142
—— contracts (ketubot), I, 113, II, 236,
IV, 195 f., V, 265 f., VI, 85, 128; and
biblical law, VI, 24 f.; and loans, VI,
132; pledge against polygamy, VI,
138
Mar Samuel, see Samuel, Mar
Marseilles, France, VI, 60
Martel, Charles, III, 199
Martha, daughter of Boethos, I, 262

Marthad-ilan Ahsan, see Dhu Nuwas
Martial, II, 156
Martini, Raymond, II, 296, 427, VI, 196,
VIII, 33; compilation of aggadic sav-
ings, VI, 171 f.; Pugio fidei, V, 357
Martyrologies, I, 190, II, 100; in folk
plays, V, 116; of Jewish people, VIII,
345; use of, in sermons, VI, 167 f.
Martyrs and martyrdom: Christian, I,
230, 399, 400, II, 167, 383, 394;
"heathen," I, 190, 248, 381, II, 108
—— Jewish, I, 230-33, 399-400, II, 100,
139, 215, III, 39, 57, 125, VI, 193 f.;
child martyrs, IV, 135 f.; in Crusades, IV, 95 f., 103 f., 133, 138, 144-
47, 218, 309-11; first urge to, I, 48;
four martyrs, VIII, 19; glorification of,
VIII, 127; Isaac prototype of, II, 383;
Pharisees, II, 100, 371; records of, VI,
234; seven Maccabean, I, 230, 232;
the Ten, I, 231, II, 370, IV, 285, VIII,
283; see also Massacres of Jews; Per-
secutions; Pogroms
Mar 'Uqba, see 'Uqba, Mar
Marut, fallen angel, III, 265
Marwan II, caliph, III, 288
Mar Zutra, see Zutra, Mar
Masada, I, 252, II, 370, VI, 193
Masarjawaih, Jewish medical writer,
VIII, 236, 256; medical works, VIII,
242 f., 393
Masawaih, Christian doctor, VIII, 234
Masbotheans, sect, II, 348
Masgeda (mosque), VI, 13
Masha'allah, Jewish mathematician,
III, 99 f., 152, VIII, 148; astronomic
works, VIII, 166 f.; building plans for
Baghdad, IV, 170, VIII, 59
Mashal le-mah ha-dabar domeh, para-
ble, VI, 167
Mashiah, biblical term, V, 157; see also
Messiah and messianism
Mashqin, tractate, VI, 62
Maslama al-Majriti, VIII, 355, 363
Masliah b. Elijah ibn al-Bazaq, R., of
Sicily, VII, 30
Masons, IV, 170, 321, VIII, 159
Masorah, II, 145, 386, III, 72, V, 176,
195 f., VI, 20, VII, 28; details of, VI,
247; final formulation, VI, 251; spell-
ing and pronunciation (ketib and
qeri), VI, 293, 443; Syriac, VI, 443;
and systematic rules of grammar, VII,
32

Masorites, I, 336; contribution to Jewish life, VI, 253; detailed monographs, VI, 252; early generations, VI, 424; linguistic decisions and meaning of words, VII, 13; Palestinian, VI, 245 f.; principles of Creation, VIII, 15; refinement of biblical text, VI, 249-55, 449-53; on the seven "kings," VII, 53; symbols for cantillation, VII, 126 f.; Tiberian school, V, 305, VI, 253, 262

Massacres of Jews: commemoration of, IV, 89 ff., 144 ff.; in England, IV, 124 ff.; in Germany, IV, 104 f.; memorial services, VII, 99; reaction to, IV, 139 ff.; theme of liturgical poets, VII, 179; see also 'Aqedot; Pogroms

Masses, the: adherence to the commandments, VIII, 81; Aramic speech replaced by Arabic, VII, 67, 223; attitude toward, V, 238 f.; exploitation of, I, 84; illiterate, V, 394, see also 'Am ha-areş; inequalities and suffering, I, 276, V, 238 ff.; obstacle to professionalized medicine, VIII, 232; and religious philosophy, VIII, 67 ff., 137; suspicion of merchants, IV, 184

Mass hysteria: in age of Crusades, IV, 100 ff.; and mass suicide, IV, 104; and messianism, V, 167

Mas'udi, Arab geographer, V, 84; on chess, VIII, 356; on Khazar tribunal, III, 200; "Meadows of Gold," III, 182, VIII, 215; popular saying on the mawali, III, 149

Materialism, VIII, 78 ff.

Mater synagogae, II, 240, 413

Mathematics: Jewish students of, II, 306 f., 433, VIII, 146-60, 349-57; and astronomy, VIII, 167; definition, VIII, 144 f.; Kaspi's program of education, VIII, 361; in Mishnat ha-Middot, II, 307, 433; and music, VII, 209; orthodox objectors to, VIII, 142

Matilde, queen of England, IV, 81

Mating, festival of, I, 294

Matrand, Saracen "king," IV, 46

Matriarchal society, I, 43, 310; surviving vestige of, VIII, 275

Mattathias of Modein, I, 229, 231

Matter, VIII, 101; eternality of, II, 311, VIII, 94; and form, VIII, 114, 325; primordial, VIII, 87 ff., 93 f., 322 ff.

Matthew, Saint, II, 66

—— Gospel of, II, 68, 72, 73, 74, 359, V, 348

Matthew of Edessa, Armenian chronicler, III, 184

Mattiah b. Heresh, II, 56

Maulana Jalalu'ddin Rumi, Muslim opponent of rationalism, VIII, 83

Mauretania, I, 169; see also Morocco

Maurice, Byzantine emperor, II, 399, III, 17; persecution of Jews, III, 19, 236

Mausolea, see Tombs

Mawali, Arabic term, III, 148 f.

Maximinus, Roman emperor, II, 400

Maximus, Valerius, II, 24

Maximus Confessor, VI, 304

Mayence, Germany: academy, IV, 7, VI, 74 f.; 'aqedot, IV, 103 ff., 144 f., 292, 309 f., VI, 193; attempts to protect Jews of, IV, 99; burghers and Jews, IV, 100; congregation of ghosts, IV, 103 f., 292, VIII, 46; Diet of, IV, 130; expulsion of Jews, IV, 26, 73; Jewish community, IV, 66, 103 f., VI, 48; martyrdom of a Jewess, IV, 96; pun on name, IV, 67; residence permits, V, 69; return of Jewish refugees, IV, 116; "sages of," VII, 30

Mayence Anonymus, IV, 102, 287 f., 290, VI, 218

"May he rest in peace," formula, II, 333

Mazdaism, see Parsees and Parsiism

Mazdak and Mazdakites, II, 182, 222, 231, 251, 409, III, 55, 69, 255

Meal-offering, I, 129

Meals, blessings associated with, VII, 115

Me'am zar, term, II, 409

Meat, I, 254; and milk, VI, 258 f.; prohibitions on, III, 42, 51, 84, IV, 61, V, 92 f., 218, 249; tax, VIII, 386

Meaux, Abbey of, IV, 204; Council of, IV, 18

Meborakh, nagid, V, 41 f.

Mecca, V, 86; flood, and letter from Caliph, VII, 4; Jewish community, III, 263; Ka'aba stone, III, 86, V, 86; Mohammed's relations with Christians and Jews in, III, 76 f.; pilgrims to, III, 88, 302, VIII, 211; turning toward, during prayer, III, 296

Mechanics, VIII, 159 f.; Muslim knowledge of, VIII, 356

Media, I, 102, V, 178, 183, 223; association with Babylonia, II, 205; "remnant" in, I, 106

Mediators, see Intermediaries

Medicine: ancient, II, 306–7, 412, VIII, 251
—— medieval, VIII, 221–66; 384–405;
'Anan on practice of, V, 259, 282;
Arab historians and biographers, VIII,
254; book ascribed to Ibn Ezra, VIII,
361; discrimination in practice of, III,
146 f.; Jewish reliance on non-Jewish
authors, VIII, 253 ff., 265; and theology, VIII, 259; toleration of study of,
VIII, 265; tradition vs. experience,
VIII, 234 ff.; see also Physicians; also
under individual doctors, e.g., Asaph;
Moses b. Maimon

Medievalism: incipient, II, 172-214, 396-
407; Babylonian supremacy, II, 204-9,
405; Christianity's authority after
Constantine, II, 172; decline of Hellenism, II, 173-75, 396; intergroup
relations, II, 187-91, 400-402, 427;
Jews' new legal status, II, 176-87,
396 ff.; local autonomy, II, 198-204,
403 f.; in Roman and Sassanian em-
pires, II, 172 ff., 396 ff.; segregation
and self-government, II, 191-98, 402 ff.;
shrinkage in Jewish population, II,
209; widening of geographic basis, II,
210-14, 406 f.

Medina (Yathrib), III, 63; Jewish tribes
in, III, 76, 78, V, 109; pilgrims to, III,
88; refugees from, III, 87, V, 179 f.

Medinah, term, V, 298

Mediterranean Sea: islands of eastern,
I, 169; Maccabean drive for access to,
I, 255; Phoenician ships sailing, I, 64;
trade routes, IV, 172 f.

Mediterranean world: Assyrian shadow
over, I, 67; Jewish expansion through-
out, I, 167 ff., 210, VII, 13, 107; Palestine's political position, I, 215 ff.;
Phoenicia's contact with, I, 39; proselytes and their descendants in, I, 283;
see also under names of countries and
cities

Megiddo, I, 183; archaeological excavations, I, 122, 317, 320, 350; stables, I,
326

Megillat (or Sefer) bene Ḥashmona'i, VI,
188 f., 269, 416 f.

Megillat Ta'anit (Scroll of Fasts), II, 140,
384

Meḥasiah, academy, and annual fast, VI,
330

Meir, R., I, 255, II, 9, 119, 133, 145, 148,

224, 230, 316, VI, 31, 155; aggadic
notes, VI, 158; as author of unnamed
mishnah, VI, 204; and Beruriah, legend of, VI, 408; on the hundred benedictions, VII, 110; moves against waste,
II, 273; quoted, II, 124; sermon, II,
280; "Story of R. Meir," VI, 168 f., 185,
408; wife, II, 239, 408

Meir b. Baruch: on Rashi's ordinances,
V, 64; on taxation, V, 78

Meir b. Isaac, R., cantor of Worms, V,
376, VII, 144, 193; liturgical poems,
VII, 246

Meir b. Isaac Katzenellenbogen, I, 302

Meir b. Simon, Narbonnese scholar, V,
115; on the Book of the Bright Light,
VIII, 37; on interest, V, 128; on usury,
IV, 224

Me'iri, Menaḥem, VI, 37

Meisterlein, Sigmund, IV, 117

Melakhah, I, 9

Melcart, god, I, 322

Melchizedek, king of Salem, I, 45, 312;
David's claim to succession of, I, 322

Meleager of Gadara, I, 194

Melitene, Armenia, III, 18, 58

Melito of Sardis, V, 126

Mellitus, abbot, II, 154

Melody, see Tunes

Melons, tale of Elijah and, VI, 415

Memor books, IV, 287, 310, VI, 213, 217

Memory: and knowledge, VIII, 79 f.;
masoretic aids to, VI, 251; see also
Mnemotechnical devices

Memphis, Egypt, I, 111

Memra, I, 389

Men: preponderance over women, I,
113 f.; supremacy in family, I, 146; see
also Man

Menahem, king of Israel, I, 77

Menahem, Zealot leader, II, 58

Menaḥem (b. Hezekiah), name of Messiah, V, 357

Menaḥem b. 'Ammiel, messiah, V, 157

Menaḥem b. Ḥelbo, VI, 294

Menaḥem b. Jacob b. Saruq, VI, 278;
controversy with Dunash, VII, 21 ff.,
147, 195, 237 f.; dictionary written in
Hebrew, VII, 7, 20 f., 48; Hebrew
style, VII, 237; letter to Ḥisdai, VII,
228; on power of the pen, VII, 149;
rhymed prose, VII, 201 f.

Menaḥem b. Jacob of Worms, IV, 124

Menaḥem b. Michael, V, 260

Menaḥem b. Simon of Posquières, VI, 468

Menaḥem b. Solomon, Italian homilist, VII, 244, 277; encyclopedic philological-exegetical work, VII, 48

Menahem b. Solomon Al-Roḥi, see Alroy, David

Menaḥem ibn Zeraḥ, see Ibn Zeraḥ

Menasseh, tribe, III, 208

Menasseh b. Ibrahim al-Qzaz, Jewish governor of Syria, III, 154

Mendelssohn, Moses, VI, 337

Mendicancy, II, 272

Menelaus, high priest, I, 229

"Men of the Great Synagogue," I, 162, 367, 397

Menstruation, V, 250; alleged Tannaitic work on, VI, 181 f.; laws of, VI, 73 f., 86

Mental hygiene, VIII, 229, 258, 260 f.

Merab, name, VI, 293

Mercenaries, I, 326; Israelitic, employed by Assyrians, I, 346

Merchants, I, 60, 256, II, 250; bankers, as, IV, 201; communal ordinance re, VI, 139, 395; custom duties paid by, IV, 65 f.; death of, and 'agunot, IV, 184; discrimination against, IV, 183; divorce of, IV, 184; knowledge of writing, III, 82; multilingual, IV, 181; new route opened to, I, 64; non-Jewish, IV, 50, 179 f., 327; in Poland, III, 218; privileges to, IV, 48, 50, 62, 179, 182, 327; proportion of population, IV, 171; as religious propagandists, I, 173; suspicion of, among the masses, IV, 184; Syrian, IV, 173, 323; taxation of, III, 169; and competitors, I, 260, II, 431; transfer of holdings, VIII, 224; treaty of racial equality, IV, 63; widespread business deals, IV, 174; see also Peddlers

Mercy: attribute of God, VIII, 42; and justice, see Justice

"Merit of the Fathers" doctrine, I, 135, II, 42, 346

Merkabah (Ezekiel's vision), II, 315

Merkabah mysticism, VIII, 11-29, 55, 58, 277-87, 355; ascent of the soul to heaven, VIII, 105; German pietists and, VII, 44; Maimonides and, VIII, 73; see also Chariot

Merneptah, pharaoh, I, 307, 308; stele, I, 41

Meroe, built by Moses, VIII, 382

Merovingians: attitude toward Jews, III, 47-54, 250-54, VIII, 43; decree of 614, III, 250

Merseburg, Germany, provision for Jews, IV, 65 f.

Merv, Persia, III, 166

Mesene, district, II, 208, 405, V, 179

Mesha, king of Moab, I, 90; inscription, I, 336

Mesharsheya Gaon, VI, 446

Meshekh, Khazaria, III, 202

Meshullam b. Kalonymus of Lucca, VI, 117 f.

Meshullam b. Moses of Béziers, VI, 89

Meshullam b. Nathan of Melun, VI, 118 f.

Mesopotamia, I, 57, II, 96; democracy, I, 325; deportations to Asia Minor, I, 373; "remnant" in, I, 106; see also Assyria; Babylonia

Messenger: and the Messiah, V, 185, 191; see also Mohammed

"Messenger of the people," see Cantor

"Messenger to Zion," VI, 110

Messiah and messianism, I, 7, 10, 12, 17, 18, 21, 31, 99, 118, 164, 180, 208, 215, II, 58-62, 351 f.; III, 97, 176, IV, 57 f., 294, V, 118 ff., 138-208, 353-87, VII, 201, VIII, 123; apocalyptic-aggadic, V, 139-50, 185, 353-60, VI, 170 f.; Arius and doctrine of, V, 379; astrological computations, VI, 231 f., 439 f., VIII, 183; "breath" of, V, 145; and belief in second coming of Christ, III, 15; and contemporary events, V, 162; and the Crusades, IV, 302; date of advent, V, 119 f., 153, 161, 164, 167 ff., 199, 225, 363, VI, 230 f., 232, 309, 439 f., VII, 61, 178, VIII, 183, 186, 206 f., 361, 372; differing outlooks, II, 31, 58 ff.; and "end of days," II, 61, 73, 122, 139, 312 f., 351, V, 147 ff., 359, 371; expectations and downfall of Rome, I, 210, II, 397; false messiahs, III, 16, V, 168, 182-205, 366 f., 374-87; as goal of creation, VIII, 322; Graeco-Roman, II, 5, 329; and idealization of past, I, 99; Innocent II re, IV, 10; interfaith, V, 168 f.; Karaite speculations, V, 260 f., 409; Khazars and, III, 204; "lowly" ('ani), I, 152, 364; and magic arts, VIII, 47; and Mohammed, III, 77 f.; Moses and, I, 99, V, 174 f., 371; and

Messiah and messianism (*Continued*)
nationalism, V, 155 f., 184-91, 344 ff.,
name of Messiah, VIII, 273; oriental
view, I, 97; and Persian conquest of
Palestine, III, 21; poetic and exegetical derivations, V, 150-59, 360-63;
portents, V, 142 ff., 201, VI, 402; preexistence, V, 120 f., 141, 146 f., VIII,
126; prophets and prophecies, I, 98,
157, 159, 180, 339, II, 61 f., 68, 72, VI,
309; in Psalms, I, 339; rationales, V,
159-66, 363-66; as realization of Jewish
political aspirations, V, 160; and reestablishment of Jewish state, V,
184 ff.; and religious martyrdom, IV,
96 f.; and revolutionary action, II, 95,
101, 121, 372, III, 263, V, 144 ff., 191 ff.,
353 f., VII, 97 f.; in Salonica, IV, 107 f.;
and sanctification of the Temple and
Jerusalem, VIII, 41; and sectarianism,
V, 166-70, 182-97, 366 f., 374-82; super-
human nature of Messiah, V, 141 f.,
146 f.; timelessness, II, 81; Torah "abrogated," II, 161, V, 122, 124, 347; two
messiahs, V, 144 f., 160, 185, 191, 356,
see also Messiah b. Joseph; "watches"
at the Temple, VII, 90; Yinnon, V,
153; *see also under* individual messiahs, *e.g.*, Bar Kocheba; Jesus
—— beliefs: of Abraham ibn Ezra, V,
156 ff., 363; of Abraham bar Ḥiyya,
V, 162 f., 364; of Hai Gaon, V, 161 f.,
364; of Ibn Gabirol, V, 152 ff., 361 f.,
364; of Maimonides, V, 164 ff., 364 ff.;
of Philo, I, 208, II, 5 f., 329; of Saadiah,
V, 160 ff., 363 ff., VI, 481; of Samaritans, II, 31, 341, V, 170 f., 174 f., 367 ff.;
of Virgil, II, 329
Messiah b. David, V, 160, 168; and
Elijah, V, 144 f.
Messiah b. Joseph (or b. Ephraim), II,
351, V, 143 f., 160; and Armilus, V,
364
Messina, Sicily, IV, 23
Metals: evasion of duty on, IV, 329; in
Palestine, I, 256, VII, 48
Metal workers: Alexandrian, I, 260;
Kenite, I, 60
Metaphor, in Hebrew poetry, VII, 198
Metaphysics, Greek: adapted by Jewish
philosophers, VIII, 138; *see also* Phi-
losophy
Meṭaṭron, angel, I, 335, V, 142; deriva-
tion of name, VIII, 281; identified

with Enoch, VIII, 282; mystic school
of, VIII, 16
Metempsychosis, *see* Transmigration of
the soul
Meter: Arabic, VII, 193 ff.
—— Hebrew, VII, 194 ff., 313 f.; biblical,
VII, 194 f.; forms of, VII, 196; and
music, VII, 202 f.
Methodius, apostle, brother of Cyril, III,
187, 209 f.; in Moravia, V, 339; possible
fate of Moravian followers, IV, 194
Methodology, talmudic, VI, 27-35, 63 f.,
332-36; concern with chronology, VI,
201 f.
Metibot, authorship of, VI, 373 f.
"Metonic cycle," VIII, 189, 195
Metronymic, use of, VIII, 275
Metropolis, Jewish, I, 212-15, 392-93
Metuens, *see* Semiproselytes
Metz, Germany, IV, 91
Mezuzot, door-post inscriptions, V, 59
Mhebodh, Persian general, III, 58
Mibtaḥiah, I, 113, 114
Micah, prophet, I, 87, 99, 352
Michael, archangel, II, 18, 19, V, 142
Michael, Monophysite patriarch, III, 136
Michael II, Byzantine emperor, III, 178,
193
Michael III (the Drunkard), Byzantine
emperor, III, 179
Michael Basilius, Christian monk, VII,
183
Michael the Syrian, VI, 263
Michaes, Treves convert, IV, 293, 310
Middot, hermeneutic rules, V, 213; *see
also Mishnat ha-Middot*
Midianites, I, 46, 57, 313, V, 353
Midrash: aggadic, II, 294, 296, 316, 320,
III, 16, 235, 240, VI, 6, VIII, 277 f.;
anthropomorphic legends, V, 259;
apocalyptic, III, 93, 235, 237, 239, VI,
170 f.; attributed to Elijah, VI, 160;
on books of the Bible, VI, 161 f.;
halakhic, II, 294, 301, VI, 38; hermeneutics, II, 144, 427, 429; heyday
of, VI, 154 f.; and martyrdom, IV, 96;
measurements of the earth, VIII, 214;
messianic, V, 146; on number of stars,
VIII, 163; origin of, VI, 407; problem
of dating, VI, 407; supernaturally ori-
ented, VIII, 278; tannaitic, theory of,
VI, 409; transition from, to historical
literature, VI, 233
Midrashim: *Abba Gorion*, VI, 188; *Agur,*

VI, 160; *Bereshit rabbati,* V, 146; *Ekhah rabbati* and *Ekhah zuṭa,* VI, 167; *ha-Gadol,* V, 72; *Hashkem,* VI, 40, 339 f.; *Konen,* VIII, 214; *Leqaḥ ṭob,* III, 210; *rabbah,* V, 91, VI, 406; *Sod ha-'ibbur,* VIII, 193; *Tanḥuma,* V, 217, VI, 40, 409; *Va-Yosha',* VI, 188; *Yelamdenu,* VI, 170

Mieszko II, king of Poland, III, 217, 218
Mieszko III, king of Poland, III, 218
Migdol, Egypt, I, 111
Migratory movements, I, 172, 373; among subject races, I, 106 f.; and biblical narratives, I, 37; from Palestine, I, 393, II, 173, 204, 208, 210, 405 ff.; measures to stem, II, 123, 377; of Nestorians to Persia, II, 164
Milan, III, 30
Mile, and parasang, VIII, 213 f.
Milestones, Roman, I, 378
Miletus, inscription, II, 9, 330
Milḥemet miṣvah, II, 100, 372
Military colonies, I, 348, 394; *see also* Elephantine
Military movements: messianic, V, 192 ff., 203 f.; sectarian, V, 191 ff.
Military service: ancient, I, 14, 84, 121, 313, 350, 352, II, 90 f., 93, 179, 368; Deuteronomic laws, I, 332; in Egypt, I, 110, 346; soldier-farmers, II, 266; subjects sold to serve, I, 95; titles of commanders, II, 403; *see also* War
—— medieval: of Jews, III, 7, 236; and Byzantine Empire, II, 179, 398, III, 7 f., 18 ff., 236 f.; Jews excluded by Roman law, II, 179, 186; in Faṭimid campaigns, III, 107; freedom from, and taxation, III, 310; at Gaza, III, 87; in Germany, IV, 70; Khaibar, III, 79; in Khwarizm, III, 326; in Palmyra, III, 104; in Persian campaigns, II, 179, 398, III, 18 f., 57, 73; in Spain, III, 92 f., IV, 36; at Tyre, III, 19 f.
Millenary movement: Christian, as antecedent to Crusades, IV, 91 f.; Jewish, V, 354; *see also* Messiah and messianism
Millennium, "day of the Lord," VIII, 191
Minerals, I, 257; names of, VIII, 253; study of, VIII, 225
Mines and mining, IV, 169 f.; gold and silver, IV, 211 f.; salt, IV, 169
Minet el-Beida, I, 49, 306

Minim, I, 376; *see also* Heresies and heretics
Minorca, Spain, I, 370, III, 245
Minorities, religious: in Latin kingdom, IV, 114 f.; legislation on religious rights, III, 128 f.; V, 97; polemics and apologias, V, 83-94, 326-33; primacy of society over, VIII, 120 f.; protected, III, 57, 120-72, 288-312, IV, 42, 86, 185, V, 4, 82; *see also* Dhimmis; in Sicily, IV, 115
Mintmasters, IV, 29, 210 f.; in royal employ, III, 218, IV, 72; transfer of holdings, VIII, 224
Minucius Felix, II, 382
Miracles, VI, 300; biblical tradition of, VII, 201, VIII, 28 ff.; commentary on, VI, 310 f.; intervention, VIII, 179; of Jesus, II, 67; legends of, IV, 136, VIII, 47; in messianic tales, V, 192, 199; performed by Mohammed and Moses, V, 91 f.; performed only through men, I, 98; as proof of veracity, V, 205; rationales of, VI, 177, VIII, 128 ff., 342 f.
Miriam, prophetess, I, 365; false accusation of Moses, VI, 179
Miriam, daughter of Naqdimon b. Gurion, II, 113
Mishael, biblical hero, I, 116
Mishael b. 'Uzziah, VI, 248
Mishawayh (or Mesvi) al-'Ukbari, V, 182, VI, 254; approach to Jewish calendar, V, 382; syncretism, V, 196 f.
Mishawayhites, V, 182, 195 f.
Mishnah, I, 114, 270, III, 3, V, 256, VIII, 278; availability of, VI, 201; Babylonian, VI, 456; codification, II, 206 f., 294, 301, V, 254, VI, 258; commentaries on, VI, 28, 61, 76, *see also* Moses b. Maimon; concordance to, VII, 29; description of Temple service, VII, 90; dictionary of, VII, 15; divisions omitted from comment in Gemara, II, 305; ethical or juristic interpretation, VI, 35; on intermarriage, II, 232; Justinian's ban on reading of, III, 12, 233; language of, VII, 11, 15, 56 ff., 223, 242 f.; laws governing economic relations, IV, 217; legal code of Pharisaism, II, 44, 344; merits of decisions, VI, 30 f.; oral vs. written transmission, II, 425, VI, 205, 258, 426; and proselytes, I, 376; Saadiah Gaon on, V, 26;

Mishnah (*Continued*)
on sacrifices and Onias priests, I, 219;
sequence of tractates, VI, 204; spelling
and interpretation, VII, 12 f.; study of,
VI, 267, VII, 71; unraveling various
strains in, II, 295 ff.; warning against
philosophic speculation, VIII, 5 f.;
writing and chronology of, VI, 203 ff.
Mishnah of R. Eliezer, see under Eliezer,
R., author
Mishnaic-Greek glossary, VI, 333
Mishnat ha-Middot, II, 307, 433, VIII,
154, 354
Mishnat Massekhet Kallah, VI, 182 f.
Misrepresentation, "law" of, II, 255, 303
Missionary efforts, *see* Conversions;
Proselytes and Proselytism
Mithraism, II, 151; VIII, 31; initiation,
I, 181; spread of, II, 164
Mithridates I, king of Parthia, II, 229
Mitridates Potions, VIII, 257
Mizraim, Noah's grandson, I, 335; *see
also* Egypt
Mnaseas, I, 382
Mnemotechnical devices, VII, 3, 42, 234,
251; Hebrew cyclic formulas, VIII,
190, 370 f.; in oral transmission, VII,
88, 149; rules, VII, 32
Moab and Moabites: biblical, I, 55, 56,
57, 307, VI, 303; ancestry, V, 90; copper, I, 60; displaced by Nabataean
Arabs, I, 190, VI, 308; endogamous
exclusion of, I, 158, II, 232; Israel's
animosity toward, I, 156; Israelites'
dominion over, I, 345
Mobeds, see Magi
Mob violence, and the Crusades, IV,
90
Modestinus, Herennius, II, 375
Mohammed, VIII, 134; alleged will, III,
262; ascension, V, 94, VIII, 284 f.;
blasphemies against, III, 137, V, 94;
called an impostor, V, 104; circulation
of sayings attributed to, VI, 201; declaration of belief, III, 86; importance
of Abraham to, III, 81, 85 f., 266, VI,
8; imputed biblical allusions to, V,
89 f., VI, 307; on individualistic interpretation of the Qur'an, VI, 471; Islam
as political movement, III, 94; and
Jewish sectarians, V, 171, 192, 264;
Judeo-Christian influences on, III,
81 ff., 263, 265 ff., V, 168; legend of
assassination of, III, 262; linking of

with biblical prophecy, V, 86 ff., 89 f.,
117 ff., 157, 186, 219, VIII, 133; on
lunar year, VIII, 370; the "madman,"
V, 94, 264; in Medina, VII, 191; miracles, V, 91, 92; and Moses, I, 41, II,
27, III, 81, 85; numerical value of
name, V, 100; origin of enmity toward
Jews, III, 76; professed illiteracy, III,
263; on religious toleration, III, 124,
131; and tombs of the prophets, III,
136; traditions and Muslim law, VI,
24; treaties with Christians, III, 86 ff.,
163; treaties with Jews, III, 79 f., 86 ff.,
262, 264, 274; and unification of Arabian Peninsula, III, 75; victory of, as
a miracle, V, 99 f.
Mohammed ibn Musa al-Khwarizmi, *see*
Khwarizmi
Mohar, II, 220, 236; *see also* Marriage,
contracts
Moisevich, Ephrem, Kievan Jew, III, 216
Monarchy, I, 91; opposition to, I, 93 f.;
power and drawbacks, I, 64-66, 320-22;
rise of, I, 61; Saadiah on, V, 72; and
prerogatives of patriarch and exilarch,
II, 200; *see also* Kings; Rulers
Monasticism: Damascus sect, II, 52;
Essenes, II, 49
Monastic orders and monasteries, II, 269;
Cistercian, IV, 84; privilege to, IV, 65;
and transfer of land, IV, 13
Monenergism, III, 21, 24, 248
Money: embezzlement of sacred, I, 245;
exchange of, VIII, 385; Maimonides
on accumulation of, IV, 220 f.; in
precapitalistic system, I, 69, 318; Saadiah on the power of, IV, 217; and
social differentiation, I, 60; trade in,
I, 132, 214, II, 250, 414, IV, 197-215,
338-49; transfer of, IV, 209 ff., 212 f.;
see also Banking; Capitalism; Coins
and coinage; Currency; Poverty;
Wealth
Moneylenders and moneylending, I, 20,
109, 261, 265, 346, II, 250, III, 217, IV,
75, 197-207, 338-44, V, 128; attitude
of pietists toward, VIII, 48 f.; Byzantine legend, V, 348; Christian, IV, 121;
and coreligionists, IV, 199, 203, 205;
in France, IV, 62, VI, 128 f.; Karaite,
V, 258; pledges, IV, 202 f., 341 f.; and
political rivalries, IV, 82; religious
laws, IV, 198 ff., 338 ff.; royal protection, IV, 78, 82 f.; and state officials,

IV, 201 f.; *see also* Banking; Interest; Usury

Mongols: in Baghdad, III, 123; conquest of Khazaria, III, 206

Monogamy, I, 347, II, 223-29, 409 f.; and R. Gershom's ordinance, V, 135 f., 393 f.; in Roman society, II, 226; sects practicing, II, 408; *see also* Polygamy

Monophysites, II, 168, III, 259, V, 7, VI, 263; in Arabia, III, 268; and Council of Chalcedon, III, 240; in Egypt, III, 239, 268; massacre of, in Edessa, III, 19, 239; on the nature of Christ, III, 5

Monopolies, royal, IV, 113

Monotheism, V, 105, VI, 229, 234, VIII, 16; antecedents, I, 43-48, 83, 310-13; in ancient Gentile world, I, 313; conflict between faith and reason, VIII, 80 ff., 87 ff., 319 ff.; and emancipation from nature, I, 31; ethical, I, 10, II, 5; Hellenization of Semitic, I, 196; historical, I, 4-10, 13, 31, 61, 294, II, 5; and pagan spouses, II, 232, 411; influence on Zoroaster, I, 341; Judeo-Christian-Muslim, III, 82, 93, 221, VIII, 56; Mosaic, I, 43, 51, 314, 315, 316; of Philo, I, 208, II, 5; primitive I, 44, 311; treaties of religious toleration, III, 130; and Trinitarianism, VIII, 95 f.

Monotheletism, III, 21

Mons Judaeorum, IV, 29

Monsters, eschatological, V, 148, VIII, 10

Montanists, III, 176, 186; martyrdom, III, 177

Montesquieu, Charles Louis, baron de, III, 43

Monteverde catacomb, II, 331

Months: Jewish, VIII, 188; Babylonian names adopted, I, 118; and creation, VIII, 368; intercalation, II, 125; length of, V, 224 ff., VIII, 187 ff., 196 f., 369 ff.; lunar, V, 218; solilunar harmonization, VIII, 184 ff., 368 ff.; two New Moon days, VIII, 374; *see also under* names of months, *e.g.*, Nisan

Montpellier medical school, VIII, 298

Moon: association of Sabbath with, I, 359; calendar based on, I, 44, II, 125, 206; creation of, VIII, 203; linked with sun, I, 45; and rise and fall of prices, VIII, 361; size, VIII, 162 f.; worship, I, 44, 45, 311

—— new: controversy over basis of proclamation, VIII, 194 f.; and dating of religious holidays, V, 28 f., 217, 227, 248; nativity, VIII, 196 f.; observation of, V, 94, 211, 246, VIII, 205; proclamation of, VI, 216, 253, VIII, 186, 200; sanctification of VIII, 193 f., 228; services, VII, 73

Moon god, I, 44, 45, 311

Moors: Jewish aid to, in Sicily, IV, 244; Spanish, IV, 30, 335; *see also Mozarabs*

Morality, *see* Ethics; Marriage; Sex

Moral law: authority of priest, I, 81; equality of ritual and, II, 307-9, 433; source of all law, I, 227; *see also* Ethics

Moravia, IV, 72

Mordecai, I, 119, 136; reply to Esther, I, 116

Mordecai b. Hillel ha-Kohen, V, 60, 118; quotations from Gershom, VI, 385

Mordecai's Dream, VI, 167, VIII, 278

Moriscos, *see* Moors

Morning Ablutionists, II, 51

Morocco: Abu'l Kamal Tamim's rebellion, III, 122; Arab-Jewish relations, III, 90 f.; charges of Jewish conspiracy, III, 46; communal elders, V, 51; Jewish communities, II, 108, 281, VI, 24; and Mohammed's decrees of religious toleration, III, 124; Mozarab churches, III, 126

Mörs, Germany, IV, 104 f.

Mortality rate, II, 220

Mortara, Edgar, V, 113

Mortgages, I, 109, II, 303, 304; laws on, VI, 83

Mosaic law, *see under* Moses; *also* Old Testament; Pentateuch

Mosaics, II, 10, 285, 330, 402

Moses, prophet, I, 16, 22, 43, 142, VIII, 134; and Meroe, VIII, 382; apotheosis, II, 27; Arab legends of, III, 63, 161, 280; Assumption of, II, 47, 59, 346; Blessing of, II, 31; called an impostor, V, 104; center of religious controversy, VI, 479; "curses," I, 85; descendants of, V, 192; desire to view divine Glory, VIII, 129; distinguished Israel from other Hebrews, I, 56; divine name revealed to, I, 13, 309, VIII, 132; elevation of, VIII, 127 f.; enduring work, I, 40, 59, 62, 143, 205, 295, 315; and ethnic society, I, 43; historicity, I, 341; humility of, VIII, 121; identified with Hermes Trismegistos, VIII, 10; in-

Moses (*Continued*)
voked deeds of the Fathers, II, 42;
law of, I, 79, 150, 178, 204, II, 159,
319, IV, 49; legend on homage to
Jesus, V, 138; levitical ancestry ques-
tioned, I, 318; list of Edomite kings,
VI, 309; Maimonides on, VI, 229; midrashic apocrypha on, VIII, 278; miracles, V, 91; and Mohammed, I, 41, II,
27, III, 81, 85; mosques associated
with, III, 161, 280; name, I, 315; names
in family, I, 38, 305; "prayer of," VIII,
126; priests' claim to descent from, I,
330; reception by heavenly hosts, VII,
182; religion, I, 4, 41, 44, 46-53, 58,
59, 65, 313-16; religious league organized by, I, 51; reputed knowledge
of alchemy, VIII, 223; return as Messiah looked for, I, 99, V, 174 f.; role
of, in mysticism, VIII, 20; and Samaritans, II, 31, 32, V, 174 f.; saved Israel,
I, 90; Sinaitic revelation, II, 161, V,
93, VI, 8, 91, 100, 228, 232, 269, 300,
356, VIII, 6, 41, 294; snake symbol, I,
66; source of calendar computations,
VIII, 205; status as prophet, VIII, 132,
229; synagogue of Damwah and, III,
106; tradition of astronomic calcula-
tions, VIII, 196; traditions of burial
place, III, 161, 308; wife, II, 38, 39;
woman's position in family improved
by, I, 58; *see also* Exodus; Law; Pentateuch
Moses, Chronicle of, VIII, 179
Moses, Jewish scholar of Cyprus, III, 184
Moses, R., Kievan scholar, III, 217; Commentary on the Mishnah, VI, 61
Moses b. Asher, *see* Ben Asher, Moses
Moses b. Elijah Bashyatchi, *see* Bashyatchi, Moses
Moses b. Ḥanokh, captive scholar, V,
46 f., 53 f., VI, 332
Moses b. Jacob of Cordova, VI, 361
Moses b. Joseph ha-Kohen of Mayence,
IV, 128 f.; use of magic, VIII, 7
Moses b. Joseph of Narbonne, VI, 354;
and the written Halakhah, VIII, 38 f.
Moses b. Joshua Narboni, VIII, 115
Moses b. Kalonymus, R., of Lucca, VII,
181, VIII, 44
Moses b. Maimon, I, 408, II, 221, 255,
381, 408, 424, III, 106, 119, 222, IV,
114, V, 49; and Aaron Ben Asher's
biblical manuscript, VI, 247; on ablu-

tions, VI, 14; on Abu 'Isa, V, 380; on
age of talmudic scrolls, VI, 21; on
the Aggadah, VI, 177 ff., 412 f.; anatomical observations, VI, 103, 379,
VIII, 230, 387; animosity toward
Zuṭṭa, VI, 432; on Arab historical
writing, VI, 199; Arabic stylist, VII,
8, 221; on Aristotle, VIII, 82, 93; on
astrology, VIII, 111, 180 ff., 335, 366 f.;
astronomic writings, VI, 103, 379, VIII,
162, 164 f., 199 f., 357; authority over
Fusṭaṭ community, VI, 11, 432; auto-
graphs, VI, 351, 388, VII, 8, 280; basic
doctrines of Judaism, I, 408, V, 229,
VI, 101 ff., VII, 175; on biblical synonyms and homonyms, VI, 297; on
capital crimes, V, 17, 45, 280 f.; castration of slaves, IV, 191; on cause of
death, VIII, 259; on charges of biblical falsification, V, 92; on Christians,
III, 161, V, 57 f., 118 f., 365, VI, 11;
codification of liturgical observances,
V, 28, VII, 81, 108, 118 ff., 276; commentaries, I, 376, VI, 297, 352; on
concluding lines of Torah scroll, VI,
253 f.; concordance between faith and
reason, VIII, 81 f., 321; controversy
over, VI, 104 ff., VII, 175, VIII, 40, 68;
on Daniel's prophecies, V, 87; debt to
Saadiah, VII, 119; vs. deviations from
talmudic law, V, 52; on diabetes, VIII,
262; disagreements with predecessors,
VI, 26, 133, 378; on disposition of
private property, V, 320; on divorce
and marriage, III, 112; doctrine of
God, VIII, 87 ff., 322 ff.; on domestic
employment, IV, 196, V, 240; on economic status and religion, IV, 217;
on enforced conversion to Islam, III,
125; on commandments, VI, 143, VIII,
115, 118; esteem for exilarch, V, 12;
on ethics of Judaism, VIII, 117 f.,
122 f.; exegetical methods, VI, 297;
family, III, 115, 126, false messiahs,
V, 198 ff., 382 ff.; on figures of speech,
VII, 317; on individual rights and
public welfare, IV, 222; influence of,
V, 49, VI, 106, VIII, 137; influence of
Ḥefeṣ on, VI, 96; and Jewries of western Europe, III, 173; on the Karaites,
V, 266, 280; on length of seasons, VIII,
201; life as physician, VIII, 232 ff.,
249 ff., 388 f., 398 ff.; on linguistic
techniques, VI, 294; on lowly trades,

IV, 167; on magic, VIII, 29; on man's
freedom, VIII, 110; on man's love of
God, VIII, 115 f.; marriage ordinance,
VI, 134 f., 138 f.; on music, VII, 205 f.,
208; Muslim denunciation of, VIII,
250; Muslim physician's tribute to,
III, 147 f., VIII, 249 f.; *negidim* descendants, V, 48; octocentennial, VIII,
398 f.; opinion of his own work, VI,
99, 106, 120 f., 380, VIII, 71; on Palestinian land ownership, IV, 160 f.,
316; "perpetual" ordinance, VI, 136;
physicians' oath ascribed to, VIII, 239;
on physician's qualifications, VIII, 260;
poems, VII, 105, 271; on political
power, V, 72; on preaching, VI, 156;
prohibition of teaching Torah to Gentiles, VI, 275; on prophecy, V, 87, VIII,
131 f.; propositions requiring no proof,
VIII, 80; on psychological factors in
healing, VIII, 261, 404; on purposes
of Jewish law, VI, 142; on qualifications of a messenger, VII, 129; quoted,
II, 252, VIII, 82, 101 f., 115, 120, 124,
164 f.; on ransoming captives, IV, 177;
rationale of suffering, V, 101 f.; on
rational law, V, 78, VI, 144, VIII, 338;
reaction to *piyyuṭim*, VII, 102, 133;
reconstruction of transmission of oral
law, VIII, 210 f.; rejection of Arab
arguments on creation, VIII, 89 f.; re-
production of his writings in Hebrew,
VII, 7; restrictions on Jewish trade,
IV, 220; on sale of Jewish house to
Gentile, III, 146; and Samaritans, V,
172, 177; on scholars, V, 76; semi-
oracular style, VI, 104; on a translator,
VIII, 65 f.; on sexual transgressions,
III, 143; on site of Temple, VI, 228;
on slaves, IV, 190 ff.; on the soul, VIII,
108; sources of decisions, VI, 104 f.,
380; Spanish collections of essays on,
VI, 378; on state and local authority,
V, 71 f.; and Sultan Al-Afdhal, VIII,
260 f.; support of local customs, VI,
127; on testing drugs, VIII, 257; theory
of "negative attributes" of God, VIII,
98 f., 327 f.; theory of sacrifices, VI,
147 f.; thirteen principles, V, 229, VII,
175; on the Universe, VI, 146, VIII,
161 ff., 357 ff.; use of allegory, VIII,
86; use of alternate talmudic readings,
VI, 413; on use of knowledge of the
sages, VIII, 142; use of the sciences,

VIII, 135; on verbal charms, VIII, 234;
warning to Torah scribes, VI, 254
—— works, VIII, 250 ff., 308 f., 398 ff.;
editions by American Academy for
Jewish Research, VIII, 307 ff.; Anti-
dotarium, VIII, 257; *Book of Commandments*, VI, 26, 59, 97 ff., 178 f.,
375 ff.; *Code*, III, 143, IV, 218, 223,
316, V, 164 f., 261, VI, 31 f., 99-107,
376 ff., VII, 280, VIII, 71; commentary on the Bible, VI, 297; *Commentary on the Mishnah*, III, 143, V, 166,
VI, 57-61, VII, 185, VIII, 116; correspondence, VI, 119 ff., 388, VII, 54;
"Epistle on Conversion," VIII, 126;
Epistle to Yemen, III, 291, V, 78, 198,
VIII, 64; "Glossary of Drug Names,"
VIII, 252; *Guide for the Perplexed*,
IV, 218, VII, 220, VIII, 64, 70-73,
306 f.; "Medical Aphorisms," VIII,
238 f., 250, 261 f., 388; "Regimen
Sanitatis," VIII, 260 f.; supplement
to Alfasi's work, VI, 88 f.; "Treatise of
Logical Terms," VIII, 144 f.; treatise
on fits, IV, 318
Moses b. Naḥman, R., of Barcelona, V,
114, VIII, 24; kabbalist exegete, VI, 26,
VII, 306; defense of Alfasi, VI, 88; on
month of Tishre, VIII, 184; and
recitation of *Musaf 'Amidah*, VII,
107 f.; refutation of Maimonides, VI,
98; and Tosafists, VI, 56
Moses b. Napthali, *see* Ben Naphtali
Moses b. Samuel, Karaite, V, 411
Moses b. Solomon of Salerno, VIII, 315
Moses b. Yehudah, VI, 89
Moses b. Yequtiel the Elder, IV, 142
Moses ha-Sefardi, former name of Petrus
Alphonsi (*q.v.*), VIII, 174
Moses Khalfo, R., of Sicily, VII, 30
Moses of Castoria, Jewish scholar, III,
210
Moses of Crete, false messiah, III, 16, V,
168, 366 f.
Moses of Khorene, Armenian historian,
I, 169, II, 204; on origin of Armenian
Jews, III, 110
Moses of Pavia, Jewish martyr, IV, 105
Moses the Preacher (ha-Darshan), of
Narbonne, V, 146, VI, 171 f., 196, 405,
410, VII, 30, VIII, 32, 38; Book of the
Bright Light and, VIII, 33; influence
on Qimḥi, VI, 280
Mosque, I, 15; associated with Moses,

Mosque (*Continued*)
III, 161, 280; center of secular life,
VI, 154; churches and synagogues
converted into, III, 123, 136, 140,
148, 297; derivation of term, VI, 13;
and height of neighboring buildings,
III, 138, 145; imitation of synagogue,
III, 297; interruption of service, V,
67; libraries, VII, 138, VIII, 246; mag-
nificence of structures, III, 134
Mosque of the Footprints, Damascus,
III, 161
Mosque of the Rock, Jerusalem, III, 101,
134, 269, 272
Mosul (Ḥesna Ebraya or Ashhur), III,
99; cantor-preacher of, VII, 81; Jew-
ish provincial administration, V, 43;
Jews' greeting to 'Ali, III, 276
Mother: supremacy of, I, 43, 310; *see
also* Family
"Mother Church," designation, II, 168
"Mother earth," I, 57, 318
Mother-goddess, I, 318
Motion, eternality of, VIII, 90
Mountain, holy, *see* Gerizim, Mount
"Mourners for Zion," V, 32, 185, 257,
258, 271, 376, VI, 10
Mourning: days of, I, 294; over destruc-
tion of the Temple, II, 111 ff., 375 f.,
V, 27; external signs of, V, 27; laws
on, VI, 63, VII, 267; marriage during,
VI, 120; Naṭronai on, VI, 382;
qaddish prayer, V, 59, VII, 67; for a
scholar, VI, 83
Movement, freedom of, IV, 32 f., 63 f.,
78, 85, V, 68, 78, VIII, 211 f.
Movements, planetary, effect on earth,
VIII, 185
"Moyses Hall," Bury St. Edmunds, IV,
282
Mozarabs (Christian Moors), III, 155;
Bodo and, IV, 52; employed by Al-
Manṣur, III, 126; in Spain, IV, 27;
and Jews, IV, 31; Visigothic code and,
III, 127
Mu'awiya: founder of 'Umayyad dynasty,
III, 88; concentration of landholdings,
III, 163; destruction of Colossus of
Rhodes, III, 235; and Jews in Tripolis,
III, 104
Mubarrad, Baṣran philologist, VII, 234
Mubashshir ha-Levi, Rabbanite scholar,
VI, 270, VII, 15 f.
Muḥammad 'Ali, VI, 13

Muhammad b. Zakariva ar-Razi, *see*
Razi, Muhammad
Muḥibb b. 'Atiqa, VIII, 233
Mu'izz, al-, Faṭimid caliph, VIII, 246
Muktafi II, al-, caliph, charter to Nes-
torian *catholicos*, V, 6; offer of al-
liance from Berta di Toscana, IV, 245
Mula Ismael, Moroccan sultan, III, 94
Mulla Yaḥya, Arab author, VIII, 244
Mundhir, Lakhmid king, III, 68
Municipalities, *see* Cities
Münster, Sebastian, VI, 191
Muntafil, Arab poet, III, 157
Münzenberg, castle, IV, 304
Muqaddasi, VI, 192; on Christian and
Jewish occupations, IV, 166, VIII, 236;
on minorities in Jerusalem, III, 102;
on mixed population of Persian towns,
III, 109; on paper manufacture, IV,
169; on sects in Arabia, III, 72
Muqtadir, al-, *see* Al-Muqtadir
Murabba'at, cave, V, 188
Murals, *see* Painting
Murashshu Sons, I, 109; records, I, 110,
118, 120, 349
Murder: Crusaders' attitude toward, IV,
101; indemnities for, IV, 39 f.; of in-
fidels as righteous act, IV, 133, 140 f.;
penalty for, III, 132, IV, 35, 39, 48 f.,
50, 69, 128; of a priest, IV, 281; punishment for, VI, 134
Murviedro, Spain: alleged inscription on
tombstone of Adoniram, III, 34, 244,
VII, 313
Musa al-Uswari, Iraqi orator, VII, 10
Musa ibn al-Azar (b. Eleazar), Jewish
court physician, VIII, 246
Musa ibn Nuṣair, governor of Morocco,
III, 91
Musar, term, VIII, 348
Mushkhanites, V, 192 ff.
Music, I, 123 f.; Arabian, VII, 204 f.,
207; Hebrew origin of Christian, VII,
84, 130; hymns and psalms, I, 52, 123,
150, 395; natural and artificial, VII,
210; of Jews, Greeks, Christians, II,
8 f., 155, 330, 389; secular, VII, 128,
129 f., 206; therapeutic value, VII, 206,
208 f.; at Temple, I, 123; trends and
theories, VII, 125-31, 202-11, 281-85;
318-21; *see also Ḥazzan;* Israel Moses;
Cantors; Singers; Singing
Musiv style, VII, 202
Muslim-Christian relations: commerce

and, IV, 172; conflicts, V, 199; era of Crusades, VIII, 256; hostility in, IV, 186; Nestorians and, V, 6; political and economic issues, V, 95 ff.; religious disputations, V, 326; in Spain, IV, 37 f., 93 f.

Muslim-Jewish relations, see Arab-Jewish relations; Judeo-Muslim relations

Muslims: academy leadership and hereditary principle, V, 297; Arab-Berber rivalries, III, 155 f.; and Arabic speech, VII, 18; arguments re Bible and Qur'an, V, 86 ff., 327 ff., VI, 298; on castration, IV, 191 f.; charges against Jews and Christians, III, 145, IV, 243, V, 95 ff.; and the Crusaders, IV, 102, 107 ff., 295; demagogic religious appeals to, III, 123; on descent from house of David, V, 38; economic theories, IV, 218 f.; emphasis on ceremonial laws, VIII, 17; employment of Christians, IV, 15; ethnic strains, III, 103; and faith of "infidels," V, 82 f.; and foreign languages, VII, 9 f.; inheritance rights, and infidels, V, 18; Jewish charge of licentiousness, V, 134; and Karaites, V, 263 f.; mechanical knowledge, VIII, 356; messianic belief, V, 200 f.; need to feel superior, III, 4, 96, 138, IV, 28, V, 99; Norman campaigns vs., IV, 23; and Nubians, IV, 181; and Palestine and Jerusalem, III, 269 f.; possibility of rise in social status, III, 149; and prayer, VI, 13 f.; prestige-mindedness, III, 170 f.; rejection of anthropomorphism, VIII, 100; relations with Samaritans, V, 171 f., 176 f.; resentment of non-Muslim officeholders, III, 154 f.; and Saturday, V, 91 f.; and "slaves," III, 302, IV, 42, 333; Spanish, massacre of, IV, 132; status in foreign lands, III, 129; taxation of, IV, 114; see also Arabs; Islam; Law, Muslim

Mustanṣir, Faṭimid caliph, III, 158

Mutakallimun, see Kalam and Mutakallimun

Mutawakkil: decree re behavior of "protected peoples," III, 139 f.; destruction of synagogues, III, 135; use of church as mosque, III, 148

Mu'tazilites, Arab rationalists, V, 198,

VI, 187, VIII, 60 ff., 66 ff., 72, 103, 298; on attributes of God, VIII, 96, 328; on the Hereafter, VIII, 104; on predestination and free will, VIII, 109

Mutilation, as punishment, III, 186 f.; of slaves, IV, 191

Mysteries: of existence, VIII, 7 ff.; religious, VIII, 80 f.; of the universe, VII, 172

Mystery religions, ancient, I, 387, VIII, 31; pagan cults, I, 388

Mystic communion with God, I, 202

Mystics and mysticism, I, 201, VIII, 3-54, 58, 273-95; and alchemy, VIII, 225; astrological, VIII, 179 ff.; and biblical interpretation, VI, 297 f.; ecstasy, VIII, 82 f., 116; in Hebrew liturgy, VII, 78 f., 131; interfaith borrowings, VIII, 112 f.; literature, VIII, 11 ff., 25, 27 ff., 277 ff.; magic square, VIII, 354; on meanings of numbers and letters, VIII, 151, 191; Muslim, V, 103, VIII, 15 f.; nomistic, VIII, 52; poetry of, VII, 181 ff., 272 f.; reception by leaders and public, II, 314, VIII, 24 ff.; She'ur qomah, VI, 177 f., VIII, 25 f., 286; use of Arabic, VII, 193; yorede merkabah, V, 146; see also Chariot; Gnosticism; Kabbalah; Merkabah mysticism

Mythology: Babylonian, I, 294, VIII, 10; Greek, II, 4

N

Nabataeans, I, 57, 167, 254; inscriptions, III, 64; spread of, III, 60

Nablus, Samaritan center, V, 171 ff.; Crusaders and, V, 172; emigration from, V, 176

Nabonidus, king of Babylonia, I, 119, 132, 349, 355, III, 64 f.

Naboth, I, 68, 93

Nag-Hammadi, II, 435

Nahawend, Persia, III, 110, V, 223; sects in, V, 183

Nahawendi, Benjamin b. Moses, see Benjamin b. Moses

Naḥman (b. Jacob), R., Babylonian Amora, II, 198, 240, 259, III, 62; temporary marriages, II, 226, 410; wife, II, 239

Naḥman b. Isaac, R., II, 222

Naḥmani, Rabbah b., II, 243, 413

Nahmanides, *see* Moses b. Nahman

Nahor, I, 33

Nahrawani, Nissi al-, liturgical poet, VII, 144, VIII, 13

Nahshon b. Zadok Gaon, of Sura, V, 14, VI, 425; "circle" of 247 years, VIII, 192; commentaries, VI, 42; denunciation of *piyyut*, VII, 101; on local customs, VI, 124 f.; mystic writing attributed to, VIII, 25; on sale of slaves to Gentiles, IV, 193; on scholars of Kairuwan, V, 22, 77 f.

Nahum, prophet, I, 338, VI, 309

Nahum of Gimzo, VI, 186

Nahum of Media, I, 221, II, 205

Nahum the Libellarius, II, 37

Najara Israel, mystical poet, VII, 204

Najran, Arabia, III, 163; attacks on Christians of, III, 66; Christian community and Mohammed, III, 78, 80; evacuation of Jews to Kufa, III, 271

Names: of angels and demons, VIII, 8 f., 21, 275; Arabic and Jewish mixture, III, 148; Aramaic, I, 120, 121, 349; compounded with Baal and Yahweh, I, 59, 318; in Elephantine, I, 121; forms used for Jesus, II, 357; identification of biblical, VII, 16, 18, 25, 29; as key to history, I, 121, 350; means of protection, II, 20, VIII, 8 f., 21, 275; in Palmyrene inscriptions, II, 211, 407; personal and place names, I, 33 f.; Semitic, among Hyksos rulers, I, 304; substitutions, VI, 293 f.; talmudic, VII, 14; theophorous, I, 129, 352; transliteration of, under Islam, III, 303; *see also* Place names

—— adoptive, I, 349; Babylonian, I, 118 ff., 349; double, I, 310; Hellenistic, I, 373, II, 174; Hebrew and Roman, III, 207; Persian, VIII, 277

—— divine: appellations and circumlocutions, I, 46, 229, 244, 312, 352, II, 17 f., 162, 311 f., 314, 335, 357, 361, 394, 434, 435, V, 120, VI, 130, 249, 409, 449 f., VII, 12, 21, VIII, 26; components of, VIII, 152; derivatives of attributes of God, II, 314, 434 f.; in Elephantine papyri, I, 352; Greek equivalent, I, 229; improper use of, VIII, 29; in incantations, VIII, 8, 27 ff., 284; in liturgical selections, VII, 247 f.; magic power, II, 22 f., 314, 434, VIII, 9; in mystic schools, VIII, 16;

precentor's omission of, VIII, 294; reverence for, VII, 139; sanctification of, VI, 83, VII, 65; used in Samaritan oaths, II, 434

—— Hebrew, I, 6, 119, 120, 302, 349; adopted by Khazars, III, 202

—— Jewish, I, 119, 120, 392, II, 211, 407; paucity of in Edfu ghetto, I, 392

Naples, IV, 24; Jewish defense of, III, 7, 25; population, IV, 243

Naqdimon b. Gurion, II, 114, 221

Narbonne: Council of, II, 423, III, 253, IV, 154, 157; Jewish community, IV, 45-48, 58, 258-60, VIII, 38 f.; Jewish "king" of, IV, 46 f., 259, VI, 421; Moses the preacher, VI, 171 f., 410, VIII, 32; Natronai and, IV, 258 f.; scarcity of books, VII, 139; surrender to the Franks, IV, 45 f.; taxation, IV, 154; tombstone inscription, III, 48

Narsai, Nestorian, VIII, 275

Narses, exarch of Italy, II, 178, 398

Narses, Syriac poet, VII, 199

Nash papyrus, I, 186, 379, VI, 238

Nasi, title, V, 48, 59, VIII, 69, 370; *see also* Patriarchate

Nasiruddin at-Tusi, on astronomy, VIII, 145

Nasr b. Sayyar, III, 166

Nathan, prophet, I, 65

Nathan, R., II, 14, 381, VI, 17

Nathanael of Yemen, VII, 47

Nathan b. Abraham, V, 34, 274, 295; commentary on the Mishnah, VI, 57 f.

Nathan b. Abraham, Gaon, VI, 57

Nathan b. Isaac, the Babylonian, VI, 36; on the appointment of local chiefs, V, 50; description of exilarchic installation, V, 7 f., VI, 36, VII, 284; "Report," VI, 213, 430 f.

Nathan b. Yehiel, of Rome, Hebrew lexicographer, II, 411, VI, 28, VIII, 227; Arabic and Greek etymologies, VII, 232; dates of birth and death, VII, 231; lexicon for Babylonian Talmud, IV, 308, VI, 340, VII, 29, 231 f.; quotations from Natronai, VI, 383; synagogue in Rome, V, 59; Tanhum's supplementary work, VII, 31; on use of Semah's work, VII, 224

Nathan of Sosita, VI, 186

Nation, Jewish: importance of, I, 8, 12 f.

Nationalism: ancient: definition, I, 27, II, 372; emancipation from state, I,

25, 31, 93-96, 237, 338; failure to secularize Jewish life, I, 28; Jesus' aloofness, II, 69, 73; Jewish conception accepted by world at large, I, 28; national-religious ideology, I, 5, 28, 96, 163, 225, 228; Pharisees representatives of, II, 344; reality of, II, 214; safeguard against national extinction, I, 163; and territory, I, 16-25 *passim*, 53-61; and universalism (*q.v.*), I, 31, 158

—— medieval, VII, 168, 211 f., VIII, 125 ff.; in Jewish philosophy, VIII, 86 ff.; Karaite, V, 219, 258, 268, 282; in poetry, VII, 163; upsurge of, V, 184-205, 375-87, VII, 211 f.; and voluntary segregation, III, 144

—— modern: in Russia and Poland, I, 29

Nations, family of, Yosephon on, VI, 226

"Nations, seventy," VIII, 216

Naṭroi (Naṭronai) b. Emunah Gaon, VI, 37

Naṭrona (or Neṭirata), name, II, 178, 397

Naṭronai b. Ḥabibai (Ḥakhinai), exilarch, IV, 47, 258 f., V, 15, 47, VII, 21

Naṭronai I b. Nehemiah, gaon, on followers of Severus, V, 190, 193 f., 207

Naṭronai II b. Hilai, gaon, V, 14, 227, 382, VI, 31, VII, 65; correspondence with Spain, VI, 41; on debts collectible from property, VI, 132; on the hundred benedictions, VII, 110 f.; on intercourse with a slave, IV, 195; on Lucena, III, 109; mystic writing attributed to, VIII, 25; on neglect of biblical studies, VI, 236 f., 313; on prayer, VI, 15, VII, 76; reaction to Karaite schism, V, 276; on recitation of the Aramaic Targum, VI, 264; on suppression of *hafṭarah*, VI, 42; on study of the Talmud, VI, 34 f.; on vineyards, IV, 163; on vocalized Torah scrolls, VI, 244

Natural causes, and actions of man, VIII, 111 ff.

Natural law: doctrine of, II, 136, VI, 5, 144 ff.; Greek vs. Judeo-Christian background, VI, 397; increasing role in legal philosophy, II, 432; Saadiah's discussion of, VIII, 335; unchanging, VIII, 90

Natural sciences, VIII, 142, 222-30, 384-87

Nature: antinomy between spirit and, I, 296; control of forces of, VIII, 4; defiance of, I, 163-64, II, 321; emancipation from, I, 8, VIII, 46, 111 f.; healing powers, VIII, 260; and history, I, 5 ff., 12, 18, 101, 296; Paul's use of word, II, 81; in poetry, VII, 163 f.

Naubakht, an-, Persian astronomer, III, 99, 100, 152

Naubakhti, translator, V, 84

Naukratis, I, 190

Navicularii, guild, II, 249

Nazirites, sect, I, 42, 78, II, 51, 348

Nazis and Nazism, I, 18, 296, 324, II, 427, IV, 270 f., VIII, 386; impact upon Jews, I, 347, II, 356 f.

Nea Moné, monastery, III, 192

Neapolis, formerly Schechem, II, 28; *see also* Nablus

Near East, I, 394; circulation of Mohammed's sayings, VI, 201; concepts of nature of ruler, VIII, 18; corruption of nations of, I, 284; cultural synthesis, VII, 59; eschatology, V, 358; ethics, III, 283; ethnic movements, I, 36, 305; feudalism and landholding, IV, 152, 318; folklore, VI, 183, 415 f.; Greek emporia, I, 184; Hebrew deeds, IV, 320 f.; Jewish craftsmen, IV, 167 f.; popular philosophies, VIII, 5, 151; power of the word in, VII, 87, VIII, 14; rigidity of court etiquette, III, 171; role of Jews in cultural exchange, VIII, 255 f.; sectarianism and biblical interpretation, VI, 276 f., VII, 223; socioeconomic changes, IV, 26, 186, 337, V, 96 f., 126 ff.; synagogue readers, VII, 58 f.; *see also under* countries and cities

Nebiim, I, 59, 78

Nebukadrezzar, I, 115, 130, 344, V, 119, 132, VIII, 26; Jephet b. 'Ali's comment on, VI, 308; Jewish refugees from wars of, III, 64; places chosen for settlement by Jews, I, 107; and Tadmor, III, 62

Necho, pharaoh, I, 183, 327

Neck, tax receipt stamped upon, III, 168

Necropoles, *see* Cemeteries and catacombs

Nedarim, commentary on, VI, 53

Negev, ancient, I, 252, II, 368
Negidim, provincial leaders of Jewry, in Egypt, V, 39 ff., 56, 308 f.; Kairuwan, V, 51; term, V, 39 f.
Nehardea, Babylonia, I, 168, II, 206, 207, 247, 317, 405, 435; academy, VI, 455; adherence to Galilean custom, VI, 124 ff.; Jewish principality, III, 62 f.; and Pumbedita, VI, 24; work on biblical text, VI, 239
Nehemiah, R., II, 127, 307, 378; *Mishnat ha-middot*, VIII, 147
Nehemiah b. Hacaliah, I, 73, 85, 114, 116, 118, 144, 151, 160, 180, 353; concludes covenant, I, 161; historicity, I, 341; racialist extremism, I, 147, 163, 361; on reading the law "distinctly," VI, 258; restoration under, I, 103; service to mankind, I, 158
—— Book of, I, 104, 343, III, 61
Nehemiah b. Hushiel, messiah, V, 143, 157
Nehemiah b. Kohen Zedek, V, 23 f.
Nehorai, R., physician-shopkeeper, II, 121, IV, 179
Nehuniah b. ha-Qanah, R., VIII, 33 f.
Nehushtan, I, 66
Neighbors, legal protection, II, 252
Neo-Babylonian Empire, I, 102; *see also* Babylonia
Neoplatonism, V, 381 f., VIII, 61, 76; and Christianity, II, 159; influence on Ibn Gabirol, VIII, 325; rise of, VI, 258
Neo-Phythagoreans, I, 208
Nero, Roman emperor, II, 57, 96, 100, 103; persecution of Christians, I, 191
Nerva, Roman emperor, II, 83, 106
Nesi'im, Karaite, V, 263
Nestor, III, 215
Nestorians, II, 164, 188, 191, III, 259 f.; *catholicos*, III, 88 f., V, 6; charge of John Rufus vs., III, 229; equation with Jews, III, 8, 243; religion and law, VI, 4; in Sassanian Empire, VI, 271; school of Jundeshapur, VIII, 236; Trinitarian doctrine, VIII, 96, 326
Nestorius, III, 5
Netira, house of, Jewish bankers of Baghdad, III, 152 f., 167, V, 10 f., VI, 214
Neumes, VII, 282
Neuss, Germany, IV, 134
Neutrality: of Jewry, on Islam and

Christendom, IV, 91; political, of Jews, III, 235
Neva, Transjordan, VI, 381 f.
New Antioch, III, 6 f., 58, 255
"New Christians" (forced converts), III, 177; *see also under* Christians and christianity; Converts and conversion
New Covenanters, V, 188, 215, 219, 380, VI, 78; *see also* Damascus sect
New Moon, holiday, I, 6, 44, 286
New Testament: anti-Jewish polemists and, V, 108; Arabic versions, VI, 265; Jewish attitude toward, V, 85; language of, I, 186; late interpolations and canonization, II, 73, 131; Muslim charges of Christian falsification of, V, 88; scholarship divided, II, 358; social aspects, II, 356; "translation Greek," VII, 4, 7; *see also* Bible; Gospels; *also under* names of books and versions
New Year's Day, I, 5, 144, 294, VIII, 188; animal sacrifice, VII, 78 f.; dating of, V, 31, VIII, 195; customs, VI, 125; fasting on, VI, 330; *Musaf 'Amidah*, VII, 107 f., 127, 172; observance, V, 248, VII, 107; prayers, VII, 76; *Tashlikh* ceremony, III, 241; two-day celebration, V, 29
Nibridius, archbishop of Narbonne, IV, 52
Nicaea, First Council of, II, 188, 401; decision on date of Easter, III, 248, VIII, 369
—— Second Council of, III, 177-78, IV, 5 f., 189
Nicanor of Alexandria, I, 262
Nicephoros I, Byzantine emperor: and banking, IV, 198; on calling Arabs Saracens, III, 302
Nicephoros II (Nicephoros Phokas), Byzantine emperor, III, 193; conquest of Crete, IV, 190
Nicetas, son of Jason, II, 24
Nicetas Choniates, Byzantine historian, IV, 166, VI, 212; on Constantinople fire, IV, 130 f.
Nicholas, Byzantine monk, VIII, 246
Nicholas I, pope, III, 209
Nicolaus of Damascus, I, 218, 242, 272, 401, II, 342; on descent of Antipater, VI, 193
Nichomachus of Gadara, VIII, 151
Nicon Metanoites, Saint, III, 184, 318

Nies Babylonian Collection, Yale University, I, 332
Nihavend, Persia, V, 223; see also Nahawend
Nihilism, V, 103
Nile, river, III, 116; canal, III, 155
Nilus, abbot of Rossano, VIII, 245
Nineveh: fall of, I, 96, 338; Petaḥiah's visit to, VI, 435; repentance in, II, 384
Ninos, see Nineveh
Ninth of Ab, IV, 145, VI, 167; liturgy, V, 152, VIII, 82 f., 257; mourning for Temple on, II, 112, 193, VII, 82 f.; poems for, VII, 143; replaced by 'Anan, V, 214; yearly gathering, II, 108, 118, 374; Zionide poem in ritual for, VII, 168 f.
Nippur, city, I, 107; banking and commerce, I, 108, 109, 346; exilic community around, I, 134; incantations, VIII, 21; magicians of, VIII, 10
Nisan, month, I, 294, V, 217, 224
Nishmat, prayer, II, 75
Nisibis, VI, 245; academy, VIII, 58, 392; center of biblical studies, VI, 240 f.; Ezra synagogue, VI, 436; history of, VI, 443; school of, VI, 256 f.
Nissi b. Nuḥ, Karaite, V, 229, 253; "Commentary on the Ten Commandments," VII, 220
Nissim b. Jacob ibn Shahin of Kairuwan, III, 298, V, 48, 312, VI, 205; folkloristic collection, VI, 184-88, 414-16, 420, VII, 183, 311, VIII, 50; introduction of shabbata de-rigla, V, 40; Secret Scroll, VI, 33, 335 f.; on The Scroll of Antiochus, VI, 416 f.; works on the Talmud, VI, 33, 45, 335 f., VIII, 97
Nissim b. Moses, V, 8
Nissim of Qaṭiyah, III, 138
Niẓam al-Mulk, vizier, III, 151 f.
Noah, patriarch, I, 44, 307, II, 223, V, 87, VI, 39, VIII, 134; astrology and, VIII, 176
—— Book of, II, 336
Noahide commandments, I, 375, VI, 5, 145
Nomadic ideals, I, 89, 335, 336
Nomads: and agriculture, I, 55, 301; and religion, I, 47; seminomadic tribes, I, 33, 41, 315, 333; see also Tribes
Nomenclature, theophorous, I, 129

Nomism, VI, 141, VIII, 32
Nomocanon, III, 187, 191, 319
Noph, Egypt, I, 111
Normandy: Church of, IV, 269; Jews in, IV, 77
Normans: policy in Palestine, IV, 113 f.; rule in Sicily, IV, 21 ff.; taxation of, III, 191, 193
North Africa, see Africa, North
Northampton, England: Council of, IV, 277; donum, IV, 303
Norwich, England, IV, 135, 306 f.
Notation, musical: Byzantine, VII, 282; ekphonetic, VII, 282
Novel, VI, 187 f.; see also Historical literature
Novellae, VI, 62, 353 f.; see also Justinian; Leo VI
Novgorod, excavations, III, 334
Nubia, IV, 181
Nu'man III, Lakhmid king, III, 70
Numbers, Book of, V, 219; and firstborn males, VIII, 149; scholion on, V, 175
Numenius, I, 199; attitude to Judaism, II, 157
Numerals, VIII, 146-60, 349-57; Hindu, VIII, 150, 360; letters as, VIII, 150 f.; symbolism, VI, 157 f.; systems of, VIII, 150 f.
Numerical principle, in cosmic structure, VIII, 284
Numerical values: of Arabic and Syriac letters, VIII, 150; of biblical words and phrases, V, 86 ff.; of divine name, VIII, 281; and the gates of Understanding, VIII, 294; of Hebrew letters, V, 167, VI, 164, 166, 242, VII, 250, VIII, 14 f., 147, 150, 290; of Messiah's name, V, 357; of Mohammed's name, V, 100; of opening line of poem, VII, 289; in riddles, VIII, 357; of words, V, 167; see also Gematrias
Nuns: expulsion from Sens, IV, 56; Sister Catherine, Jewish convert, V, 113
Nuremberg, Germany, IV, 117, 299
Nurses, Christian, of Jews, IV, 269
Nuzi tablets, I, 302, 327

O

Oaths: in criminal vs. civil litigation, IV, 253, 255; of Damascus sect, II, 52,

Oaths (Continued)
54; of Essenes, II, 48, 347; of fidelity,
II, 36; IV, 49, 163; Hai's monograph
on, VI, 71, 359 f.; in interfaith part-
nerships, IV, 331; in Judeo-Christian
litigation, IV, 41 f.; more judaico,
III, 149, 194 f., 322, IV, 41 f., 49, 61;
of office, II, 110, 375; physicians', VIII,
238 f., 242, 391; and readmission of
Karaites, V, 274; relating to end of
days, II, 312; Samaritans' use of divine
name in, II, 434; taken by Saadiah
Gaon, V, 20; three imposed on man by
God, II, 115; see also Blasphemy;
Curse
Obadiah, prophet, VI, 229; Book of,
V, 158 f.
Obadiah, Khazar king, III, 201
Obadiah (Johannes), Norman proselyte,
III, 141, 169, 190, 320, IV, 294, V,
202, 260
Obadiah, see Abu 'Isa al-Isfahani
Obedience: to divine law, VI, 142; to
will of God, VI, 218
Obscurantism, and conservatism, VIII,
68
Observation, astronomic, VIII, 173; and
calendar computations, VIII, 194, 369;
difficulties of, VIII, 161 ff.
Observatories, astronomic, VIII, 161
Occult sciences: and astrology, II, 15 f.,
44, 334; and German pietism, VIII,
50 ff.
Occupations, industrial, IV, 165 f.; ratio
of Jews employed in, IV, 171, VIII,
236; see also under individual occupa-
tions, e.g., Crafts and craftsmen;
Trade
Oceans, geographic knowledge of, VIII,
214 f.
Oculist, Jewish, VIII, 237
Odenath of Palmyra, II, 177
Odo (Eudes), French king, IV, 43
Odo, scholastic, VI, 273, 463
Odors, V, 327; industrial, II, 248
Oescus (Gigen), III, 207
Office, public, see Public office
Officials, Jewish: in royal service, III,
150-61, 303-8, IV, 15 ff., 29 ff., 36-39,
45, 251-53
—— communal: appointment, V, 71;
election, V, 67 f.; hereditary principles
and, V, 73 f.; number, V, 60; special-
ized, V, 51

Oikonomia, term, IV, 218
Oikumene, V, 117 f.
Oinomaos of Gadara, II, 281
'Olah, I, 353
'Olam, term, II, 389
'Olam ha-ba, term, V, 148
Oldenburg, see Sopron
"Oldest Collection of Bible Difficulties
by a Jew," VI, 305 ff.
Old Testament, IV, 51; Arabic translation, VI, 264; canonization, II, 144 f.,
V, 262; Christians' use of, II, 144, 145,
170, VI, 241, 257, VIII, 77, 95 f.; critique of Mardan Farukh, V, 106; controversy over interpretation, V, 85 ff.,
129, 135, 136, see also Interpretation,
biblical; deviations from law of, V, 93;
doctrine of Chosen People (q.v.), V,
125 ff.; "Hebrewisms" in translations
of, VII, 10; Latin and other late translations, II, 144, 385, VI, 272 ff., 462 f.;
messianic allusions, V, 157, see also
Messiah and messianism; on moneylending and usury, IV, 199; Muslim
arguments based on, V, 86 ff.; Paulicians and, VIII, 288; poetic rhythm,
VII, 313 f.; prophecies, V, 174, see also
Prophets and prophecy; reevaluation
of postexilic period demanded, I, 103,
341; references to divine attributes, V,
120 f.; stabilization of text, VI, 292,
442; strictures on, II, 167 f., 394, V, 88,
106, 330 f., VI, 298, 303, VIII, 128;
subjects in liturgical poems, VII, 85;
taboos, V, 250; tendency to give greater
credence to records, I, 32; see also
Bible; also under names of books,
e.g., Esther; and under versions, e.g.,
Septuagint; see also Masorah; Maso-
rites
Olive oil: quality, II, 246; uses, I, 253,
II, 247
Olive press, use in forced conversion, III,
180, 315
Olivet, Mount: Rabbanite pronounce-
ments from, V, 279; site of worship by
Jews, III, 101
Olive tree, Jews likened to, II, 173
Olympic games, I, 236
Omar, Covenant of, see under 'Umar I;
'Umar II
Omnipotence, of God, VIII, 96 f.
Omniscience, of God, VIII, 96 f.; see also
Attributes, divine; God

Omri, king of Israel, I, 73, 322; dynasty of, rebellion against, I, 89

Ona'ah, term, II, 255

One, number, VIII, 151 f.

Onias, military commander, II, 94

Onias IV, high priest, I, 14, 200, 386; temple of, I, 219, 394, II, 12, 93, 126; temple priests, I, 219

Onias the Just, identified with Righteous Teacher, II, 349 f.

Onkelos, Targum, II, 146, 346, 386, VI, 256; Aramaic counterpart to Aquila ('Aqilas), VI, 256, 260 f.; concordance to, VII, 29; decline of use in Fez, VII, 5 f.; masoretic recension, VI, 258 f., 312; Rabbanite reverence for, VII, 227; and Targum Jonathan, VI, 456

Onkelos the Proselyte, VI, 260

Onomatological studies, I, 350; see also Names

Ontology, and the existence of God, VIII, 324

Ophir, I, 321; identification of, III, 116, VII, 18

Ophthalmology, VIII, 405

Opportunity, equality of, II, 279

Optics, VIII, 159

Oracles, I, 154, 210, 391; attributed to Balaam, I, 313; fallen into desuetude, I, 82, 152

Oracular lots, I, 49, 314

Oral Law (Deuterosis), II, 65, 207, 294, 314, III, 189, V, 188 f., 209, 374, VI, 22 f.; Byzantine suppression of, III, 12 f., 233, V, 26, VI, 261, VII, 83, 94 f., 256; esoteric, II, 314, VIII, 52; influence, II, 294; Karaite repudiation of, V, 213, 218, 246, 251 ff., 272, 274, VI, 275; Maimonides on transmission of, VI, 100, VIII, 210 f., 380; memorizers of, VI, 37; Pharisaic defense of, VI, 438; Rabbanites and, V, 218, 282; sectarians and transmission of, VI, 201; see also Law; Talmud

Oral study, II, 275, 281, 421

Oral transmission, see Transmission, oral

Oran, battle of, III, 127

Orations: device used by Yosephon, VI, 193; Graeco-Roman, VI, 163 ff.

Orators, Greek, employment of tachygraphoi, VI, 157

Orchards, IV, 162

Ordeal: trial by, I, 329, IV, 40, V, 205; by combat, IV, 40, 92; exemption from, IV, 49, 69, 77 f.; water, IV, 137 f.

Ordinances (taqqanot): communal, V, 64, VI, 46, 131-41, 392-95; termination of, VI, 136; see also Decrees

Ordination: ancient, II, 201, 419; of judges, VI, 9; restoration of, VIII, 191

Ordoño III, of Leon, III, 155 f.

Orestes, prefect, II, 402

Oria, Italy: capital punishment in, V, 57; Jewish community, III, 180

Orient, mass migrations to, II, 210

Oriental art, see Graeco-Oriental art and music

Oriental factor in decline of Hellenism, II, 173 ff.

Oriental renaissance led by Jews, I, 210, 212

Origen, II, 23, 81, 131, 151, 391; VI, 157; Christian doctrine and theories, II, 161; Egyptian citizenship, II, 412; estimates of converts, II, 163; Hexapla, VI, 248; written transmission of works, VII, 258

Original sin, doctrine of, II, 433

Orléans, France: fairs, IV, 325; Jewish community, IV, 57; synagogue, III, 53

—— Second and Third Councils of, III, 50, 51, 252, IV, 156 f.

Orosius, Paulus, VI, 429

Orphans, V, 321; economic and social status, I, 275, II, 271; legal protection, II, 253; writ of appointment for guardians, VI, 67

Orthodox Eastern Church, V, 109, VII, 65, 84; attitude toward Jews, III, 185; commemoration of Najran martyrs, III, 67; formula on nature of Christ, III, 5; linguistic freedom, VII, 68; vs. Monophysites, III, 259; Romanos I and, III, 182; Russian conversion, III, 221; Russian sectarianism, III, 216; theological controversies in Palestine, III, 21

Orthodoxy, Jewish, I, 31; departure from, as apostasy, II, 292

Oshaiah or Oshaya, R., II, 21, 247

Osiris, I, 335

Ossuaries, II, 63, 287

Ostraca, I, 78, 213, 252, 318, 334

Othniel, son of Kenaz, II, 37

Otot ha-Mashiah, V, 143

Otranto, Italy, IV, 24, VI, 119

Otto I (Otto the Great), emperor, III,

Otto I (*Continued*)
155, IV, 65, VI, 222; ambassadors in
Cordova, VI, 435; coronation, VI, 420
Otto II, emperor, IV, 47, 65; and Ka-
lonymide family, IV, 273
Otto III, emperor, IV, 238
Otto of Freising, chronicler, VI, 434
Ouargela, *see* Warjalan
Outhouses, Persian, VI, 344
Outlawry: of Christianity, III, 132; of
forced conversion, IV, 236; of Islam,
III, 212 f.; of relapse to Judaism, IV,
61; of violence, IV, 70
—— of Judaism, III, 24, 174, 186, 193;
under the Almohades, III, 111 f.,
124 ff., 290 ff.; by Dagobert, III, 47; by
Heraclius, III, 32, 174 f., 220; by Leo
III, III, 313; by Phokas, III, 237; by
Trajan in Cyprus, III, 19 f.
Ovid, I, 382, II, 241
Oviedo (Coyanza), Council of, IV, 43
Ownership, *see* Landownership; Prop-
erty
Oxford, England, IV, 81
Oxyrhynchus papyri, I, 395, II, 244

P

Pacific Ocean, VIII, 214 f.
Pactum, term, III, 249
Paganism, II, 310; and Christian Church,
II, 140, 151 ff., 154 f., 163, 169 ff.; de-
ities identified with the God of Jews,
II, 24; intellectual counterattacks, II,
156 ff., 390 ff.; "pagan revival," II, 160
Pagan temples: adornment and worship
in, II, 6, 7; contributions by Jews, II,
24
Paganus, term, II, 166, 393
Painting: frescoes in Dura-Europos, II,
11, 14, 331; in synagogues, II, 11 ff.,
154, 331, 402
Palaestina, new name for Judaea, II, 123,
380; *see also* Palestine
Palaestina Tertia, III, 61
Palermo, Sicily: Muslim capital, IV,
20 f.; synagogue, III, 30; transfer of
Jews to clergy, IV, 22
Palestine: Ancient, Israelitic: agriculture, I, 55 ff.; celebration of Jubilee
years, VIII, 210; copper-producing
areas, I, 60; early ties with Arabia,
III, 61; education in, I, 323; Egypt's
relations with, I, 35, 67, 316, 322; eth-

nological make-up, I, 34, 57, 104, 307,
320; geography, I, 33, 53 f.; handicrafts, I, 69, 323; influence, I, 53-61,
316-19; Israel's birthplace, I, 32 ff., 42,
53 ff., 101, 161, 302, 308, 316; invasions
of, I, 63, 344; myth re emigration of
Canaanites, I, 374, III, 214 f., 271,
335; Phoenicia's relations with, I, 306,
374, III, 214 f.; population, I, 64, 320;
sacrificial and nonsacrificial worship,
I, 123; trade and industry, I, 77, 327;
urbanization, I, 71, 85
—— postexilic and talmudic: agriculture,
I, 250-55, 406-7, II, 104 f., 245, 246, 373,
406 f.; Alexander's conquest of, I, 184,
228, 338, VIII, 205; ancient Hebrew
dialects, VII, 40; and Babylonia, I,
282, II, 205, 207 f.; burial in sacred
soil of, II, 289; calendar and festivals,
I, 220; cattle raising, I, 301; cemeteries of Jews, I, 378; center of Jewish
life, I, 116, 165, 212-49, 277, 392-405,
II, 82, 204, 206 f., 321; centers of
learning: students, II, 207 f.; charter
granted to Jews, I, 216, 369, 393; Christianity (*q.v.*), II, 62, 82, 164, 204;
churches, II, 392; controls over, II,
125 f.; economic conditions, I, 108,
258, 262-71, II, 102, 246; emigration
from, I, 172, II, 123, 204, 208, 210, 377,
405 ff.; effect of antisemitic movements
in other lands, I, 219, *see also* Antisemitism; freedmen within Jewish
communities, I, 269; Greek funerary
inscriptions, I, 378; harlots' quarters,
II, 225; and Hellenism, I, 228 f., 398;
Herod's fiscal reign of terror, I, 262,
410; historic importance, I, 392; internal animosities, I, 162, 281, 284,
367, II, 116; Jewish bourgeoisie, I, 280;
Jewish state, I, 250; "Judaea," a con-
fusing term, I, 397; Judaism, formulation of, I, 133; land measures, II, 104,
372, 373, *see also* Land; law formulated again outside the country, I,
162; marriage laws and customs, II,
221, 226, 227; patriarchate (*q.v.*), II,
126, 192-206 *passim*, 209, 403; and
Persian Empire, I, 160, 162; population, I, 168, 371, 372, II, 27; Restoration, I, 105, 112, 114, 157-63, 366-68;
resurrection from the dead in, II, 40;
and Rome, I, 237 ff., 247 ff., 263, 402-5,
II, 89, 96 ff., 102 f., 104 ff., 368-73

passim; Sadduceeism, II, 36; sculptures, II, 9; sectarian divisions, II, 3 ff.;
self-determination of coastal Greek
cities, I, 225; slaves and free workers,
I, 267-71, 412, IV, 190; social stratification, I, 262-67, 271-76, 413-14, II,
279, 343; social turmoil, I, 249-85, 349,
406-15; Syriac-Aramaic dialect, VII,
84; taxation, I, 411, II, 185 f., *see also*
Taxation; theocratic regime, I, 163,
165, 221-27, 395-97; trade and industry,
I, 255-58, 407-8, II, 248 f.; value of
residence in, VI, 230 f.; weaknesses
undermining, I, 212; woman's social
status, I, 114; *see also* Judaea and
Judaeans
—— High medieval: academic independence, V, 24-32, 302-5; Arab conquest, II, 179, III, 62, 102 f., V, 99,
VII, 97; attachment of Jews to, IV, 94,
V, 26 ff., 198, VI, 230 f.; Babylonian
Jews in, V, 303; banking, IV, 198;
Book of Precedents, VI, 64 f., 355 f.;
Charlemagne's alleged protectorate
over, IV, 257 f.; under the Crusaders,
IV, 109 ff., 295 ff.; desertion of land by
farmers, III, 168; earthquakes, IV,
153; emigration from, III, 48, 113, IV,
221; evolution of Jewish law, VI, 5 ff.;
exilarchate, VI, 199 f.; four ells of
land, VI, 134, V, 27, 303, VII, 63; as
geographic lodestar, VIII, 211; God's
gift to Israel, VI, 51; Jewish expansion, III, 100 f.; Judeo-Christian relations (*q.v.*), III, 77; Karaites in, V,
222 f., 271, 395, VI, 288 ff., 472 f.; VII,
18, 37 ff.; Khazar hope of military conquest, III, 204; as land of Israel, VIII,
125; landownership, IV, 151 ff., 312 f.;
law codes, VI, 82 f.; loss of direct contact with, V, 58; merchants, IV, 327 f.;
messianic hope of return to, V, 27, 155,
185, 202, 221, 282, 358, VII, 168 f., 178;
messianic movement, V, 202, 384 f.;
Muslim respect for holiness of, III,
269; mutual hostility of Christian
sects, III, 161; Persian-Jewish collaboration in, III, 20; pilgrimages to, IV,
131, V, 31 f., VI, 225 f.; plant life cycles, V, 246; poll tax, III, 191 f.; population, III, 103, 237; proclamation of
new moon, VIII, 186, *see also under*
Moon; ritualistic autonomy, VII, 24 ff.,
65, 94 f., 246, 302 ff.; sectarian strife,

III, 102; self-assertion of Jewish com-
munities, V, 24-32, 302-5; Seljuk rule,
III, 104, IV, 94, 285; spread of Arabic,
VI, 256; spread of Hebrew liturgy
from, VII, 101; Tobiah's letter for
pilgrim to, VI, 174 f.; Tulunide rulers,
V, 222; variations in local customs, V,
26 f., 302 f., VI, 122 ff., 389; *see also*
Academies; Exilarchs and exilarchate;
Latin Kingdom of Jerusalem; Rabbis
and rabbinate; *also* place names
Pallughta (Pumbedita?), messianic movement in, V, 184
Palm-trees, I, 253; grove of Frederick II,
IV, 160; plantations limited, I, 262; as
symbol, II, 11, III, 70
Palmyra and Palmyrenes: caravan trade,
II, 417, III, 62, VIII, 168; communal
leaders, V, 50; conversions and reli-
gious syncretism, II, 159; exclusion
from Judaism, II, 222, 232; god Hyp-
sistos, III, 62; inscriptions, II, 211,
407; Jews in, II, 210, III, 104; legend
on descent of Palmyrenes, II, 222, 232,
III, 62; repulse of Shapur I, II, 177,
III, 62
Palṭiel b. Shefaṭiah, Jewish leader, III,
154, V, 40 f.
Palṭoi Gaon, VI, 27, 108
Pamphlet literature, I, 87, 334, VI, 214 f.
Panaetius, II, 4
Pannonia, Hungary, II, 210, III, 206
Pantheism, Babylonian, I, 314
Panticapaeum, *see* Kertsh
Papa, R., II, 248, 249, 251, 288
Papacy: attempts at supremacy, II, 198,
401, IV, 95; attitude toward Jews, III,
27 ff., IV, 14, 47; *Constitutio pro
Judaeis,* IV, 7 f.; Jewish appeals to, for
redress, IV, 17, 97 f.; and Jewish com-
munity of Rome, IV, 4 ff.; protection
for Church holdings, IV, 59; revenue,
IV, 12 ff., 239 f.; sociopolitical rela-
tions with Jewish communities, IV,
7 ff.; *see also* Christian Church; *also
under* names of popes
Papal States, III, 243; ecclesiastical
tithe, IV, 13, 239
Paper: introduction of, IV, 169, VI, 184;
and production of books, VII, 136
Papias, Christian teacher, II, 66, 75, 361
Papias, R., VIII, 36
Papiscus, II, 133
Pappus b. Judah, II, 239

Pappus, revolutionary, II, 96, 370
Papyri, Aramaic, I, 347, 360, see also under Elephantine; Greek, I, 213, 255, 266, 378, 392, see also under special collections, e.g., Oxyrhynchus papyri; preserved in Egypt, I, 213
Papyrus, I, 252; cost of, and book production, VII, 136; trade monopoly, I, 261 f.
Parables, in sermons, VI, 166 f.
Paradise, preexistence of, VIII, 125 f.
Paran, Mount, identification of, V, 86, 89
Parasang, unit of length, VIII, 213 f.
Parasitic class, I, 275
Parchment, I, 252; production of, IV, 319; requirements in use of, VII, 286
Parents, see Family life
Pariah status of Jews, I, 23, 24, 297
Paris: Benjamin of Tudela on, IV, 60; conversionist pressure on Jews in, III, 52; Fifth Council of, III, 51
Parlor games: poetic improvisations, VII, 150 f., 162; riddles, VII, 4
Paroikia, term, II, 381
Parousia, II, 73
Parsees and Parsiism, II, 180, 183, 184, 190, V, 375; and burial, II, 290; eschatological computations, II, 318, 342, 435; expansion, I, 102, II, 251; incest encouraged, II, 229; interrelations with Judaism, I, 159, 366, II, 317 f., 436; law a basic constituent, I, 227; marriage, II, 219, 229, 231; rejection of sacrifices, I, 127; religious exclusiveness, I, 117, 159, 348, II, 150, 257; see also Persia; Zoroaster; Zoroastrianism
Parthia, II, 95 f., 97; and Hellenism, II, 174; marriage and incest, II, 229; and Sassanian empire, II, 174
Particularism, religious, I, 96-99, 339; see also Nationalism
Partnerships: interfaith, IV, 177, 185 f., 338; lenders and borrowers as, IV, 200 f.; Muslim law on, IV, 331; among shopkeepers, IV, 327
Pascal, Blaise, V, 101
Paschal II, pope, IV, 114
Passover (Pesaḥ), I, 5, 148, 214, 254, 361, 381, III, 202, V, 227, 236, 246; agricultural labor and, IV, 315; association with blood accusation, IV, 135 ff., 306 f.; coincidence with Easter, II, 188,

209, 401, III, 11, 248, V, 303, 346, 410; date of, VIII, 185 f., 187 ff., 195; Haggadah, I, 189, 197, 381, II, 119, III, 289, V, 392; laws relating to, V, 122 f.; lambs, I, 148, 221, 372, V, 173, 217, 223, 236; prayer for dew, VII, 98; ritual, II, 119; sectarians and, V, 196, 217; theme in sacred poetry, V, 153, VII, 181; wine drinking, VII, 116
Passport (aman), dependent on poll tax, III, 166
Past, idealization of, I, 99-100, 340; see also History
Pateressa synagogae, II, 413
Patriarchal society, I, 43, 310
Patriarchate: Christian: Cyril elevated to, II, 190; Juvenal, III, 20
—— Palestinian: control of calendar proclamation, II, 206, 209, VIII, 186 ff., 368 ff.; disaffection and resentment toward, II, 269; office, its functions and decline, II, 126, 192 ff., 195, 197, 200 f., 209, 268, V, 179; rabbis' cooperation with, II, 291; reestablished by Karaites, V, 32; rivalry between "dynasty" of exilarchs and, II, 198, 205, 403
Patriarchs, biblical, I, 32 ff., 301; divine pledge to, I, 335, V, 99; dualist attack on, V, 106; God of the, I, 43; influenced by earthly trigon, VIII, 180
Patrons, literary, VII, 147 ff., 186
Paul, Saint, I, 170, 209, 221, 294, II, 70, 74, 80, 151, 164, 265, 381, 383; Athenian disputes, II, 79 f., 362, 363, 389; attitude toward nature, II, 81; burned magic books, II, 23; and Catholic Church, II, 86, 366; and the Chosen People, V, 126; controversialists on, V, 119; cooperation with Jerusalem community, II, 82; disciples, II, 365; epistles, II, 78, 81, 84, 85 f., 362, 365, VII, 109; failure in Rome, II, 165; father of, II, 36, 56; and Hellenistic Jewry, II, 76, 80, 84, 85, 366; history as means of propaganda, II, 80; leadership, II, 76-87, 361-67; missionary efforts, II, 76, 78, 79 f., 82, 83, 86, 165, 362, 365; reputed knowledge of alchemy, VIII, 224; on Savior's sonship and timelessness, II, 81, 364; use of Hebrew and Greek, I, 185, 187
Paul, patriarch of Antioch, III, 5 f.
Paulicians, III, 179, 183, IV, 107, VIII, 31

Paul of Samosata, II, 407

Paulus, Roman jurist, III, 35

Paulus Aemilius of Verona, III, 250

Paulus Alvarus, IV, 53; and convert Bodo, V, 126

Pauperes, IV, 106

Pavia, Italy: Council of, III, 32; disputation, IV, 26

Pax Romana, I, 250, II, 6, 57, 58, 249

Peace: concessions made, I, 23, II, 188, 400; efforts to establish international and domestic, II, 115 f., 376; formulas used for the dead, II, 424; prayers for, II, 115, VII, 265; proclamations, royal, IV, 70 ff.; treaties with church and state, IV, 89 f.

Peasants: in ancient Palestinian towns, I, 71; equation with *paganus*, II, 166, 393; exploitation of "free," I, 85, 260; freeholders under Vespasian, I, 265; as tenants, II, 105; taxation and flight, II, 245, 414; *see also under* Agriculture; Farmers

Pedagogy, *see* Education

Pedaiah (Shenazzar), I, 349

Peddlers, IV, 180, 184; of "elixir of life," VI, 154

Pedro II, king of Aragon and Sicily, IV, 132; decree on tax exemptions, IV, 39; privilege to Huesca, IV, 39

Pedro Alfonso, *see* Petrus Alphonsi

Pehlevi records, I, 341

Pekah, I, 155

Pelagonia, *see* Macedonia

Pella, I, 225; Christians' removal to, II, 82, 99, 132

Penalties, *see* Punishments

Penance, German system of, VIII, 52

Penitence: in Judaism and Christianity, IV, 95 f.; period of national mourning, IV, 145; *see also* Poetry, liturgical

"Penitential tariff," VIII, 52

Pentagram of Solomon, II, 11

Pentateuch (Torah), I, 140 ff., 359, II, 30, 135, IV, 47; 'Ananites on, V, 212 f., 393; on angels, II, 18; canonical material, I, 317; children's lessons in, II, 275; commentaries on, V, 212, VI, 51, 479, VII, 114; copies for study and recitation, VI, 244; division of commandments, II, 421; Eleazar b. Pedat on, V, 163 f.; ethical sanctions, I, 357; excommunication before scrolls of, V, 17; and Ezekiel's law, I, 154; as first

written book, VIII, 77; fragments, I, 331; *Hekhalot rabbati* on, VIII, 17; Ibn Ḥazm's study of, V, 85, 88; known through Ezra, I, 345; Masoretic, V, 197; modes of interpretation, V, 254, *see also* Interpretation, biblical; Mosaic authorship, I, 330; number of letters and verses, VI, 237 f., 442, VIII, 15, 149, 238; on observation of the Sabbath, V, 92, *see also* Sabbath; official readers, II, 283; "Onkelos" (*q.v.*) to, VI, 258; Persian manuscript of, V, 183; Philo on, I, 199; preservation of, and precision of speech, VII, 3; punishment for burning scroll of, I, 239; reading cycle, V, 28, 405; reading of, in Hebrew and Aramaic, VI, 256; references to the Messiah, V, 118; Samaritan Pentateuch, II, 30, 32, 340, VI, 442; Samaritan Triglot, VI, 271; segregationist prohibitions, V, 100, 335 f.; sorcery denounced, II, 17; summary of rational and divine law, VI, 142 f.; translation inadequate, II, 143; weekly readings, in synagogues, II, 280, 281, 422, VII, 72; on women, I, 111; *see also* Bible: Law; Old Testament; Torah; *and under* names of books, *e.g.*, Exodus

Pentecost, I, 5

Peons, Persian, II, 257; *see also* Agriculture; Peasants

"People of the book," III, 81, 164, V, 82, 236, 400, VI, 19; warning against, VI, 444

Pepin the Short, Frankish king, IV, 259

Pepper, as medium of payment, IV, 182, 347

Perctarit, Langobard king, III, 32, IV, 25

Peregrini, II, 226

Perfet, nephew of Saltel, IV, 159

Perfet (Profet), Sheshet b. Solomon, IV, 36 f.

Peroz Shapur, Persian emperor, III, 55, 109

Persecutions: of Christians by pagans, I, 400, IV, 57, VII, 256; by Almohades, III, 122 ff.

—— of Jews, II, 215 f., IV, 89 ff., 105, V, 108 f., VI, 427, VII, 177; Byzantine, III, 199; under Caliphate, III, 122 ff., 289 ff., *see also* names of caliphs; history of Jews as series of, I, 400;

Persecutions (Continued)
inescapability of, II, 215; "lachrymose conception of Jewish history," VI, 234, VII, 247; and liturgical creativity, VII, 83 f.; local or individual, VI, 218 f.; pogroms, I, 191, 266, II, 189; for possession of Bible, VII, 86; see also Antisemitism; Atrocities; Martyrs and martyrdom; Massacres of Jews, Murder

Persia: Achaemenid and Parthian, I, 102 f., 106 f., 169, II, 26, 206, III, 18, V, 119 f.; Aramaic used in, I, 159; assimilation of racial and religious groups, I, 111, 131, 181; and Egypt, I, 190; family distinction valued, I, 125; imperial policy, I, 129-32, 142, 162, 184, 353-55; and Judaism, I, 228, 341, II, 317; Phoenician ghettos, I, 176; policy toward Jews, I, 103, 116, 129 ff., 163, 348, 354 f., 372; Samaria as a district capital, II, 27; self-determination under, I, 166; semicapitalist economy, I, 109; see also Achaemenids; Parsees and Parsiism; Parthia

—— Sassanian, V, 230, VI, 54, VII, 255; admixture of names in, VIII, 275; Arab penetration of, III, 88 f.; attitude to burial, II, 290; caste system, II, 176, 181, 279, 403; changing attitudes, II, 213; Christians in, II, 164, 181, 399, III, 89, VI, 271; dates borrowed from eschatology of, II, 318; destruction of Antioch, III, 6 f.; exilarchate, II, 195 ff., 200 f., 205, 291, 403, VI, 200; expedition to India, II, 212, 407; family distinction valued, I, 125; fiscal reforms, III, 56; immigration of Nestorians into, VI, 271; influence after decline of Hellenism, I, 283, II, 174; intergroup relations, II, 190, III, 128 f.; invasion of Armenia, III, 18; and Jewish refugees, III, 8, V, 180, VIII, 241; Jewish revolt, II, 182 f., 399, VI, 199 ff.; 423 f.; Jewish schools, VI, 54; Jews in, II, 172-214 passim, 317 f., 396-407, III, 8; "king of kings," VIII, 18; and Lakhmids, III, 61, 63; last king of, III, 19; legal system, II, 299, 302 f., 429 f., 431; legislation against Shema', VII, 95; Magi, II, 181, 183, 190, 317, 347; medical literature, VIII, 235 f.; polygamy and incest, II, 226, 229; rank and titles of officials, II, 196, 403; religious beliefs and policy, II, 173, 213, VI, 3; religious controversies, V, 106; Rome and, II, 176 ff., 213, 396 ff.; rule by religious fanatics, II, 213; Samaritan refugees in, III, 255; status of minority groups, III, 54 ff., 120, 254 ff.; tax system, II, 180, 184 ff.; see also Babylonia; Exilarchs and exilarchate; Lakhmids; Parsees and Parsiism; Parthia; Sassanians; Zoroaster; Zoroastrianism

—— under Islam: autonomy of local usages, VI, 126; and the catholicos, III, 89; dualism in, V, 104; expansion of Jewry in, III, 109; inquiries to geonim, VI, 113; Jewish traders in, IV, 174; Karaites, V, 397 f.; messianic movement, III, 204, V, 203 f.; poetry and music, VII, 318; reading of haftarah, VI, 42; reversal of policy toward Jews, III, 239; sectarianism, III, 57, V, 183 ff.; taxation system, III, 162, 255; traveler's report of population, VI, 224; see also under cities, e.g., Isfahan

Persian language, II, 146, 147; classical forms vs. dialects, VII, 5; talmudic loan words, II, 206, 405, VII, 141; translation of Bible into, VI, 271

Perso-Byzantine wars, III, 17, 18 ff., 74 f.; and the Caliphate, III, 86 ff.; Jewish participation, III, 18-24, 57, 236-40, VIII, 235; Samaritans and, III, 17 f., 235 f., V, 170 f.

Personality, inner conflicts, I, 21

"Personality principle," II, 265

Perushim, the, II, 342, 343; see also Pharisees and Pharisaism

Pesaḥ, I, 5; see also Passover

Pesaḥ, Khazar commander, III, 203

Pesaḥim, tractate, VI, 86, 382

Pescennius Niger, I, 263, II, 400

Pesher, commentary, VI, 158

Peshiṭta: canonical Syriac, VII, 4; origin of, II, 386 f., VI, 257, 454 f.; textual exactitude, VI, 241; see also Aramaic language; Syriac language

Pesiqta de-R. Kahana, VI, 162

Pesiqta rabbati, midrash, VI, 165, VII, 130, 182

Pesiqta zuṭrata, VI, 175

Petaḥiah b. Jacob of Ratisbon, Jewish traveler, VII, 129; chronological framework of journey, VI, 437; on Jewish communities in Byzantium, III, 195;

Jewish population, III, 104, 113; on Khazaria, III, 201 f.; messianic computation, VIII, 47 f.; travels, VI, 222-26, 435-37
Petcherskii Monastery, III, 215
Peter, Saint, II, 70, 71, 82; crucifixion and burial, II, 74, 361; Epistles, II, 74, 362; espouses nomistic Judeo-Christianity, II, 74 f., 361; Hebrew prayers ascribed to, II, 74 f., VII, 92; identification with Cephas and others, II, 74 f., 361
Peter the Hermit, IV, 98; bridge over the Danube, IV, 107
Peter the Venerable of Cluny, V, 116, 341; on "Alphabet of Ben Sira," VI, 169; antisemitism, IV, 122, 301 f.; on Jews and farm labor, IV, 155
Petra, III, 61
Petronius, and Caligula's statue, I, 219, 231
Petrus II (Candiano), doge: antisemitism, IV, 25
Petrus Alphonsi (Pedro Alfonsi; formerly Moses Sefardi), Christian convert and scientist, V, 115 f., VIII, 173 f.; on the attributes of God, V, 345; on Jesus' word on the cross, V, 120
Phanagoria (Sennaja), III, 202
Pharaohs: and the *Apiru* (Hebrew), I, 38, 56; *see also under* individual names, *e.g.,* Akhenaton
Pharisees and Pharisaism, I, 142, 166, 226, 234-38, II, 35-54, 342-50, V, 250, 255; Christians and, II, 70 f., 75, 343; contemporary sects, II, 46-54, 346-50; democratic trends, I, 175; doctrines elaborated, I, 221, 226, 237, II, 38, 308 f., 310-14, 320, 344 f., 434; educational system, II, 46, 274; and enslavement of Jews, I, 267; and era of Creation, VIII, 208; Essenes, II, 48-51, 342; expansive and popular force, II, 36, 344; and government, I, 216, 223, 237, 401, II, 56, 117; influence on Islam, VI, 8; Jesus' denunciation of, I, 173, II, 67, 336, 356; Mishnah a legal code of, II, 44, *see also* Mishnah; Talmud; name, II, 35, 342; number, II, 36, 342; priestly revenues, I, 272, 280; and proselytism, I, 181; and rebellions against Rome, II, 90, 100 f.; ritualistic implements displayed, II, 336; strengths and weaknesses, II, 56;

struggle with Sadducees, I, 180, 234, 402, II, 35, 36, 38-46, 343 f.; subjection to law, I, 11; Zealotic faction, II, 47 f.
Phatir, III, 52
Philanthropia, Graeco-Roman, VIII, 263
Philanthropy, *see* Charity; Humanitarianism
Philip II (Philip Augustus), king of France, IV, 128 f.; expulsion of Jews, IV, 61, 80, 156, V, 78; "extradition" treaty with Count Thibaut, IV, 204; moneylending charter, IV, 204-6, 393; treaties re Jews, IV, 62 f., 204, 269 f.
Philipp, archbishop of Cologne, IV, 275
Philipp, eunuch, fraternization with Jews, IV, 21 f.
Philipp, landgrave, IV, 341
Philippopolis, Transjordan, II, 174, 175
Philip "the Arab," emperor, II, 174, 177
Philistines, I, 39, 53, 55; disarming of Israel, I, 60 f.; infiltration of Palestine, I, 63, 320; use of iron, I, 320
Philo Judaeus of Alexandria, I, 66, 177, 181, 199-207, 386-90, II, 8, 9, 55, 137, 198, 315, 391, 409, VIII, 85; apologetic interests, I, 391; on authenticity of biblical text, VI, 236 f.; definition of name "Israel," I, 182; delegate to Caligula, I, 241; description of Jewish congregations, VII, 125; doctrine of creation of time, VI, 469, VIII, 91; doctrine of intermediaries, V, 226; on Essenes, II, 49, 51, 347; exegesis, I, 202, 387, VI, 35; extra-Jewish sources of, I, 388; on Golden Age, I, 209; on imagery, II, 15; on immortality, I, 207, 390; on incest and intermarriage, II, 233; on Jewish expansion, I, 171; on law, I, 204, 387, II, 253, 280 f., 415, 418; on *logos,* II, 202, 389, V, 121; on marriage, II, 229; meaning of "father," II, 309; meaning of *philanthropia* transformed, II, 269; and Midrash, II, 320; monotheism and messianism, I, 208, 232 f., II, 5 f., 329; on Moses, I, 199; and natural law, VI, 144; on *nouveaux riches,* I, 266; on Palestine's historic importance, I, 392; Paul's indebtedness to, II, 85; and Pharisaism, I, 206, II, 36, 56, VII, 80; on pilgrimages, I, 214; quoted, I, 200, 203, 205, II, 152; on sabbatical year,

Philo Judaeus of Alexandria (*Continued*) II, 271; static philosophy, I, 205 f., VIII, 76; on status of Jews in Alexandria, I, 403; survival of doctrines and concepts, II, 206 f., V, 188, VI, 410, VIII, 4; symbolism, II, 13; use of Greek, I, 186; views on prophecy, VIII, 344; on women, II, 241, 413; writings, I, 201, 387, V, 216, 380

Philology: Arabic, VII, 9 f., 15, 19, 234; analogistic and anomalistic approaches, VII, 34, 52, 58, 224 f.

—— Hebrew: acceptance of discoveries in, VII, 46 ff., 238 ff.; classifications, VII, 36; comparative linguistics, VII, 11 ff., 60; debates over, VII, 23, 46, 165; historical shortcomings, VII, 55 ff.; independent research, VII, 49; neglected in Babylonia, VII, 19; and poetry, VII, 211; schools of, VII, 21; Spanish, VII, 19-28, 41-46, 227-31, 236-38; talmudic, VI, 28

"Philomena," and Narbonne, IV, 46

Philosophy: Arab, VIII, 89 f.; German, I, 296

—— Greek: influence on Jewish thinkers, VIII, 55 ff.; letter symbolism, VIII 284; and Moses, I, 174; and reinterpretation of Jewish tradition, VIII, 76 f.; *see also under* individual philosophers, *e.g.*, Aristotle; Farabi

—— Jewish, VIII, 55-137, 296-346; commentaries on, VIII, 65 f.; dilemma of translators of, VII, 220; diverse elements in, VIII, 3 ff.; Ibn Daud's references to, IV, 218 f., VI, 209; and medieval thought, I, 206; messianic ideology, V, 159-66, 363-66; and music, VII, 207 f.; neglect of works of, VIII, 137; pietistic and nationalistic, VIII, 39; poets and, VII, 151, 171 f.; and prophecy, VIII, 127-35, 342-45; rationalistic, I, 201; and science, VIII, 222 ff.; speculation vs. revelation, VIII, 85; subservience to religion, VIII, 81; written in Arabic, VII, 8; *see also under* individual philosophers, *e.g.*, Moses b. Maimon; Philo Judaeus; Saadiah Gaon

Philo the Elder, I, 198, 386, II, 31, 341; epic on biblical themes, VII, 167

Phineas, I, 38; longevity, VIII, 211

Phineas, head of Rabbanite academy of Jerusalem, VI, 245

Phinehas b. Meshullam of Alexandria, VI, 380; and Maimonides, VI, 98

Phocylides, I, 184

Phoenicia and Phoenicians, I, 55; and Canaanites, III, 91; circumcision, I, 6; colonies, I, 39, 175; conversion to Judaism, I, 176, 374; expeditions in Far East and Africa, III, 116; relations with Palestine, I, 61, 306; religion, I, 374

Phokas, Byzantine emperor, III, 16; outlawry of Judaism, III, 19, 237

Phonetics, Hebrew, VI, 242; masoretic development of, VI, 249 ff.

Photius, patriarch, III, 181; commendation of Cyril, III, 210

Phrygia, I, 216

Phylacteries, II, 189, 335 f., V, 59, 122, 215, 218; manual of laws on, VI, 65, 93, 475, VII, 21; Qumran, VII, 244

Physical education, II, 421

Physicians, I, 275; *dhimmis*, Muslim attitude toward, III, 152, V, 96 f., VIII, 254; Muslim, status of, VIII, 237, 398

—— Jewish, II, 185; access to medical literature, VIII, 235 f.; all-round knowledge of patient, VIII, 260; canon law on treatment by, III, 175, 194; charity practice, VIII, 258; to Christian lord, IV, 113 f.; court, IV, 37, 253, VIII, 232 ff., 246, 248 f., 255; ethics of, VIII, 234, 238; fees, VIII, 254 f.; Hippocratic oath, VIII, 238, 242; humility of, VIII, 391; interfaith cooperation in medical studies, VIII, 265; musical therapy, VII, 208 f.; number of, VIII, 255, 389 f.; professionalization of, VIII, 232 ff.; training, VIII, 221 f., 255; *see also* Surgeons and surgery; *also under* individual physicians, *e.g.*, Asaph Judaeus; Moses b. Maimon

Physics: definition, VIII, 145; interest of philosophers, VIII, 222 f.; as a science, VIII, 142

Piast dynasty, Poland, III, 217

Pierleoni, Peter, *see* Anacletus II

Pierre de Lubières, archbishop, IV, 58

Pietism: Jewish compared with Christian, VIII, 48 ff., 295; heterogeneous elements in, VIII, 45 f.; Italo-German, VII, 175-83, 205, 303-7, VIII, 14, 32 f., 42-50, 293-95; on medical interference with God's will, VIII, 231 ff.; *see also* Ḥasidism

Pigeon-fanciers, **I**, 254; disapproval of, **I**, 275

Pig symbol, **II**, 152; "in Zion," **VII**, 97

Pilgrimages: and geographic knowledge, **VIII**, 211; leap year and, **VIII**, 376; to Mecca, **III**, 88, 302, **VIII**, 211; to Medina, **III**, 88; to Palestine, **I**, 213 f., 258, 392, **II**, 108, 118, 374, **IV**, 94 f., 131, 283, 284 f.

Pinḥas, Palestinian poet, **VII**, 268

Pinḥas b. Yair, R., **VI**, 410

Pioneers: Jews as, **III**, 222, **IV**, 161, **V**, 62, 319, **VIII**, 159; in Khazaria, **III**, 197

"Pious, Book of the," **VI**, 404; on care of the sick poor, **VIII**, 258, 265; on medical fees, **VIII**, 233; on preventive medicine, **VIII**, 261; *see also* Pietism

Pi-Ra'amses (House of Raamses), **I**, 38

Pirates, **I**, 256, 407; capture of slaves by, **IV**, 192; raids on shipping, **IV**, 184; ransom from, **IV**, 177 f.; scholars captured by, **V**, 46 f.

Pirqe de-R. Eliezer, **II**, 296, **III**, 163, **VI**, 168, 170, **VII**, 66, **VIII**, 147; on calendar proclamations, **VIII**, 194; on chronological problems, **VI**, 307; cycle of 84 years, **VIII**, 191

Pirqoi b. Baboi, **V**, 181, 282 f., **VI**, 22, 65, 81, 253; on liturgical deviations, **VII**, 65; on Palestinian scrolls, **VII**, 286; on *piyyuṭim*, **VII**, 103, 125; on Yehudai, **VI**, 79; on religious restrictions of Jews, **VII**, 84, 95

Pisa, Italy, **IV**, 26

Pishon, river, **III**, 116, **VI**, 266, 281

Piyyuṭim, **V**, 151, 249, **VII**, 63 ff., 89-105, 259-71; acceptance of, **VII**, 100 ff., 132 f.; in Aramaic, **VII**, 192 f.; on attributes of God, **VII**, 178; debt of Spanish poets to, **VII**, 270; German mysticism in, **VIII**, 44; imitations, **VII**, 104; improvisations, **VII**, 82 f., 86, 143, 255; language of, **VII**, 103 f.; melodies for, **VII**, 125 f.; opposition to, **VII**, 100 ff., 149; popularity of, **VII**, 269; posttalmudic, **VII**, 57; refrains, **VII**, 127 f.; *see also* Liturgy; Poetry

Place names: biblical, **VI**, 211; Hebrew transliteration of, **VI**, 223; identification of, **VI**, 266, 281; Jewish, in France and Poland, **III**, 218, 251, 338; talmudic, **VII**, 14

Placitum, term, **III**, 42, 249

Plagiarism, **VII**, 299, 308; by translators, **VII**, 312

Planets: comparative sizes, **VIII**, 162 ff., 360; conjunctions of, **VIII**, 180 f.; distances from earth, **VIII**, 184; position of, **VIII**, 164

Plantations, **I**, 252

Plants: identification of biblical, **VI**, 474; life cycles of, **V**, 246; names of, **VIII**, 253; poisonous, **VIII**, 258

Plato, **I**, 174, 199, **II**, 4, 6, 157, **VIII**, 57, 61; *Laws*, **VIII**, 61; legendary meeting with Jeremiah, **VIII**, 320; on negative attributes of God, **VIII**, 98; neoplatonism (*q.v.*), **V**, 381 f.; *Republic*, **VIII**, 61; Semitic pronunciation of name, **VI**, 449; social ideal, **I**, 295; superiority of Torah, **VI**, 142

Plato of Tivoli, **VIII**, 148; collaboration with Bar Ḥiyya, **VIII**, 266; translation by, **VIII**, 155

Pledges, laws of, **VI**, 68 f.

Pleonasms, in mystic writings, **VIII**, 14

Pliny the Elder, **I**, 210, 250, 251, 252, **II**, 5; *Natural History*, **VIII**, 253; quoted, **II**, 49, 151

Plotinus: method employed by, **II**, 320; theory of emanations, **VIII**, 91 ff.

Plural forms, interpretation of biblical, **V**, 120

Plutarch, **I**, 251, **II**, 24; ignorance of Jewish customs, **II**, 390

Pneumatikoi (spiritualists), **II**, 85, 365

Pocoke, Edward, **VI**, 60

Poetry: Egyptian, **VIII**, 325; Greek, **VII**, 314; non-Hebraic by Jews, **VII**, 190 ff.; Syriac, **VII**, 203

—— Arabic: biblical reflection of, **VII**, 201 f.; homosexuality as theme, **VII**, 158 ff.; influence of, **VIII**, 325; quest for innovation, **VII**, 142; written by Jews, **VII**, 191 ff.

—— Jewish, **IV**, 38, 216, **VII**, 89-105, 140-83, 259-71, 288-307; acrostics, **VII**, 14; "adornments," **VII**, 197 f., 201 f.; antipathy of jurists to, **VII**, 149; in Arabia, **III**, 72, **VII**, 191 f.; art of, **VII**, 193-202, 313-18; astronomic themes, **VIII**, 168 f.; biblical influences, **III**, 261, **VI**, 292, **VII**, 201 f., 316; chain verse, **VII**, 179 f., 306, 316; chastity of, **VII**, 212; decline in the East, **VII**, 47; development in Spain, **VI**, 188, 255, **VII**, 146-75, 291-303; didactic, **VII**, 192;

Poetry (*Continued*)

distinction between sacred and secular, VII, 98 f.; figures of speech, VII, 198; lines reading backward and forward, VII, 151, 185, 197 f.; linguistic devices, VII, 34, 57 ff., 199 ff.; and martyrs, VI, 218; meter in, VII, 22, 41, 194 ff., 313 ff.; names of Palestinian poets, VII, 259; praise of great leaders, VII, 147 f.; priestly poets, VII, 90 f.; rhymed, VII, 88 ff., 261; in Rome, IV, 238; Saadiah's book of grammatical rules, VII, 15; secular themes, VII, 155-69, 296-300; of self-praise, VII, 153, 292; theme of national history, VII, 166 ff., 211, 300; use of, for teaching grammar, VII, 49 f.; of vengeance, IV, 143 f.; vocalized, VI, 260; Zionide elegies, V, 260, VII, 168 f., 298 f.

—— liturgical, III, 233, V, 362, 376 f., VI, 44, 92, 263, 372, 424, VII, 89-105, 169-83, 260-71, 300-307; Arabic meter, VII, 195; Aramaic versions, VI, 263; *Ashirah ve-azamrah*, VII, 182; background, VIII, 30; biblical themes, VII, 134, 167 f.; Christian, VII, 84; composed by synagogue readers, VII, 58; distinguished from secular, VII, 143; effect of music, VII, 209; Franco-German, IV, 309, VII, 144 f.; imitators, VII, 268; improvisations, VII, 82 ff.; individualistic, VII, 132 f.; innovations in terms and forms, VII, 40; as link among communities, VII, 144 f.; on martyred English Jews, IV, 124; and messianism, V, 150 ff.; mystical, VII, 252, VIII, 12 ff.; penitential, IV, 93, 106, 138, 145, 286 f., VII, 145, 170, 173, 179 f.; *qerobot*, VII, 66 f., 318; *Sefer Qerobah*, VII, 202, 318; *selihot*, VII, 99; *see also Piyyutim*

Pogroms: Alexandrian, I, 191, II, 189; catastrophic results, I, 266; *see also* Massacres of Jews

Poitiers, battles of, III, 91

Poland: Jewish communities, III, 206, 217 ff., 338, VII, 178; leader of Slavonic tribes, III, 217; secular Jewish nationalism in, I, 29

Polemics: anti-Jewish in Christian liturgy, VII, 85; religious, V, 83 ff.; *see also* Controversies, socioreligious

Political conditions: moneylending and, IV, 82; and Palestino-Babylonian struggle for communal control, V, 47 ff.

Political power, I, 116, 164, 192; emancipation of nationality and religion from, I, 22, 237; Israelites' weakness vs. democracy, I, 325; lack of, rationalized, I, 23; prophets' deprecation of, I, 96; *see also* Civil rights; Self-government

Political reverses following Judeo-Roman conflicts, II, 102-8, 110

Political rights, IV, 7 ff., 69

Political science, VIII, 144; Arab contributions, VIII, 122

"Political Zionism," I, 28

Politics: Jewish influence on, under the Caliphate, III, 154; and literary talent, VII, 147, 149; liturgical allusions to, VII, 97; participation in by Kievan Jews, III, 216

Polybius, I, 229, 248

Polycarp, Saint, II, 167, 394

Poll tax (*gulgolet, jizya, kephaleiton*), I, 240, 242, II, 373, 375, 399, III, 96, 163 f., 170, 191 f., IV, 151 f., V, 18; in Arabia, III, 80; *aurum coronarium*, III, 191; collection of, V, 5; and estimates of Jewish population, III, 113; exemption from, III, 113, V, 76; in Fez, III, 263; humiliation, III, 167; in Muslim Babylonia, III, 99, 191; and residence permits, V, 69; in Sicily, IV, 23; *see also* Taxation

Polygamy, I, 112, 347, II, 223, 410; Christian Rome's opposition, II, 226; 231; legal theory, II, 227; outlawed, VI, 135 ff., 393 f.; *see also* Monogamy

Polytheism, I, 45, 202, 352; assailed, I, 177, VI, 298; monarchical, I, 44, 312

Pomegranate, I, 253

Pompeii, II, 332

Pompey, Roman general, I, 167, II, 13, 103; occupation of Palestine, I, 223, 237, II, 27

Pontius Pilate, I, 238, 368; cruelty to Samaritans, II, 33; Jesus' trial before, II, 70, 72

Poor, the: charity and social welfare, II, 269 ff., 420, V, 37, 414; communal responsibility, V, 178, VIII, 295; funerals of, II, 287; landless, I, 68; medical care, VIII, 258, 391; Rabbanites and, V, 178, 238; standard of living, V, 239; terms for, II, 269; tithe for, V, 235; a

title of distinction, I, 152; troubled by
need to disregard laws, II, 77; see also
Charity; Poverty; Slaves and slavery

Pope, see Papacy

Population: ancient: biological balance,
I, 156, 171-79, 373-75, II, 219, 238, 408;
Christian and Jewish ratios, II, 163,
165 f., 393; decrease in Jewish, II, 210,
243; Israelitic, I, 64, 320; numerical
and geographical expansion, I, 167-71,
369-72; of Roman Empire, II, 183,
209, III, 283 f.; urban and rural, I,
276

—— medieval: of Byzantine Empire, III,
195, 322 f.; under the Caliphate, III,
99 ff., 113 f., 293; in England, IV, 277;
increase in, IV, 70 f.; Persia, III, 110;
reports of travelers, VI, 224; of Rome,
IV, 240; see also specific countries and
cities

Pork, consumption of, III, 43, V, 131,
VI, 14

Porphyry, Bible critic, II, 158 f., 391,
401

Portugal: Crusaders in, IV, 132; Jews of,
IV, 35; Judeo-Christian relations, III,
160

Poseidonius, I, 194, II, 5, 188, 400

Post mortem examination, VIII, 230

Pothos, son of Straton of Gorgippia, III,
200

Potiphar, and his daughter Asenath, VI,
170

Pottery, I, 320, 326

Poverty, I, 262 ff.; Babylonia's wealth
and, II, 247; extremes leveled, II, 242;
and learning, II, 256; varied attitudes
toward, II, 46; see also Poor, the

Power: attitude toward, I, 22, V, 101;
Jewry's lack of, V, 176, 194; political,
effect of, V, 72 ff.

Praeparatio evangelica, III, 221; see also
Eusebius of Caesarea

Prague, III, 217, 218; admission of Jews
to, IV, 274 f.; forced conversion of
Jews, IV, 100; transferral of holdings
by Jews of, IV, 118; visited by Jewish
traders, VI, 222

Prayer books, V, 26, 28, VII, 63 ff., 105-
18, 271-78; attributed to Rashi, VI,
75; Karaite, V, 248, 408; nucleus in
Natronai's responsum on benedictions,
VII, 110; oral transmission, VII, 85 ff.;
printed, VII, 81; Saadiah's, V, 31, VI,

15, 69, 92; scarcity and high cost of,
VII, 123 f.; Ṣemaḥ, V, 248; Sephardim,
VI, 15; see also Amram; Saadiah
Gaon

Prayers, I, 186, 379, II, 146; against heretics, II, 135, 381; antiquity of, VII, 65;
Arabic, VII, 101; Aramaic, VI, 453 f.,
VII, 192, 244 f.; avoidance of controversial subjects, V, 151; basic, VII, 79,
105 f., 112, 131 f.; composed by synagogue readers, VII, 58; concentration
on meaning, VII, 74, 128, VIII, 14;
daily, VII, 245; deviations from talmudic practices, V, 59; for economic
betterment, II, 256; enumeration of
commandments, VI, 92; forbidden,
V, 26, 302 f.; freedom to recite in any
language, VII, 66; geonim on, VI, 43 f.;
Habdalah, V, 153, 155; Hallel, VII,
69; improvisation, VII, 82 f., 86, 143,
255; influence on heavenly intermediaries, VII, 76 f.; interruption of, II,
286, 423, V, 66 f., 321; Karaites and, V,
248; Kol Nidre, VI, 389; of laudation,
VII, 131; loud-voiced, VII, 74 f.;
memorization of, VII, 85 ff., 124, 257 f.;
Mishawayh's injunctions on, V, 196;
music and, VII, 125-31, 207, 281-85;
in Muslim practice, III, 266, VI, 13 f.;
for Ninth of Ab, II, 112, 375; order of,
VII, 106; orientation toward Jerusalem, I, 213, 392, III, 81, VII, 78, VIII,
211; penitential, VII, 178; of petition, VII, 70, 74, 86 f., 114, 120, 140 f.;
posture, I, 351, VII, 74 ff., 141, VIII, 3;
private, VII, 72, 108; pro perfidis
Judaeis, II, 169, 395, V, 351 f.; proselytes', I, 182; prostration in, VII, 74 f.;
from the Psalms, VII, 44; public recitation, II, 7, 134, 281; qaddish, II, 84,
146, V, 59; for rain, II, 40, 345, 349;
regulations concerning, I, 376, II,
119 f., 138, 282, VI, 69, VII, 84, 133;
for ruler, I, 130, 245, 404, V, 293;
and sacrifices, I, 123 f., 350; for "the
scholars of Babylonia," V, 25; "secret
lore" in, VII, 64; silent, VII, 248; of
Simon b. Yoḥai, III, 274, IV, 296, V,
353; standardization, II, 119, 377; and
study, VII, 143; of thanksgiving, VII,
109; tunes for, VII, 127; variations in
local customs, VI, 122, 125 f.; Yigdal,
VII, 175; Yismaḥ Mosheh, VI, 327; see
also .Liturgy; Piyyuṭim; Poetry;

Prayers (*Continued*)
Ritual; *and under* individual prayers, *e.g., 'Alenu; Azharot*
Preachers: invention of detail, VI, 170 f.; itinerant, VI, 156; rabbis as, VI, 155 ff.; *see also* Homilists and homiletics; Sermons
Precentor, *see* Cantor
Precious stones, medicinal value of, VIII, 225
Predestination, II, 41, VIII, 108 ff., 333 ff.; and life span, VIII, 259; *see also* Free will
Predicables, list of, VIII, 329
Predictions, astrological, VIII, 179 f.; according to astronomic doctrines, VIII, 181 f.; *see also* Prophets and prophecy
Preemption, houseowner's right of, III, 145 f.
Preexistent things, VIII, 125 f.; talmudic enumeration of, V, 147
"Prefect, Book of the," IV, 170, 183, 321 f.
Pregnancy, intercourse prohibited during, II, 221
Premonstratensians, V, 112 f.
Přemysl Ottokar II, king of Bohemia, IV, 137
Presbyter or episcopus: office of English Jewry, V, 63; women as, II, 240
Prester John, III, 205, VI, 434
Preventive medicine, VIII, 261
Prices: and calendar cycles, VIII, 209, 361; gyrations of, II, 247, 414; just, II, 254 f., 416, IV, 222 f.; regulation of, I, 85, II, 261, 417
Priest cities, I, 146, 360
Priestesses, Vestal, I, 146
Priestly Code, I, 111, 142, 150, 156, 359, II, 308; *see also* Leviticus, Book of
Priestly dynasty, founder of, in Jerusalem, I, 330
Priests and priesthood: Egyptian, I, 149, II, 107; Muslim, VI, 9 f.; Persian, II, 317; *see also* Magi
—— Jewish: anointment of, I, 152, 364, 414; aristocracy, I, 149, 272, 274; authority of, I, 74, 76, 81, 140, 149 ff., 153, 271, 281, II, 117; chain of ordination, V, 36; cleavage, I, 273; coinage right in Jerusalem, I, 130, 166, 353; continuity of, after the fall of Jerusalem, VII, 259; and continuity of law, I, 82; culture and character, I, 154;

custodians of Scripture, VI, 236; gifts to, VI, 69; high-priestly office, I, 216, 271, 273, 393, 414; and house of David, VI, 215; Karaite, V, 235 f.; *ha-kohen ha-levi*, V, 174; learning and educational opportunities, II, 117, 120 f.; in Leontopolis, I, 219 f.; marriage, II, 234, V, 18, 240; as masons and carpenters, I, 258; and Mosaic religion, I, 59; nation of, I, 163, VII, 80, 125; numbers of, in Palestine, I, 272, 413; Pharisees, I, 237, II, 45 f., 52, 117; poets among, VII, 90 f.; priestly blessing and other rituals, II, 119; and prophets, I, 149 ff., 365; relations with levites, I, 329, 362, 413; resisted conversion to other creeds, I, 414; ritualistic segregation, I, 149, II, 282; Samaritan, V, 173 f.; as state officers, I, 229; tax exemption, II, 413; tithes and dues paid to, I, 130, 272, 280, 413, II, 105, 118, *see also* Tithes; titles conferred at ordination, II, 120; vestments, I, 239, II, 284, VII, 145; the Wicked Priest, II, 53 f., 349; *see also Kohen and Kohanim;* Levites; Rabbis and rabbinate
—— *see also* Clergy
Prime Cause, VIII, 110
Primum mobile, VIII, 164 f.
Princes, and Jewish property, IV, 15 f.
Princes of captivity, *see* Exilarchs and exilarchate
Printing presses, Hebrew, VI, 279
Priscus, court jeweler, III, 52; debate with Gregory of Tours, V, 114
Prison, Jewish, V, 43
Prisoners of war, I, 95, 259, 325; as slaves, II, 258; treatment of, III, 150
Private ownership, *see under* Property
Privileges: to cities, IV, 23, 35 f., 38, 42, 67 f., 71 f.; to Jews, I, 240 ff., IV, 78 f., 164, 170, 205, V, 62, 324; to merchants, IV, 48, 179, 182; monastic, IV, 65; payment for, IV, 142 f.
Prochownik, Abraham, alleged Polish king, III, 217
Proclus, VIII, 57, 61
Procopius, II, 142, 179, 393, III, 7; on Iberians, III, 22; and portentous disasters, III, 16; on the Samaritans, V, 367 f.
Procreation: duty of, I, 31, II, 210, 218, 219, V, 134

Procurators, *see* Roman Empire
Produce: agricultural, and taxes, IV, 151 f.; and tithes, IV, 314
Produit de Juifs, department in French Treasury, IV, 62
Professions, IV, 197 ff., 215 f.; specialization, VIII, 160
Profiat Duran, *see* Duran, Profiat
Profits, II, 255, 416
Pro (perfidis) Judaeis, prayer, II, 169, 395, V, 351 f.
Proletariat: free, I, 324; landless, I, 76; urban Jewish, I, 281
"Promised land," I, 42, 46
Promotus, Jewish convert to Christianity, V, 126
Pronunciation, Hebrew: changes in, VI, 240; difference between Karaites and Rabbanites, VI, 247 f.; double, VI, 450 f.; and meaning, VI, 443; regional variations, VI, 239, VII, 28; "Sephardic," VIII, 233; and spelling, VI, 243 f., 293; system, VI, 259 f.; of transliterations, VI, 248
Propaganda, anti-Jewish: I, 188, 192, IV, 133 ff.; *see also* Antisemitism
—— Christian, VIII, 48, 177 f.; *see also* Converts and conversion
—— Jewish religious, I, 172 ff., 272, 274, 372, 375; and attitude toward converts, II, 147 ff.; economic and social forces, I, 174; Christian fears of, IV, 9; Gentile reaction, I, 209, 246; *see also* Proselytes and proselytism
—— political: court poets and, VII, 147
Propedeutics, VIII, 142
Property: accumulation by small minority, I, 68; acquisition by Jews, IV, 42, 116 f.; attitude of princes toward Jewish, IV, 15 f., 50; Church, IV, 204 f.; communal, V, 18; confiscation of, III, 45 f., 169, 193, IV, 13, 34, 82, 156; damage or destruction prohibited, II, 254; debts collectible from, VI, 132; of *dhimmis,* III, 143 f., 146; disposal of, IV, 79, 203 f., V, 320; interfaith, III, 301 f.; legal protection for women's, II, 236, 412; mortgages, II, 303, VI, 83; private ownership vs. communal control, I, 89, II, 252, 415, IV, 221 f., 351; registration of, IV, 83; sales and leases to Gentiles, II, 124 f., 261; seizure of debtor's, II, 303; tax, IV, 81; and the tithe, IV, 13; transfer of, IV,

22, 59f., VI, 358; 'Umar I re captured lands, III, 95 f.; urban, IV, 161; *see also* Houses; Land
"Property of iron sheep," II, 236, 412
Prophets and prophecy, I, 22, 84-91, 104, 153, 197, 199, 339; activities, I, 87 ff.; addressed to Gentile nations, VI, 280 f.; 'Anan's attitude toward, V, 212; applied to contemporary events, VI, 308 ff.; attempts to punish, I, 78; bands of, I, 153; biblical, V, 86 ff., 140, VI, 228 ff., 310; cessation of, I, 152, 364, II, 139, VI, 230; on "day-star," V, 132; degrees in, VIII, 132, 344; on deliverance from Egypt, I, 16; enumeration of, VI, 197; false or true, I, 87, 333; gift of prophecy, VI, 228 f., VIII, 125; grasped meaning of abnormal situation, I, 98; individual aspirations, V, 198; interfaith recognition, V, 186; interpretation, V, 150 ff., 175; and kings, I, 63-101, 320-40; and laws, I, 82, II, 319, 436; and massacres by Crusaders, IV, 110; messages of, and historic tact, VI, 234; messianic, I, 98, 339, II, 68, V, 117 ff., 165 f., 200; and miracles, VIII, 28; Mohammed and, V, 90; Muslim doctrine of transmission, V, 21; opposition to imagery, I, 335; philosophic argument for, VIII, 127-35, 342-45; qualifications of, VIII, 131 f.; radical concepts of survival, I, 90; rank of, VIII, 132; return of prophetic gift to Israel, V, 384; revelation through, VIII, 85; role in theological debates, V, 86 ff., VIII, 28; and sages, chronology of, VI, 202; sectarian recognition of, V, 192; silenced, I, 79; social ideals, I, 84-91, 295, 332-36; supernatural death of, I, 339; tombs, II, 286, 423, III, 136; transmission of gift, VIII, 134
—— books of: I, 345; in Aramaic, VI, 260; Cairo and Leningrad manuscripts, VI, 245, 253, 446; *haftarot,* VI, 41, 244; philological notes on, VII, 23, 43; number of verses, VIII, 149; as source of Jewish law, VI, 244; textual transmission, VI, 237
Prosbol, II, 262, 302, 304, 417, IV, 200, VIII, 209
Prose, rhymed, VII, 201 f.
Proselytes and proselytism, I, 172 ff., 179 ff., 283, 373, 375, 376, 382, II, 147-

Proselytes and proselytism (*Continued*) 50, 387 f., III, 46, 110 f., 118 f., 178, 215, IV, 9, V, 112, 135 f.; Christian, III, 52, 65 f., IV, 54 ff., V, 111, 112 f.; descendants of, I, 274; differing attitudes toward, I, 180; Egyptian, I, 190; effect upon Jewish thought, II, 150; female, II, 233; Jewish-Gentile relations affected, II, 148; Karaite, V, 267-75, 411-14; legal fiction about, II, 231; Muslim, III, 94, V, 89; place in social scale, II, 234; and public office, I, 243; semiproselytes, I, 415, II, 149; treatment, I, 181, 203, II, 282 f.; tests of genuine conversion, II, 149, 388; *see also* Converts and Conversions; Propaganda

Proselytos, I, 155, 177, 375

Prostitute: children of, II, 218; definition of, V, 240

Prostitution, religious, I, 405

Protection, royal, IV, 35 f., 40 f., 60, 66, 70 ff., 79, 80 f.; Carolingian charters, IV, 48 f.; of cities, IV, 60 f.; ecclesiastical vs., IV, 73 f., 98 ff.; of merchants, IV, 185; of minorities (*q.v.*), III, 120-72, IV, 42, 86, 185; *see also* Privileges; Rights, legal

Protective intermediaries, *see* Intermediaries

Proto-Sinaitic inscriptions, I, 35

Provence, V, 61, VI, 280; anti-Maimonidean controversy, VIII, 68; bridge between east and west, VIII, 229; court poets, VII, 146, 151; dialects, VII, 20, VIII, 229, 386; reception of Bar Ḥiyya's works, VIII, 361; scholars, VI, 468, VIII, 55, *see also under* individual scholars, *e.g.*, Abraham b. David; schools of Gershom (*q.v.*) and Rashi (*q.v.*), VI, 87 f.; sectarianism in, IV, 132, VIII, 32

Proverbs, Aramaic, in northern Iraq, VII, 220

Proverbs, Book of, VII, 163, 164 f.; authorship, VI, 160, 308; commentaries on, VI, 285, 289 f.; individualistic tinge, I, 357; priestly influence, I, 150; reconciliation of nationalism and universalism, I, 158; Saadiah's Arabic translation, VI, 268; use in sermons, VI, 167; *see also* Wisdom

Przemyśl, Poland, III, 219

Psalmody, *see* Singing

Psalms, biblical, I, 123, 340, 362; attribution of authorship, I, 322, VI, 307 f., 310; in Canaanite ritual, I, 350; commentaries on, VI, 288, 310, VII, 38; effect of mispronunciation on meaning, VI, 443; individualistic tinge, I, 357; king's, I, 130; Leningrad manuscripts, VI, 288, 472; liturgical use, I, 363, VII, 41, 69 ff., 247 f.; messianic, I, 339; number of verses, VI, 238; pre-exilic, I, 340; Psalm 2, V, 157, 239 f.; Psalm 90, VIII, 126; Psalm 91, VII, 282 f.; Psalm 139, VIII, 78; recited to music, I, 150; VII, 129, 203, 320; symbols for cantillation of, VII, 126; texts of, III, 265; translations, VI, 273; Zionist aspirations, VII, 247; *see also* Wisdom

Psammetichus I or II, I, 110, 346

Pseudepigrapha, I, 385, II, 145; contribution to mysticism, VIII, 5; messianic speculation, V, 139; preserved in Slavonic translations, III, 211; *see also* Apocrypha

Pseudo-Baḥya: eschatological punishments, VIII, 105; "Investigation of the Soul," VI, 478 f., VIII, 303; reference to Ḥivi, VI, 302

Pseudo-Clement, II, 166, 393

Pseudo-Dionysius of Tell-Maḥre, III, 237; tale about Severus, V, 193

Pseudo-Empedocles, VIII, 324

Pseudo-Eupolemus, II, 16, 31, 334

Pseudo-Ezekiel, *see* Ezekiel

"Pseudo-Isidorian Decretals," IV, 241

Pseudo-Jonathan, II, 346; as commentary, VI, 457; *see also* Targum Jonathan

Pseudo-Philo, VI, 196 f., 421 f.

Pseudo-Saadiah: Commentary on Canticles, VI, 157, 362; Commentary on *Yeṣirah*, VIII, 45, 95, 326

Pseudo-Scylax, I, 367

Psyche, Greek term, II, 14

Ptolemais (Acre), I, 190, 225

Ptolemies, dynasty, I, 224; Jewish supporters, I, 190; religious exemption granted to Jews, I, 244

Ptolemy I (Ptolemy Soter), king of Egypt, I, 172, II, 34

Ptolemy III (Ptolemy Euergetes), king of Egypt, II, 331

Ptolemy IV (Ptolemy Philopator), king of Egypt, I, 244

Ptolemy VI (Ptolemy Philometor), king of Egypt, I, 196, 220, II, 34

Ptolemy VIII (Ptolemy Lathyrus), king of Egypt, I, 215

Ptolemy (Claudius Ptolemaeus), VIII, 139, 187 f.; *Almagest*, VIII, 172; astronomical tables, VIII, 170; fractions of hour, VIII, 373; on humility, VIII, 340; system, VIII, 164 f.; *Tetrabiblos*, VIII, 178, 376

Publicans, I, 275, 279; status among Jews, II, 185

Public office: II, 186; Al-Muqtadir's decree re, VIII, 236; and art of literary composition, III, 156 f.; classes excluded from Jewish, V, 73 f.; and converts, III, 179 f., V, 74; corruption, V, 5, 178; effect of quest for, V, 72 ff.; honors and responsibilities, II, 201 ff.; Jews' participation, I, 243, II, 110, 180, 181, 375, III, 120, 150-61, 187 f., 213, 303-8, 319, V, 95 ff., 333 f., IV, 9 f., 19, 226 f.; judges and other court officials, II, 268 f., 419; local, V, 50; oath of fidelity and, II, 110, 375, IV, 49

Public opinion, appeals to in services, VI, 139

Public welfare, individual rights and, IV, 222

Public works, Jewish corvée labor on, IV, 56

Puento del Castro, Spain, IV, 33

Pufendorf, Johann, V, 229, 272

Pumbedita, academy, II, 207, III, 59, V, 13 ff., 24, 276; archives, VI, 112 f.; and Babylonian Talmud, VI, 17 f.; controversy with exilarchs, V, 10 ff., 15; and fasts, VI, 330; preeminence and decline, V, 18 f., 23 f.; Rab at, VI, 428; *see also* Pallughta

Punctuation: antiquity of, VII, 60; Babylonian system, VI, 241, 259; old Palestinian, VI, 249, 446; and pronunciation, VI, 239; system of Syriac Christians, VI, 241; Tiberian system, VI, 245, 253; *see also* Masorah

Punishments: after death, VIII, 47; geonic methods, V, 16 ff., 298 f.; inflicted on family of criminal, I, 136; mutilation, III, 186 f.; prayer for remission of, VII, 92; or rewards after death, I, 137, II, 31, 38, 40, 41; as seen by prophets, I, 90; sin and, I, 136; to uphold authority of courts, II, 267,

419; *see also* Capital punishment; Excommunication; Fines; Flogging

Purification rites, V, 173

Purim, I, 5, 169, 220, IV, 139, V, 214; charitable dues, VI, 139

Purity, in family life, I, 147, 149, 159; Karaite, V, 250; laws of, I, 147, VI, 60, 69; *see also* Ethnic unity

Puteoli (Dicaearchia), I, 261, 409

Pyrrhos, patriarch, III, 174

Pythagoras, I, 233; doctrine of numbers, VIII, 151; geometric theorem, VIII, 354 f.

Pythagoreans, and numerical principle, VIII, 284

Q

Qaddish, prayer, II, 84, 146, V, 59

Qadhi, VI, 9; *see also* Judges and judiciary

Qadosh, I, 358; *see also* Holiness

Qalir, Eleazar (Eliezer), R., liturgical poet, V, 151 f., VII, 40, 58, 82, 96-100, 263-66, VIII, 60; charged with linguistic errors, VII, 58, 104; cycle of jubilee years, VIII, 191 f.; derivation of name, VII, 96; on duration of world, VIII, 372; identity confused, VII, 104, 264 f.; improvisations for benedictions, VII, 86; influenced by mysticism, VII, 97, VIII, 12; legendary account of death of, VII, 270; liturgical poems, VII, 96 ff., 133, 263 ff.; *see also* Piyyuṭim

Qalon, term, V, 94

Qamḥi, see Qimḥi, David

Qara, Joseph, VI, 262; on the Aggadah, VI, 294

Qara, Simon, *Yalquṭ Shime'oni*, VI, 161 f., 404, VIII, 43 f., 50 f.

Qarafi, Aḥmad as-Sinhaji al-, Muslim controversialist, V, 119; list of scriptural passages, V, 329 f.; use of Christian Jew-baiting, V, 108 f., 346

Qarmatians, V, 103 f.; and messianic expectations, VI, 485; revolt, III, 88; and the "three imposters," VI, 301

Qaṭiyah, Sinai, III, 138

Qayyara, Simon, VI, 26, 174; *Halakhot gedolot*, VI, 77 f., 81 f., 91 f., 333, 339, 364 f., 372 f., VII, 278; Ḥefes' criticism of, VI, 374 f.; on intercourse with a slave girl, IV, 195; on liturgical problems, VII, 68, 110; and the Pales-

Qayyara, Simon (*Continued*)
tinian Talmud, VI, 22; reformulation of Jewish law, VI, 91 ff., 372 f.; on the *sefirah*, V, 283; six hundred and thirteen commandments, VII, 172
Qedushah, prayer, VII, 78
Qeṭina, R., VI, 45
Qi'as, analogy, V, 213 f.
Qiddushin, tractate, VI, 98
Qimḥi (Qamḥi), David b. Joseph, V, 132, 159, VI, 280 f., 467 f.; on authorship of Psalms, VI, 307 f.; commentaries on Jeremiah and Isaiah, VI, 468 f.; commentary on Exodus, VI, 296; commentary on Hosea, VI, 289 f.; grammatical works, VII, 53 f., 241; lexicon, VII, 26; rationalist approach, VI, 467; translations into Romance dialects, VIII, 386
Qimḥi, Joseph b. Isaac, V, 128, 130; collaboration with his sons, VII, 53 f.; on family life, V, 134, VIII, 53; Ibn Ezra's influence on, VII, 52; on Jacob Tam, VII, 53; rating of the sciences, VIII, 143; *Sefer ha-Berit*, V, 111, 339; on the Torah, V, 349
Qimḥi, Moses, doctrine of paradigms of Hebrew verb, VII, 53, 241
Qirqisani, Abu Yusuf Ya'qub, V, 232, VI, 244, VIII, 26; on 'Anan and Karaism, V, 229 f., 254, 259 f., 387 f., 395 ff.; on anthropomorphism, VIII, 100; "Book of Lights," V, 398, VIII, 60, 130, 247; on Christianity, V, 118 f., 263; on circumcision, V, 215; debate with Jacob b. Ephraim, VII, 223 f.; defense of Judaism, V, 84; description of sects, V, 172 f., 182 f., 191, 206, 261 f., 380; exegetical propositions, VI, 36 f., 287; Ibn Daud vs., VI, 207; influenced by Saadiah, VI, 211, 460; on Jewish translators into Arabic, VI, 265; liturgical use of Psalms, VII, 70; on magic and divination, VIII, 28 f.; on Palestinian Hebrews, VII, 235; on prophets and miracles, VIII, 130; reference to mystical writings, VIII, 12; on Sabbath regulations, V, 244; on suicide, VI, 194; writings, V, 398
Quackery, medical, VIII, 233 ff., 237 f.
Quadratic equations, VIII, 158
Quakers, *see* Friends, Society of
Queen of Heaven, goddess, I, 104, 112, 311, 347; *see also* Astarte

Quietism, political, VIII, 109
Quinisext of 692, III, 175; *see also* Councils, Church
Quintillian, II, 368
Quirinius, census, I, 263, 410
Qumisi, Daniel b. Moses al-, Karaite Bible commentator, V, 185 f., 223, 228 f., 233, VII, 274, VIII, 26; on 'Anan, V, 256 f.; condemnation of mystic writings, VIII, 12, 32, 283; exegetical works, VI, 276, 283 f.; on inheritance rights, V, 243; on mathematical calendar computations, VIII, 194 f.
Qumm, battle of, V, 193
Qumran sectarians, VI, 409, 442; *see also* Dead Sea Scrolls
Quraiẓa, tribe, III, 261
Qur'an, III, 263 ff., 268; alleged absence of contradictions, V, 87; attitude toward anthropomorphism, VIII, 114; on attributes of God, VIII, 96, 99; ban on retelling stories from, VII, 167, 180; and biblical predictions re Mohammed, V, 90; copy "written" by Abu'l Munajja, III, 155; "createdness" vs. preexistence of, VI, 307, VIII, 341; debates over, V, 83, 85 ff., 327 ff., VI, 236; 254; decrees on religious toleration, III, 124, 167, 169; exegesis of VI, 165, 275, 282, 292, 471 f.; on the Greeks in Arabia, III, 75; *hamza* sign, VI, 250; Hebrew script, V, 329; on the Hereafter, V, 148, VIII, 105; and Isthmus of Suez, IV, 173; Judeo-Christian influences on, III, 80 ff., 265 ff., 269; language of, III, 81, VI, 460, VII, 4, 10, 220; as law, VI, 7 ff.; Mohammed and, VI, 8 f.; moneylending on copy of, IV, 340 f.; Muslim praise of, V, 87; praise of David, V, 7; *qalon* and *qolon*, V, 94, 410; relation to Bible, V, 83, 90; source of Jewish folk tales, VI, 187; standard text, VI, 242 f.; translations of, III, 263, VI, 11
Qurra, Theodore abu, V, 122
Qurra b. Sharik, Egyptian governor, III, 165 f.

R

Raamses II, king of Egypt, I, 37
Rab, title, II, 201
Rab (Abba Arikha), I, 175, 176, II, 21, 133, 190, 205, 315, 316, 417, 422, 424,

VI, 124, VII, 62; animosity to Persians, II, 176, 396; business advice, II, 260; on correct spelling, VII, 12; feats of piety, VII, 285; founder of Sura academy and synagogue, II, 207, VI, 24, 239, 428, VII, 108; grave of, VI, 436; improvised prayers, VII, 89; market supervisor, II, 254; marriage regulated by, II, 218; own marriages, II, 226, 239, 410; Palestinian teachings in Babylonia, VIII, 6 f.; on precision of speech and preservation of Torah, VII, 3; on purchase and revision of scriptural texts, VI, 441; quotation from the "secret scroll," VI, 41; quoted, II, 239, 273; on secular music, VII, 129; the wealthy anathemized, II, 242, 274, 277

Raba, II, 133, 208, 264, 272, 277, 278, 283, 308, 406, 417; advocate of proselytism, II, 149; on conduct of women, III, 112; on correct spelling, VII, 12; and measurements of the earth, VIII, 213; poem improvised for, VII, 89; quoted, II, 209, 254

Raba (R. Abba), disciple of Yehudah Gaon, VI, 65, VIII, 187; juridical tract, VI, 40, 80 f.

Raban Maur, IV, 44, 256

Rabbah bar bar Ḥana, II, 176, 306, 396, 433

Rabbah b. Aboah, II, 149

Rabbah b. Naḥmani, II, 243, 316

Rabbah b. R. Huna, II, 268

Rabban, title, II, 120

Rabbana, title, II, 198

Rabbanites, III, 203, IV, 253; adherence to Aramaic, VII, 6; al-Baqillani on, V, 84; attitude toward magic, VIII, 12, 29, 283; on attributes of God, VIII, 100; biblical exegesis (q.v.), VI, 235 f., 244, 277 ff., 288 ff.; "Book of Stars," VIII, 364; chronology of Creation, VIII, 203; and circumcision, V, 215; in Constantinople, IV, 294; and the Crucifixion, V, 118; Egyptian, VII, 120, 137; Ibn Daud on, VI, 207; intercalation based on computations, VIII, 194; in Jerusalem, IV, 111; legal codes, VI, 78, see also Law; lexicographic interpretation, VII, 51; liturgy (q.v.), VII, 70, 73 f., 110 f.; medical law, VIII, 247; neglect of the poor, V, 178, 238; on oral tradition and reading of Scrip-

ture, VI, 243; on prophets and miracles, VIII, 130; reconstruction of history of Jewish tradition, VI, 203; religious observances, V, 191, 244 f.; return to Palestine, V, 186; and Saadiah's translation of the Pentateuch; VI, 269 f.; sectarian opposition, V, 375; Spanish, advances in grammar and lexicography, VI, 290 f.

—— and Karaites (q.v.), VI, 173; borrowings from, V, 281 f., 413, VI, 461; controversies, V, 56, 211, 228 ff., 275-85, 414-16; intermarriage, V, 265 ff.; joint worship, VII, 280; on origins, V, 255; separation and readmission, V, 9, 273 ff., 413 f.

Rabbi, title, II, 120, 201, V, 60, 283

Rabbis and rabbinate: aggadic works ascribed to, VI, 159; allegations of biblical falsification, V, 92; and 'ame ha-areṣ (q.v.), I, 278; and Arabic language, VII, 6 f., 46, VIII, 263; and Aramaic written translations, VI, 257; astronomic teachings, VIII, 193; on biblical laws, V, 122 ff.; on biblical prophecy, V, 87; on choice between conversion and death, IV, 146; commandments enacted by, VI, 98; condemnation of corrupt provinces, V, 178 f.; on corporal punishment, IV, 261; and dairy products, IV, 315; on deposits with bankers, IV, 208 f.; dialect of, as independent language, VII, 56 f.; education, II, 117, 306; emigration to Persian Babylonia, II, 405; essentials of Judaism, VI, 91; establishment of, in Western Europe, V, 63; ethical ideals, VIII, 120 ff.; expansion of learning, VI, 25; farmers, II, 414; foreign influences, II, 319; Franco-German, V, 60 f., VI, 50, 55 f., 94, 117 f., 205, 295, 336, 371, 387, 427, 441; and God as king, VIII, 18; on interfaith partnerships, IV, 331; and Julian the Apostate, V, 350; and labor, I, 258; leadership, II, 129-71 passim, 197, 204, 242, 261, 276, 279, 291, V, 56, VI, 3; on levitical tithes and heave-offerings, IV, 313 f.; on liberal professions, IV, 215 f.; and local judges, V, 20; on love of God, VIII, 116 f.; and magic (q.v.), II, 317, VIII, 233 f.; Maimonidean chronology of, VI, 202; manumission of slaves discouraged, II,

Rabbis and rabbinate (Continued)
269; on marriage and procreation, V,
134; martyrs, (q.v.), IV, 96; and medical practice, VIII, 238; on Messiah
(q.v.), V, 119 f., 357; on moneylending
(q.v.), IV, 197 ff., 338 ff.; on money
transfers, IV, 212 f.; music banned by,
VII, 319 f.; and mysticism (q.v.), VIII,
283; as national heroes, VI, 168; a new
sort of theocracy, II, 279; ordinances,
VI, 134 ff., 392 ff.; ordination, II, 120,
201, 419; and personal slaves, IV, 193;
polygamy among, II, 227; and physicians, VIII, 231 ff.; and piyyuṭim, VII,
101 ff.; on loyalty to the state, IV, 270;
poverty and wealth, II, 265 f., 277, 278;
on prayers in Hebrew, VII, 68; preachers (q.v.) among, VI, 155 ff.; on price
structure, IV, 222 f.; as professional
class, VIII, 232 f.; proselytism (q.v.)
discouraged, I, 175; religious observances, IV, 310; and religious speculation, VIII, 69; responsa (q.v.), VI,
109 ff., 116 ff., 381 ff.; rules of interpretation, VI, 287, 297; on sacramental
wine, IV, 165; and the Samaritans, V,
172; and shepherds, I, 254; on slave
trade, IV, 188 ff., 193; social control,
IV, 222; on span of evildoers in Hell,
VIII, 104; on speech clarity and precision, VII, 3; on supernatural world,
VIII, 27; talmudic commentary of Italian, VI, 353; on tanners, IV, 166 f.; as
tax collectors, V, 65 f.; tax exemption,
II, 243, 244, 277, 413; theory of state
and local government, V, 71 ff., 77 ff.;
tombs glorified, II, 279; views of the
earth, VIII, 212; on viticulture, IV,
162 f.; see also Amoraim; Elders; Geo-
nim; Priests; Rabbanites; Scholars;
Talmud; Tannaim
Rabbula, bishop of Edessa, III, 57; and
the Peshiṭta, VI, 454
Rabina, II, 251, 276; on recitation of
psalm, VII, 69; redactor of Babylonian
Talmud, II, 296, 426
Rabina the Younger, VI, 17 f.
Rab Raba, Mar, VI, 132 f.
Races, human, VI, 192, 226
Rachel's tomb, II, 14
Racial equality, Islamic theory of, III, 98
Racial mixtures, I, 39
Radegund, princess, III, 22
"Radhanites," IV, 328

Radicalism, ancient, I, 228
Radulph, Cistercian monk, leader of
Second Crusade, IV, 120 f.
Raffelstetten, Germany, IV, 65 f., 301
Raḥem, prayer, II, 375
Raḥmi'el, angel, VIII, 8 f.
Rain: as messianic portent, V, 201; and
moon, VIII, 175; prayers for, II, 40,
345, 349, 385, III, 260, V, 27, 303, VIII,
202
Rainer papyrus, I, 378
Ra'is, Arabic title, V, 48
Ralph de Diceto, IV, 124
Ralph of Coggeshall, IV, 85
Ramadan, V, 246
Ramah, "guest house" in, II, 285
Ramleh, Palestine: commercial center,
IV, 180; evacuation of, IV, 109; Ka-
raites in, VI, 246; Muslim administra-
tive capital, III, 102 f.; Samaritans in,
V, 171 f.; Solomon b. Yehudah vs.
Nathan b. Abraham, V, 34; syna-
gogues, V, 28
Ramlites (or Malikians), V, 182
Ramon Berenger III, count of Barce-
lona, IV, 37
Ramon Berenger IV, count of Barcelona,
IV, 30 f., 37, 42, 207; writ of indebt-
edness, IV, 252
Ram's horn, II, 256, 333, 383, 416
Ransom of captives, IV, 109, 110 f.,
177 f.
Raqqa, Mesopotamia, VIII, 139; birth-
place of Al-Muqammiṣ, VIII, 393;
center of learning, VIII, 243; Jewish
"philosophers" of, VIII, 67
Rashbam, see Samuel b. Meir
Rashi (or Yiṣḥaqi), Solomon b. Isaac,
R., II, 289, 424, IV, 144, 157, 162; aggadic interpretations, V, 157 f.; on
ban of settlement, V, 68 f.; date of
birth, VI, 245; on days of the Messiah,
V, 148 f.; exegetical work, VI, 49-53,
61, 180, 278 ff., 344-49, 465 f., 475;
French translation of technical terms,
VIII, 227; on local customs, VI, 128 f.;
methodological approaches, VI, 348;
ordinances, V, 64, 319 f.; on peculiar
formation of verbs, VII, 47; prayer
book attributed to, VI, 75, 362 f.;
responsa by, VI, 118, 385 f.; school of,
VI, 34, 53 ff., 75 f., 202, 278, 362 f., 386,
467; student days, VI, 345; talmudic-
geonic learning, VI, 173 f.; on Targum

of Hagiographa, VI, 262; use of Hebrew dictionaries, VII, 20, 31

Rashid, ar-, see Harun ar-Rashid

Rashid ad-Din, execution of, V, 97

Ras Shamra (Ugarit), I, 45, 52 f., 302, 306, 309, 312, 401; bread and wine offerings, I, 316; *Keret* legend, I, 301, 401; marriage, II, 229; school for scribes, I, 315; Ugaritic alphabet, I, 307; Ugaritic poems, I, 48, 63, 306, 311, 312, 334, 350; worship of Athtar and Astarte, I, 318

Ratherius, bishop of Verona, IV, 25; *De qualitatis conjectura*, IV, 26

Rationalism: Arab, VIII, 66, 129; Muslim opponents of, VIII, 83 f.

—— Jewish, VIII, 55-137, 296-346; in biblical exegesis, V, 259, VI, 259, 267, 274-81, 298-306, 463-68, 478-84; denial of astrological predictions, VIII, 176; and messianic expectations, V, 159-66, 363-66; and moral values, VIII, 113 ff.; opposition to mysticism, VIII, 37 ff.; and prophecy, VIII, 132; in religious poetry, VII, 175; see also Philosophy; Reason

Rational power, VIII, 107

Ratisbon, Germany: mass baptism of Jewish community, IV, 100; privilege, IV, 67, 71 f., 272, 274; trading center, IV, 175 f., 325

Ravenna, Italy: exarchate, III, 24; Judeo-Christian relations, III, 241

Raw materials, production of, IV, 163

Rawandi, ar-, Muslim agnostic, V, 103, 337, VI, 298, 477, VIII, 129

Raymond, archbishop of Toledo, IV, 32 f.

Raymond, count of Sens, V, 114

Raymond de Bollène, archbishop of Arles, IV, 59

Razi, Aḥmad ar-, IV, 159

Razi, ar- (Rhazes), Muhammad b. Zakariya ar-, VI, 301, VIII, 225, 242, 390

Reader, see Cantor

Real estate, see Land; Property

Reason: and faith, VI, 108 f., VIII, 55-137, 296-346; and nature, VI, 285 f.; reliability of findings of, VIII, 78 ff.; see also Rationalism

Rebirth, see Immortality of the soul

Reccared, king of Spain, III, 32, 36, 245 f.

Recceswinth, king of the Visigoths, III, 41

Rechabites, I, 42, 78, 89, II, 48

Rectangle, formula for measuring, VIII, 157

Redeemer: personal, in Jewish theology, I, 118, V, 168; see also Messiah and messianism

Redemption: atonement and, V, 217; communal, I, 259; computation of date of, V, 149 f.; as cosmic cataclysm, II, 59; individual and collective, VII, 132 ff.; of Israel from Egypt, VII, 115, see also Exodus; messianic, V, 141 ff., VIII, 127; poems of, V, 153, VII, 181; via penitence and martyrdom, IV, 95

Red Sea: crossing of, VI, 300; Song of the, VII, 279

Reform, Catholic, IV, 10, 28

Reformation, Israelitic, see Deuteronomic reformation; Protestant, VI, 306

Reformers, III, 110, VII, 64

Reform Judaism, I, 26, 228, II, 344; and nationalism, I, 28, 361

Refuge, cities of, I, 360; see also Asylum

Regimentation, II, 260-65, 417 f.

Rehoboam, king of Israel, I, 74

Reḥomai, R., VIII, 37

Reims, Council of, III, 252

Rekhub-el, god, I, 357

Relics, Christian, pilgrimages in quest of, IV, 283

Religion: comparative study, I, 102-3, 103-4, V, 84, VII, 11; disputations, II, 133, 136 ff.; "eternal" elements, I, 16; Persian, I, 129, see also Parsees and Parsiism; and political power, I, 22, 237; and science, VIII, 219; Semitic settlers' influence on, I, 175

—— Jewish: Antiochus IV and apostasy, I, 217, 229; autonomy under Christian emperors, II, 191; civic duty, I, 234; conflicts, I, 61 f., 228; crucial test in Exile, I, 102-33, 341-55; cultural influences affecting, I, 46, 58; in declining Second Commonwealth, II, 54; fertility cults, I, 318; genius of Israel's, I, 41; hegemony of Jerusalem, I, 219; and history, I, 4 ff., 99 ff., 295 ff., 340; imageless worship, I, 322; Israel's "popular," I, 4, 59, 62, 83, 98, 104 f., 128, 161, 219; Jews relieved of imperial worship, I, 244; and law, I, 77-84, 142, 227, 327-32, II, 293 ff., 307, 425 ff., VI, 3 ff.; monotheism (*q.v.*), I, 4-10, 43-46, 294; Mosaic, I, 4, 41, 44, 46-53, 58, 59,

Religion (*Continued*)
65, 313-16, *see also* Moses; and music,
VII, 207 f.; and nature, I, 4 ff.; opti-
mism of, I, 8; Palestinian controls
over world Jewry, II, 125 f.; a *religio
licita*, I, 117; sacrificial worship condemned, I, 123-29 *passim*, *see also*
Sacrifices; Samaritan (*q.v.*) a relapse
into the preprophetic, II, 28; and society, I, 3-31, 59, 123 ff., 132, 258,
293-97; sources of, I, 161, 298-99; syncretism (*q.v.*) and sectarianism (*q.v.*),
II, 3 ff., 23 ff., 26 ff., 330-50; synthesis
of a national and universal religion, I,
28, 31; and territory, I, 17, 99-100;
theocratic state founded in Palestine,
I, 165; unifying bond in Egypt, I, 36;
and woman's position in family, I, 58;
and worship, VII, 62
—— *see also* Christians and Christianity; Converts and conversion; Gnosticism; God; Judaism; Law; Parsees and
Parsiism; Priests and priesthood; Proselytes and proselytism; Rabbis and
rabbinate; *also under* names of sects,
e.g., Sadducees
Religious holidays, *see* Holidays
Religious liberty, II, 191; in ancient em-
pires, I, 117; relative immunity of
synagogue, II, 284; *see also* Rights,
legal; Self-government; Toleration,
religious
Religious objects, ransom of, VI, 447
Religious observances, IV, 60 f., 310; in
Babylonia, V, 246; Byzantine laws on,
III, 190; charge of Jewish laxity in, V,
124 f., 135 f.; of Christian servants
employed by Jews, IV, 314 f.; controversy over, V, 122-25, 346 f.; differences
between Babylonia and Palestine, V,
28 ff., 246, 255; farm workers and, IV,
156 f.; followers of Severus, V, 193 f.;
Karaite, V, 214 ff., 282 ff.; in Khazaria,
III, 202 f.; local variations in, V, 59,
VI, 121 ff., 389 ff.; ritualistic, and blood
accusation, IV, 135; Samaritan, V,
173 f.; Scriptural recitations, V, 151;
sectarian, V, 190 ff., 195 f.; *shabbata
de-rigla*, V, 40; and trade, IV, 219 f.;
see also Law; Liturgy; Ritual; Sabbath; Synagogue
Religious toleration, *see* Toleration, religious
Religious unity in times of crisis, I, 61

Religious universalism and particularism, I, 96-99, 339
Remigius of Auxerre, IV, 257
"Remnant," doctrine of the, I, 30, 97,
106
Renaissance: Hebrew, reconsideration of
liturgical formulas, VII, 67; of Islam,
III, 117-21, V, 83, 103, 170, 197, 231,
VII, 3 ff., 60 f., 176, VIII, 147, 255 f.,
262 f.; Italian, VIII, 147; twelfth cen-
tury, IV, 311
Repatriation, forced, of Jewish exiles,
IV, 62 f.
Repentance, I, 294, II, 308 f., 384, 433;
doctrine of, VIII, 105; fasting and, VI,
16; preexistence of, VIII, 273; and
redemption, V, 160; Ten Days of, VIII,
74
Repetition, ritualistic import of, VIII,
284
Rephidim, battle, I, 317
Research Institute for Hebrew Poetry,
Jerusalem, VII, 261, 271
Res gestae divi Saporis, II, 238, 380, 397
Reshep, I, 49
Resh kallah, title, V, 59
Reshut ha-rabbim, II, 252
Residence permit (*ḥerem ha-yishub*), IV,
71, 185, V, 68 f.; and excommunication, V, 17; Gershom b. Yehudah and,
IV, 65, 213
Responsa: in Arabic, VII, 6; authority
of, VI, 115; authorship, VI, 114 f.,
384 f.; compilations of, V, 115, VI,
29 ff., 113; geonic, V, 32, VI, 29 ff.,
109-16, 339, 381-85, VIII, 229, *see also
under* names of geonim; and origin
of talmudic commentaries, VI, 41;
preservation of, VI, 383 f.; rabbinic,
VI, 116-21, 386-88, *see also under*
names of rabbis; to series of related
questions, VI, 382; in support of local
customs, VI, 122 ff.; talmudic, VI, 110,
381 f.
Responsibility, communal, for common
welfare, II, 251, 269, 270, 271, 273, 291,
see also Communities, Jewish; individual, II, 41, 44; mutual, I, 10, 135 f.,
146, 356, II, 217
Restoration to Palestine in antiquity, I,
157, 158-63, 366-68
Resurrection, doctrine of, I, 9, 12, 207,
208, 390, II, 14, 111, 312, 318, V, 175,
228, 260, VIII, 104; Maimonides on,

V, 22, VI, 119, 413; messianism and, V, 166; in Muslim creed, VI, 8; Pharisaism's conception, II, 38, 344 f.; poems on, VII, 267; and return of Jesus, II, 71, 73, 359; Saadiah's interpretation, VI, 286; sectarian opinions of, II, 31, 39, 345, V, 196; stressed above immortality (*q.v.*), I, 208

Retaliation, law of, I, 79

Retribution, I, 136-37; *see also* Punishments

Reuben, Jacob's blessing of, VI, 259

Revelation: Bible as, VI, 294, 307 ff., VIII, 127; Judeo-Christian reliance on, II, 159, VIII, 85, 113; media of, VIII, 342; and reason, VIII, 82; relationship to history, I, 296; Sinaitic, II, 161

Revenues: clerical, IV, 58, 65 f., 74, 153 f.; exilarchic, V, 12; farming of public, I, 262; imperial, from Jews, V, 5; papal, IV, 14; priestly, I, 272; state, IV, 87, 89 f., 201, 203 f., 213, 225 f.; in Temple treasury, II, 44; under the Caliphate, III, 150; *see also* Taxation

Revivalists, Crusading fanaticism engendered by, IV, 102, 120

Revolts: in Northern Israel, I, 95; against Romans, I, 212, 265, 266, II, 90-102, 368-72, *see also* Judeo-Roman wars; *also under* names of wars, *e.g.*, Great War

Rewards, I, 137; after death, I, 137, II, 31, 38, 40, 41; *see also* Punishments

Reziel, Book of, VIII, 11 ff., 27

Rezin of Aram, I, 155

Rhazes, *see* Razi, ar-, Muhammad

Rhetoric, Greek, influence on Jewish homilies, VI, 163 f.

Rhodes, I, 236; Colossus of, III, 16, 235

Rhyme: in alphabetic order, VII, 142, 294; forms of, VII, 200; in Hebrew poetry, VII, 197 ff., 314 f.; as mnemotechnic aid, VII, 88

Rhythm, *see* Meter

Rice, cultivation of, IV, 161

Rich, the, *see* Wealth

Richard I (Richard Lion-Heart), king of England: appointment of first Jewish presbyter, V, 63; on Crusaders in England and Normandy, IV, 127 f.; debt to Aaron of Lincoln, IV, 303; policy toward Jews, IV, 78 f., 163 f., 304; riot at coronation of, IV, 124 ff., 140

Richard, son of Nigel, *Dialogus de Scaccario*, IV, 80 f., 205

Richard of Devises, IV, 125, 136, 140

Richard Strongbow, *see* Strongbow

Richulf, archbishop of Mayence, IV, 45

Riddles: linguistic, VII, 4; poetic, VII, 162; use of numerical value of letters, VIII, 357

Righteous Teacher, II, 53, 349, 350

Rights, legal of Jews, III, 13, 24 ff., 294, IV, 22 f., 49; in ancient Babylonia, I, 115-17, 348 f.; Barcelona custumal, IV, 41 f.; in Byzantium, III, 13, 153, 173-90, 313-20; in Carolingian Empire, IV, 43-53, 256-64; in early Roman Empire, I, 239 ff., II, 398; in England, IV, 75-86, 276-82; in France, III, 47-54, 250-54, IV, 53-64, 264-70; inequality of, IV, 35, 39 f.; in Germany, IV, 64-75, 270-76; in Hungary, III, 211-13, 332 f.; in Italy, III, 24-33, 240-44, IV, 5-27, 235-45; royal alliance and, IV, 50 ff.; in Spain, III, 33-46, 244-50, IV, 27-43, 245-56; under the Caliphate, 120-72, 288-312; of women, I, 111, II, 303, 304, 306; *see also* Charters; Inheritance; Privileges; Property; Toleration, religious

Ring, use of at weddings, V, 283

Rites, Sacred Congregation of, V, 351

Ritual: Christian, II, 71, 84, 154, 155, 365

—— Jewish: appeal of ceremonial, II, 149, 189, 191; of blood, I, 51; and chronological cycles, VIII, 209; deviations from, I, 200, 351, II, 7, 182, 399; equality of moral law and, II, 307-9, 433; food requirements, I, 189, II, 217, 306, *see also* Sacrifices; funerary, II, 340; Graeco-Oriental contrasts and influences, II, 6 ff.; Jeroboam's innovations, V, 254; link between synagogue and Temple, II, 119, 376; local customs, VI, 59, 123 f.; origin of, VI, 392; Palestinian vs. Babylonian, V, 28 ff., VIII, 228; prayers for rulers, VII, 265; reinterpretation of ancient, I, 315; segregation of priests, I, 149; *see also* Liturgy; Prayers

Ritual murder, *see* Blood accusation

Robbery, II, 46; distinguished from theft, VI, 147

Robert, count of Normandy, IV, 289

Robert I, king of France, IV, 92

Robert II (Robert the Pious), king of France, V, 114
Robert of Gloucester, IV, 140
Rodoam, Haly, see Ibn Ridhwan
Roger I, king of Sicily, IV, 22, VIII, 215; silk robe, IV, 168
Roger II, king of Sicily, IV, 11, 21; attack on Thebes, IV, 168 f.; privilege to Messina, IV, 23
Roger de Moulins, IV, 114
Roman-Byzantine emperors, anonymous list of, III, 317 f., V, 354, VI, 211 f., 430
Roman Catholic church, see Church, Christian
Romance languages: Jewish influence, II, 406; translations of Bible and prayer book, II, 144; see also under individual languages, e.g., French
Romances, fictional, VII, 183 ff.
Roman Empire: agricultural supply sources, II, 246; anarchical conditions in society, II, 225, 234; anti-Jewish sentiment, I, 190, 246, II, 103; burial customs, I, 382, II, 423; caste system, II, 176, 242; Catholicism the heir of, II, 85 ff.; Christianity, II, 63, 83, 85, 86, 150, 152, 165, 366, 393; circumcision outlawed, II, 97, 107, 109; class differences, II, 242; continuity of traditions, IV, 4; controversies with Palestine, I, 238, 248, 250, 263, II, 104; decline of, II, 213, III, 4; dictatorial regime, II, 57, 420; economically most advanced region of, I, 258; Edom identified with, II, 152; family degrees and marriage laws, II, 230; fiscal system, I, 262 ff., II, 100, 105 f., 183 ff., 399, see also Taxation; Hellenism and, II, 173 ff., 396; and Jesus, II, 70; Jewish attachment to emperors, I, 190; Jewish communal freedoms, V, 58 f., VIII, 193; and Jewish law, II, 300, 430; Jewish population, I, 171, III, 283 f.; and Jewish religious customs, I, 179, 238, 382, II, 284; Jewish settlements, III, 49; Jews in, I, 166, 170, 371, II, 210; "kingdom of wickedness," II, 153; law courts, II, 266, 419; legal and political status of Jews, I, 240, 403, II, 108 ff., 320; marriage, I, 226-34 passim; morals, I, 191; Persia and, II, 176-86, 213, 396-98; pessimism, II, 57 f., 89; Phoenician ghettos, I, 176; policies toward Jews, I, 195, 209, 248, II, 89, 97,

100, 106 ff., 118, 120, 187 ff., 213; political-military world mission, II, 329; polygamy opposed, II, 226, 231, VI, 137; population, I, 371, II, 183, 209; proselytism, I, 176, II, 150; provincial administration, II, 103 f., 373; religious inspiration of imperialism, II, 152, 388; revolts against, I, 212, 219, 265, 266, II, 90-108, 368-72, see also Judeo-Roman wars; robbery and piracy preserved as source of slave supply, II, 46; Samaritans in, II, 33, 342; self-control of officials, I, 239; seven day week, I, 6, VIII, 185, 368; slaveholding by Jews, II, 259, 416; syncretistic tradition, II, 11 ff., VIII, 32; treaty of alliance with Judaea, I, 218; unfolding and fusion of religions, II, 86; in vision of Daniel, II, 59, V, 140 ff.; Yosephon on, VI, 192; Zealotic faction's resistance to oppression of, II, 47; see also Byzantine Empire; Holy Roman Empire; and under names of emperors, e.g., Hadrian; Trajan
Romanos, Christian melodos, VII, 82, 127, 142
Romanos I (Lekapenos), Byzantine emperor, III, 179; attempts to suppress Judaism, III, 179, 182, 203, 317 f., IV, 25
Romanos II, Byzantine emperor, VIII, 65
Romanos III, Byzantine emperor, VIII, 246
Roman roads, I, 172
Rome, city: alien groups in, I, 248; Christians in, III, 31; Church Councils of, IV, 9; council of Jewish elders, V, 55; Eleazar's observations in, II, 113; equated with Edom, V, 145, VI, 407; equated with a pig, V, 131; evil power of, VIII, 19; Jewish community, I, 284, II, 199, 332, IV, 4 ff., 11, 13 f., 240, V, 55, 59 f., VI, 216, VII, 29 f.; Jewish exile, VII, 290; Jews expelled and readmitted I, 246; Judeo-Christian relations (q.v.), III, 27; Menaḥem b. Saruq's work, VII, 48; messianic predictions, V, 143 ff., 354; public schools, II, 279; success of Jewish religious propaganda, I, 191; "synagogue of Severus," VI, 401
Rom family, publishers, VI, 348 f.
Romizanes Shahrabaz, III, 22

Romualdus, IV, 21

Romulus, equated with Armilus, V, 145, VI, 481

Roots, Hebrew, VII, 41; alphabetical listing by last letters of, VII, 27; biliterality or triliterality of, VII, 39, 42, 46 f.; "Book of," by Ibn Janaḥ, VII, 24 f., 45, 229, 237

Rosh ha-Shanah, tractate, VI, 352

Rossi, Azariah de', V, 365, VI, 210, 422, VIII, 183

Rossi, Giovanni Bernardo de, VI, 255

Rostov, Russia, archaeological investigations, III, 213

Rothschild, Edmond, baron de, III, 232

Routes, trade, IV, 172 f., 180 f., VIII, 212

"Routes, Books of," VIII, 212; see also Ibn Khurdadhbah

Royal alliance, IV, 28 ff., 87; and disposition of Jewish property, IV, 59 f., 203 f.; and economic enterprise, IV, 36-43, 45, 225 f.; and legal status, IV, 50 ff.; protection through, IV, 45, 141

Royal grants, of Jewish persons and property, IV, 59 f.

Royal power, see Kings; Monarchy

Rüdiger-Huozmann, bishop of Spires, IV, 74, 98 f., V, 79; privilege to Jews, IV, 74, 205, 275

Rudolf Brugensis, VIII, 363

Rufinus, Christian exegete, VI, 292

Rulers: ancient worship of, I, 244, 404, II, 5, 99, 109; concepts of nature of, VIII, 18; jurisdiction of local, IV, 72; oath of allegiance to, II, 36; patrons of poets, VII, 148 f.; the perfect, I, 199; prayers for, VII, 265; see also Emperors; Kings; Monarchy

Russia: archaeological findings, III, 333 f.; conversion to Greek orthodoxy, III, 221; Jewish settlements, III, 213-17, 336 f.; meat tax, VIII, 386; name for Khazars, III, 204; origins of first Slavic state, III, 334; pig symbol, II, 152; secular Jewish nationalism in, I, 29; Slavonic Josephus, II, 379; see also Josephus

Ruth, V, 90
—— Book of: commentary on, V, 400, VI, 472; date, I, 366

Ruthard, archbishop of Mayence, IV, 99, 116 f.

Rutilius Namatianus, Claudius, II, 188, 400

S

Saadiah Gaon, III, 119, 197, 221 f.; acrostic of name, VII, 141, 144; on Agur, VI, 402; "analogistic" approach, VII, 34; appointment to Sura, V, 21, VI, 356; on atomistic theory, VIII, 88; attitude toward Arabic meter, VII, 194; on attributes of God, VIII, 96 f.; on authorship of mystical literature, VIII, 25; on authorship of Psalms, VI, 307; on biblical chronology, V, 120; calendar regulation, V, 30 f., VIII, 196; on character of the universe, VIII, 78 f., 165 f., 213 f.; chronology of the Mishnah, VI, 203 f.; the community and Jewish law, V, 4 f.; computation of date of Messiah, V, 164; concentration on meaning of prayer, VII, 74; controversy with Ben Meir, V, 181, 196, 212, VI, 126, 430, VII, 115, VIII, 195, 196 ff.; controversy with David b. Zakkai, V, 10, 21 ff., 74, VII, 277; on creation ex nihilo, VIII, 89; on darkness and light, VIII, 34; debates on lexicographic contributions of, VII, 15 ff.; and decisions of the exilarchic court, V, 200 f., 297 f., 300 f.; defense of Judaism, V, 84, 126, VIII, 100; on deviations from biblical law, V, 93; doctrine of the "second air," VIII, 342; vs. dualists and Christians, V, 107, 126; exegetical principles and methods, VI, 296; on faculties of human soul, VIII, 117; formula for confession, VII, 253 f.; geographic observations, VIII, 217; Ibn Ezra's epigram on, VI, 279; on immutability of Torah, VI, 145; influence of, VI, 271, 276 f., VIII, 45; on interpretation of ketib and qeri in the Masorah, VI, 292 f.; on Israel as a nation, VI, 231; on Jewish skeptics, V, 104 f.; on Jewish sufferings, VI, 439; and Karaites, V, 277 f., 295, 397, VI, 276, 471; lack of historical criticism, VI, 269; on laws of nature, VIII, 335; literary use of personal experiences, VII, 289; on magic practices, VIII, 29; on man's love of God, VIII, 115; medical observations, VIII, 244; messianic rationale, V, 159 ff., 363 f.; on miracles, VIII, 128 f.; motivations for behavior, VIII, 120; on Musaf,

Saadiah Gaon (*Continued*)
VII, 91; nature of the Hereafter, VIII, 104; on neglect of ritual tradition, VII, 106; on number of commandments, VI, 92 f.; on perfect government, V, 71 f.; on physiological reactions to music, VII, 208; on the power of money, IV, 217; on prohibition of murder, VIII, 113; quest for innovation, VII, 142; quest for office, V, 72 f.; on recital of Scripture, VII, 69; rejection of transmigration of souls, VIII, 36; religious disputation, V, 121; reply to Ḥivi, VI, 302 ff., 478 f., VII, 143, VIII, 58; request of aid from Jewish banking families, III, 154; vs. ritualistic divergences, VI, 125 f.; on the soul, VIII, 107; on sources of knowledge, VIII, 79 ff.; style, VII, 142; theories of creation and eternity of the world, VIII, 78 f.; theory of exile, V, 100 f.; theory of prophecy, V, 21; use of Aramaic, VII, 67

—— works: Arabic translation of Hebrew Bible, VI, 265 ff., 312 f., 458 f.; *Beliefs and Opinions*, VI, 195, VIII, 59 ff., 313; Book of Chronology, VI, 211; Book of Commandments, VI, 95; commentaries on Mishnah and Talmud, VI, 28, 42; Commentary on Book of Creation, VI, 242, VIII, 24 (alleged), 59, 151; Commentary on the Thirteen Hermeneutic Modes, VI, 32, 304 f., 335; correspondence, V, 16, VI, 208; Dictionary of the Mishnah, VII, 15; exegetical works on the Bible, VI, 114, 284 ff.; halakhic monographs, IV, 209, VI, 65 ff., 356 ff., VII, 117, VIII, 153 f.; handbook for Hebrew poetry, VII, 15, 89, 99, 197; *Kitab at-Tamyiz*, dispute over date of, VIII, 203 ff.; linguistic works, VII, 14 f., 33 ff., 234 f.; liturgical poems, VII, 87, 104 f., 141, 219, VIII, 150; methodological treatise, VI, 32; monographs on chronology and calendar, VI, 307; polemical poem against Aaron Ben Asher, VI, 246; polemical poem against Ḥivi, VI, 304; prayer book, V, 150 f., 248, VI, 15, 69, 92, VII, 70, 100 f., 113 ff., 115 f., 140 f., 302; story of the Children of the Hasmoneans, VI, 189; variations on the theme of the Ten Commandments,

VII, 141; works neglected by public, VI, 96; *see also* Pseudo-Saadiah
Sabbath: academic joint sessions on, V, 19; association with moon and planets, I, 359, VIII, 184; birth of child on, I, 120; drinking on, V, 245; fasting on, VI, 330 f.; and the Festival of Weeks, V, 195; first, V, 357; Jews not called as witnesses on, I, 245; of Repentance, VI, 165; special lessons, VI, 162, 172 f., 338, VIII, 208

—— observance, I, 71, 153, II, 132, III, 31, 83 f., IV, 26, 156, 183, 268, 283, V, 122, 216, 223, 283, 350, VI, 80, 119 f., 396, 475 f.; carrying objects on, III, 62, IV, 70, VI, 178; censured by Seneca, I, 192; Christians', II, 188; cooking on, VI, 42; eternal law of, V, 91 f.; Graeco-Roman attitude toward, I, 6, 382, II, 107, 109; Jesus' utterance about, II, 67, 69, 356; Karaite rules, V, 217 f., 243 f.; new prominence, I, 143 ff., 359 f.; origin, I, 6, 143, 382; Pharisaic, II, 45, 46, 50; poems devoted to, VII, 90; Saadiah on, VI, 15 f.; violation of, VI, 134

"Sabbath of Sabbaths," I, 144
Sabbatical millennium, II, 318
Sabbatical year, I, 279, II, 271; abolished, II, 263; dating by, II, 116; legal cancellation of debts, I, 261, II, 262, 417; produce of, and betrothals, V, 29
Sabbazius, god, I, 128, II, 24, 25
Sabians, III, 130, VIII, 217; etymology of, VI, 437
Sabionetta, edition of the Targum, VI, 259
Saboraim, VI, 17 ff., 110, 204, 334; and amoraic sayings, VI, 40; liturgical works, VII, 63 ff.; period of, III, 58, 73; rabbinic succession, VI, 426; recension of Babylonian Talmud, VI, 240; source of geonic tradition, VII, 108
Sacrifices, I, 51, 179, 254, 362, VI, 147 f., 300; animal, II, 50, 52, 154, 155, 306, 353; and burnt offering, III, 29; in Christian ceremonies, II, 154; consistent with patriarchal and Mosaic religion, I, 50 f.; ideas underlying Israelitic, I, 315 f.; justification of, VIII, 118; laws of, VI, 95, VIII, 228; limited to Temple at Jerusalem, I, 123, 129, 133; in name of ruler, I, 244, 404, II,

99; obliterated by burning of Temple, I, 179, II, 155, 284; opposition to, I, 123-29 *passim;* Passover (*q.v.*), II, 45; Persian attitude, I, 353; prayer as substitute for, I, 124, 132, 350, II, 125; preeminence of priest in worship, I, 81; of primitive tribes, I, 51, 127; replaced by prayers, VII, 249; and ritual murder (*q.v.*), IV, 135 f.; spiritualization of, II, 308; and temple of Onias, I, 219; for unsolved crime, I, 79

Sadducees and Sadduceeism, I, 142, 221, 234-38, V, 228, 261, VI, 236, VIII, 205; absorbed in mainstream of Judaism, I, 237, 271, II, 129; anti-Syrian revolt, I, 234; and era of Creation, VIII, 208; and Karaites, V, 255; legal code, VI, 78; name, II, 342; priesthood, I, 271 f., 280, II, 46; punishment of, V, 280; rebellions against Rome, II, 90, 99; representatives of priestly and lay aristocracy, II, 35, 36; responsibility for slaves, I, 412; struggle with Pharisees, I, 180, 234, 402, II, 35, 36, 38-46, 343 f.; survival of teachings, II, 117, 129, V, 187 ff., 215, 377 ff.; unable to guide dispersion, II, 55

Sa'd ibn Abu Waqqas, III, 95

Sa'd ibn Manṣur ibn Kammuna, *see* Ibn Kammuna

Ṣafiya, Jewish wife of Mohammed, III, 76, 262

Safra, R., prayer of, VII, 76 f.

Ša-Gaz, *see* Ḥabiru

Sages, ancient, I, 136, 153, 307; innate gifts, VIII, 139; "language of," and the language of Scripture, VII, 56 f.; *see also* Rabbis and rabbinate; Scholars and scholarship

Sahel, *see* Sahl b. Bishr

Sahlal b. Abraham, liturgical poet, VII, 12

Sahl b. Bishr (or Zahel), astrologer, VIII, 148; astronomic works, VIII, 166 ff.; poem on the stars, VIII, 168; variants of name, VIII, 167

Sahl b. Maṣliaḥ, IV, 167, V, 186, 233; biblical interpretation, V, 264; on the calendar, V, 30 f.; charges against rabbinic leadership, V, 236, 238 f., 246; missionary journey, V, 269; on sectarian intermarriage, V, 267

Sahl b. Neṭira, III, 153

Saḥoq b. Esther Israeli, IV, 92

Sa'id ibn Sina al-Mulk, Muslim physician, III, 148, VIII, 250

Saif Dhu Yazan, III, 69

Sailors, Jewish, II, 249

Saint-Denis, Abbey of, IV, 59

Saint Edmundsbury, monastery, IV, 13, 84, 204

Saint Lo, France, IV, 239

Saint Moritz, monastery of, IV, 65

Saint Sophia, *see* Hagia Sophia

Ṣala', meaning, I, 351

Saladin, Seljuk caliph, III, 106; coins, VIII, 255; founder of Nasiri Hospital, VIII, 248; reconquest of Jerusalem, IV, 115 f.; tithe, IV, 81, 279, 297

Salama (Solomon) ibn Mubarak (Meborakh) ibn Raḥamun, *see* Ibn Raḥamun

Salar, term, V, 309

Ṣalat, prayer, VI, 13

Salbit (ancient Shaalbim), synagogue at, II, 29

Salem, *see* Jerusalem

Salerno, Italy: medical school, IV, 24, VIII, 245; population, IV, 244; transfer of Jewish property to archbishop, IV, 22

Salic law, IV, 263

Sallam, interpreter, VII, 12

Salmon b. Yeruḥim, Karaite author, III, 102, 297, V, 363, VII, 16, VIII, 26; vs. 'Ananites, V, 259; biblical commentaries, VII, 27 f., 288; on the exilarchate, V, 236 f.; grave of, V, 408; identified with Ibn Saqawaihi, V, 406; on Karaism, V, 232, 253; liturgical use of Psalms, VII, 70; on Sabbath drinking, V, 245

Salome-Alexandra, I, 223

Salonica, Greece: communal council, V, 55 f.; messianic movement, IV, 107 f., V, 200, VI, 173; taxation of Jews, III, 192

Saltel, Jewish landowner in Spain, IV, 159

Salt mine, IV, 169, 222

Salvation, *see* Redemption

Samael, Rome's angelic "prince," V, 134, VIII, 19

Samareia, village, I, 266, II, 34, 341

Samareitikon, Greek translation of Pentateuch, II, 30

Samaria, I, 72, 99, 167, II, 339; alien in-

Samaria (*Continued*)
flux, II, 27; deportations from, I, 95, 345; fall of, and jubilee years, VIII, 209 f.; fate under foreign rulers, II, 27; high ecclesiastical officers, I, 81; Jewish settlements in postexilic, I, 225, 370; kings assassinated, I, 74; uprising of peasantry of, I, 89; *see also* Israel, Northern
Samaria-Sebaste, I, 280
Samaritans, II, 26-35, 339-42, V, 170-77, 367-73; address king as *theos epiphanes*, I, 229; adoption of Saadiah's translation, VI, 271; alphabet, V, 176; biblical text, II, 30, 32, 340, V, 175, VI, 236, 442; and Caesarea, V, 171; choice of allegiance, II, 30; "contamination" by unbelievers, V, 409; delegation to king of Persia, III, 17, 56; descent, II, 27, 30, 31; Diaspora settlements, II, 34 f., 339, 342, V, 177; edicts, III, 9, 14, 231; Hebrew of, II, 340, VII, 224; heterodox wings, II, 32 ff., 341; historical literature, VI, 212; history of earliest sect, II, 26, 28; and Jewish era of Creation, VIII, 206; and Judaism, I, 162, 167 f., II, 318; and Karaites, V, 261 f.; on levirate, V, 332; liturgy, VI, 372, VII, 64; messianism, V, 170-77, 367-73; observance of biblical laws, V, 173 ff.; physicians, VIII, 248; priesthood, V, 235; rabbinic attitude toward, II, 339; refugees in Persia, III, 255; segregation, V, 172, 174, 219, 409; sources of history and religion, II, 29, 31, 339; sub-sects, V, 369; temple on Mount Gerizim, II, 26 ff., 339, V, 170 f., 367 f.; use of the divine name, II, 434
Samarkand, Persia: Jewish population, III, 110; Muslim defeat at, VI, 434
Samau'al ibn 'Adiyah, Jewish Arabic poet, III, 72, VII, 191
Samau'al ibn Yaḥya al-Maghribi, Jewish convert to Islam, V, 85 ff., 202, VII, 155, VIII, 249; anti-Jewish tract, V, 93, VI, 303; on beauty of the Qur'an, VII, 8; description of *piyyuṭ*, VII, 96; on expansion of knowledge, VIII, 139; interpretation of Scripture, V, 99 f.; and Karaites, III, 112, V, 285; on liturgical changes and Persian persecutions, VII, 82, 255 f.; on melodies for *piyyuṭim*, VII, 125 f.; on Muslim

toleration, V, 335; and story of Lot, V, 90
Sambari, Joseph b. Isaac, chronicler, III, 123, V, 38 f., 308
Sambation, mythical river, III, 205
Sambethis, Sibylla, I, 197
Samkartsh, *see* Kertsh
Sampseans, sect, II, 51, 348
Samson, I, 376; as prophet, VIII, 132
Samson, Christian apologist, III, 160
Samuel, prophet (the Seer), I, 317, II, 114; antimonarchical, I, 91; Israelitic unity promoted by, I, 61, 63; prayers at tomb of, VII, 76
—— Books of: authorship, I, 340; interpretation, VIII, 95 f.
Samuel, Armenian scholar, III, 184
Samuel, exilarch of Baghdad, conflict with Samuel b. 'Ali, V, 12, 40
Samuel, Mar (of Nehardea), II, 74, 219, 221, 302, 417, VI, 17 f., 124; on abrogation of a biblical law, II, 262; *Baraita de-Shemu'el*, VIII, 147, 350; formula for solar year, VIII, 198; interpretation of the Mishnah, VII, 13; maxims, II, 208, 313; a Persian patriot, II, 177, 397; on purity of Jewish family, I, 234; school of, II, 207; as scientist, II, 206, 307, 433, VIII, 231; substitute for '*Amidah*, VII, 263
Samuel, R., gaon, V, 15
Samuel b. 'Ali, gaon of Baghdad, III, 217, 222, VI, 119, 224; on appointment of judges, VI, 9 f.; on the exilarchs, V, 10; letter of authorization to Zechariah b. Berakhel, V, 52 f.
Samuel b. David Moses ha-Levi, V, 363
Samuel b. Ḥananiah, V, 42
Samuel b. Ḥofni, gaon of Sura, IV, 212, V, 24, 40, VI, 30, VIII, 287; attitude toward the Aggadah, VI, 176 ff.; correspondence, VI, 42 f.; interpretation of Saul's vision at Endor, VIII, 130; "Introduction to the Talmud," VI, 33; legal monographs, VI, 69 f.; "Letters of Authorization," IV, 217 f.; on miracles, VIII, 128; modes of interpretation, VI, 406 f.; and prohibition of Jewish prayers, VII, 255; prolixity, VI, 94; and Saadiah's Book of Commandments, VI, 93
Samuel b. Hosha'nah the Third, liturgical poet, VII, 100, 167, 262; imitator of Saadiah, VII, 278

Samuel b. Joseph ibn Nagrela, *see* Ibn Nagrela, Samuel

Samuel b. Meir (Rashbam), R., VI, 53, VIII, 371; on meaning of Amen, VI, 130; on opening and closing verses of Scripture, VIII, 192; rational criticism, VI, 294 ff.; student's comment on, VI, 467; supplements to Alfasi's work, VI, 90; on trade with Christians, IV, 220

Samuel b. Naḥmani, R., II, 177

Samuel b. Netanel, II, 117

Samuel b. Palṭiel, IV, 23

Samuel b. Shalom, poet, VII, 167

Samuel di Medina, Salonican rabbi, VI, 136

Samuel ha-Nagid, *see* Ibn Nagrela, Samuel

Samuel of Bemberg, VII, 280

Samuel the Little, *Baraita de-Shemu'el*, VIII, 147, 350

Samuel the Pious, VII, 253

Samuel the Small, II, 220, 275, 421

Sanballat the Horonite, I, 349

Sancha, queen of Aragon, IV, 166

Sancho, king of Leon, III, 156

Sancho I (Sancho Ramirez), king of Aragon, IV, 318

Sancho IV, king of Castile, IV, 160

Sancho VII (the Wise), king of Navarre, IV, 253; protection of Jews of Tudela, IV, 35 f.

Sancho VIII, king of Navarre, IV, 253

Sanctuaries, I, 14, 58, 59, 76, 332; Hebrew, as depositaries and fiscal agencies, I, 333; punishment for desecration, II, 93, 369; Tabernacle in Mosaic age, I, 49, 314; women in, I, 146; *see also* Synagogue; Temple at Jerusalem

Sanctus, VII, 65, 77; Christian, VII, 252; daily recitation, VIII, 12 f.; from Isaiah, VIII, 9; *see also* Qadosh; Qedushah

Sanhedrin, I, 222, 396, 401, V, 315, VI, 24, 132; and the academies, II, 120, 126, 197, 378, V, 19 f.; and ascent of Jewish king, V, 75; proclamation of leap year, VIII, 194, 206; reconstitution of, and calendar reform, VIII, 191

—— tractate: commentaries on, VI, 60, 349, VIII, 64

Sanjari, Isaac, Bulan's teacher, III, 326

Santa Cruz, monastery, Coimbra, III, 160

Santa Maria Maggiore, church, II, 11

Saracens, *see* Muslims

Saragossa, Spain, III, 158, IV, 39; Muslim treaty with Alphonso I, IV, 30

Sarah, I, 58

Sardes, Jewish quarters, I, 188

Sardica, *see* Sofia

Sardinia, I, 246, 248

Sargon, I, 106; inscription, I, 95

Ṣarot, term, II, 225

Sar Shalom Gaon, IV, 187 f.; on late arrivals at services, VII, 250; on Onkelos, VI, 260

Sar Shalom, *nagid*, *see* Zuṭṭa

Sassanians, dynasty, II, 172 ff., 180, 317; *see also* Persia, Sassanian

Satan (or Asmodaeus), I, 139, II, 19, 43; as Evil principle, VIII, 290; meaning of "delivery unto," II, 85; view of Jew as ally of, IV, 139, V, 132

Satanas, family name, V, 45

Satire, poetical, VII, 149 f.

Saturday, Muslim prejudice re, V, 91; *see also* Sabbath

Saturn, I, 374, 382

Saturnalia, I, 382

Saturninus, C. Sentius, II, 91

Saul, king of ancient Hebrews, I, 63; celebration of double holiday, VIII, 375 f.; vision at Endor, VIII, 130

Saul b. 'Anan, V, 222 f.

Saul of Tarsus, *see* Paul, Saint

Savasorda, *see* Bar Ḥiyya

Sawad, province, III, 163, 168

Ṣawafi, term, III, 163

Saxony, or "As-Skandz" and Ashkenaz, IV, 4

Sayings of the Fathers, VI, 203, VII, 281, VIII, 21, 64

Scaccarium Aronis, IV, 203 f.; *see also* Aaron of Lincoln

Scaevola, Mucius, VI, 232

Schechem-Neapolis, *see* Nablus

Schedia, synagogue inscription, II, 331

Scholars and scholarship, II, 204-8, III, 184, 195; Arabian biographers, VIII, 223; attribution of mystic classics to ancient, VIII, 18; captured by Arab pirate, V, 46 f.; conflict between people and, II, 241; confused by philosophic controversies, VIII, 70 f.; control over community, II, 120, 197, 403, V, 13 ff., 21, 49; dispersal, II, 119, 126; economic position, I, 265, II, 240, 243 f., 256, 269, 277 f.; education, II,

Scholars and scholarship (*Continued*) 117, 306; exemption from taxation, V, 75 f.; Ḥananel on, VI, 47, 83; intellectual debates, VIII, 72; Karaite, V, 233 f., 275; and marriage, II, 221, 235; molders of tradition, VI, 26 f.; and moneylending, IV, 199; posttalmudic biblical learning, VI, 312, VII, 249, 275 ff.; preachers' attitude toward, VI, 172 f.; preferential treatment for students, II, 221; prestige of, II, 201, 235, 276, 279, III, 85, IV, 221, V, 32-38, 75, 305-8, VI, 30; priestly function of, VI, 9; prolixity of style, VI, 94; reaction to criticism, VI, 120 f.; reliance of Christian authors on, IV, 256; talmudic, liturgical poems, VII, 170 f.; titles, II, 120, 201, 419; visits to foreign communities, V, 53 f.; and women, II, 239 f.; *see also* Academies; Education; Rabbis and rabbinate; *and under* respective disciplines

Scholasticism: Christian, VIII, 61 f., 322, 324; Jewish, VIII, 55 ff.; on "natural" and "positive" laws, VI, 144; questions raised by, VIII, 51; *see also* Philosophy

Schools, elementary, and the "new" Torah, VI, 302

Sciences, VI, 169, VIII, 140, 384; classification of, VIII, 121 f., 141-46, 347-49; communities interested in, VI, 422; effect of differences of opinion among scientists, VIII, 172 f.; expanding study of, VIII, 264; Graeco-Roman, VIII, 56 f., 121; handmaiden of law and exegesis, VIII, 218; Ibn Daud's references to, VI, 209; Jewish contribution as intermediary between East and West, VIII, 219 f., 255 f.; Jewish exploration in, VIII, 68, 138-230, 347-87; opposition to, V, 97, 259, 282, VIII, 142; physician's grounding in, VIII, 222; rabbinic training in, II, 306; "seven," VIII, 145; theory vs. practice, VIII, 138 ff., 143, 159, 218 ff.; *see also* Scholars and scholarship; *also under* respective disciplines

Scientia media, VIII, 128

Scina, North Africa, I, 410

Scipio Africanus Minor, I, 176

"Scorched earth" policy, I, 406

Scorpion, symbol of Jew, V, 132

Scribes, ancient: attitude toward state, I, 238; functions of priests taken over by, I, 271; origin, I, 153; Pharisaic, I, 225, 397; *soferim*, VIII, 149; status, I, 142; temple, I, 397

—— professional, I, 334, II, 422, IV, 215, VII, 138; and accuracy of scriptural texts, VI, 237, 254, 441, VII, 150; halakhic works and, VI, 63; important role of, III, 156 f.; school for, I, 315

Script, so-called "Rashi," VI, 345; *see also* Alphabet

Scripture, *see* Bible

Scrolls: of Abiathar, V, 31, 37; Abisha, V, 372; of Fasts (*Megillat Ta'anit*), II, 140, 384, V, 189; "five," VI, 244

—— of law: colophon, IV, 112; in greeting ceremony, IV, 10, 12, V, 39, 41; ransomed from the Crusaders, IV, 111 f.; swearing on, IV, 83; for synagogue services, VII, 73, 286

—— secret: cited by Hai Gaon, VI, 23; Ḥiyya's school's, VI, 41; Nissim b. Jacob's, VI, 33, 335 f.; *see also* Abiathar; Dead Sea Scrolls; Esther; Hasmoneans, Scroll of

Sculptures: barred from temple buildings, II, 9; human and animal figures, II, 9, 10, 13, 15, 154, 402; in synagogues, II, 154, 330

Scythia, I, 96, 338, II, 336

Scythopolis (Beth-shan), I, 225, II, 27; church, II, 392 f.

Seal cylinders, I, 323

"Seal of Prophecy," V, 377

"Seal of Solomon," III, 204

Seals in a Western Semitic alphabet, I, 346

"Sea peoples," invasion of, I, 320

Seasons, and climate, VIII, 200, 216

Sea trade, I, 255 f., II, 249, IV, 175 f., 333 ff.

Ṣebaot, II, 311

Sebaste, I, 225; rebuilt, 236; *see also* Samaria

Sebastes (Augustus, *q.v.*), I, 236

Sebomenoi, *see* Semiproselytes

"Second air," doctrine of, VIII, 342

Sectarianism: Christian, III, 160 f., 216, 220, 259 f., 279, V, 136, 188 f., 374, VIII, 31; Bulgarian, III, 209, 330; in Byzantine Empire, III, 176; Russian, III, 216

—— Jewish, II, 26-56, 339-50, III, 11,

78 f., 220 f., V, 84, 170-285, 367-416, VIII, 66 ff.; Al-Ma'mun's decree, V, 9 f., 222; in Arabia, III, 71 f.; attacked by al-Baqillani, V, 84, 327; and biblical texts, VI, 235 f., 243, 254, 298 ff.; controversies, VI, 5 f., 243, 267, 298 ff., VIII, 203 ff.; Damascus sect (q.v.), II, 52-54, 348-50; divisive force among minority groups, III, 57; equalization among, V, 186 f.; Essenes (q.v.), II, 48-51, 347 f.; forces shaping ideologies, II, 23-26; independent research, VI, 79; influence on Muslim and Christian, V, 136, 374; and intermarriage, V, 265 ff.; internal conflicts, V, 177-84; in Khazaria, III, 203; legal codes, VI, 78, 108; and magic arts, VIII, 11; and messianism, V, 166 ff., 170 ff.; military and ideological movements, V, 191 ff., 347 ff.; and mystery religions, VIII, 31; names of obscure sects, II, 51, 348; in Persia, III, 254 f., V, 105 f., 183 f., 231; Pharisees and Sadducees (q.v.), II, 35-46, 55 f., 342-46; Qirqisani's study of, V, 369, 374 ff., VI, 211; religious importance of grammar to, VII, 4; religious syncretism and, II, 3, see also Syncretism; repudiation of oral tradition, V, 188 f., VI, 201, VIII, 57 ff.; Samaritans (q.v.), II, 26-35, 339-42, V, 170-77, 367-72; unity within, V, 205 ff.; zealotic faction, II, 47; see also under respective sects
—— Muslim, III, 123, 133, 148 f., V, 180, 189; number of sects, V, 374; philosophers' assemblies, VIII, 56; and segregation, III, 145 f.

Security, personal, III, 172; in England, IV, 85 f.; of exilarchs, V, 7; instability of, in era of Crusades, IV, 35, 89 ff., 141; and property, IV, 68 f; under the Caliphate, III, 121-27; under Frankish rule, IV, 50

Ṣedaqah, see Charity

Seder, term, VII, 111

Seder Eliyahu rabbah, VI, 229

Seder 'Olam (World Chronology), II, 141, 376, 384, V, 256, 366; VIII, 203 f.

Seder tanna'im va-amora'im, VI, 21

Sefarad, and Hesperia, IV, 4

Sefardi, Moses, see Petrus Alphonsi

Sefardim, see Sephardim

Sefer Eliyahu, V, 353

Sefer Gezerata, V, 189

Sefer ha-Bahir, see Bahir

Sefer ha-Ma'asim, Palestinian, II, 283, 422, III, 111 f., VI, 64 f., 355

Sefer ha-Yashar, VI, 197 f.

Sefirat ha-'omer, period of national mourning, IV, 145

Sefirot, ten, VIII, 22 f.

Segelmessa, Africa, III, 281; IV, 170

Segregation, ancient, II, 173, 187, 191-214 passim, 402; in Byzantine Empire, III, 194 f., VIII, 31; and canon law, IV, 9 f., 42 f., 51, 54, VI, 54, 137; of converts to Islam, III, 126; effect on Jewish and Christian doctors, VIII, 254; and hospitals, VIII, 240; of the "impure," V, 250 f.; integration of Jews in Spain, III, 35; and intellectualization, II, 319; of Jewish quarter, III, 11, 232 f., 301, IV, 35, V, 79 ff., 325; Jews coresponsible for, I, 131, 188, 380, II, 12, 430, V, 79 ff., 100, 131, 186, 219 f., VIII, 49; Karaite, V, 261, 265; occupational, IV, 166, 171; of religious minorities under Islam, III, 97 ff., 142, 144 ff., 300 ff., V, 79 ff.; of Samaritans, V, 172, 174, 219

Se'ir, Palestine, VI, 301

Sejan, councilor, I, 246, II, 368

Sekenoi, I, 410

Selah, VI, 257

Seled, childless, VII, 158

Seleucia, destruction of, II, 174

Seleucid era, II, 118, 376, VIII, 378, 379; and birth of Jesus, VIII, 206; dispute over date, VIII, 203 ff.

Seleucids, dynasty, I, 220, 224, 382, II, 98; charter extended to Jewish subjects, I, 216, 244, 369, 393; Jerusalem under, I, 229, 230; story of ritual murder, I, 193; tax on crops, I, 279

Seleucus, story of, VI, 187

Seleucus of Babylon, VIII, 163 f.

Self-determination, individual, II, 41

Self-government, ancient: under Persia (Achaemenid), I, 166; and citizenship, II, 108 ff., 372, 374; coastal Greek cities, I, 225, 280; communities' local autonomy, I, 228, 231, II, 198-204, 265, 403 f.; Hadrian's attack on, II, 106 ff., 108, 118, 120; individual offices, II, 200; patriarchate and exilarchate (q.v.), II, 192-98; Pharisee program, I, 401; protected by imperial legislation, I, 240, 245; segregation and, under

Self-government (Continued)
Rome and Persia, II, 187, 191-214 passim, 402-7
—— medieval, III, 102, V, 3-81, 293-325; areas of, IV, 86; under Byzantine law, III, 190 ff.; congregational, VII, 131 f.; judicial, V, 62, VI, 135; of local usages, V, 48, VI, 126; for merchants, IV, 260; and the messianic age, V, 118; municipal, influence on communal organization, V, 319; political, VI, 172, 214; ritualistic, IV, 55, VII, 65, 94 f.; state attitudes toward, V, 69 ff.
—— see also Civil rights; Communities, Jewish; Rabbis and rabbinate; also under respective offices, e.g., Exilarchs and exilarchate
Self-mortification, and Day of Atonement, VII, 122
Self-sacrifice, I, 399; Graeco-Roman emphasis upon, I, 233
Seljuks, III, 106, V, 37, 194; occupation of Jerusalem, III, 104, IV, 94; in Palestine, IV, 285, 295
Ṣemaḥ b. Ḥayyim (?) Gaon, VI, 108; and Eldad's Halakhot, VI, 221, 241; and Spanish scholars, VII, 13 f.; support of local customs, VI, 122
Ṣemaḥ b. Joshua, VII, 288
Ṣemaḥ b. Palṭoi Gaon, VI, 23, 27, 28, 31; dictionary of talmudic terms, VII, 13 f.
Ṣemaḥ b. Solomon, VII, 111 ff.; on piyyuṭ, VII, 101; prayer book, V, 248
Semaḥot, tractate, VI, 63
Semantics, biblical, VI, 296 ff.
Seminomadic life, I, 55
Semiproselytes, I, 284, 415, II, 149
Semiramis-Astarte, cult, II, 30
Semites, ancient: altars, I, 48; in Egypt, I, 37; influence in Europe and Africa, I, 175; Jewish leadership, I, 210; migration into Palestine, I, 33; monotheism, I, 44; religion expressed in art, I, 14; see also under respective nations, e.g., Babylonia
Semitic languages, and Hebrew, VII, 11
Seneca, philosopher, I, 192, 193, II, 16, 170
Sennacherib, king of Assyria, I, 123, 318; campaign against Judah, I, 95; deportees, I, 95, 338; Edomite expansion set in motion by, I, 106

Sennaja, see Phanagoria
Sens, France, IV, 61
Senses: internal, VIII, 226; location of, VIII, 79; perception of, VIII, 78 ff.; and the soul, VIII, 108
Separatism, see Segregation
Sephardim, VI, 87; and Ashkenazim, IV, 3 f., 43, V, 61, VI, 25 f.; collections of penitential poems, VII, 170; congregational recitation of Yigdal, VII, 175; Hebrew pronunciation, VI, 250, VII, 233; New Year's day services, VII, 172; prayer book, VI, 15; talmudic manuals, VI, 34; "Thirteen Principles," VI, 60; see also Spain
Sepphoris, II, 99, 108, 123, 164, 175, 179, 224; congregation in, II, 199, 285; Ḥanina's ordination opposed, II, 243; kohanim in revered class, I, 413; leadership, V, 179; partial burning of, II, 179, 398; rabbis' struggle for power, II, 242, 413; renamed Diocaesarea, II, 108; theater, I, 401
Septimania, province, III, 245, IV, 52; acquired by the Franks, IV, 43; Jews of, III, 46 f.; Stephen II's letter to prelates of, IV, 47; see also Narbonne
Septuagint, I, 186, 187, 196, 199, 379, 383, 384, III, 189, V, 345, VI, 238, 256; antianthropomorphisms, I, 196, 383 f., VI, 258 f.; Arabic translations, VI, 264; Christians' use of, II, 385, III, 12 f., 233; growing hostility of Jews, II, 142, 385; hermeneutic elaboration, VI, 155-63; interpretations of, and the Peshiṭṭa, VI, 257; Latin paraphrase from, II, 143 f.; "translation Greek," VII, 4, 7; see also Bible; Old Testament
Sepulveda, Spain, fuero, IV, 39
Seraḥ, wife of Bulan, III, 199
Seraphim, V, 142
Serapists, II, 133
Seren, I, 63
Serenus-Severus, see Severus, pseudo-Messiah
Serfdom: of Jews, IV, 22, 41, 63, 70 ff., 87, 141, V, 78, 128 f.; see also Vassals; Villeins
Sergius, commander of Gaza garrison, III, 87
Sergius, monk of Amida, III, 230 f.

Sergius, patriarch of Constantinople, III, 248

Sergius Paulus, I, 243

Sermon on the Mount, II, 67

Sermons, II, 144, 280, 294, 316, 422; aggadic-halakhic, VI, 36, 169; Christian missionary, forced attendance of Jews, IV, 55, 57; content and development of, VI, 152-75, 399-412; exegetical, VII, 81 f.; poetic, VII, 82; scarcity of compilations, VI, 157; threefold division of, VI, 163 ff.; use of tales and parables, VII, 183; see also Homilists and homiletics; Preachers

Serpent: allegorical meaning of, VIII, 86, 339; brazen, I, 66, 322

"Servant of the Lord," I, 157, 365

Servies, term, V, 129

Seth, god, I, 37, 304

Settlements, see Communities, Jewish

Set-Typhon, god, I, 382

Seven, number, VIII, 145; cosmic importance, VII, 244

Seven-branch candelabrum, see Candelabrum

Seven-day week, I, 6, 120, 192

"Seven times seven years," I, 332

Severan dynasty, II, 187

Severus, patriarch of Antioch, III, 5; "fear of the Jews," III, 17

Severus, pseudo-Messiah, III, 16, V, 182, 184 ff., 193 f.

Severus, Julius, general, II, 98

Severus, Lucius Septimius, Roman emperor, II, 109, 110, 150, 375, 400

Seville, Spain: employment of Muslims by dhimmis, III, 146; Jews in, III, 109; Muslims vs. dhimmi scientists, V, 97

Sex, VI, 182 f.; abstinence of the Essenes, II, 218; appetites reproved by Paul and rabbis, II, 85, 365; extramarital relations, II, 218, III, 142 f., V, 240 f., VIII, 53; "false" prophet and, VIII, 131 f.; and interfaith rules, III, 142 f.; and Karaites, V, 241 ff.; magic arts and, VIII, 283; menstruating women and, V, 250; morality of Jews, II, 225, V, 133 f., VII, 180; penalties for transgressions, III, 111 f., 143, 300, V, 57; pregnant wife safeguarded, II, 221; relations with foreign women, I, 194; restraints on, I, 146, 147, II, 217, 290,

319; and the Sabbath, V, 217; with slaves, IV, 191, 195, 334; theme in Arabic literature, VII, 187; theme in poetry, VII, 169, 176

Shabbat, designation, I, 143, VI, 267; see also Sabbath

Shabbat, talmudic tractate, VI, 41, 80, 382

Shabbata de-rigla, V, 40

Shabbetai, name, I, 6, 120, 121, 349

Shabbetai b. Abraham Donnolo, see Donnolo

Shabbetian movement, antinomianism in, VIII, 18

Shabbetit, name, I, 121

"Shabur," generic title, VI, 428

Shaddai, divine name, I, 158, VIII, 179

Shafi‛i, Muslim jurist, V, 212 f.; on convert's property, III, 144; Muslim confiscation of property, III, 169; on sunna of the Messenger, VI, 330; and wergeld of Zoroastrians, III, 295

Shafi‛ites, III, 123, 168, VI, 16; in Cairo, V, 268

Shaf ve-Yatib, synagogue, II, 317, 435

Shahrastani, III, 254, V, 327; censure of Ibn Hudail, VIII, 96; on changeability of laws, V, 332; on number of Jewish sects, V, 183, 194 f., 207 f.; religious studies, VIII, 301

Shakespeare, William, V, 348

Shalom, I, 146; see also Peace

Shalosh, word, VI, 351

Shalosh regalim, I, 5; see also Holidays

Sham‛atiyya, V, 84

Shammai, I, 180; controversies with Hillel, V, 255

Shammaite school, I, 114, II, 228, 410

Shapur (Shahpuhr) I, king of Persia, II, 177, 178, 195, 238, 290, 380, 397, 433, III, 55; checked at Palmyra, III, 62

Shapur II, king of Persia, II, 179, 181, 204, 405; and Isfahan, III, 109, 110

Sharecropping, I, 111, II, 258; coloni and, III, 31, 244; and concentration of landholdings, III, 163; by dhimmis, III, 146

Shari‛ah, term, and halakhah, VI, 12

Sharon, Valley of, IV, 154

Shaṭbi paper, IV, 169

Sheba, queen of, II, 212

Shebu‛ot, tractate, VI, 86

Shechem (Nablus), I, 35, 61; covenant concluded at, I, 308, 325; renamed Flavia Neapolis, II, 123; "sacred town" of Samaritans, II, 28, 31, 35
Shechem Decalogue, II, 29
She'eltot, book, VI, 337 f.; *see also* Aḥai of Shabḥa
Sheep raising, I, 253, 263, 301
Shefaṭiah b. Amittai, Hebrew poet in Italy, III, 180, VIII, 60
Shefelah, Palestine, IV, 153
Sheḥiṭah, ritual slaughtering, VIII, 386; *see also* Slaughter, ritualistic
Shekhinah, I, 389, II, 317
Shelamim, I, 316
Shem, VI, 192
Shemaʿ prayer, I, 186, II, 119, 349, V, 26, 126, 248, VI, 47, VII, 66 ff., 96 f., 120, 244; accuracy of oral transmission, VII, 112; incorporation in the *Qedushah,* II, 182; *piyyuṭim,* VII, 102; prohibition of, VII, 95; recitation of, II, 7, 8, VI, 93, 123, 131, 450, VII, 72
Shemariah, captive scholar, V, 46
Shemaya, ancient sage, II, 203, 346
Shemayah, R., Rashi's pupil, VI, 53 f., 348 f., VII, 281
Shem Ṭob, false claimant to Davidic descent, V, 39
Shem Ṭob b. Joseph ibn Falaquera, *see* Ibn Falaquera
Shemuel, acrostic, VII, 262; *see also* Samuel b. Hoshaʿnah
Shenazzar, I, 119, 349
Shepherd, messianic connotation, V, 379
Sheqalim, tractate, VI, 336, 349
Sherira Gaon: on Aramaic prayers, VII, 66 f.; on authority of the geonim, V, 23; commentaries on Talmud, VI, 43; on conduct of religious services, VI, 9; Davidic descent, V, 9; "Epistle," VI, 30, 81, 112, 204 f., 233; on geonim and Talmud, VI, 23; loss of pupils, V, 24; on marriage settlement, VI, 24; and Muslim robbers and thieves, III, 122; on "new light on Zion," VII, 116; responsa, III, 111 f., VI, 29 ff.; and R. Yose, VI, 18
Sheshna Gaon, VI, 446; advice re extortion, V, 5
She'ur qomah (Measure of the Divine Stature), VIII, 11 ff., 25 ff., 32 f., 179; Maimonides on, VI, 177 f.

Shiʿa, Muslim sect, V, 168, 183 f., 211, VI, 10, 363; accessions among Persians, III, 150; attitude toward Enoch, VI, 437; in Baghdad, III, 123, 133; Idriside dynasty, III, 108; rites, VII, 308; in Tiberias, V, 180
"Shield of David," III, 204
Shilo, identified with messiah, II, 139, 140, V, 118
Shiloh, sanctuary, I, 59
Shimei, I, 324
Ship, as symbol of Israel, V, 361
Shipping: restrictions on Jewish merchants and owners, IV, 183 f.; and shipowners, II, 249, 261; Venetian, exclusive rights to, IV, 24; *see also* Piracy; Trade, international
Shipowners' guild, II, 261
Shirin, Persian wife of Khosroe II, III, 57, 60
Shopkeeping, IV, 179 f.; *see also* Trade
Shoshan-Dukht(?), city built by, II, 204, 404
Shoshenk (Shishak) I, king of Egypt, I, 322, 327
Shouting, congregational, VII, 125 f.
Showbreads, in the Temple, VII, 78
Showfringes, V, 218, 219, VII, 76
Shpsh, god, I, 45
Shrines, Jewish: in Egypt, III, 106; portable, I, 49
Shrouds, II, 273, 287
Shuraiḥ ibn ʿAmram, Jewish poet, III, 78
Shureiḥ, Muslim exegete, VI, 471
Shurpu, I, 50
Sibawaihi, Baṣran philologist, VII, 34
Sibylline Oracles, I, 204, 385, 390, II, 397, III, 15, 234
Sicarii (assassins) of Zealotic faction, II, 47, 347
Sichardus, John, editor of pseudo-Philo apocryphon, VI, 196 f.
Sicily, III, 24, IV, 24, 115; Graeco-Byzantine tradition, VIII, 256; Jewish communities, III, 109, IV, 20-24, 242 f.; Jewish converts, III, 28; Jewish landowners, IV, 160; languages, IV, 21; service of fleet in the Crusades, IV, 298; synagogues, III, 30, 175
Sicut Judaeis, IV, 7 f., 235 f., 240; *see also Constitutio pro Judaeis;* Papacy
Siddur, term, VII, 274; *see also* Prayer books

Sidon and Sidonians, I, 162, 176, 374 f.; economic blockade, I, 277

Sidonius Apollinaris, V, 125 f.

Sifre, term, IV, 338

Silano, R., VI, 156, 400

Silk: as currency, IV, 347; industry, II, 249, IV, 168 f.; trade, IV, 169, 183

Silver, I, 256; artificial production of, VIII, 224; mines, IV, 211; standard, IV, 209 f.

Simeon, anchorite, IV, 245

Simeon of Beth Arsham, III, 67 f.

Simeon Stylites the Elder, III, 6

Simḥah b. Samuel, R., of Vitry, VI, 75, 202, 356; liturgical works, VII, 122 ff., 144 f., 281; on Qalir's poems, VII, 103

Simlai, R., II, 162, 278; Mosaic commandments, VI, 90 f.

Simon, patriarch, I, 39; tribe of, I, 317, III, 208

Simon, R., and Hai, VI, 364; on individual prayer, VII, 74

Simon, Richard, VI, 306

Simon, son of Boethos, I, 216

Simon, son of Giyoras, I, 231, 268, 412, II, 347

Simon an der Pfort, R., VI, 162

Simon b. Abba, R., II, 253

Simon Bar-Jona, II, 74

Simon b. Eleazar, II, 419

Simon b. Gamaliel, R., II, 14, 15, 117, 141, 237, 253, 408, 430, VI, 31; academy head, II, 126, 127; as patriarch, II, 193, 403; on translation of Torah, II, 143

Simon b. Isaac "the Great," cantor of Mayence, VII, 144

Simon b. Laqish, R., II, 44, 148, 194, 206, 237, 283, 305, 392, VI, 181, VII, 62; epigrams, II, 276; on eternity of Jewish law, II, 161; homily against separateness, II, 241; pun on the law, II, 277; quoted, II, 172, 184, 246

Simon b. Megas the Priest, VII, 92

Simon b. Menasya, R., II, 67, 356

Simon b. Ṣemaḥ Duran, *see* Duran

Simon b. Shetaḥ, I, 219, 221, 395, II, 21, 236, 409, 421, 422, V, 255, VI, 207

Simon b. Yoḥai, II, 96, 124, 125, 185, 265, 309, 426, IV, 157, VIII, 283; book of "Mysteries," V, 148 f.; on Islam, III, 93; legends, I, 9, V, 140; prayer, III, 274, IV, 296, V, 353; tomb, II, 279; on Torah vs. economic endeavors, II, 251

Simon b. Zoma, R., II, 218, 248

Simonias, Palestinian community, VI, 36, VII, 81

Simon Maccabee, Jewish ruler, I, 220, 222, 223, 229, 235, 255, 368, II, 98; numismatic sovereignty, I, 369, *see also* Coins and coinage, Maccabean; political sovereignty recaptured by, I, 166

Simon Magus, II, 32, 341

Simon the Hasmonean, *see* Simon Maccabee

Simon the Just (or the Pious), II, 120, 421, VI, 155; encounter with Alexander the Great, VI, 207

Simony, II, 268; Church legislation vs., III, 249

Simon Zealotes, II, 74, 346

Simson b. Abraham of Sens, VI, 54 f., 349 f.

Sin, Babylonian moon deity, I, 44; worship, in Arabia, III, 64

Sin, desert, I, 45

Sinai, Mount, I, 45, 48, II, 139, 161, V, 92; Moses on, V, 93, VI, 8, 91, 100, 228, 232, 269, 300, VIII, 6, 41, 294; *see also* Revelation

Sinaitic Peninsula, I, 36

Sinaitic slaves, I, 36

Sinan, Sabian medical commissioner, III, 146; vizier's order to, VIII, 240

Sindbad, Parables of, VII, 189

Sind b. 'Ali, Arab astronomer, VIII, 167 f.

Singers: among returning exiles, I, 124; prophesy, I, 153

Singing: in synagogue and church, I, 125, II, 8, 155, 330, 389, VIII, 3; in Temple, I, 123; *see also* Music

"Singing girls," VII, 205

Sins: avoidance of, as preventive medicine, VIII, 261; biblical synonyms for, VI, 296; Crusades as expiation for, IV, 101; doctrine of original, II, 433; exile and, V, 100 f.; extinction of, in messianic era, V, 165 f.; forgiveness of, II, 308, V, 17, VII, 92; interrelated origins of death and, I, 139; and penitence, VIII, 52, 105; and punishment, I, 136, *see also* Punishments; remedy, I, 294; responsibility for, I, 135, II, 41, 346; and transmigration of souls, VIII, 36; *see also* Confession of sin; Redemption

Siqariqon, law of, II, 104, 372

Sirach, Jesus, I, 6, 151, 185, 198, 228, 252, 255, 265, 272, 386, 397, II, 34, 222, 228, 313, V, 188, VII, 66; beliefs of, II, 19, 38, 44, 45, 346; epigram on the physician, VIII, 221; medieval knowledge of works of, VII, 260; prayer, II, 342; quoted, II, 129, 379, 420

Siroe, son of Khosroe II, III, 239

Sisebut, king of the Visigoths: anti-Jewish decrees, III, 37, IV, 5, 155 f.; effect of intolerance of, in France, III, 47

Sivan 20, fast of, IV, 138, 145, V, 217

Sixth century, I, 103-5, 341-44

Skeletons, at Montjuich, IV, 33, 249

Skepticism, VIII, 79; Jewish spokesmen for, V, 104 f.; religious, VIII, 66 f.; *see also* Philosophy; Rationalism

Slaughter, ritualistic, II, 306, IV, 104, V, 93, 249, VI, 70, 359, VIII, 227; of half cow, half dog, VI, 183 f.; house, IV, 39; monopoly on, IV, 244; nonsacrificial, I, 148, 150; poems on, VII, 192; regulations, IV, 60 f., VI, 70, 359, VIII, 386

Slaves and slavery: children of bastards and, II, 223; circumcision of, IV, 188, V, 219; conversion, III, 179, IV, 49, 52, V, 219; of converts to Islam, III, 126; and debts or fines, II, 257, 258, 303; decree on clothing, III, 139; Egyptian, I, 259, 260; employment, IV, 196; Ethiopian, II, 238; female, I, 71, 85, 112, 259, 269, 324, II, 224, 230, III, 89, *see also* Concubines and concubinage; freedom of, through baptism, III, 14; and free workers, I, 267-71, 412; fugitive, I, 71, 85, 324; Gentile, I, 70, 71, 268, 269, 324, II, 259; in industry, II, 247; Jewish ownership, I, 110, 181, II, 259; laws affecting, I, 70, 85, 88, 267, 324, II, 259, III, 89, VI, 84; Muslim attitude toward, III, 302 f., IV, 195; Negro, mother of Mustanṣir, III, 158; Pharisaic-rabbinic aversion toward, I, 269; prisoners of war sold as, I, 95, II, 102, IV, 110; ransom of, I, 259, 268, 281, III, 200, IV, 188 f., 255; reference to, in Jewish prayer of thanksgiving, VII, 109; religious instruction, IV, 190, VI, 12; responsibility for damages inflicted by, I, 269; run-away, IV, 190; Sabbath observance by, IV, 156; Sinaitic, I, 36; Slavs as, III, 214, IV, 172, 194; state, I, 324; Syrian, I, 409; taxation, II, 105; tax receipt as mark of, III, 168; temple, I, 324; treatment on basis of equality, II, 258; treatment of freed, I, 269, II, 223, 286, *see also* Freedmen; unrest of, II, 57

—— Christian, III, 32, 36, 51; Arian, in North Africa, III, 234; circumcision, IV, 188; owned by Jews, III, 30 f., 188, 219, 243, 252 f., IV, 19, 154 ff.

—— Jewish, II, 258 ff., 416, III, 45; accretions to community through, III, 110; 'Anan on, V, 219; Hebrew, I, 57, 69, 70, 85, 267, II, 114; and Israelites, I, 57; perpetual slavery, III, 43

Slave trade and traders, I, 70, II, 259, 262, III, 30 f., IV, 187-96; ban on sales to Jews, IV, 9; fraudulent, IV, 192 f.; and labor shortage, IV, 172; Phoenician, I, 176; prices, I, 268, 324, IV, 188 f., 255; self-sales, I, 324

Slavonic countries: Jewish merchant traders, IV, 175 f.; source of slavery, IV, 194

Slavonic dialect, Old, IV, 177; Christian writings in, III, 211; *see also* Josephus

Slavs: and "Canaan," III, 214 f., IV, 177, VI, 437; contributions to Christian literature, III, 211; Jewish settlers among, III, 206 ff., 330 ff.; legal codes, III, 187; as slaves, III, 214, IV, 172, 194; in Syria, III, 98

Smallpox, VIII, 242 f.

Smiths, Palestinian, I, 60

Snake bite, verbal charms for, VIII, 234

Snake symbol, I, 66, 322

Ṣobah, *see* Aleppo

Social classes, *see* Classes, social

Social justice, I, 25, 332; Essenes' preoccupation with, II, 48; an essential of religion, I, 88; preachment of Islam on racial equality, III, 98

Social science, VIII, 121 f.

Social unrest, I, 67-72, 322-25; Graeco-Roman period, I, 250-85, 406-15; and prophecy, I, 73, 84-91, 332-36; *see also* Revolts

Social welfare: in talmudic age, II, 269-74; 420; pietism and, VIII, 48 f.; *see also* Charity

Societies, friendly, II, 288, 289, 424

Society: cleavages in Israelitic, I, 275; moral foundation, I, 50, 319; primacy over individual, IV, 222, VIII, 120; and religion, I, 3-31, 189, 277, 293-97

Socioeconomic conditions, IV, 150-226, 312-52; and changes in law, VI, 63, 146 f.; class distinctions in Muslim society, III, 148 f.; effect on aggadic study, VI, 152 ff.; in England and Normandy, IV, 76 ff.; interfaith, III, 50, 147, IV, 14 f., V, 95 ff.; Karaites and, V, 238 f., 400 f.; leisure class, VIII, 72; medical practice and, VIII, 254; Paul's acceptance of, II, 77; and pessimism under Rome, II, 57; protection of rights by papacy, IV, 7 ff.; and rabbis' insistence upon procreation, II, 210; regional variations, IV, 158-64; and religious propaganda, I, 174; reported by Benjamin of Tudela, VI, 223 f.; and sectarianism, V, 177 ff.; and type of occupation, IV, 167, 179 f.

Socrates, Greek philosopher, I, 233, II, 259

Socrates, Byzantine chronicler, V, 167 f., 366 f.

Sodom, punishment of, VI, 482

Soferim (scribes), VIII, 149

Soferim, tractate, II, 143, VI, 34 f., 238 f.

Sofia (Sardica), Bulgaria, III, 210

Soklos, Pannonia, III, 207

Soldiers, *see* Military service

Solomon, Hebrew king, I, 22, 67, II, 212, III, 244 f., VIII, 77; authorship of biblical books, II, 145, VI, 285, 308; breach of law of succession, I, 149; centralized controls, I, 74 f., 326; collaboration with Tyre, I, 64, 321; *corvée*, I, 70, 84, 324; eulogized as king of magicians, II, 17, 21, VIII, 223 f., 283; expeditions, VII, 16; figures in palace and Temple decoration, II, 15; foreign gods served by, I, 65, II, 160; harem, III, 201; identification with Agur b. Jakel, VI, 160; industrial and commercial undertakings, I, 326; influenced by earthly trigon, VIII, 180; knowledge of natural sciences, VIII, 387; mystical midrash, VIII, 18 f.; Northern Israel as continuation of kingdom of, I, 73; and Palmyra, II, 407, III, 62; population under, I, 29, 320; prayer, II, 60; as prophet, VIII, 132; seal of, III, 204; splendor of court, I, 77; taxes and payments in kind, I, 318; wives, I, 65, II, 226, III, 201

Solomon, governor of Africa, III, 230

"Solomon," acrostic used by Saadiah, VII, 141, 144

Solomon, Song of, *see* Song of Songs

Solomon, Testament of, VIII, 283

Solomon Abu'l Munajja ibn Sha'ya, constructor of Nile canal, III, 155

Solomon b. Aaron of Troki, V, 272

Solomon b. ha-Yatom, VI, 62

Solomon b. Ḥisdai, exilarch: and academy of Sura, V, 9; appointments to gaonate of Sura, V, 15

Solomon b. Isaac or Yiṣḥaqi, *see* Rashi

Solomon b. Kuji, V, 203

Solomon b. Saron, apologist for Karaism, V, 229

Solomon b. Simson, chronicler of First Crusade, IV, 94 ff., 285 ff., V, 199 f., VI, 193, 217 f.; vs. Christians, IV, 143; and forced converts, IV, 106; on Jewish martyrs, IV, 96 f., 144 f.

Solomon b. Yehudah, Palestinian gaon and poet, III, 295, V, 33, 48, 233, VII, 268; career, V, 34; and Karaites, V, 280; Nathan b. Abraham's campaign against, V, 274; prayer for fellow Jews, III, 104

Solomon ha-Kohen, messianic pretender, V, 202, 260

Solomon ibn Adret, *see* Ibn Adret

Solomon ibn Parḥon, *see* Ibn Parḥon

Solomon's Temple, *see* Temple at Jerusalem, First

Solomon-Sulaiman, of Sanjar, liturgical poet, VII, 100, 268

Solomon the "Babylonian," IV, 14

Solomon the Egyptian, Jewish court physician, III, 185

Song, synonyms for, VIII, 279

Song of Deborah, I, 141, 317, 318, VI, 261

Song of Moses, II, 330; pronunciation, VI, 250

Song of Songs, I, 336, 340, II, 145, 386, V, 282, VII, 158, 213; eschatological interpretation of, V, 156 f.; Judeo-Christian controversy, VI, 161; Midrash on, VII, 81; Targum of, VI, 160, 403

Songs, secular, VII, 203

Sons, younger, in biblical legend, I, 22
Sonzolo, Shem-Ṭob, IV, 12
Sophism, VIII, 78 f.
Sophronius, patriarch of Jerusalem, III, 87, 277
Sopron (Oldenburg), Hungary, III, 211
Sorcery: prohibition of, VIII, 276; *see also* Magic arts
Soul, I, 390 f., VIII, 318 f.; and Adam's body, I, 52; ascent to heaven, VIII, 21 f., 23, 105, 284 f.; and body, VIII, 36 f., 226; faculties of, VIII, 82 ff., 105 ff., 117, 331 f.; Greek concept, I, 208; Hebrew synonyms for, VIII, 338; hygiene of, VIII, 339; immortality of, VIII, 104; location, VIII, 107; meaning of words as, VII, 51; prophetic, transmission of, VIII, 134; well-being of, VI, 142; *see also* Immortality of the soul; Resurrection
Sovereignty of the people, I, 91
Space: four ells in, V, 303; philosophic discussions of, VIII, 88 ff.
Spain, I, 169, 170, III, 33-46, 244-50, IV, 27-43, 245-56; Alfasi in, VI, 86 f.; apocalyptic tract, V, 145 f.; Arab conquest, III, 91 f., 272; Babylonian Talmud in, V, 47, VI, 332; biblical commentaries, VI, 277, 284 f., 309; capital punishment in, VI, 45, 134; Christian-Muslim relations, IV, 93 f.; Council of Elvira, II, 188, 210; court poets, VII, 146 ff.; Crusades against Jews and Muslims, IV, 131 f., 148; emigrés to Italy, IV, 21; evolution of Jewish calendar, VIII, 199 f., 204; *ghubar* numerals, VIII, 150; Golden Age of Jewish literature, VI, 188, VII, 136 ff., VIII, 263; identification with Sefarad, IV, 4; international trade, III, 156; Jewish agriculture, IV, 158 ff.; Jewish communities, II, 210, III, 27-43, 33 ff., 108 f., IV, 44 ff., 148, V, 51, 58; Karaites, V, 241, 271, VII, 228; liturgy, VII, 107 f., 116, 118, 272 f.; manuscript of Aḥimaaz' chronicle, VI, 432; massacre and pillage, IV, 39 f.; medical science, VIII, 248; merchants, IV, 179 f.; mishnaic commentaries, VI, 61 f.; Mohammed's decrees of religious toleration, III, 124; moneylending, IV, 206 f.; Muslim prohibition re slaves, IV, 194; New Christians, III, 176 f.; paper manufacture, IV, 169;

philosophic speculation, VIII, 39, 63 f., 135, 311; Phoenician ghettos, I, 176; recitation of Aramaic version, VI, 262; record of postgeonic century, VI, 208; responsa collections, VI, 117; rise of Jewish influence and power, III, 155 ff.; slaves in, IV, 194 f., 337; spread of influence of Muslim Golden Age, IV, 3 ff.; taxation of Jews, III, 169; Tosafists, VI, 56; use of Hebrew language, VII, 47, 54 f.; and vernaculars of east and west, VIII, 229; vineyards and orchards, IV, 162
—— Visigothic, III, 33-46, 244-50; Babylonian influence on Jewry of, V, 61; laws on Jews, III, 33 ff.; number of Jews, III, 245; weakness of the monarchy, III, 44
Sparta and Spartans: affinities with Jews, I, 185, 377; delegation to St. Nicon Metanoites, III, 184, 318
Spartianus, II, 109
Speculations, metaphysical, II, 314; attitude toward, VIII, 68 f.; vs. revelation, VIII, 85
Speculations: regulations against economic excesses, II, 254; *see also* Business transactions; Economic conditions
Speech: Aramaic supplanted by Arabic, VII, 67; divine, VIII, 129; "levantinization" of, VII, 10; purity of, and environment, VII, 3, 223
Spelling: in biblical texts, VI, 238; in the Masorah, VI, 293; and pronunciation, VI, 243 f.
Spheres, celestial, VIII, 93 ff., 163, 213; and the Hereafter, VIII, 105; influence on man, VIII, 111
Spices, Book of, VIII, 235
Spice trade, IV, 44
Spinoza, Baruch: *scientia intuitiva*, VIII, 131; and Trinitarian creed, VIII, 96
Spires, Germany: Jewish community, IV, 67, 68, 74, 96, 134, VI, 345; Jewish quarter, IV, 275, 347, V, 79
Spirits, world of, VIII, 180; *see also* Demonology
Spiritual exercises, II, 315, 316
Sports and games, II, 421
Spring, miraculous, V, 367
Staff called Graciousness, V, 264
Stars: Abraham's knowledge of, II, 16; Hebrew names of, VIII, 358; influence

of, VI, 231, VIII, 94, 111, 175; movements of, VIII, 169; trepidation of,
VIII, 164 f., 173; *see also* Astrology;
Astronomy; Planets
State: artificial, I, 122; attitudes of Jews
toward, I, 4, 16-25, 27, 235; coercion
vs. Jews, V, 70 f.; vs. communal autonomy, V, 69 ff.; Jesus and, II, 69, 73;
loyalty to, V, 77 f., VIII, 263; and
nationality, I, 17-25, 93-96, 234, 338;
Sadducees and, II, 99; scholastic theory
of, V, 71 ff.; *see also* Political power;
Rights, legal; Self-government
Steer, eschatological monster, VIII, 10
Status: of burghers, IV, 23; of farmers
in Byzantium, IV, 153; of Muslims in
foreign lands, III, 129; change in so-
cioeconomic, V, 126 f.; *see also* Rights,
legal; Socioeconomic conditions
Stephen, Saint, II, 74, 83
Stephen III (IV), pope, IV, 42, 47
Stephen V (VI), pope, IV, 260
Stephen VI (VII), pope, IV, 260
Stephen, king of England, IV, 81
Stilicho, Teuton ruler of Rome, III, 234
Stobi (Yugoslavia), II, 210, III, 207; syna-
gogue, II, 10
Stone quarries, I, 257
Stone structures, built by English Jewry,
IV, 85, 170
Stoning, V, 241
Stories and storytelling, VI, 168-74, 181-
88, 408-16; art of, III, 71; intermingled
with history, VI, 233; popularity of,
VI, 167; in synagogue and mosque, VI,
154; types of, VI, 180 f.
Strabo, I, 180, 252, 255, 262, 266, 396, II,
13, 266
"Strange woman" of the Proverbs, I, 151,
363
Straton of Gorgippia, III, 200
Strikes and strike breakers, I, 270
Strongbow, Richard (Richard de Clare,
2d earl of Pembroke), IV, 82
Strophe, Hebrew, VII, 199
Students: books supplied to, VII, 137 ff.
Study: time for, and employment, IV,
221, 223; *see also* Education
Style, Hebrew, purification of, VII, 50 f.,
54
Subotniki, Russian sect, III, 216
Suetonius, Paulinus, I, 178, II, 57, 104,
105 f.
Suez, Isthmus of, IV, 173

Suffering: divine compensation for, VIII,
103; of Israel, V, 144, 160; values in,
I, 257, II, 215, IV, 146 f., V, 101 f., VI,
439, VIII, 126 f.
Ṣufism, Muslim, VI, 143, VIII, 51, 112;
and alchemy, VIII, 225; influence on
Judaism, VII, 78; *see also* Mystics and
mysticism
Suftaja, draft, IV, 213
Sugyot, lessons, VI, 20
Suicide, V, 241; as alternative to enforced
baptism, IV, 96; exhortation vs., VI,
193 f.; funeral rites, II, 287
—— mass: in England, IV, 125 f.; in
Mayence, IV, 104; public reaction to,
IV, 144
Suidas, VIII, 57; on Agapios, VIII, 241
Sulaiman, caliph, III, 102
Sulaiman al-Sanjari, *see* Solomon-
Sulaiman
Sulaiman of Andalusia, III, 115
Sumer, Jewish fiscal expert, III, 150
Sumerian law codes, I, 327
Sun: creation of, VIII, 203, 368; posi-
tion, VIII, 201; rotation, VIII, 163;
size, VIII, 162 f., 360; worship of, I,
45, II, 50, 51
Sunday, II, 134, 380; Judeo-Christian
trade on, IV, 220; observance of, IV,
60 f., 157, V, 123 f.
Sun goddess, I, 311
Sunna: in Fez, V, 79; and Jewish *halak-
hah*, VI, 7; judicial summaries, VI, 363
Superman, doctrine of, VIII, 344 f.
Supernatural: attraction of, VII, 76 ff.;
formulas for control of, VIII, 8 ff.; and
man, VIII, 27; *see also* Angels; Demonology; God; Intermediaries; Magic
arts; Miracles
Superstition: Karaites on, V, 258; religious, VIII, 26
Supreme Being, I, 174; *see also* God
Sura, Babylonia, II, 207, 405, III, 114;
discriminatory rules on medical treatment, III, 146, VIII, 240; Jewish majority, III, 99; synagogue, VII, 108
—— academy, III, 59, 154, V, 9, 13 ff.,
276, VI, 201 f., 425, 455; adherence to
Judaean custom, VI, 124 ff.; archives,
VI, 112 f.; Babylonian Talmud, VI,
17 f.; enrollment, V, 19; and the exilarchate, V, 14 f.; Palestinian traditions, VI, 24; revenue, V, 14; superiority over Pumbedita, VI, 430; weaver

Sura *(Continued)*
as presiding officer, V, 74 f.; *see also*
Amoraim; Geonim and gaonate
Surgeons and surgery, VIII, 238, 260
Surveyors, methods of mensuration, VIII,
157
Survival, after death, VIII, 104; *see also*
Immortality of the soul
Survival of Jews, I, 9, 105, II, 215; de-
pendent upon fulfillment of covenant,
I, 90
Susa: exiles at royal court, I, 115, 132;
Ezra and Nehemiah in, I, 116; re-
building of, II, 204
Suyuti, Arab historian, III, 153; history
of Qur'anic exegesis, VI, 468
Sviastoslav, duke of Kiev, III, 205 f.
Sviatopluk, duke of Prague, IV, 118
Swastika, emblem, II, 11
Swiatopolk II, of Kiev, III, 216
Swinthila, king of the Visigoths, III,
39 f.
Switzerland: multilingualism, VII, 223;
outlawry of *shehitah*, VIII, 386
"Sword of Moses," VIII, 11, 281
Symbolism, VIII, 284; of letters, VIII,
15; numerical symbolism, VI, 157 f.;
phonetic, VI, 249 ff.; and tombstone
inscriptions, IV, 33; *see also* Images
and symbols
Symmachus, Bible translation, II, 143
Synagoge (Johannes Scholasticus), III,
187
Synagogue, I, 351, 410, II, 280-86, 422 f.;
architecture, II, 9, 284 f.; benefactors,
II, 187, 191, 242, 333, 338, 402; benefactresses, II, 24, 240, 338, 413; books
discarded, VII, 139; Caesarea, II, 423;
chief works on, II, 423; churches converted into, III, 280; communal life
in, I, 15, 126, 133, 214, II, 45, 285 f.,
291, VI, 154, VII, 62 ff.; construction,
III, 232; converted into churches, III,
8, 30, 136, 296; customs concerning, VI,
123 f.; decorated with signs of Zodiac,
VIII, 184; dedication to pagan digni-
taries, II, 4; destruction of, II, 189, 284,
III, 6; at Dura-Europos, I, 14, II, 241,
346; equality with church and mosque,
I, 24; exemption from billeting of
soldiers, III, 192; Galilean, in which
Jesus taught, II, 67, 355; and Graeco-
Oriental arts, II, 6 ff., 9 ff., 146, 285,
330 ff., 402; hospice and, I, 214, VIII,

239 f.; Karaite, V, 247 ff.; location and
autonomy, II, 199, 403 f., IV, 266 f.;
oldest known, II, 10; orientation toward Jerusalem, II, 285, *see also* Jerusalem; origins, I, 351, VI, 392; outlawed in North Africa, III, 8 f.; papal
attitude toward, III, 29 f.; pre-Islamic,
II, 175, 242, III, 136; prohibition of
new, II, 181, 192, 398, III, 9, 10,
134-39, 188, 230; preparation of scrolls,
VII, 73, 286; professional readers, VI,
237, *see also* Cantor; protective laws
for property, II, 189, 192; rebuilt, III,
175; Samaritan, V, 174, 177; segregation of sexes, II, 241; separate, of
Palestinian and Babylonian rituals,
V, 28, *see also* Ritual; and Temple,
I, 132, II, 125, VII, 128, 274; use of,
to denounce Islam, III, 123; violation classified, I, 245; woman's role
within, II, 240, 413; worship of Christians in, II, 188, VII, 84, 128
—— Great, Men of the, VI, 203 f., 206,
230, VII, 65 f., 101, 251, VIII, 21
—— services, II, 280 ff., III, 72, VII, 128;
attendance and length of, VI, 139 f.,
VII, 69, 71, 130 f., 246 f.; books neces-
sary for recitation, VII, 135; cantillation of weekly lessons, VII, 126; congregational leader, VII, 79-85; congregational responsoria and singing, VII,
125 ff., 284; educational and devotional
aspects, II, 280, 281, VII, 73 f., 271 f.;
interruption by public appeal, V, 66 f.,
VI, 139; music, II, 8, 155, 330, 389,
VII, 125-31, 281-85; procedure, VI,
41 f.; recitation of Aramaic version,
VI, 262; regional autonomy in use of
piyyutim, VII, 104; scriptural lessons,
VI, 257, 262, VII, 81, 94; sermons in,
IV, 55, V, 112; *see also* Liturgy;
Preachers; Rabbis and rabbinate;
Worship
"Synagogue Greek," I, 186
Syncretism, II, 292; astrology, magic, and
ritual, II, 15-23, 334, 336 f.; bridges be-
tween Jewish and Gentile worlds, II,
3-6; geographical centers, II, 24 f.;
Graeco-Oriental art, II, 6-15, 330-34,
402; Islamic, III, 80-86, 265-68; Israelitic, I, 349; Judeo-Christian, V, 367;
Khazar Judaism, III, 200-206; Misha-
wayh's, V, 196 f.; and Second Common-
wealth, II, 23-26, 54-56, 338 f.; and

sectarianism (*q.v.*), II, 3, V, 179; shaping forces, II, 23-26, 338
Synods, Catholic, *see* Councils, Church
Synods, communal, V, 64 ff., 70 f.; of Usha, II, 126, 271, 378, 420
Synonyms, biblical, VII, 12; multiplication of, VIII, 14
Syracuse, Sicily, III, 175
Syria and Syrians, I, 217; ancient Christians in, II, 83, 164, 165, 393; antisemitism, I, 176, 283, II, 89; apotheosis of royal power, I, 398; army's desertion of Jews, I, 218; bronze, I, 318; Byzantine campaign, III, 317; concentration of landholdings, III, 163; Crusaders in, IV, 297; ethnic and racial groups in, III, 98; extortions of Ventidius, I, 264; industry, II, 248 f.; Jews in, I, 169, 170, 283, 393, III, 103 ff., 279, IV, 108 f.; Maccabean uprising, VI, 189; merchants, I, 260; migrations to, II, 210; Palestine a province, II, 94; political stupor of ancient Jewish communities, I, 247, II, 96, 99; proselytes, I, 183, 283; religion, I, 229, II, 3, 165 f.; Sadducees leaders of revolt against, I, 234; *see also* Seleucids
Syriac Christians, VIII, 76; Al-Muqammiṣ and, VIII, 97 f.; doctrine of divine attributes, V, 120 f.; emphasis on ceremonial laws, VIII, 17; influence of religious philosophy of, V, 120 f., VIII, 58; in international trade, III, 49, 53, IV, 44; law codes, II, 432, VI, 4 ff., 321 f.; liturgy, VII, 65; poetry related to current events, VII, 99; Trinitarian creed, VIII, 96; version of Bible, VI, 241, 263, 454; works of translation, VIII, 64; *see also* Peshiṭta
Syriac language, II, 146, VI, 256, 453, VII, 4, 84, VIII, 393; church use of, VII, 68; medical works, VIII, 242; poems in, VII, 196; *see also* Aramaic
Syria Palaestina, official name for Judaea, II, 123, 380
Syro-Roman Code, VI, 4
Syrus, Michael, III, 177, V, 8
Szabolcs, Council of, III, 212

T

Ta'abod, term, V, 129
Taanach, I, 313

Ṭabari, 'Ali b. Rabban al-, I, 341; interpretation of biblical prophecy, V, 87; "Paradise of Wisdom," medical work, VIII, 243; self-appraisal as controversialist, V, 88; use of Syriac version, VI, 263
Ṭabari, Mohammed ibn Jarir aṭ-, V, 86, VI, 170; commentary on the Qur'an, VI, 282; on ordinary meaning of scriptures, VI, 463
Tabeel, I, 348
Tabernacle, I, 49, 314, VI, 147, VIII, 147; in desert, VIII, 7, 94; Moses' building of, IV, 167, VI, 163
Ṭabit ibn Qurra, *see* Ibn Qurra
Tables of testimony, I, 314
Tabrizi, at-, VIII, 346
Tacitus, I, 193, 248, 262, 372; anti-Jewish bias, I, 175, 181, 183, 191, 194, II, 170; despair of Roman future, II, 57; on Great War and after, II, 90, 92, 102, 106, 368, 372; ignorance of Israel's preexilic history, I, 192; on Jews, I, 382, 411, II, 5, 109, 219, 223, 394
Tadmor, *see* Palmyra
Taḥpanḥes, Egypt, I, 111
Ta'if, Arabia, introduction of viticulture, III, 70
Tajo, bishop of Saragossa, III, 248
Taku (of Tachau), Moses b. Ḥisdai, VIII, 39, 286; report of legend re Ibn Ezra's death, VIII, 368
Tales, fantastic, II, 306, 433; *see also* Stories
Talismans, protective, II, 20; used during childbirth, I, 329; *see also* Magic arts
Talmidim, term, VI, 342
Talmud: II, 207, 215-321, 408-36; on agriculture, IV, 157; allusions to moon's nativities, VIII, 161; on *'am ha-areṣ* (*q.v.*), IV, 167, V, 178; anatomical observations, VIII, 228; antitalmudic movements, II, 264; on appointment of officials and judges, V, 71; on asceticism, II, 435; and astrological approach, VIII, 176, 178; on bans imposed by *nasi,* V, 48; biographical material, VI, 24; borrowings from the Persian, II, 206, 405; bulwark against forces of nature, II, 293 f., 319-21, VI, 19 f.; burning and suppression of, VI, 90; capital punishment, V, 45, 57; cemeteries, II, 286-90, 423 f.; and Christianity, II, 130, 297, 427, V, 110;

Talmud (*Continued*)
chronology, II, 297; circumcision of slaves, IV, 187 f., 189; community, II, 290-92; concentration of study on, VI, 236; on consumption of butter, IV, 315; on darkness and light, VIII, 34; "days of the Messiah," V, 148; designation of Meṭaṭron, VIII, 281; deviations from, V, 52, 59; discussions of ritual, VII, 108 f.; distinction between theoretical and practical laws, VI, 77; economic trends and policies, II, 241-55, 262, 264, 413-18, IV, 209, 217; education, II, 274-79, 421 f.; eugenics, II, 229-35, 411; exegetes, VI, 50, 347, *see also* Exegetes and exegesis; few anthropomorphisms, VIII, 100; few anti-Gentile polemics, II, 111, V, 110; Gemara, II, 295, 305; Gentile prophets, VIII, 133; geographic references, VIII, 215; Gnosticism opposed, II, 314-18, 434-36; Graeco-Roman words used, II, 300, 302; "great things," VIII, 71; *Hekhalot rabbati* on, VIII, 17; and Hellenism, I, 388; and history, II, 296, 320; ignorance of Khazar Jews, III, 202; intellectualization, II, 319-20, 436; "introductions" to, VI, 32 f.; judiciary, II, 265-69, 418 f.; *jus divinum*, V, 78; Karaite study of, V, 253; Karaites vs. supporters of, V, 230 f.; labor, appreciation of, II, 256-60, 416; language of, II, 147, 387, VI, 27 ff., 256, VII, 28-32, 56 ff., 60, 192 f., VIII, 263; law and religion, II, 293-321, 425-36; list of preexistent things, V, 147; literature, II, 294-98, 425-29; on liturgy, VII, 69 ff., 170 f.; logic, II, 297; magic formula from, VIII, 9; manuscripts, editions, and translations of, II, 297, 427 ff.; marriage, II, 217-23, 408 f.; and martyrdom, IV, 96; on medical fees, VIII, 232; messianic folklore, V, 165; monogamous trends, II, 223-29, 409 f.; on music, VII, 206, 283; on mutilation of slaves, IV, 191; names of plants and animals, VIII, 226 f.; number of bones in body, VIII, 230; number of communal officials, V, 60; obscure literary allusions to, VII, 142; Pharisaic doctrines elaborated, II, 310-14, 434; on pilgrimages, I, 213, 214; prohibition of tax stamp, III, 168; protection of tradesmen, V, 68; reason

for supplying biblical names, VI, 281; references to God's love, VIII, 114; references to older halakhic works, VI, 63; regimentation, II, 260-65, 417 f.; on rights of settlers, V, 68 f.; ritual and moral law, II, 307-9, 433; rules concerning debates, VI, 30, *see also* Debates, talmudic; on sale of slaves to non-Jews, IV, 193; scarcity of copies, VI, 21, 111 f., 201; Sirach quoted in, II, 129; situation out of which born, II, 214; social welfare, II, 269-74, 420; study of, V, 3, VI, 34 f., VII, 71, VIII, 219; supremacy of law, II, 298-307, 429-33; synagogues, II, 280-86, 422 f.; tanning, IV, 166; tax legislation, V, 65 f.; urban vs. farm property, IV, 316; warning on pronunciation, VI, 240; women's status, II, 223, 235-41, 412 f.

Talmud: Babylonian, II, 294, 295, 297, 302, 316, 320, III, 3, 99, VI, 230; circulation of, VI, 441; commentaries on, VI, 35-56, 336-50, 352; geonim and, V, 212; lexicon, VII, 29; oral transmission, VI, 19, VIII, 7; Saboraic recension, III, 54, 73, VI, 240; in Spain, V, 47; supremacy, V, 22, 25 f., VI, 17, 34, 100, 242 ff., VII, 29; text, VI, 237 f.; translation into Arabic, VI, 264; uniform recension, VII, 28; unifying influence, V, 180 f.

—— Palestinian, I, 376, II, 13, 294 ff., 302, 333, 426, VI, 331; Arabic translation, VII, 29; area of dissemination, VI, 346; commentaries on, VI, 88 f.; Ḥananel and, VI, 47; Maimonides' reliance on, VI, 104 f.

—— *see also* Aggadah; Amoraim; Law; Mishnah; Rabbis and rabbinate; Religion; Tannaim

Tam, Jacob b. Meir, R., of Rameru, France, III, 217, IV, 48, 119, 162, V, 70, VI, 295, VII, 47, VIII, 43; on ban of settlement, V, 68; collection of northern responsa, VI, 117 f., 121; on early halakhic works, VI, 63 f.; on escape of slaves to Palestine, IV, 190; on geonic teachings, VI, 133, 332; on lack of door-post inscriptions, V, 59; and local customs, VI, 129; on Menaḥem-Dunash controversy, VII, 228; on purchase of land, VI, 147; reaction to criticism, VI, 121; on R. Simḥah's work, VII, 123; on study of the Tal-

mud, VI, 34, 55; on synagogue attendance by workers, IV, 155; on use of dairy products, IV, 315

Tamid, offering, I, 316, 404

Tamim Abu Ḥarb, leader of Palestinian peasant revolt, III, 166

Tana de-be Eliyyahu, III, 198

Tancred, IV, 110

Tanganyika, Lake, III, 116

Tanḥuma, Midrash, V, 217, VI, 40

Tanḥum b. Ḥanilai, VI, 164

Tanḥum Yerushalmi, Egyptian scholar: lexicographic works, VII, 31 f.; mistaken historical views, VII, 242

Tanis, I, 35

Tanit, deity, I, 374

Tannaim, I, 386, II, 295, 425, VI, 19, 30, 334, VIII, 147; agricultural controls, II, 263; and Amoraim, VI, 29, 201; ban on written recensions, VI, 454; controversy over intercalations, VIII, 371; economic controls, IV, 219 f.; on emigration from Palestine, IV, 221; Hai on, VI, 176 f.; interest in masoretic problems, VIII, 280; law on acquisition of books, VII, 135 f.; literary allusions to lives of, VII, 142; prophecy re end of age, VI, 17; R. 'Aqiba's compilation of law, VI, 107; sayings in halakhic works, VI, 63; teachings re number of commandments, VI, 91; works ascribed to, VI, 159, VIII, 18; *see also* Mishnah; Rabbis and rabbinate; Talmud; Tosefta; *and under* names of teachers

Tannaitic and Amoraic Sages, Order of, VI, 201 f.

Tanners and tanning, I, 275, IV, 166 f.

Tarfon, R., II, 117 f., 205, 222, 227, 409; quoted, II, 133

Targum, Aramaic (Onkelos): V, 159, 213, VI, 239, 264 f., 421, 444, VII, 17, 249; Babylonian revision, VI, 256; Masorah for, VI, 259 f.; replaced by Saadiah's translation, VI, 270; use of, by synagogue reader, VI, 257; *see also* Onkelos

—— Jonathan, II, 146, 387, 411, VI, 260 f., 456

—— Palestinian, VI, 160, 261 f., VII, 94, 263; aggadic accretions, VII, 82; dates of, VI, 456; and Onkelos, VI, 262

—— Samaritan, VI, 455

—— *sheni:* of the Book of Esther, VI, 188

Tarichaea, I, 255, 407

Tarragona, Spain, IV, 34; "city of Jews," III, 109

Tarshish, III, 34; location of, VII, 16; ships of, I, 321

Tarsus, and Tarshish, VII, 16

Tartar dialect, V, 247

Tartessus, Phoenician colony, I, 321, III, 34

Tashlikh ceremony, III, 241

Taurus, constellation, VIII, 177 f.

Taxation: ancient Israelitic, I, 76, 160, 326; Byzantine, III, 190-94, 320 f.; in Caliphate, III, 96 f., 150, 161-70, 308-12, VI, 112; collectors and farmers of taxes, I, 190, 274, 275, 279, 414, II, 105, 110, 184, 185 f., 194, 373, III, 152, 165 f., IV, 151, 201 f., V, 5 f., 18, 65 f.; communal responsibility for, II, 243, 245; concessions to converts, III, 242, 295; in England, IV, 81; evaders, II, 243; and flight from land, II, 245; indirect, III, 192 f.; in Jerusalem, III, 101; land tax, III, 162 f., 274 f., IV, 152, 214; in Latin Kingdom of Jerusalem, IV, 114 f.; loss of land by defaulters, II, 242; Norman system, IV, 23; paid in kind, I, 318; patriarchate's collection of, II, 193 ff.; of peasants, II, 245, 414, IV, 151 f.; poor tax, III, 274; property tax, IV, 81; punishment for default, III, 309 f., 312; resources of Jewish communities, I, 175; receipt stamped on neck of taxpayer, III, 168; revenue sources for religion and charity, II, 194; on sales at fairs, IV, 325; Temple tax, I, 394, II, 105, 118; under Persia, II, 180, 184 ff., III, 56; under Rome, I, 248, 262 ff., 279, 411, 415, II, 100, 104, 105 f., 183 ff., 263, 373, 375, 399; *see also* Poll tax

—— exemptions from: I, 263, III, 164, 179 f., IV, 38 f., 67 f., V, 75 ff.; for officials, I, 397; for priests, II, 413; for rabbis, II, 243 f., 277, 413

Taxo, of tribe of Levi, II, 59, 346

Tchernichovsky, Saul, Hebrew poet, III, 79, 264

Teachers and teaching, II, 278, IV, 215; *see also* Education; Rabbis and rabbinate

Tebtunis, I, 266; papyrus, I, 261

Technical progress, II, 248

Ṭeharot: geonic commentary on, VI, 42, 340; introduction by Maimonides, VI, 60 f.

Teima, Arabia, I, 349; identification of, III, 257; Jewish settlement, III, 63 f., VII, 191

Teleology, and the existence of God, VIII, 324

Tella, defense of, II, 179, 398

Tell al-Yahudia, Heliopolis: inscriptions, I, 394; temple, I, 219, 394

Tell Beit Mirsim, I, 115

Tell el-Amarna, see El-Amarna

Tell en-Nasbeh, I, 326

Tell Halaf (Gozan), I, 345

Temple at Jerusalem: First (Solomon's), I, 48, 83; abominations worshiped, I, 88, 335; building of, I, 14, 66; date of founding, I, 321; destruction, I, 102, 126, II, 87, 131, III, 62; Ezekiel on gates of, I, 122, 350; as fiscal agency, I, 333; incense (q.v.), I, 352; music, I, 123; orientation toward, I, 213; orientation within, I, 392; sacrificial worship, I, 123-29 passim, 148, 219, 352; symbol of freedom and power, I, 126

—— Second, III, 23, VIII, 125, 211, 273; Caligula's statue ordered, I, 219, 231; computations based upon, V, 366, VIII, 205; conflicting views of, II, 44 f., 74, 82, 305; construction, I, 258, VIII, 372; correctors of biblical books, VI, 235; Day of Atonement worship, VI, 390; desecration, I, 192, 217, II, 34; elaborate ceremonies, II, 6; figures in decoration, I, 238, 402, II, 13, 15; focus of Jewish intellectual life, I, 161 f.; gates, I, 262, 263; Gentiles excluded, I, 157, 239, 258, 402; gratitude for rebuilding dissipated, I, 237; Greek influence, II, 9 f.; heqdesh, VIII, 240; high priesthood of Hyrcanus denounced, I, 227; high priest's confession, VII, 79; holiness of, II, 28; Jesus' reference to himself as temple, II, 83, 364; Julian's promise to rebuild, II, 154, 160, 392; Maccabean rededication of, VI, 163, see also Ḥanukkah, festival of; and messianic age, V, 147 ff., VIII, 40; and Mosque of the Rock, III, 272; pilgrims in, I, 213, 392; plan to rename temple of

Zeus, I, 229; poems on the "watches," VII, 90; position of implements in, VII, 78; restoration, I, 160, 161, 367; revenue, I, 272, 273, 413, II, 82, 194; sacrificial system, I, 271, II, 33, 284, V, 218, VII, 72, VIII, 41; scribes, VI, 441; separation of sexes, II, 240; special privileges for property of, II, 252; site of, III, 277 f., VI, 228; state's main exchequer, I, 215, 333, II, 44, 82; and synagogue (q.v.), II, 282, V, 247, VII, 62, 293; tax, I, 215, 393, 394, II, 105, 118; tables in outer and inner courts, III, 29; world marvel, II, 9; yearly gathering at Wailing Wall, II, 108

—— destruction of, I, 166, II, 131, III, 62, 283 f., VI, 447, VIII, 379; antecedents to, II, 34, 341; and Christians, II, 74, 83, 364; dating events by, II, 116, 376, III, 237, IV, 283 f.; as homiletical theme, VI, 167; long-lasting effects, II, 90; loot from, I, 217, II, 113, 375, III, 11, 232; mourning over, II, 8, 111 ff., 375 f.; people's beliefs about, II, 112, 113 f.; responsibility for, II, 93, 369; vision of Third, V, 140 f.

Temples: Greek, in Palestine, II, 8; of Jupiter Capitolinus, II, 13, 106, 373; pagan, II, 6, 7, 24; Parsee, I, 353; and private banking in Assyria, I, 108; Samaritan, II, 26, 29, 30, III, 9, V, 173; see also Gerizim, Mount

—— Jewish, I, 132; in Elephantine (q.v.), I, 129

Temuda, Arab official, III, 63 f.

Tenan, term, VI, 65

Tenancy, see under Landlords

Ten Cities, I, 225

Ten Commandments, see Decalogue

Ten Days of Repentance, VIII, 74

"Ten horns," V, 158

Ten Martyrs, I, 231, II, 370, IV, 285

Ten plagues, I, 189

Ten Tribes, III, 117, 205, 329, VI, 434; cause of loss, II, 338; redemption of, II, 61, V, 144, 151, 200; see also Israel, Northern

Tents, I, 72

Terah, Abraham's father, I, 33, 302, 311

Terah, word, I, 302

Terahites, I, 311

Terefot, term, VIII, 387

Terminology, biblical: requisite for exegesis, VII, 12; grammatical, lists of, VII, 51; legal, VIII, 338; Rashi's work on, VI, 52, VII, 31; scientific, difficulty with equivalents in translation, VII, 6 ff., 220 ff., VIII, 75 ff., 227, 245; talmudic, VI, 27-35, 332-36; *see also* Words

Terracina: religious rights of Jews in, III, 29 f.; synagogue, III, 31

Territory: attempt to reconquer minimum of, I, 164; clan society and territorial society, I, 55; Jewish attitudes toward, I, 4, 16-25 *passim;* and nationalism, I, 53-61

Tertullian, II, 136, 396; on Christian officials, I, 243, 404; on history of Israel, II, 80; on prayer, VII, 79

Teruel, Spain, *fuero*, IV, 41

Teshubah, see Repentance

Testamentary dispositions, II, 253

Testament of Abraham, II, 4

Testaments of the Twelve Patriarchs, II, 345, 351

Testimonies against the Jews, II, 386; compilations of, V, 345; messianic, V, 157

Tetragrammaton, V, 120, VI, 249, 409, VIII, 275; in incantations, VIII, 281; meaning of the two *he*'s in, VIII, 36; misspelling and mispronunciation of, VI, 449; numerical value, VIII, 152; ritualistic repetition of, VIII, 284; *see also* Yahweh

Teutons, as mercenaries, II, 238

Textile industry, I, 257, 408, II, 248, 249; growth of, IV, 165; and international trade, IV, 327; *see also* respective branches, *e.g.* Linen

Thanksgiving, formula for daily, VII, 109

Theater: Greek, I, 189, II, 9; Jewish attitude toward, II, 9

Thebes, Greece, communal council, V, 55 f.; silk industry, IV, 168 f.

Theobald, count of Champagne, *see* Thibaut

Theobald, tale of martyred children, IV, 135 f.

Theocracy, I, 163, 165, 167; vs. old aristocracy, II, 279; regime, I, 130, 152, 221-27, 395-97; term coined by Josephus, I, 152, 223, 271

Theodicy, I, 136, 356 f.

Theodora, wife of Justinian II, III, 7, 198

Theodore of Mopsuestia, Syriac author, VI, 257, VII, 136; exegetical works, VI, 282

Theodoret of Cyrrhus, II, 434, V, 133, 338, VI, 271, 304

Theodoric the Great, king of the Ostrogoths, II, 398, III, 25 f.; *Edictum Theoderici*, III, 25 f.; policy toward Jews, III, 240

Theodorus, Byzantine commander, III, 23

Theodosian Code, II, 192, 398, III, 13, 187, 243; domination of, in western Europe, III, 25; Jewish status under, III, 49, IV, 50 f.

Theodosians, Coptic sect, III, 9

Theodosius, abbot of Petcherskii Monastery, III, 215

Theodosius I, Roman emperor of the East, II, 193, 399; Ambrose's victory over, II, 189, 401; economic moves, II, 250, 254, 261; legal decrees, II, 266, 267, 419, III, 8; quoted, II, 192

Theodosius II, Roman emperor of the East, II, 180, 186, 398, III, 11; on Nestorians and Jews, III, 229; *Novella* 439, III, 35

Theodosius of Alexandria, III, 17

Theodotion, Greek translator, II, 143; and Targum Jonathan, VI, 261

Theodotos, son of Vettenos, I, 214, II, 202, 285

Theodotus, poet, II, 31

Theodulf of Orléans, IV, 257

Theology: Christian controversies re, III, 21; interfaith debates, V, 83 ff.; and medicine, VIII, 259 f.; and messianism, V, 163 ff.; attributes of God in Muslim, VIII, 96; and politics, VIII, 349; rank of, as science, VIII, 142 f., 160; *see also* Philosophy; Religion

Theophanes: on forced conversion, III, 176; on Jews in Jerusalem, III, 103; on tax stamps, III, 168

Theophilus, Christian missionary, in Ḥimyara, III, 65 f.

Theophilus of Antioch, II, 73, 136, 138

Theophrastus, I, 377, 404

Theophylactus Simocatta, III, 58 f.

Theophylaktos, son of Romanos I, III, 182

Theosophy, pietism and, VIII, 50 f.

Theotonio, founder of monastery of Santa Cruz, III, 160, 308

Therapeutae, sect, II, 347, 349; compared with Essenes (q.v.), II, 51

Theriak the Great, VIII, 257

Thessalonica, Paul in, II, 79; see also Salonica

Theudas, false messiah, I, 221, 395, II, 36, 61

Theudas of Laodicea, VIII, 241

Thibaut, count of Champagne, IV, 62 f., 269

Thietmar, IV, 271

Thieves, I, 268

"Third communion," Jews as, II, 173, 396

"Third order": claim of Christians to be, II, 396; term, II, 366

Third Wall, Jerusalem, II, 369

Thomas à Becket, Saint, IV, 277, 280 f.; loan for flight to France, IV, 82

Thomas Aquinas, Saint: on imposition of taxes on Jews, V, 77 f.; on royal alliance with Jews, V, 348

"Three imposters," VI, 301

Throne of Glory, VIII, 6, 82, 273; preexistence of, VIII, 125 f.; song of, VIII, 13

Thucydides, I, 25

Thutmes III, king of Egypt, I, 38

Tibbonide family: "translation Hebrew," developed by, VII, 7; see also Ibn Tibbon

Tiberias, city, II, 99, 108, 123, 164, 175, IV, 113, 169, V, 180; academy, II, 196, III, 102, V, 32 ff., VI, 245, 446; aid to Persian army, III, 21; Byzantine commander and, III, 23; vs. Christians of Ḥimyara, III, 67 f.; center of masoretic research, VI, 239, 245; congregations, II, 199, 404; exilarchate, VI, 200; guardian of Hebrew language, VI, 245, VII, 33, 47; Ḥimyarites and, III, 67 f., 260, V, 180; leadership of Jewish communities, III, 20; rabbis' struggle for power, I, 242; riot against ordination of Ḥanina, II, 277; Saladin's conquest of, IV, 298; starvation in, II, 245; textile industry, IV, 323

Tiberius, Roman emperor, I, 178, 264; and Jews of Rome, I, 246, 248

Tiberius Alexander, II, 91, 93, 110, 368, 369

Tiberius Claudius Balbillus, II, 369

Tiberius Claudius Fatalis, II, 368

Ticino, Council of, IV, 26

Tiflis, Armenia, III, 110

Tiflisites, V, 182, 195, 219

Tigranes I, king of Armenia, I, 169

Timagenes, I, 396

Time, II, 158, VI, 469; philosophic discussions of, I, 295, VIII, 88 ff.; see also Chronology

Timothy I, patriarch, V, 378

Timothy III, patriarch of Alexandria, III, 68

Tiridates, king of Armenia, II, 165

Tishre, month, I, 294, V, 224, VIII, 184

Tithes: for academies, V, 14; of animals, V, 399; charitable, II, 241, 271; ecclesiastical, IV, 13, 43, 58, 153 f., 239, 256; ḥomesh, V, 14; Karaite, V, 235; priestly, I, 272, II, 118, IV, 13, 313; Saladin, IV, 81, 279, 297

Titles: honorary, V, 48, 59, 60, 283, 313, 314; princely, V, 311; used by Jewish leaders, III, 233

Titus, Roman emperor, II, 92-93, 102, 108, 113, 120; love affair, II, 92, 369; policy toward Jews, I, 248

Tmutarakan, duchy of, III, 205

Ṭob 'Elem (Bonfils), Joseph b. Eliezer, VIII, 362 f.

Ṭob 'Elem (Bonfils), Joseph b. Samuel, IV, 157, V, 62, VI, 48; on communal responsibility, V, 65; collection of responsa, VI, 113; copy of Seder tanna'im, VI, 34, 202; on intercommunal noninterference, VI, 393; liturgical works, VII, 121

Tobiah b. Eliezer, Jewish scholar, III, 210, V, 200; aggadic learning, VI, 173; mystical teachings, VIII, 30; works, VI, 174 f., VII, 82

Tobiah b. Moses of Constantinople, translator, III, 195, V, 233 f., 252 f., VI, 173, VIII, 301; on conversion to Karaism, V, 274; similarity of original work and translations, VII, 220; translation of Arabic works into Hebrew, VII, 7, 48

Tohu va-bohu, VI, 302

Toledo, Spain, IV, 28, 132; Arabic documents on moneylending, IV, 206; collaboration of Jews in Arab capture of,

III, 92; Councils of, III, 36-46, 246-50, IV, 241, V, 129; Jews of, III, 34; Mozarabs, III, 127; privilege to Mozarabs, Castilians, and Franks, IV, 40
—— Third Council of, IV, 19; on circumcision of Christian slaves, III, 36; on clergy and temporal powers, III, 41; on mixed marriages, III, 36
—— Fourth Council of, III, 41; on converts, III, 43, 248; on forced conversion, III, 39
—— Sixth Council of, III, 41, 54, IV, 241
—— Eighth Council of, III, 41; on sale of slaves to Jews, IV, 188
—— Eleventh Council of, III, 43
—— Twelfth Council of, IV, 19; Erwig's appeal to, III, 44
—— Sixteenth Council of: on property of Jews, III, 45
—— Seventeenth Council of, III, 43, IV, 41
Toledot Adam, VI, 197 f.
Toledot Yeshu (Life of Jesus), II, 140, 384, V, 348
Toleration, religious, IV, 114 f., V, 103 ff., VI, 6, VIII, 136; abrogated by Philip Augustus, IV, 61 f.; 'Anan and, V, 218 f.; in Byzantine legal codes, III, 187 f.; Church policy of, IV, 53 f., 56, 121, 141; equality in Spain, IV, 28; in Italy, III, 29 f.; of Jewish observances, III, 148, V, 124; juristic interpretation of, III, 124; in Khazaria, III, 200; Mohammed's decree, III, 124, 131; and nationalist revival, V, 186; separate ethnic-religious groups, IV, 86; under Theodoric, III, 26; Theodosius I and, III, 8; treaties, III, 130 f.; under the Caliphate, III, 123 f., 133, 171 f., V, 82, 210, 264, 335; under the Sassanians, III, 57, 128 f.; see also Persecutions; Religious liberty
Tolls, Roman, I, 279, 415
Tombs: decorative motifs and inscriptions, II, 11 ff., 14, 63, 146, 331, 353, 376; psyche, II, 14; of rabbis, II, 279; studies of ancient, II, 333; violation of, I, 410; see also Cemeteries and catacombs
Torah: contradictory biblical statements on, VI, 305; on economic matters, IV, 162; equality of parts, VIII, 318; eternity of, II, 319, 320, V, 91 f., 130, 229; VI, 146; fenced around by elaboration, II, 319, 436; festival of Rejoicing, V, 26; Ḥuqqe ha-torah (Laws of the Torah), VI, 140 f.; jus divinum, V, 78; Karaite concept of, V, 251 f.; language, VI, 248; Midrash Sar Torah, VIII, 19 ff.; neglect of, VI, 100 f.; new, VI, 302; preexistence, VI, 228, VIII, 6, 19 f., 125 f.; rejected by Esau and Ishmael, V, 134; as revelation, VI, 307 f.; study of, IV, 221, 223, V, 162 f.; Western Jewry and, III, 173; see also Bible; Law; Old Testament; Pentateuch
Torat kohanim, I, 150; see also Priestly Code
Torlonia, Villa: tombs, II, 11, 146, 331
Tortosa, Spain, IV, 132; Jewish community, IV, 332; Judeo-Christian debate, VI, 172; Muslim treaty with Ramon Berenger IV, IV, 30
Tosafists and Tosafot, V, 61, 78, VI, 53-56, 88, 172, 202, 278, 348 ff., 363; compilers of, VI, 350; on conclusion of Torah scroll, VI, 253; on dairy products, IV, 315; on division of earth's surface, VIII, 214; measuring circular field, VIII, 157; and talmudic methodology, VI, 34
Toscana, Berta di, IV, 245
Tosefta, I, 273, II, 123 f., 294, 295, 425, VI, 53 f., 104; ancient, VI, 413; compilation of, II, 301, VI, 76, 204; concordance to, VII, 29; on physician's responsibility, VIII, 238
Tota, queen of Navarre, III, 155 f., IV, 29
Ṭoṭafot, term, VII, 21; see also Phylacteries
Totalitarianism, I, 325
Totressia, and Tetragrammaton (q.v.), VIII, 284
Toulouse, IV, 55
Tours, battle of, III, 91
Town, Israelitic, I, 71, 325; responsibility for unsolved crimes, I, 327; see also Cities; Urbanization
Toys, mechanical, VIII, 356
Trachonitis, I, 172
Tracts, controversial, V, 83 ff.; see also Apologetics; Controversies, socioreligious
Trade: ancient, I, 60, 64 f., 69, 255-58,

Trade (*Continued*)
318, 323, 360, II, 262; advance of, II, 247, 249-51, 260, 414; anti-Jewish regulations, IV, 13, 24 f.; associations, IV, 185, *see also* Guilds; barter, IV, 214; charters, IV, 48 f.; Jews attracted to, I, 108, II, 123; laws of sales and purchases, VI, 67 f.; local, VI, 126; Muslim law on, III, 126, IV, 351; in Near East, III, 339; in Palestine, II, 244; rabbinic restrictions on, II, 262, IV, 219 ff., 351; and Sabbath observance, I, 360; in Spain, III, 156; taxes, IV, 152; women engaged in, I, 113, II, 237; *see also* Business transactions
—— international, III, 49, 284 f.; effect on family relationships of traders, VI, 395; effect on Jewish unification, VII, 136; elimination of Jews from, V, 25; influence on geographic knowledge, VIII, 212 f.; Italian republics and, IV, 4 f., 186; Jewish settlement on routes, IV, 175, 266 f., *see also* Routes, trade; legal aspects, IV, 176 f.; as medium of cultural exchange between East and West, VIII, 256 f.; military aspects, IV, 186; rabbinic control of Palestine's export trade, II, 262; restrictions on Jewish shipping and shipowners, IV, 183 f.; role of Jews in, IV, 44, 171-96, 322-36; routes (*q.v.*), IV, 172 f., 175, 180 f., 266 f.; Russo-Norman, IV, 181; talmudic law and, V, 27
Trades: and manufactures, II, 248 ff.; specialization, I, 257; *see also* Crafts and craftsmen
Tradition: adherence to, and scientific progress, VIII, 138 f.; agnostics and, VIII, 90; historic continuity, VIII, 31; vs. innovations, V, 109 f.; and medical science, VIII, 234 f.; as source of knowledge, VIII, 80 ff.
—— Jewish, V, 188; adjusted to new demands, VII, 131 ff.; chain of, VI, 205, 230, VIII, 20 ff.; conservatives and, VIII, 68; departure from, in legal codes, VI, 77 ff.; historical accuracy of oral, I, 305; Karaites and, V, 235, 251 ff., 261; legal, VI, 16-27, 327-32; Mosaic, VI, 8, 334; mystic roots in, VIII, 20 ff., 25; preservation of, by Franco-German Jewry, VIII, 42 ff.; proof of, by reasoning, VIII, 82; and

Scripture, V, 209 f., VI, 460; sources of, VI, 267; talmudic vs. posttalmudic, VI, 100 f., 210; proponents of written, VI, 427; *see also* Oral Law
—— Muslim, VI, 7; collections, VI, 26 f.; historic validity and, III, 308 f.; oral, III, 273
Trajan, Roman emperor, II, 121, 156; outlawry of Judaism in Cyprus, III, 19 f.; revolt against, II, 94-97, 100, 370 f.
Trance, ecstatic, II, 315
Trani, Italy, Spanish refugees in, IV, 21, VI, 167
Transjordan: cattle raising, I, 57, 72, 253; cities in hands of Greeks, I, 224 f.; conquest of, I, 250, 308; historic intermissions, I, 33; iron in, I, 320; Jewish settlements, I, 167, 370; modern, I, 307; Nabatean-Roman domination, III, 61
Translation: of Arabic classics, IV, 3, 32; of entire literature, I, 187; free vs. literal, VII, 7; of philosophic works, VIII, 64 f., 75 ff.; and transliteration of names and terms, VIII, 172, 174; use of like-sounding words, VII, 8
"Translation Hebrew," VII, 7, VIII, 316
Translations, biblical: Jewish and Catholic collaboration in, VIII, 265 f.; *see also* *under* Bible *and* respective versions
Transmigration of the soul, V, 211, 228, 259, VIII, 36, 104 f.
Transmission, oral, VI, 37, 194, 205, 426 f., VII, 87, VIII, 7; Decalogue, VI, 427; generations of transmitters, VIII, 210 f.; of historical chronicles, VI, 433; of learning, Jewish role in, VIII, 256; of linguistic material, VII, 243; mnemotechnic aids, VII, 88, VIII, 149; and opposition to written, VI, 37, 110 f., 205, 426 f., 454, VII, 107, 124; of prayers, VII, 85 ff., 112, 124
Transport associations, II, 257, 261, 417
Transportation, II, 249; difficulties caused by famines, II, 245; by sea, II, 249
Transport workers, I, 275
Trapezite banking, I, 410; *see also* Banking; Moneylenders and moneylending
Traveler: conditional divorce of, VI, 139; role in cultural exchange, VIII, 256

Travelogues, VI, 219-26, 433-37, VIII, 211 f.; value of, VI, 225 ff.

Treason: charges of, vs. Jewish converts, III, 46; political, in Visigothic Spain, III, 40 f., *see also* Loyalty; religious, VIII, 263, *see also* Heretics and heresies

Treasures, concealed, IV, 211

Treaties: between city and conqueror, IV, 30; between city and Jews, IV, 27; between Rome and Judaea, I, 218; extradition, IV, 80, 204; with merchants, IV, 63; Muslim, of religious toleration, III, 97, 130 ff., 161 ff., 269, 293 f.; peace, IV, 70 f., 89 f., 141, 236; regional, IV, 63; royal, re Jews, IV, 62 f.

Trebonian, III, 13

Tree of knowledge, I, 253; size of, VIII, 26

"Tree of Life," I, 363; size of, VIII, 26

Trees: in Jewish iconography, I, 253; symbolism, II, 13, 332, 333

Trent, Council of, IV, 19

Treuga Dei, IV, 236

Treves: burning of effigy of bishop, IV, 283; early Jewish settlers in, II, 406; expulsion of Jews, IV, 92, 283; forced baptism, IV, 106, 293, 310

Triangle, equilateral, VIII, 157

Tribes, Arabian: I, 41; and Abraham, V, 137, *see also* Ishmael; desert, I, 46; *see also* Kenites; Midianites

—— Hellenic, amphictyony of, I, 61

—— Israelitic, I, 41, 47, 61, 317; ethnic unity, I, 39 ff., 55, 61; God of, I, 47, 313; groups, I, 317; led by Joshua, I, 53; racial mixtures, I, 39; role in messianism, V, 144, 355; sacrifices, I, 51; seminomadic, I, 33, 41, 315; seven-year redistribution of land, I, 333; system of twelve, I, 61, 319; ten lost: II, 61, 338, III, 117, 205, 208; *see also* Ten Tribes

—— Jewish: in Arabia, III, 64, V, 168; exiled from Medina, III, 78 f.; Jeraua in North Africa, III, 91, 271 f.

—— Slavonic, in Poland, III, 206 ff., 213 ff., 330 ff., 333 ff.

—— Turkic, V, 162, VI, 226

Tribute, I, 263; payment of, for protection, IV, 38 f., 55 f., 74, 81, 99, 102 f., 142 f., 152; to escape discrimination, III, 147; *see also* Taxation

Trigon, earthly, conjunctions of, VIII, 180 f.

Trilingualism, dictionaries, VII, 17

Triliterality, VII, 41 ff., 48

Trinity, doctrine of, II, 161, V, 26, VI, 5 f., 303, VII, 179, VIII, 30, 95 ff., 279; Maimonidean view, V, 365; Mohammed's view, III, 83; religious debate over, V, 120 f.; separation of God the Father, VIII, 42

Tripolis, Syria, IV, 113; Jewish community, III, 104; treatment of prisoners of war, III, 150

Tripolitania: Jewish settlement, III, 107 f.; and Roman synagogue, I, 410

Trito-Isaiah, I, 103

Troki, Karaite settlement, V, 285

Troubadour, in Spain and Provence, VII, 151; *see also* Poetry

Troyes, France: Rashi's school in, VI, 49, VII, 121 f.; synods, IV, 48, V, 64 f.; tanneries, IV, 319

Trullan Council, III, 175; anti-Jewish canons, III, 194; on bathing in public places, III, 142; canon re traditional interpretation of Bible, V, 109; injunction on preaching, VI, 154, 159

Truth, quest of scientists and philosophers, VIII, 173

Tryphon, R., *see* Tarfon, R.

Tryphon, name, II, 380

Tryphon, of Justin's dialogue, II, 133

Tubal-Cain, first smith, I, 60

Tübat (Tibet?), tribe, III, 115

Tudela, Spain, IV, 248; privilege from Sancho VII, IV, 35 f.; treaty with Alphonso I, IV, 30; *see also* Benjamin of Tudela

Tulunides, rulers of Palestine, V, 222 f.

Tumai, Egypt, III, 23, 105

Tummim, I, 49, 82

Tunes: Jewish aversion to foreign, VII, 205; as mnemotechnical aid, VII, 125 ff.; secular, for religious poems, VII, 204

Tunis, and Tarshish, VII, 16

Turbo, Marcius, II, 95, 96

Turkestan, I, 322

Turkey: law on forced conversion, III, 132; public officials, III, 151; treatment of minorities, III, 137, 160; tribes, V, 162, VI, 226

Turkish language, III, 324

Tustar, III, 165

Tyrannos, I, 63, 320

Tyre, I, 162, 176, 322, 375; alliance with Solomon, I, 64, 321; economic blockade, I, 277; glassblowers, IV, 168; Jerusalem academy transferred to, V, 37; Jewish community, III, 104, IV, 113; Jewish "siege" of, III, 19 f., 236; relationship with Delos, I, 377; surrender to the Crusaders, IV, 113

U

'Ubaid-Allah al-Azdi, VI, 165

Ucles, battle of, IV, 36

Ugarit, see Ras Shamra

Ugrians, III, 204; see also Hungary

'Ukbari, Isma'i al-, V, 182, 262, VI, 299; biblical interpretation, V, 195 f.; tombstone inscription, V, 195

'Ukbarites, V, 182, 195 f., VI, 475

Ulpian (Domitius Ulpianus), VI, 55; quoted, II, 110, 375

'Umar I, caliph: career of world conquest, III, 86 ff., 94; disposition of captured lands, III, 95 f.; on inheritance rights, III, 144; mosque of, III, 103, 134, 269, 272; revival of exilarchate, V, 141; successors in the Caliphate, III, 152; supported by Jews and Nestorians, III, 89 f.; suppression of Arabian Jews, III, 76, 80, 274; treaties, III, 97, 101, 269, 293 f.; violent death, III, 122

—— Covenant of 'Umar, III, 97, 129, 131, 269; ban on unbelievers in public office, III, 151; injunction re family names, III, 148; provisions restored under the Latin Kingdom, IV, 115 f.

'Umar II, caliph: and the Covenant of 'Umar, III, 131, 294; decree against infidels, III, 97, 176; discharge of dhimmi officials, III, 151 f.; and Jewish medical writings, VIII, 236; on price fixing, IV, 223

'Umayyad dynasty, III, 88; and Byzantium, III, 198; dissolution of, VII, 147; period of transition to 'Abassids, III, 121 ff.; status of Jewish minority under, III, 120; status of judges, VI, 9; support of fatalism, VIII, 109; see also under names of caliphs, e.g., Mu'awiya

Ummi, term, III, 263

Understanding, gates of, VIII, 294

Unemployment, I, 70, 412

Unitarianism, VIII, 98

Unity: absolute character of, VIII, 152; ideological, of Jews, V, 198; in Jewish sectarianism, V, 205 ff.; see also Ethnic unity

Universalism, I, 23; and nationalism (q.v.), I, 31, 158; and particularism, I, 96-99, 339; prophetic, in Exile, I, 157

Universe: divine government of, VII, 172, 174; duration of, VI, 146, 232; image of, VIII, 160-66, 313-15; plural nature of, I, 202, II, 310, 311; see also World

Unleavened bread, I, 148

Unmoved Mover, VIII, 90 f.

'Uqba, Mar, ancient exilarch, II, 198, 272

'Uqba, Mar, medieval exilarch, III, 107, V, 40, 213; controversy with Pumbedita academy, V, 10 ff.; in Kairuwan, V, 39

Ur, city, I, 33, 44

Urban II, pope, IV, 94, 97 ff.

Urbanization: under the Caliphate, IV, 152 f.; and changes in Jewish law, VI, 147; growth of, VI, 132, V, 177; of Jewish population, IV, 274; rise of leisure class, VII, 69; role in ethnic-religious conflicts, I, 372; see also Cities; Town, Israelitic

Uriah, prophet, I, 79, 324, 327

Uriah the Hittite, I, 326

Urim, I, 49, 82

Urine, VIII, 244

Urraca, daughter of Alphonso VI, IV, 38, 252 f.

Usama ibn Munqidh, Muslim emir, VIII, 398

Usatges, custumal of Barcelona, IV, 41

Usha academy, V, 14; synod at, II, 126, 271, 378, 420

Usury, I, 20, 194, 265, II, 250, 302, IV, 75 ff., 88, V, 128; bans on, IV, 79, 197 ff.; charge of, against Jews, IV, 121; and foreigners, I, 156; interest considered as, I, 109; Jewish aversion to, I, 85 f., 261, 409; Meir b. Simon on, IV, 224; "open" vs. "concealed," IV, 205; Saadiah's tract on, VI, 69; see also Banking; Interest; Loans; Moneylenders and moneylending

'Uthman, caliph: efforts re Qur'anic text, VI, 243; violent death, III, 122

Utopian thinking, II, 58
'Uzziel, R., viceroy of Ḥamat, III, 159

V

Valens, Roman emperor, II, 188
Valerian, Roman emperor, II, 177, 380
Vandalism, sepulchral, IV, 236
Vandals, III, 7
Vannes, Council of, III, 50
Varro, Marcus Terentius, I, 251, 254
Varuna, ethical deity, I, 45
Vassals: Christian and Jewish, IV, 163; status of, IV, 49 f.; see also Serfdom
Vecelin, clerical convert to Judaism, IV, 9, 66
Vegetables, names of, VIII, 229
Vegetative power, VIII, 107
Ve-hizhir, midrash, VI, 23, 40
Veil, wearing of, III, 142, 283, 299
Venafro, church of, III, 31
Venereal disease, V, 250
Vengeance, I, 134, 135; motive of Crusaders, IV, 102; and Day of Recompense, II, 31, 341
Venice: ban on Jews in shipping trade, IV, 183; Jewish community, IV, 25; shipping rights in Byzantium, IV, 24
Venosa: inscriptions, IV, 20, VIII, 204; itinerant preacher, VI, 156
Ventidius Cumanus, I, 239, 264
Venus, I, 311; planet, I, 57
Veracity, consent of masses as proof of, VI, 145 f.
Verbs, Hebrew: doctrine of paradigms, VII, 53; forms of, VII, 35 ff., 49; triliterality of, VII, 42 f.
Verdun, Treaty of 843, IV, 43, 64
Verona, Italy, IV, 26
Verses, biblical: hermeneutic elaboration of, VI, 164 f.; in prayers, VII, 69; number and division of, VI, 238; see also Bible
Vespasian, Roman emperor, I, 391, II, 57, 103, 131, 369; all land taken over by, I, 265; campaign in Palestine, II, 91 f., 245; Commentaries of, II, 372; coronation, VI, 420; execution of all who claimed Davidic descent, II, 121; Jewish fiscal tax enacted by, I, 266, II, 106, 186, 373, III, 191; Jewish rights under, I, 248, II, 100, 108; R. Johanan's demand of, II, 120, 377; sympathy for

Jewish faith, II, 92; Temple of Onias closed by, II, 93; witticism, I, 244
Vestal priestesses, I, 146
Vetus Latina, Bible version, II, 144, 385 f., VI, 272 f., 462 f.; see also Bible; Jerome, Saint
Ve-yitqales, usage of, VII, 246
Vibia, wife of Vincentius, II, 25
Vienna, Austria, IV, 72
Villages: agricultural, IV, 157; celebration of High Holidays, VII, 79; collective tax responsibility, IV, 152; contrasted with towns, I, 325; owned by Jews, IV, 161 f., 163
Villa judaica, IV, 29
Villa Torlonia tombs, II, 11, 146, 331
Villeins and villeinage, II, 258; and Jewish "serfdom" (q.v.), IV, 63 f., 70 ff.; labor, IV, 155; see also Peasants
Vincentius, tomb, II, 25, 338
Vine: productiveness, I, 251; symbolism, I, 253, II, 13
Vineyards: royal and ecclesiastical, IV, 317; talmudic innovation, IV, 163; work in, on half holidays, IV, 315
Violence, outlawry of, IV, 70
Viper, flesh of, VIII, 247
Virgil: "messianic" eclogue, II, 5; indebtedness to Judaism, II, 329
Virginity, V, 241 f.; of bride, V, 29, VI, 59
Virtue, I, 201
Vishehrad, Czechoslovakia, IV, 103
Visigoths: in Spain and Gaul, III, 33-46, 127, 176, 244-50, IV, 5; anti-Jewish legislation, III, 33 ff., 127; areas of influence in Christian Spain, IV, 27 ff.; "bigotry," IV, 19; Byzantine influence, III, 246; vs. forced conversion, IV, 5; Jewish collaboration with Arab invaders, III, 91 f.; laws, on land tenure, IV, 155 f.; Leges Visigothorum, III, 36, 42, 44; Lex Romana Visigothorum, III, 35, 49; and Mozarabs, III, 127
Visions: apocalyptic, V, 149 f., 353; of Daniel, III, 179, 183, 315; prophetic, VIII, 129 f., 133; Ibn Gabirol on, VIII, 333
Vitalism, VIII, 226
Vital power, VIII, 107
Vitellius, Lucius, I, 238-39, II, 10
Viticulture, IV, 162; in Arabia, III, 70; in France, IV, 317; see also Grape culture; Vineyards

Vivisection, VIII, 203 f.
Vladimir I, duke of Kiev, III, 215
Vladimir II (Monomakh), duke of Kiev, III, 216, 217
Volkmar, see Dithmar
Vowels, Hebrew: analysis of, VII, 36; antiquity of, VII, 60; in Arabic and Hebrew, VII, 194 f.; points, VI, 260; pronunciation of, VI, 250; ratio of, to consonants, VII, 314; slurring over, VI, 248; symbolism of, VIII, 35 f.; tenfold division, VII, 52 f.
Vows: Aḥai on, VI, 39; "All Vows and Abnegations," VI, 125; dissolution of, V, 249; laws on, VI, 95 f.; unwittingly broken, VII, 78
Vratislav, duke, of Prague, IV, 118
Vulgate, II, 144, 385 f., VI, 272 f., 462 f.; see also Bible; Jerome, Saint

W

Wadi Tumilat, I, 37
Wages, I, 270, 325, 412; community regulation, II, 261; of Jewish labor, I, 270, IV, 170, 321; see also Labor and laborers
Wahb ibn Ya'ish of Raqqa, VIII, 310
Wailing Wall, at Jerusalem, III, 101, 278, V, 236; sole remnant of Temple, II, 108
Walcher, abbot of Malvern, England, VIII, 174
Walking, on the Sabbath, VI, 80
Wamba, king of the Visigoths, III, 41, 46, IV, 47
Waqidi, library, VII, 138
War: in behalf of a commandment, II, 100, 372; Jewish leaders, III, 157; Judeo-Roman, I, 212, II, 89-102, 106, 121, 368-71, see also Bar Kocheba; Great War; Hadrian; Roman Empire; Trajan; mass participation, I, 332; messianic, V, 144 ff., 191 ff., 353; purchase of booty, V, 317; see also Crusades; Military service; Revolts
Warjalan (Ouargela), African Karaite community, VII, 226
Warmth, loss of natural, VIII, 259
Warning, poems of, VI, 372
War of Investiture, IV, 73, 95
"War of the Children of Light with the Children of Darkness," II, 53

Wasit, Egypt, VIII, 168
Waṣiyya, term, V, 7
Water: in biblical cosmology, VIII, 6, 22 f., 336; proportion of earth's surface, VIII, 214; significance, I, 407; and wind, VIII, 217
Water Drinkers, II, 51
"Water of bitterness" ordeal, II, 222, 409
Way of life, and reproofs of instruction, VIII, 37
Wealth: acquisition of, VIII, 48 f.; a motive for joining the Crusade, IV, 101; Muslim jeweler's, IV, 214; rabbinic attitude toward, II, 256, 276 f., 278, IV, 220 f., 347; short-lived, of Romans and Jews, II, 420; term, II, 422
—— of Jews, I, 262-67, 410-11, II, 242, 247, IV, 118, 203, 214; communal, IV, 82, 85; debate re source of, IV, 211; envy of, IV, 85, 126 f., 142; of exilarchs, V, 8; expropriation of, by Vratislav, IV, 118; funerals, II, 287; Isaiah's warning, I, 68; sectarian, V, 258; short-lived, II, 420; see also Poverty
Weapons: ban on carrying, III, 62, IV, 70, 141, 303; lack of, in Jewish communities, IV, 126
Weavers and weaving, I, 408, IV, 167 f.; head of Sura academy, V, 74 f.; see also Textile industry
Wedding: Baghdad ordinance re, VI, 140; choice of day, V, 29, VI, 123, 130; customs, II, 231, VI, 75; poems for, VII, 143, 176, 180
Week, "cosmic," VI, 232, 440; seven-day, I, 6, 120, 192
Week days, designation of, I, 144
Weights and measures, I, 85, II, 254, 255
Welfare, medical, VIII, 238, 404
Weli worship, III, 137, V, 308, VII, 76
Wends, German Crusades against, IV, 131
Wergeld, III, 295, IV, 35, 39, 41, 253 f.; see also Fines; Punishments
West-Semitic dialect, I, 36
Wheat, I, 251, 252
WHWH, see Yahweh
Wicked Priest, II, 53 f., 349
Widows, V, 321; distribution of estate among, VI, 85; ḥaliṣah, V, 299; pre-

scribed settlement for, IV, 345; support of, VI, 124; *see also* Women

Wieselburg, Germany, IV, 106 f.

Will, divine, VIII, 101, 328; changeability of, VI, 145; Christian and Muslim contention re, VI, 482; media of revelation of, VIII, 342; mediation through, VIII, 91 ff.; medical practice and, VIII, 231; and miracles (*q.v.*), VIII, 129; *see also* Prophets and prophecy

Will, freedom of, *see* Free will

William, Saint, IV, 135 f.

William, archbishop of Tyre, IV, 109 f.

William I, king of Sicily, IV, 27

William II, king of England: and forced converts, IV, 106, V, 113; policy toward Jews, IV, 77

William III, count of Montpellier, IV, 63

William of Auvergne, VIII, 101; on Jewish philosophy, VIII, 72

William of Malmesbury, IV, 76

William of Newbury, IV, 76, 124, 140; on crimes of Crusaders in England, IV, 127 f.; on Jews of England, IV, 87

William Rufus, *see* William II, king of England

Wills, II, 253

Winchester, England, IV, 125, 136 f.

Wind, and water, VIII, 217

Wine, I, 251, 252; 'Ananites' consumption of, V, 218; blessing over, V, 245, VI, 123; funerary, II, 288, 424; fifth cup, VII, 116; inspirational effect, VII, 200; law re Gentiles and, IV, 162, V, 281; Muslim ban on, IV, 164; Palestinian and foreign, II, 246; payment in, by Gentile debtors, VI, 128 f.; poems to drinking, VII, 158 ff.; ritualistic requirement, IV, 158, 165; and song, VII, 203; *see also* Vineyards; Viticulture

Wisdom: beginning of, VIII, 176; and divine will, VIII, 91 f., 328; literature, I, 150, 377; religious and national heritage, I, 151, 363; schools of, I, 141, 150 f.; "seven pillars" of, VIII, 145; *see also* Education

Wisdom of Solomon, The, I, 141, 198, 204, 386, II, 222

Witches, II, 21

Witnesses: formula for, VI, 67; illiteracy of, VI, 255; in Judeo-Christian litiga-

tions, IV, 15 ff., 41 f., 49, 78; requirements, IV, 69, V, 56; warning to, II, 137

Wojtech, *see* Adalbert, of Prague

Wolf, and Joseph, story of, VI, 170

Women: agents of religious conversion, V, 267 f.; antifeminism, VII, 309; banned at public baths, III, 142; beauty, II, 237 f., 412; benefactresses, II, 24, 240, 338, 413; community of, II, 183, 222, 251; *dhimmi*, III, 142, V, 202; duties, II, 237, 239; employment of Christian, IV, 15; exclusion from public office, V, 74; freedom of, V, 224, VI, 64; in harems, III, 201, 283; intellectual pursuits, II, 239, V, 323; levirate marriage (*q.v.*), I, 79, II, 231, 411; magic arts, I, 347, II, 21; marriage of captive, V, 8 f.; menstruating, V, 250, VI, 69; Moses' Ethiopian wife, I, 38; "obstreperous," VI, 64, 133 ff., 138; pregnant, V, 283, 349; preponderance of men over, I, 113 f.; and procreation, II, 218; profanation of, V, 240; proselytes, I, 177, II, 233; reference to, in Jewish prayer of thanksgiving, VII, 109; rights, III, 283, V, 243, VI, 68; role in the Crusades, IV, 96; Roman, I, 191, 405, II, 239, 240; rules of conduct, II, 222, 228, III, 111, 139 f., 142, VI, 182 f.; in sanctuaries, I, 146; secondary wives, II, 224; "singing girls," VII, 205; status, I, 58, 111-14, 146, 191, 347-48, II, 235-41, 303 f., 306, 412 f., 421, V, 221 f., VII, 188; status in Mazdakite movement, III, 55; sufferings, I, 265; in synagogue, II, 240, 413; veils, III, 142, 283, 299; widows (*q.v.*), I, 275, II, 271, 303, 304, 420; *see also* Concubines and concubinage; Marriage; Slaves and slavery

Wool industry, I, 257, 408

"Word," divine, and *logos* (*q.v.*), V, 121

Words: biliteral and triliteral, VII, 38; as body and soul, VII, 50 f.; foreign, in Hebrew commentaries, VI, 52 f., 347, 349, VII, 31; implications of correct interpretation, VI, 166, VII, 13, 68; like-sounding, VI, 288, VII, 8, 145, 223; power of, II, 22, VII, 87, VIII, 8, 12, 14; significance of correct spelling, VI, 166, VII, 12 f.; vocabulary, and comparative linguistics, VII, 12

Words: biblical, VII, 25; alphabetical listing, VI, 252; controversy based on numerical value of, V, 86 ff.; derived from same root, VII, 25; plural forms, V, 120; substitution, VI, 293 ff.; *see also* Grammar; Lexicography

Workers, *see* Labor and laborers

World: divine government, V, 259, VIII, 16, 18, 23, 34 ff., 86, 101; duration of, VIII, 78 f., 81, 87 ff., 191 f., 372; end of, III, 15, 97, 176, V, 142 f., 360, VIII, 191, *see also* End of days; five worlds of Bar Ḥiyya, VIII, 94 f.; sublunary, VIII, 94, 102, 103, 128, 222 f.; superlunary, VIII, 162, 165; *see also* Creation; Universe

World Chronology (*Seder 'Olam*), II, 141, 376, 384; aggadic scheme of, V, 147 ff.; in messianism, V, 148 ff.

World government, I, 209

World history, VI, 198-204, 210, 423-25, 429 f.; "devolutionary" views, VI, 229 f., VII, 56; dividing point, VI, 227 f.; Judeo-Christian view, VI, 209, 227 ff.; Yeraḥmeel, VI, 195 ff.

World Intellect, VIII, 333

World Orders, VI, 200, 233

World Soul, VIII, 115, 333

World-to-come, *see* Hereafter; Immortality of the soul

World War, Second, I, 293

Worms, Germany: Jewish community, VI, 48 f.; privilege granted by Henry IV, IV, 67 f., 71; siege of, IV, 70

Worship, VII, 62-134, 244-85; ban on public, III, 14; daily participation in, VII, 62; imperial, I, 244, 404, II, 5, 99, 109; inwardness of, VII, 73 ff., 179, VIII, 3; linguistic problem, VII, 66 ff.; mystic union in, VII, 212 f.; private, I, 352, VII, 120 f., 168; proper behavior in, I, 351, VIII, 3; ritualistic dynamism, VII, 131 ff.; sacrificial, V, 173, *see also* Sacrifices; *see also* God; Liturgy; Prayers; Ritual

Writing, I, 334; Arabic calligraphy, IV, 36 f.; knowledge of, in Arabia, III, 82; knowledge of ancient art of, I, 314; Mohammed on Jews' method of, III, 85; preexilic, I, 305; Slavs' learning of, III, 208; *see also* Alphabet

Written transmission, *see under* Transmission, oral

Würzburg, Germany, IV, 120

Wydobycz, *see* Kiev

X

Xerxes I, king of Persia, I, 341, 348

Y

Yabneh (Jamnia): academy of, II, 115, 120, 126, 377, VIII, 193; debate on charities, II, 270, 420; Greek attack on Jews, I, 219

Yaho and Ḥnub, I, 352

Yahu, names compounded with, I, 78, 327

Yahweh: awe of name, I, 128, II, 17; and Baal, I, 349; image of, I, 322; kingship of, I, 93; and mercy, I, 46, II, 311; name (the holy Tetragrammaton), I, 13, 59, 138, 309, II, 18; substitute names, I, 128, 312, II, 28, 335; as tribal god, I, 39; WHWH, archaic form, II, 18; *see also* God; Tetragrammaton

Yahwism, I, 44, 64, 78; and demonology, I, 358; pure, against eclectic, I, 61

Yahwist, I, 42

Yaḥya, of Antioch, III, 103

Yaḥya b. Adam, III, 163

Yaḥya b. Yaḥya, Idrisite ruler, III, 142

Yaḥya ibn Matruḥ, vizier of Damascus, VIII, 249

Yaḥya ibn Sa'id, chronicler, III, 137

Yaḥya ibn Suleiman, *see* Zechariah b. Solomon

Yahziel, angel, VIII, 8 f.

Yalta, II, 239

Yannai, R., Amora, II, 263; and a peddler, VI, 154; suspension of years of fallowness, VIII, 209

Yannai, R., liturgical poet, VI, 248, VII, 84; acrostic of name, VII, 260, 262; halakhic content of poems, VII, 103, 262; legend on death of Qalir, VII, 270; liturgical poems, V, 276, VII, 93 ff., 261 f.; and Palestinian Targum, VII, 263

Yao (or Iao), divine name, VIII, 9

Ya'qubi, al-, *Tariḥ*, IV, 226

Ya'qub ibn Killis, vizier, III, 154

Ya'qub ibn Musa al-Nigrisi, VIII, 370

Yaqut, Muslim geographer, III, 109, VII, 14, VIII, 153, 212

Yashar, Sefer ha- (Book of the Just), VI, 197 f., 212 f., 423
Yashar b. Ḥesed at-Tustari, V, 233 f.
Yassin, Anbal, Kievan Jew, III, 216
"Yasu'," Arabic name of Jesus, III, 258
Yathrib, *see* Medina
Yaukin, king of Judah, I, 115, 348
Yazdegerd I, king of Persia: and Isfahan, III, 109, VI, 427; and Jewish wife, II, 181, 204, 404
Yazdegerd II, king of Persia, II, 181, 213
Yazdegerd III, king of Persia, III, 60, 89
Year: intercalation of lunar months, VIII, 188; length of, VIII, 189 ff., 198 f., 204, 376; lunar and solar, V, 191 f., 201, VIII, 185 ff., 188, 368 ff.; in messianic computations, V, 201; One, VIII, 202; and religious observance, V, 191 f.; seasons, VIII, 201 f.; *see also* Calendar; Chronology; Jubilee year; Sabbatical year
Yebamot, tractate, VI, 81 f.
Yedaiah b. Abraham ha-Penini, of Béziers, VII, 188, 204, 240; defense of scientific study, VIII, 264
Yeḥiel Ashkenazi, VI, 136
Yehoel (Jaoel), angel, VIII, 9
Yehudah, I, 397; *see also* Judaea
Yehudah, exilarch, VI, 214
Yehudah b. Barzillai al-Barceloni, II, 262, III, 202, VI, 113, VIII, 24, 287; and Bar Ḥiyya, VI, 149, 439, VIII, 266; "Book of Deeds," IV, 34; *Commentary on Yeṣirah*, VIII, 38, 58, 142, 279, 327, 353; compilation of halakhic works, VI, 73, 75, 89, 361; computations re Messiah, VIII, 361; linking of persecutions with literary activity, VII, 83; liturgical monograph, VI, 73, VII, 118; possible influence of Saadiah, VI, 211; on rabbinic view of *piyyuṭim,* VII, 102; on recitation of Targum, VI, 262 f.; and Simon Qayyara, VI, 365; sources for geonic period, VI, 73, 208; on traits of a local leader, VI, 324
Yehudah b. Isaac Shabbetai, mysogynist, VII, 188
Yehudah b. Joseph ibn abi'l Thanna, VIII, 243
Yehudah b. Joseph of Kairuwan, V, 309
Yehudah b. Meir ha-Kohen, VI, 48

Yehudah b. Nathan, R., VI, 53; commentary on Sanhedrin, VI, 349
Yehudah b. Saadiah, founder of Egyptian *negidim* dynasty, V, 41 f.
Yehudah b. Samuel ha-Levi, *see* Halevi, Yehudah b. Samuel
Yehudah b. Samuel he-Ḥasid (the Pious), German pietist, VI, 140, VIII, 42; attitude toward forced converts, IV, 146; "Book of Divine Glory," VIII, 45, 293; "Book of the Pious," VI, 404, VIII, 46 ff., 258, 261, 265, 294 f.; on magic practices, VIII, 46 f.; Petaḥiah and, VI, 436
Yehudah b. Solomon al-Ḥarizi, *see* Al-Ḥarizi
Yehudah Gaon on marriage customs, VI, 122, 395
Yehudah ha-Kohen, R., rabbi of Mayence, III, 219
Yehudah ibn Tibbon, *see* Ibn Tibbon, Yehudah
Yehudai b. Naḥman Gaon, head of Sura academy, V, 15, 25, 210, 212; liturgical comments, VII, 70 f.; and the Palestinian Talmud, VI, 22; on qualifications of a cantor, VII, 129; recodification of Jewish law, VI, 78 ff., 363 f.; and scholar, VI, 9
Yehudi b. Sheshet, VII, 23
Yelamdenu midrashim, VI, 182
Yeluatshi, ruler of the Kerait, VI, 434
Yemen, Arabia: Jews of, III, 69, V, 49; liturgical synthesis, VII, 120; Maimonides' "Epistle" to, III, 291, V, 78, 198, 204 f., VIII, 64, 180 f.; messianic movement, V, 198, 204 f.; midrashim, VI, 401, VII, 83; "Mourners for Zion," V, 376; reception of Saadiah's translation, VI, 270; regional Jewish chiefs, V, 43 f.; romances in sacred literature, VI, 181; route to, opened, I, 64; use of Aramaic, VII, 67; use of Babylonian punctuation, VI, 253; variations in pronunciation and meaning of talmudic terms, VII, 28
Yequtiel ibn Ḥassan, Jewish grandee, VII, 152, 159, VIII, 69
Yeraḥmeel b. Solomon, VI, 170, 195 ff., 422, VIII, 43
Yerahmeëlites, I, 57
Yerushalmi, *see* Talmud, Palestinian
Yeshu'a b. Yehudah (Abu'l Faraj Furqan

Yeshu'a b. Yehudah (Continued)
ibn Asad), Karaite theologian, V, 159,
231, 233, VI, 83, VIII, 60
Yeshubokht, archbishop, VI, 4
Yeṣirah, Sefer, see Creation, Book of
YHWH, YHW, YHH, see Yahweh
Yiddish, I, 19, 27, 186, VII, 9; biblical
renditions, VI, 272; literature, VI, 187
Yinnon, reputed name of the Messiah,
V, 153
Yiṣḥaqi, see Rashi
Yissakhar, tribe, VI, 247
Ym, god, I, 45
Yobel, I, 349
Yoma, tractate, VI, 86
Yom Ṭob b. Isaac, R., IV, 125
Yom Ṭob Kohen, V, 74
York, England: martyrdom of Jews, IV,
124, 125 ff.; Jewish community, IV,
148
Yose, R., head of Pumbedita academy,
VI, 18
Yose b. Yose, R., liturgical poet, VII, 40,
90 ff.; quoted by Ibn Janaḥ, VII, 261;
use of acrostics, VII, 88, 257, 261
Yosephon or Yosippon: aggadic collec-
tion, II, 384, III, 240, VI, 188 ff., 233,
417 ff., VIII, 43; discussion of ethnol-
ogy, VI, 226; sources, VI, 194 f.
Yoṣer ra'ash shebi'i, IV, 153
Yotabe, Jewish colony, III, 69 f.
Yudghan (Yehudah) and Yudghanites,
V, 182; messianic movement, V, 185,
191 f., 219
Yugoslavia: Jewish communities, II, 210,
III, 210 f.; synagogue, II, 10
Yusuf ibn Tashfin, Almoravid ruler of
Morocco, III, 124
Yusuf Rabban, II, 212, 407, III, 114
YW, son of El, I, 309

Z

Zacuto, Abraham, scientist-chronicler,
VII, 29; use of Ṣemaḥ's dictionary, VII,
224
Zadok, David's priest, I, 149, 330, II, 203;
house of, II, 342, 343; see also Sad-
ducees
Zadok, gaon, VI, 131
Zadok, R., II, 111, 117
"Zadokite" documents, II, 53, V, 187 f.;
see also Damascus sect

Za'frani, Musa al-, III, 110, V, 182 f., 196,
VI, 299
Zahalon, Jacob b. Isaac, VIII, 239
Zahel, misspelling of Sahl b. Bishr's
(q.v.) name, VIII, 167
Zahir, ar-, caliph, V, 271, 280
Zahirites, Muslim, VI, 463
Zaid b. 'Ali, Madjmu'a, VI, 363
Zakat, poor tax, III, 274
Zakkai b. Akhunai, exilarch, V, 9
Zakkai b. Azariah, branch dynasty in
Mosul, V, 43
Zakkai b. Ḥabibai, V, 15
Zakkai b. Joseph, V, 311
Zalaqa, battle of, IV, 36
Zangi, Imad ad-Din, V, 203
Zaradusht, Mazdakite founder, III, 55
Zarqali, al-, see Al-Zarqali
Zealots: iconoclastic fervor, II, 15, 47,
346; and Judeo-Roman conflicts, II,
94, 101, 372, 423; messianism, II, 58,
126; origins of, II, 47; Peter a mem-
ber? II, 74
Zebaḥ, I, 353
Zechariah, patriarch, III, 22, V, 141, 264
Zechariah, prophet, I, 130, 158, 354, 364,
VI, 405; and "third communion," II,
173, 396
Zechariah b. Berekhel, V, 52 f., VI, 17
Zechariah b. Solomon (Yaḥya ibn Sulei-
man), Midrash ha-Ḥefes, VI, 411
Zedek, god, I, 45
Zedekiah, king of Judah, I, 115
Zedekiah, Jewish sage, VI, 161
Zedekiah Anav degli Mansi, VII, 107
Ze'era, R., II, 182, 208
Ze'iri, R., II, 16
Zekhut abot, I, 135, II, 42, 346
Zeno, Roman emperor, I, 392, II, 189,
286, 339, III, 6
Zenobia, queen of Palmyra, II, 211, 407,
III, 63
Zenodorus, II, 14
Zenon papyri, I, 106, 255, 344, 392, 408,
409
Zephaniah b. Cushi, prophet, I, 86, 118
Zera, R., wonder worker, VIII, 21; see
also Ze'era
Zerah, Asa's victory over, I, 322
Zeraḥiah b. Isaac ha-Levi: Book of
Light, VI, 87 f., 368 f.; correspondence
with Abraham b. David, VI, 119
Zerahiah b. Isaac of Rome, translator
of Maimonides, VIII, 402

Zerubbabel, governor of Jerusalem, I, 106, 119, 354, VIII, 125, 278; restoration under, I, 103, 110, 125, 161, 367; Temple of, I, 238
—— Book of, III, 20, 239, V, 140 f., 152, VIII, 179
Zeus, I, 374; identification of Antiochus with, I, 229, 398
Zeus Xenios, II, 30
Zindiq, III, 143, V, 104, 106, VI, 482, VIII, 296; equated with Manichaean, V, 337
Zion: belief in restoration of, III, 204, VII, 97; Karaite references to, V, 260; light shining upon, VII, 115 f.; "Mourners" for, V, 32, 185, 257, 258, 271, 376; odes to, VII, 154, 168, 197; see also Jerusalem
Zionism, I, 27 f., 297, II, 296
Zirids, Moroccan dynasty, III, 108
Ziv, V, 148
Zodiac, signs of, VIII, 184
Zohar, V, 134, VIII, 278; origin of, VIII, 274; theosophy of, VIII, 51
Zoology, studies in, VIII, 226 ff.

Zoroaster and Zoroastrianism, I, 102, 315, 341; II, 173, 180, 183, 313, III, 130, V, 105 f., 183, VI, 3, 19, 299, 438, VIII, 16; burial tradition, III, 22, 297; dualism, VI, 305 f.; in Fez, III, 145; heavenly family concept, II, 317; Jewish idea re, III, 17; Ka'aba of, II, 397; on light and darkness, VIII, 34; marital unions, II, 231; relations with Judaism, II, 317 f., 436; religion of Sassanian dynasty, II, 213; Saadiah and, VI, 479; taxation of, III, 191, 193; wergeld, III, 295; see also Parsees and Parsiism; Persia
Zuṭra, Abraham, see Abraham Zuṭra
Zuṭra, Mar, II, exilarch, II, 182, 196, 213, 399, VI, 200; date of execution, VI, 424
Zuṭra, Mar, III, exilarch, II, 196, III, 20, 63, V, 32, VI, 199 ff.; emigration to Palestine, VI, 424, 446; founder of Tiberian academy, VI, 239, 243; generations of descendants, V, 305; liturgical changes in period of, VII, 255
Zuṭṭa (or Sar Shalom), VI, 110; Scroll of, VI, 215
Żydowo, Poland, III, 218

DATE DUE